1985

MANAGING FINANCES, PERSONNEL, AND INFORMATION IN HUMAN SERVICES

Social Administration: The Management of the Social Services, Second Edition
Volume I: An Introduction to Human Services Management
Volume II: Managing Finances, Personnel, and Information in Human Services

Simon Slavin is Professor of Social Administration and founding Dean Emeritus, Temple University. He established the School of Social Administration in 1968 and served as its Dean for ten years. Prior to that, he was Professor of Social Work at the Columbia University School of Social Work, where he headed the work in community organization and chaired the doctoral program. Among other responsibilities, Dr. Slavin was Executive Director of the Educational Alliance and the Mt. Vernon YM and YWHA. Currently, he is Editor-in-Chief of the quarterly journal *Administration in Social Work*, and Adjunct Professor at the Hunter College School of Social Work. He has authored many articles in the professional literature, edited *Applying Computers in Social Service and Mental Health Agencies*, and coedited, with Felice D. Perlmutter, *Leadership in Social Administration*.

Much of his time is now spent playing violin in several chamber music groups.

MANAGING FINANCES, PERSONNEL, AND INFORMATION IN HUMAN SERVICES

Volume II of
SOCIAL ADMINISTRATION:
The Management of the
Social Services, *second edition*

Edited by
SIMON SLAVIN

THE HAWORTH PRESS
NEW YORK • LONDON

Social Administration: The Management of the Social Services,
first edition, was published jointly in 1978 by The Haworth Press
and the Council on Social Work Education.

The Haworth Press, Inc.   EUROSPAN/Haworth
28 East 22 Street   3 Henrietta Street
New York, New York 10010   London WC2E 8LU England

Book design by Trudy Raschkind Steinfeld

Printed in the United States of America

Library of Congress Cataloging in Publication Data

Main entry under title:

Social administration.

    Includes bibliographies and indexes.
    Contents: v. 1. An introduction to human services management—
v. 2. Managing finances, personnel, and information in human services.
    1. Social work administration—Addresses, essays, lectures—Collected
works. I. Slavin, Simon.
HV41.S618   1985   361'.068   84-29049
ISBN 0-86656-347-4 (set)
ISBN 0-86656-348-2 (soft : set)
ISBN 0-86656-343-1 (v. 1)
ISBN 0-86656-344-X (soft : v. 1)
ISBN 0-86656-345-8 (v. 2)
ISBN 0-86656-346-6 (soft : v. 2)

Contents

PART I
RESOURCES—ALLOCATION, CONTROL, AND ACCOUNTABILITY

PART II
ADMINISTERING HUMAN
SERVICE PERSONNEL

PART III
INFORMATION, COMPUTERS, AND MANAGEMENT

APPENDIX

Contributors

LESLIE B. ALEXANDER, Ph.D., assistant professor, Graduate School of Social Work and Social Research, Bryn Mawr College, Bryn Mawr, Pennsylvania.

SHIRLEY M. BUTTRICK, D.S.W., professor, Jane Addams College of Social Work, University of Illinois at Chicago Circle, Chicago.

ANTHONY BROSKOWSKI, executive director, Northside Community Mental Health Center, and clinical associate professor of psychiatry, University of South Florida College of Medicine, Tampa.

CARL B. BUXBAUM, Adelphi University, School of Social Work, Garden City, New York.

STEPHEN R. CHITWOOD, M.P.A., Ph.D., J.D., associate professor of Public Administration, School of Government and Business Administration, George Washington University, Washington, D.C.

BERNARD DIMSDALE, Ph.D., consultant in applied mathematics and data processing, Los Angeles.

ROBERT ELKIN, Ph.D., associate professor, School of Social Work and Community Planning, University of Maryland, Baltimore.

JOANNE G. GREER, Ph.D., mathematical statistician, Office of the Inspector General, Office of the Secretary, U.S. Department of Health and Human Services.

THOMAS V. GREER, Ph.D., professor, College of Business and Management, University of Maryland.

MALVERN J. GROSS, C.P.A., partner, Price Waterhouse & Co., Washington, D.C.

CREASIE FINNEY HAIRSTON, Ph.D., coordinator/associate professor, Charleston Center, West Virginia University, Morgantown.

GLYN W. HANBERY, D.B.A., C.P.A., associate professor, School of Accountancy, University of Denver, University Park.

RICHARD L. HODGES, Ph.D., assistant professor, Department of Accountancy, College of Business, Western Michigan University, Kalamazoo.

A. RONALD KUCIC, Ph.D., C.M.A., assistant professor, School of Accountancy, University of Denver, University Park.

CHARLES S. LEVY, D.S.W., professor emeritus, Wurzweiler School of Social Work, Yeshiva University, New York.

ERNIE S. LIGHTMAN, Ph.D., professor of social policy, University of Toronto, Ontario, Canada.

CATHERINE LOVELL, Ph.D., assistant professor, Graduate School of Administration, University of California, Riverside, California.

JOHN A. MORRIS, Jr., M.S.W., director of special programs, Morris Village, Columbia, South Carolina.

EDWARD NEWMAN, Ph.D., professor, School of Social Administration, Temple University, Philadelphia, Pennsylvania.

GERARD L. OTTEN, M.S.W., planner, Division of Program Analysis, South Carolina Department of Social Services, Columbia.

MARTHA N. OZAWA, Ph.D., professor, George Warren Brown School of Social Work, Washington University, Saint Louis.

RINO J. PATTI, D.S.W., professor, School of Social Work, University of Washington, Seattle, Washington.

BRUCE A. PHILLIPS, Ph.D., assistant professor, Hebrew Union College-Jewish Institute of Religion, Los Angeles.

MELVYN C. RAIDER, Ph.D., associate professor and assistant to the dean, School of Social Work, Wayne State University, Detroit, Michigan.

MICHAEL REISCH, Ph.D., assistant professor, School of Social Work and Community Planning, University of Maryland, Baltimore.

DICK SCHOECH, Ph.D., associate professor, Graduate School of Social Work, The University of Texas at Arlington.

JAMES E. SORENSEN, Ph.D., C.P.A., professor, School of Accountancy, University of Denver, University Park.

ETHEL TAFT, M.S.W., assistant director, Jewish Family Service of Los Angeles.

MILTON TAMBOR, A.C.S.W., Michigan American Federation of State, County, and Municipal Employees, Council 25 Staff representative, Southfield, Michigan.

CHRIS L. TAYLOR, M.S.W., A.C.S.W., district director, Catholic Social Services, Diocese of Harrisburg, Lebanon, Pennsylvania.

JERRY TUREM, Ph.D., project director, Social Services Research Program, The Urban Institute, Washington, D.C., at the time this paper was written.

THOMAS W. WEIRICH, research and evaluation, J.F.K. Community Mental Health Center, Philadelphia.

STEPHEN L. WHITE, deputy director, Northside Community Mental Health Center, and clinical assistant professor of psychiatry, University of South Florida College of Medicine, Tampa.

VERNON R. WIEHE, Ph.D., associate professor, College of Social Work, University of Kentucky, Lexington.

DAVID W. YOUNG, D.B.A., assistant professor of management, Harvard University, School of Public Health, Cambridge, Massachusetts.

Acknowledgments

PART I

Gross, M. J. The Importance of Budgeting.
  Reprinted with permission of the author and The Ronald Press Company from Financial and Accounting Guide for Nonprofit Organizations, Second Edition, pp. 293–308. Copyright © 1974, The Ronald Press Company, New York.

White, S. L., and Broskowski, A. Planning and Budgeting: An Ongoing, Integrated Process.
  Reprinted with permission of Jossey-Bass, Inc. from New Directions for Mental Health, Vol. 8, 1980, pp. 69–76. Copyright © 1980 by Jossey-Bass, Inc.

Hodges, R. L. Avoiding Fiscal Management Problems in Human Service Agencies.
  Reprinted with permission of The Haworth Press, Inc. from Administration in Social Work, Vol. 6, No. 4, Winter 1982, pp. 61–67. Copyright © The Haworth Press, Inc.

Hairston, C. F. Improving Cash Management in Nonprofit Organizations.
  Reprinted with permission of The Haworth Press, Inc. from Administration in Social Work, Vol. 5, No. 2, Spring 1981, pp. 29–36. Copyright © by The Haworth Press, Inc.

Hairston, C. F. Costing Nonprofit Services: Developments, Problems, and Issues.
  Reprinted with permission of The Haworth Press, Inc. from Administration in Social Work, Vol. 9, No. 1, Spring 1985, pp. 47–55. Copyright © 1985 by The Haworth Press, Inc.

Buxbaum, C. B. Cost-Benefit Analysis: The Mystique versus the Reality.
  Reprinted with permission of the University of Chicago Press from Social Service Review, Vol. 55, No. 3, 1981, pp. 453–471. Copyright © 1981 by The University of Chicago.

Morris, J. A., Jr., and Ozawa, M. N. Benefit-Cost Analysis and the Social Service Agency: A Model for Decision Making.
  Reprinted with permission of The Haworth Press, Inc. from Administration

PART II

National Association of Social Workers, Inc. NASW Standards for Social Work Personnel Practices.
Reprinted with permission of the National Association of Social Workers, Inc. Copyright © 1968, revised 1971 and 1975 by National Association of Social Workers, Inc.

Buttrick, S. M. Affirmative Action and Job Security: Policy Dilemmas.
Reprinted with permission of the author and the publisher from The Social Welfare Forum, 1976, copyright © 1977 National Conference on Social Welfare. New York: Columbia University Press, 1977, pp. 116–125.

Lovell, C. Three Key Issues in Affirmative Action.
Reprinted with permission of the author and the American Society for Public Administration from Public Administration Review, Vol. 34, No. 3, May/June 1974, pp. 235–237.

Alexander, L. B. Professionalization and Unionization: Compatible After All?
Reprinted with permission of the National Association of Social Workers, Inc. from Social Work, Vol. 25, No. 6, 1980, pp. 476–482. Copyright © 1980 by National Association of Social Workers, Inc.

Tambor, M. The Social Worker as Worker: A Union Perspective.
Reprinted with permission of The Haworth Press, Inc. from Administration in Social Work, Vol. 3, No. 3, Fall 1979, pp. 289–300. Copyright © 1979 by The Haworth Press, Inc.

Lightman, E. S. Social Workers, Strikes, and Service to Clients.
Reprinted with permission of the National Association of Social Workers, Inc. from Social Work, Vol. 28, No. 2, 1983, pp. 142–147. Copyright © 1983 by National Association of Social Workers, Inc.

Levy, C. S. The Ethics of Management.
Reprinted with permission of The Haworth Press, Inc. from Administration in Social Work, Vol. 3, No. 3, Fall 1979, pp. 277–288. Copyright © 1979 by The Haworth Press, Inc.

Reisch, M., and Taylor, C. L. Ethical Guidelines for Cutback Management: A Preliminary Approach.
Reprinted with permission of The Haworth Press, Inc. from Administration in Social Work, Vol. 7, Nos. 3/4, Fall/Winter 1983, pp. 59–72. Copyright © 1983 by The Haworth Press, Inc.

PART III

Weirich, T. W. The Design of Information Systems.
Reprinted with permission of Temple University Press from Felice Davidson Perlmutter and Simon Slavin, eds., Leadership in Social Administration: Perspectives for the Eighties. Philadelphia: Temple University Press, 1980.

Schoech, D. A Microcomputer-Based Human Service Information System.
Reprinted with revisions with permission of The Haworth Press, Inc. from Administration in Social Work, Vol. 3, No. 4, Winter 1979, pp. 423–440. Copyright © 1979 by The Haworth Press, Inc.

Kucic, A. R., Sorensen, J. E., and Hanbery, G. W. Computer Selection for Human Service Organizations.
Reprinted with permission of The Haworth Press, Inc. from Administration in Social Work, Vol. 7, No. 1, Spring 1983, pp. 63–75. Copyright © 1983 by The Haworth Press, Inc.

Phillips, B. A., Dimsdale, B., and Taft, E. An Information System for the Social Casework Agency: A Model and Case Study.
Reprinted with permission of Temple University Press from Simon Slavin, ed., Applying Computers in Social Service and Mental Health Agencies, New York: The Haworth Press, 1982.

Young, D. W. Management Information Systems in Child Care: An Agency Experience.
Reprinted with permission of the author and the Child Welfare League of America, Inc. from Child Welfare, Vol. LIII, No. 2, February 1974, pp. 102–111.

APPENDIX

National Association of Social Workers, Inc. Code of Ethics of the National Association of Social Workers, as adopted by the 1979 NASW Delegate Assembly, effective July 1, 1980.
Reprinted with permission of the National Association of Social Workers, Inc.

Preface

The preceding volume provided a general introduction to the administration of the human services and dealt with some of its major concepts and theoretical perspectives. Major attention was given to questions of authority, to executive styles of work and to organizational conflict and change. Issues and problems surrounding the place of minority and female executives as well as participation in management were given special emphasis.

This volume turns to matters of a more technical nature, and emphasizes three essential areas of concern: financial management, administering human resources (personnel), and information handling.

Several factors have stimulated developments in these areas in recent years. The shifts in social policy engineered by the Reagan administration to a regressive view of social welfare and the financial constraints imposed on the human services have resulted in new pressures for cost containment and accountability. Parallel developments in computerized data manipulation have reinvigorated the purely technical aspects of management.

In this conservative ethos, more and more attention is directed to quantitative objectives, to efficiency rather than effectiveness, and to consideration of "the bottom line." This contrasts sharply with the professional preoccupation with standards and the quality and integrity of service. This conflict between technical and service models of the social organization represents one of the pervasive aspects of current practice in the human services. In some quarters, the move has been toward employing MBA and public-administration-trained executives in these agencies rather than those grounded in social work and the social services.

Although competent technical management of a service delivery system, buttressed by skill and knowledge about fiscal matters, is a necessary condition for administrative adequacy, it is hardly sufficient. Technology is properly to be viewed as handmaiden to client service and subordinate to it if goal displacement is to be shunned.

New material on fiscal management that has recently appeared in the literature is included in this edition. The same is true of some aspects of personnel management, particularly with respect to managerial ethics. Until recently, little has been published on problems and issues concerning ethical behavior in social agencies. A new section on this area is here included.

Perhaps the most rapid development in technology is seen in the burgeoning application of computers to fiscal, programmatic, and clinical purposes. This section has been appropriately expanded.

The material in this and its predecessor volume was prepared as an aid to teaching both prospective administrators and others who intend to work in the human services. It is intended as well for practicing executives and subexecutives who are seeking updated material on their craft and who know that managing service systems is a form of professional practice requiring knowledge, skill, and attitudes all bent to the purpose of enhancing people's ability to deal with the pressures and strains of contemporary social life.

PART I

Resources— Allocation, Control, and Accountability

Editor's Introduction

Much of the interest in administration of the social services during the seventies developed as a result of official and public concern for accountability and what were considered the uncontrolled excesses of the social programs of the sixties. In substantial part this flowed from the viewpoint of the Nixon administration that these programs were failures, and that one couldn't solve social programs by "throwing money at them." The incorporation of managerial technology into public welfare programs was seen as one way to overcome the inefficiencies that were thought to be rampant. A number of government grants were made by the Social and Rehabilitation Services of DHEW to schools of social work for projects in administration. Special encouragement was given to pursue activities jointly with schools of business. Accountability and evaluation became important preoccupations of writers in the field. For some this was seen as an opportunity to develop the professional aspects of administration. For many policy-makers this was one route to containing public expenditures on public welfare.

The sharply declining resources for public and private welfare programs in the mid-seventies and early eighties gave further impetus to this development. In a period of expansion, program innovation and initiative are readily encouraged. New efforts are simply added to the existing system of services with relatively little pressure to weigh alternatives or to focus on efficiency measures. The reverse is true during periods of curtailed finances. Emphasis goes to getting "the biggest bang for the buck." It is readily assumed that managerial know-how will curtail waste, cut out "fat," and yield greater efficiency of operation. A sharper look at the administration of social agencies should also make them more effective in achieving their objectives.

The complexities of modern-day funding of social service programs also call for a greater interest in administrative operations. Relatively few of these programs receive their financial substance from a single source. Increasingly over the years, governmental funds either supplemented voluntary efforts at income generation or became major sources of funds. Furthermore, funding streams tended to reflect the multiplicity of structural patterns among city, county, state, and federal departments and their legislative appropriations. Many programs now receive support from a variety of sources, each establishing requirements for

3

evaluation and accountability. Administering social agencies requires a quality of personnel competent to deal with these complexities and the many constituencies they represent.

Finally, the recent development of both hard- and software technology applicable to organizational management calls for a degree of sophistication not previously required. New accounting procedures and the machinery that makes them possible, new patterns of word processing, and, above all, new ways of handling data and information set partial agendas for training that are becoming widespread.

A. BUDGETING

The literature on budgeting for the social services is very meager, and serious discussion on budget theory is even more elusive. Yet an understanding of underlying concepts and approaches to budget planning and control is a necessary condition for competent management. In recent years serious questions have been raised about the cogency of conventional incremental budgeting, particularly in the public arena. Some of these new ways of doing things are discussed below. The selections in this section deal with a general view of the budgeting process.

Gross provides an overview of conventional budgeting for nonprofit agencies. He reviews its functions and procedures and cites illustrations of the use of budgets as mechanisms of financial control. Care in preparing periodic reports and in comparing actual experiences with projections is seen as essential. Deviations require specific responses and action, including periodic rebudgeting. Gross stresses the importance of planning for the future and illustrates the use of a five-year master plan as one technique to keep the organization abreast of trends and developments affecting services.

White and Broskowski present a particular view of budgeting, stressing the relation between program and resources. They see the planning function and the budgeting function as parts of an integrated process, one phase following another over an annual period. They detail a nine-step model of the planning-budgetary cycle and suggest that this process is continuous, each phase affecting and being affected by every other.

B. FISCAL MANAGEMENT

Among the reasons that managers sometimes come to grief, inadequate handling of finances undoubtedly ranks very high. Securing resources for programs and services is one of the essential administrative functions. Careful attention to their allocation and control is a cardinal requisite for organizational stability. The selections in this section deal with some canons of fiscal responsibility.

Hodges looks at some problems that inhere in the effort to achieve efficient and effective use of resources in the light of organizational constraints. He stresses the need for developing an integrated management system as a condition for the successful operation of a service delivery agency. To achieve this, the fiscal management elements (planning, action, evaluation) must be coordinated with internal control factors. After elaborating these control elements, the author explores some counterproductive management practices related to the funding process, program design, budgeting, accounting, and audit.

From her experience as a management consultant, Hairston analyzes the problems of day-to-day administration of cash flow in nonprofit organizations. Although an agency's finances may be well planned and budgeted, the exigencies of current-day funding, with the ebb and flow of periodic allocations from multiple sources, may create shortfalls in cash obligations. The author reviews ways of handling the appearance of negative cash balance and provides a number of suggestions that the nonprofit manager can apply in dealing with these recurring shortages. She stresses the importance of preparing cash budgets that follow monthly expectations of cash availability. Above all, she cautions managers to anticipate cash deficits and to make appropriate plans for dealing with them. Effective utilization of a relevant information and control system is seen as instrumental in resolving many cash flow difficulties.

C. COST ANALYSIS

Cost analysis in a variety of forms has been promulgated as a sound approach for social policy decision making, for accountability and for containing nonproductive expenditures. To budget costs without knowing the benefits to be expected has been viewed as potentially wasteful, capricious, and unsound. Relating costs to benefits may well be a rational process for resource allocation, but is not without difficulties and pitfalls in actual execution. Developing unambiguous units of measure dealing with nonquantifiable expectations (including opportunity costs), and incorporating extraneous variables are among the knotty problems one can expect to encounter.

Hairston reviews the current status of cost accounting in the nonprofit sector with particular emphasis on the voluntary health and welfare organization. Cost data and allocation studies have the potential of enhancing the effective and efficient use of financial resources, but they present a series of conceptual, methodological, and practical problems when applied to concrete situations. Hairston explores these difficulties, stressing the complications in distinguishing direct (program) costs from indirect (supporting) costs. She suggests a series of strategies to meet these issues and urges agencies to experiment with different approaches. Given the current state of the art, educational preparation and continuous training in financial management are proposed.

Buxbaum reviews the goals, procedures, and assumptions of cost-benefit analysis and asks whether, in actuality, it essentially provides a better way to allocate increasingly scarce resources or whether it is used to rationalize reduced welfare spending. He discusses a series of technical problems in both cost-benefit and cost-effectiveness analysis, and suggests that the pressures of the political environment may be as significant in their application as the cogency of the rational procedures they utilize. One conclusion drawn from the examination suggests that in a regressive policy environment, political action to alter the political context may be indicated.

Morris and Ozawa take a balanced view of benefit-cost analysis as incorporated in the Planning, Programming, and Budgeting System during the Johnson administration. They discuss both shortcomings and strengths of the procedure, present a model for adapting benefit-cost analysis to small social service agencies, and urge its increased use for rational planning and decision making. Morris and Ozawa suggest that there remains a critical role for the decision maker who, perforce, uses the results of benefit-cost analysis as an aid to informed judgment.

The Greers critically examine the assumptions and procedures involved in evaluating costs and benefits of social programs. After pointing to a series of obstacles encountered in the effort, they suggest ways of overcoming some of these difficulties. Their discussion focuses on the need for improving available data for the analysis and for better data interpretation. They imply that competent evaluation is more than a technical process, and suggest that the cost-benefit ratio should not be used as the sole criterion of program effectiveness.

D. MANAGEMENT BY OBJECTIVES

Management by objectives (MBO) has been a major managerial tool for more than two decades. Developed initially by Peter Drucker (1954), a substantial literature has developed in both business and government. More recently, social service agencies have experimented with its use. Wiehe states the case for MBO as a helpful tool in performance appraisal and program planning in social agencies. He reviews the process, both inductive and deductive, of setting agency and individual practitioner goals and objectives, and specifies the values that grow out of staff participation in that process. While Wiehe does not deal specifically with the use of MBO for budgetary purposes, its application seems self-evident, since budgets are essentially the quantification in money terms of organizational objectives.

Raider reviews the recent experience of social agencies in applying MBO, and explores both successes and failures in its use as a management tool. After identifying indicators of potential difficulty with MBO, he provides a step-by-step series of phases essential for its effective installation. The importance of adapting an MBO approach to the particular requirements of specific agencies is stressed. Ways of dealing with expected staff resistance and to paperwork overload are indicated. Raider also stresses the importance of connecting this methodology to personal growth objectives of the agency's staff as well as to the achievement of agency goals.

E. ZERO-BASED BUDGETING

Among the newest of the innovations in budgeting is zero-based budgeting (ZBB) (Pyhrr, 1973). Its essential features are in sharp contrast to conventional budgeting. In practice, traditional planning dealt with incremental changes at the margin—increasing some resources for specific items that seem to warrant expansion while reducing others. Budget justifications dealt with these marginal changes, operating on the implicit assumption that prior appropriations were given, and that only changes in amounts allocated would be rationalized. ZBB suggests that every budget year begins anew, that program planning and justification deal with total appropriations not with incremental changes alone. In the absence of a sound basis for continued operation, programs are terminated. Thus a full review of all aspects of the budget is indicated, in the course of which alternatives are probed and cost-benefit relationships are explored.

Otten presents an overview of ZBB and compares its approach to that of Planning, Programming, Budgeting System (PPBS) that preceded it in national prominence. In showing how to apply the technique to social service agencies, he provides an example of its use and suggests some of the limitations it encountered in practice. The importance of specifying and assessing program objectives and of comparing inputs and outputs are central to both ZBB and PPBS. Much less is heard of ZBB since the end of the Carter administration, yet some of its innovations are likely to be incorporated in agency budgeting of the future.

F. ACCOUNTABILITY

The hallmark of the seventies in the social services may well be the insistence on accountability, and its associated call for the evaluation of efficiency and effectiveness in service delivery and administration. The less sympathetic policy-makers became to welfare services and to welfare clients, the more they emphasized the importance of accountability. Much of the public discussion centered on two questions—accountability for what, and accountability to whom. Professional preferences for accountability to consumers of service—social welfare clients—sometimes gave way to redefinition of the client. Thus some officials in the California welfare system, joined by an academic and an official in the Department of Agriculture could write: "Who is the client for social services who must be satisfied? The critical client is the taxpayer. He pays the tabs for the programs and derives the benefits, if any, of the services. Thus he, more than the individual recipient of specific services, represents the prime target for client-satisfaction efforts. (Another important client group . . . consists of elected officials)" (Bledsoe et al., 1972, p. 800).

Elkin presents the outlines for a comprehensive review of accountability in the human services from the perspective of its administrative implications. He identifies the most salient concepts that inhere in the full cycle of the accountability process, suggesting its complex character. These deal with both technical considerations and the political context within which they operate, and concern issues of efficiency and effectiveness, of quantitative and qualitative aspects of evaluation, and of the relationship between resource providers and service deliverers. Elkin places special emphasis on the nonfinancial measures of accountability and the difficulties encountered in reporting program results and accomplishments. He notes, additionally, that when pressure for accountability leads to excessive demands and external controls, freedom of organizational action may be impeded, and organizational objectives of effective service delivery may be compromised.

Perhaps one of the clearest statements in the literature on the problems and dilemmas confronting social service accountability is that of Newman and Turem. They explore the significance of limited fiscal and human resources for policy choices, and the impact of political pressures and considerations on the scale and direction of social service provision. Because the absence of market mechanisms makes political processes paramount, they suggest that credibility must be earned through appropriate focus on effectiveness and efficiency of service delivery through highlighting results, not processes. Because this has not been the case traditionally, there is a crisis of confidence and accountability which threatens the well-being of the service delivery system. A competing view might suggest that if the crisis of accountability is in substantial part related to political dynamics, the appropriate response should in fact be political. Some programs are placed in jeopardy precisely because they achieve their stated objectives. It is their political unorthodoxy and challenge of the status quo that is often questioned—i.e., Mobilization for Youth and some poverty law programs. When police programs fail to curb crime, on the other hand, greater resources tend to be allocated. Politics overcomes rationality. This is not to suggest that accountability is not an important aspect of social service planning. But difficulties in evaluating nonobjective, nonquantifiable results, and the limitations in transforming positive results into policy initiatives ought not be underestimated.

The next selection examines a neglected aspect of program evaluation and productivity—considerations of social equity. Chitwood looks at these matters from the perspective of the political scientist and governmental social services. He contrasts the concern of public officials for expenditure accountability and operational efficiency with the equitable distribution of public services. He stresses the importance of meeting minimum levels of adequacy and of ensuring entitlements of public benefits. Furthermore, social equity requires the development of a relationship between service recipients and the administering agency that reflects respect, trust, and participation.

G. SYSTEMS ANALYSIS

Patti analyzes recent developments that are variously referred to as management science, systems analysis, or systems management, and views the ways in which their application to the social services, and particularly to public welfare, affects the social and political context of service delivery. He sees this movement as ideologically rooted, and points to the potentially negative impact they can have on clients and the agencies that serve them when indiscriminately applied. He identifies the essential features of the belief system that underlies the approach, and points to the problems and pitfalls that attend the use of the technology that they inspire. He questions the transferability of systems management to complex social welfare issues and programs. His response to the inevitable incorporation of this technology in the welfare system is to suggest approaches to the training of social administrators which include a sufficient familiarity with these technical tools, but buttressed with theoretical, empirical, and practical skills in the framework of social values and sensitivity to client needs.

REFERENCES

Bledsoe, Ralph C., Denny, Dennis R., Hobbs, Charles D., & Long, Raymond S. Productivity management in the California social services program. *Public Administration Review,* November/December, 1972.

Drucker, Peter. *The practice of management.* New York: Harper and Bros., 1954.

Pyhrr, Peter A. *Zero-based budgeting.* New York: John Wiley & Sons, 1973.

A. Budgeting

1

The Importance of Budgeting

MALVERN J. GROSS

A budget, like motherhood, is something very few would argue against. Yet, the art of preparing *and using* budgets in a meaningful manner is completely foreign to most nonprofit organizations. It is not that the treasurer or board is unaware of their importance, but more that they lack the skill necessary to apply budgeting techniques, and often are reluctant to use a budget as a tool to control the financial activities. The purpose of this chapter is to discuss the importance of budgeting, the art of skillfully preparing a useful budget, and equally important, the art of actually using the budget to control.

THE BUDGET: A PLAN OF ACTION

A budget is a "plan of action." It represents the organization's blueprint for the coming months, or years, expressed in monetary terms. This means the organization must know what its goals are before it can prepare a budget. If it doesn't know where it is going, obviously it is going to be very difficult for the organization to do any meaningful planning. All too often the process is reversed and it is in the process of preparing the budget that the goals are determined.

So the first function of a budget is to record, in monetary terms, what the realistic goals or objectives of the organization are for the coming year (or years). The budget is the financial plan of action which results from the board's decisions as to the program for the future.

The second function of a budget is to provide a tool to monitor the financial activities throughout the year. Properly used, the budget can provide a bench mark or comparison point which will alert the board to the first indication that their financial goals won't be met. For a budget to provide this type of information and control four elements must be present:

1. The budget must be well-conceived, and have been prepared or approved by the board.
2. The budget must be broken down into periods corresponding to the periodic financial statements.
3. Financial statements must be prepared on a timely basis throughout the year and a comparison made to the budget, right on the statements.
4. The board must be prepared to take action where the comparison with the budget indicates a significant deviation.

Each of these four elements will be discussed in this chapter.

Steps for Preparation

It was noted above that a budget should represent the end result of a periodic review by the board or by the membership of the organization's objectives or goals, expressed in monetary terms. Often the budget process is a routine "chore" handled by the treasurer to satisfy the board that the organization has a budget, which the board, in turn, routinely ratifies. Frequently, such budgets are not looked at again until the following year, at the time next year's budget is prepared. This type of budgeting serves little purpose and is worth little more than the paper it is written on. A budget, to be effective, must be a joint effort of many people. It must be a working document which forms the basis for action.

Here are the basic steps that, in one form or another, should be followed by an organization in order to prepare a well-conceived budget:

1. A list of objectives or goals of the organization for the following year should be prepared. For many organizations this process will be essentially a re-evaluation of the relative priority of the existing programs. Care should be taken, however, to avoid concluding too hastily that an existing program should continue unchanged. Our society is not static and the organization that does not constantly re-evaluate and update its program is in danger of being left behind.
2. The cost of each objective or goal listed above should be estimated. For continuing programs, last year's actual expense and last year's budget will be the starting point. For new programs or modifications

of existing programs, a substantial amount of work may be necessary to accurately estimate the costs involved. This estimating process should be done in detail since elements of a particular goal or objective may involve many categories of expense and salaries.

3. The expected income of the organization should be estimated. With many organizations, contributions from members or the general public will be the principal income and careful consideration must be given to the expected economic climate in the community. A year when unemployment is high or the stock market is down is a poor year to expect "increased" contributions. With other organizations the amount of income will be dependent on how successful they are in selling their program. Possibly some of the programs can be expanded if they are financially viable, or contracted if they are not. Organizations are often overly optimistic in estimating income. This can prove to be the organization's downfall if there is no margin for error, and realism must be used or the budget will have little meaning.

4. The total expected income should be compared to the expense of achieving the objectives or goals. Usually the expected expenses will exceed income, and this is where some value judgments will have to take place. What programs are most important? Where can expected costs be reduced? This process of reconciling expected income and expense is probably the most important step taken during the year because it is here that the program's blue print for the coming year is fixed.

It is important that consideration be given to the reliability of the estimated income and expense figures. Is it possible that expenses have been underestimated or that income has been overestimated? If expenses have been underestimated by 15 per cent and income has been overestimated by 10 per cent, there will be a deficit of 25 per cent, and unless the organization has substantial cash reserves it could be in serious difficulty. If the organization has small cash reserves or with little likelihood of getting additional funds quickly, then a realistic safety margin should be built into the budget.

5. The final proposed budget should be submitted to the appropriate body for ratification. This may be the full board or it may be the entire membership. This should not be just a formality but should be carefully presented to the ratifying body so that, once ratified, all persons will be firmly committed to the resulting plan of action.

The steps listed above may seem so elementary that there is no need to emphasize them here. But elementary as they are, they are often not followed and the resulting budget serves very little value to the organization.

Responsibility for Preparation

There has been very little said about "who" should follow these steps in preparing the budget. The preparation of a budget involves policy decisions. While the "treasurer" may be the person best qualified to handle the figures, he may or may not be the person to make policy decisions. For this reason, a "budget committee" should consist of persons responsible for policy decisions. Usually this means that the board should either itself act as the budget committee, or it should appoint a subcommittee of board members.

This doesn't mean that the detailed estimated cost studies for various programs can't be delegated to staff members. But the decision as to what are the goals and their relative priority has to be a board-level function.

Take, for example, a private, independent school. At first glance there might not appear to be many board-level decisions to make. The purpose of a school is to teach and it might seem that the budget would be a most routine matter. But there are many decisions that have to be made. For example:

1. Should more emphasis be placed on science courses?
2. Should the school get a small computer to help teach computer science?
3. Should the school hire a language teacher for grades 2–4?
4. Should the school increase salaries in the coming year and try to upgrade the staff?
5. Should the athletic field be resodded this year?
6. Should a fund raiser be hired?
7. Should the music program be expanded?
8. Should tuition be increased?

These questions and many more face the board. Undoubtedly they may rely on the paid staff to make recommendations, but the board is responsible for policy and the budget represents "policy." This responsibility cannot be delegated.

MONTHLY AND QUARTERLY BUDGETS

Many organizations have no real difficulty in preparing an annual budget. The real problem comes in trying to divide the budget into meaningful segments that can be compared to interim financial statements prepared on a monthly or quarterly basis. Some organizations attempt to do this by dividing the total budget by twelve and showing the resulting amounts as a monthly budget, which is then compared to actual monthly income and expense. While this is better than not making any budget comparison, it can produce misleading results when the income or expenses do not occur on a uniform basis throughout the year. Consider Table 1–1: Abbreviated Statement of a Small Church. The logical conclusion that might be drawn is that the church will have a surplus at the end of 12 months of approximately $20,000—four times the quarterly excess of $5,000. If this conclusion were reached the temptation would be to slacken off on unpaid pledge collection efforts and to be a little less careful in making purchases. This would be a very serious mistake if, in fact, the normal pattern of pledge collections were such that $36,000 should have been collected in the first quarter instead of the $35,000 actually received. A monthly or quarterly budget can produce misleading conclusions unless considerable care is taken in preparing it.

Allocating an Annual Budget to Monthly or Quarterly Periods

One of the best and easiest ways to allocate an annual budget into shorter periods is to first analyze the actual income and expense for the prior year, and then allocate this year's budget based on last year's actual expenses.

To illustrate, assume the church's income last year was $100,000 but is expected to be $120,000 this year. A budget for the new year could be prepared as in Table 1–2.

In this illustration we have assumed that the increase in income of $20,000 will be received in the same pattern as the prior year's income was received. If this assumption is not correct, then adjustment must be made for the anticipated income which will depart from past experience. For example, if it is anticipated that a single gift of $10,000 will be received in the first quarter and the other $10,000 will be received in

TABLE 1–1. Abbreviated Statement of a Small Church

Budget Item	Annual Budget	Three Months Ending March 31	
		Annual Budget ÷ 4	Actual
Contributions	$ 120,000	$ 30,000	$ 35,000
Expenses	(120,000)	(30,000)	(30,000)
Excess	0	0	$ 5,000

TABLE 1–2. Church Budget for the New Year, Based on Last Year's Actual Expenses

Income	Actual Last Year	Percent of Last Year's Total	New Budget
First quarter	$ 30,000	30	$ 36,000
Second quarter	25,000	25	30,000
Third quarter	25,000	25	30,000
Fourth quarter	20,000	20	24,000
Total	$ 100,000	100	$ 120,000

about the same pattern as last year's income, the calculations to arrive at a new budget would be somewhat different, as shown in Table 1–3.

If at the end of the first quarter income of only $35,000 had been received compared to a budget of $43,000, it would be apparent that steps should be taken to increase contributions or the church will fall short of meeting its budget for the year.

The expense side of the budget should be handled in the same way. Generally, expenses tend to occur at a more uniform rate, although this is not always so. In many ways the expense side of the budget is more important than the income side since it is easier to increase expenditures for things that weren't budgeted than to raise additional contributions. If the budget is regularly compared to actual expenditures for deviations, it can be an effective tool to highlight unbudgeted expenditures.

TABLE 1–3. Church Budget for the New Year, Based on a Pattern of Income

Income	Actual Last Year	Percent of Last Year's Total	New Budget Other Than Special	Special Gifts	Total Budget
First quarter	$ 30,000	30	$ 33,000	$ 10,000	$ 43,000
Second quarter	25,000	25	27,500	—	27,500
Third quarter	25,000	25	27,500	—	27,500
Fourth quarter	20,000	20	22,000	—	22,000
Total	$ 100,000	100	$ 110,000	$ 10,000	$ 120,000

The budget should probably be prepared on a monthly rather than on a quarterly basis to reduce the time lag before effective action can be taken. If a monthly basis appears to be too cumbersome, consideration could be given to bimonthly budgets and statements. However, if the organization's cash position is tight, monthly statements become almost a necessity.

ILLUSTRATIVE EXPENSE BUDGET

The Valley Country Club is a good example of an organization that has to be very careful to budget its income and expenses. While the club has a beautiful club house and a fine golf course, all of its money is tied up in these fixed assets and there is no spare cash to cover a deficit. Accordingly each fall when the board starts to wrestle with the budget for the following year it is aware that it cannot afford the luxury of a deficit. Since the budget is so important, the entire board sits as a budget committee to work out the plans for the following year. The treasurer, with the help of the club manager, prepares a worksheet in advance of the budget meeting. This worksheet indicates the actual expenses for the current year to date, the estimate of the final figures for the year, and the current year's budget to show how close the club will come. The board through discussion and debate attempts to work out a budget for the coming year. Table 1–4 shows the worksheet for the expense budget.

In looking at this worksheet notice first that the expenses are grouped by major function so that the board can focus attention on the activities of the club. The alternative presentation would have been to list expenses by type—salaries, supplies, food, etc.—but this doesn't tell the board how much each of the major activities is costing.

There are three columns for the proposed budget—the minimum, the maximum, and the final amount. As the board considers each item it records both the minimum and the maximum it feels is appropriate. No attempt is made at the beginning to fix a "final" budget amount. Instead all budget items are considered, listed as to the minimum and maximum cost, and totals arrived at. It is only after all items have been considered, and only after a preliminary review of potential income has been made, that the board is in a position to make a judgment.

After the board has completed this worksheet showing final figures for the year, the next step is to break down the budget into monthly budgets. As with many organizations, the Valley Country Club's expenses (and income) are seasonal. In this case, the budget is broken down into monthly segments assuming that the expenses will be incurred in the same pattern as they were for the current year, in the manner discussed earlier.

TABLE 1–4. Worksheet for Preparing 1972 Expense Budget for The Valley Country Club (in thousands of dollars)

Budget Item	Budget for Current Year			Bud-get Cur-rent Year	Proposed Budget for New Year		
	To Date (10 Months)	Esti-mate Bal-ance of Year	Esti-mate for Year		Mini-mum	Maxi-mum	Final
Maintenance of greens and grounds							
Salaries and wages	$ 47	$ 3	$ 50	$ 46	$ 50	$ 65	$ 55
Seeds, fertilizer, and supplies	14		14	13	14	14	14
Repairs, maintenance, and other	12	2	14	10	10	15	15
Maintenance of clubhouse							
Salaries and wages	20	4	24	23	24	28	26
Supplies, maintenance, and repair	10	1	11	12	11	11	11
Golf activities							
Salaries and wages	10		10	11	12	20	20
Tournament costs	14		14	15	15	15	15
Golf cart maintenance	8		8	5	5	5	5
Swimming pool expenses							
Salaries and wages	4		4	4	5	10	5
Supplies and maintenance	2		2	1	2	2	2
General and administrative salaries	35	6	41	40	44	51	44
Property taxes	33	7	40	38	42	42	42
Other Expenses	41	7	48	40	40	50	50
Subtotal, excluding restaurant	**250**	**30**	**280**	**258**	**274**	**328**	**304**
Restaurant expenses							
Food and beverages	96	13	109	67	110	150	130
Salaries and wages							
Kitchen	32	6	38	30	45	60	50
Dining room	20	4	24	19	26	39	32
Bartender	11	2	13	10	14	19	16
Supplies, repairs, and maintenance	13	4	17	8	15	25	18
Total restaurant	**172**	**29**	**201**	**134**	**210**	**293**	**246**
Total expenses	**$422**	**$59**	**$481**	**$392**	**$484**	**$621**	**$550**

TIMELY INTERIM STATEMENTS

The most carefully thought out budget will be of little value if it is not compared throughout the year with the actual results of operations. This means that the interim financial statements must be prepared on a timely basis.

What is timely? This largely depends on the organization and how much "slippage" or deviation from budget the organization can afford before serious consequences take place. If the cash balance is low an organization can't afford the luxury of not knowing where it stands on a timely basis. Guidelines are dangerous, but if an organization is unable to produce some form of abbreviated monthly or quarterly financial statement within 20 days of the end of the period the likelihood is that the information is "stale" by the time it is prepared. If twenty days is the length of time it takes then the board should plan to meet shortly after the twentieth of the month so as to be able to act on deviations while there is still time to act.

This is not to suggest that monthly financial statements are always appropriate for nonprofit organizations. But even if prepared on a bi-monthly or quarterly basis, they should still be prepared on a timely basis.

Importance of Budget Comparison

The financial statement should also show the budget, and for the same period of time. Interim figures for the three months cannot easily be compared to budget figures for twelve months. The budget must also be for three months. Last year's actual figures for the same period may also be shown, although this added information could detract from the reader seeing the deviation from the current year's budget.

Table 1–5 shows the Valley Country Club Statement of Income and Expense for both the month of June and for the 6 months, with budget comparisons to highlight deviations from the budget.

This financial statement gives the reader a great deal of information about the club's activities for the two periods. It should have the effect of alerting the reader to the fact that unless something happens, there may be a deficit for the year. For instead of having a small excess for June, there was a deficit of $6,200, and instead of having an excess of $7,500 for the six months, there was a deficit of almost $5,000. The board member reading the statement should be concerned about these deviations from the budget. This form of presentation makes it easy to see deviations. He can quickly pinpoint all unfavorable deviations and can then

TABLE 1–5. Statement of Income and Expenses and Comparison with Budget for the Month of June and the Six Months Ending June 30, 1972 for The Valley Country Club

	Month			Six Months		
	Actual	Budget	Deviation Favorable (Unfavorable)	Actual	Budget	Deviation Favorable (Unfavorable)
Income						
Annual dues	$15,650	$17,000	($1,350)	$ 81,900	$ 90,000	($ 8,100)
Initiation fees	2,100	2,000	100	6,600	4,500	2,100
Greens fees	4,750	4,000	750	11,000	8,000	3,000
Swimming	3,300	3,000	300	2,300	2,000	300
Other	6,710	8,000	(1,290)	18,250	14,000	4,250
Total, excluding restaurant	32,510	34,000	(1,490)	120,050	118,500	1,550
Restaurant	37,850	34,000	3,850	168,500	180,000	(11,500)
Total income	70,360	68,000	2,360	288,550	298,500	(9,950)
Expenses						
Maintenance of greens and grounds	14,650	12,000	(2,650)	37,650	36,000	(1,650)
Maintenance of clubhouse	3,450	3,000	(450)	18,100	19,000	900
Golf activities	13,500	10,000	(3,500)	19,500	16,000	(3,500)
Swimming pool	3,400	3,000	(400)	5,100	4,000	(1,100)
General and administrative	4,200	3,700	(500)	24,150	22,000	(2,150)
Payroll taxes	3,700	3,500	(200)	23,500	21,000	(2,500)
Other expenses	4,100	5,000	850	19,560	20,000	440
Total, excluding restaurant	47,050	40,200	(6,850)	147,560	138,000	(9,560)
Restaurant	29,550	27,000	(2,550)	145,650	153,000	7,350
Total expenses	76,600	67,200	(9,400)	293,210	291,000	(2,210)
Excess of income over (under) expenses	($ 6,240)	$ 800	($7,040)	($ 4,660)	$ 7,500	($12,160)

explore the reasons for them and determine the action that must be taken to prevent their recurrence.

Notice that both the current month and the year-to-date figures are shown on this statement. Both are important. The month gives a current picture of what is happening, which cannot be learned from the six-month figures. If only the six-month statements were shown the reader would have to refer to the previous month's statement showing the first five months to see what happened in June. Likewise, to show only the month, with no year-to-date figures, puts a burden on the reader. He will have to do some calculating using previous monthly statements to get his own total to see where the club stood cumulatively. Year-to-date budget comparisons are often more revealing than monthly comparisons because minor fluctuations in income and expenses tend to offset over a period of months. These fluctuations can appear rather large in any one month.

Restaurant Operation

Restaurant income and expenses have been shown "gross" in the statements. It would be equally proper for the club to show net income for the club before the restaurant operation was considered. Table 1–6 shows how this would look.

Another possibility is to show only the net income of the restaurant in the statements, perhaps in the income section. In condensed form Table 1–7 shows how the statements would look.

Either presentation, or the one in Table 1–5, is acceptable. The appropriate presentation depends on the importance of highlighting the restaurant activities.

TABLE 1–6.

Income (excluding restaurant)	$ 120,050
Expenses (excluding restaurant)	147,560
Excess of expenses over income excluding restaurant	(27,510)
Restaurant	
Gross income	168,500
Expenses	(145,650)
Net restaurant income	22,850
Excess of expenses over income	$ (4,660)

TABLE 1–7.

Income other than restaurant	$ 120,050
Restaurant net income	22,850
Total income	142,900
Expenses (other than restaurant)	(147,560)
Excess of expenses over income	$ (4,660)

Variable Budget

One technique that is often used in budgeting an operation where costs increase as the volume of activity increases is to relate the budgeted costs to income. For example, the final expense budget (Table 1–4) and the relationship to budgeted income for the restaurant operation is shown in Table 1–8.

If all costs increase proportionately as income increases, then it is a simple matter to create new budget figures each month based on actual income. Using the six-month figures shown in Table 1–5, our budget comparison for the restaurant activity for the six month period would look like that shown in Table 1–9.

The significant observation here is that while the original budget comparison in Table 1–5 showed an unfavorable deviation from budget of only $4,150, the unfavorable deviation using this variable budget is significantly higher, $13,925. Obviously if the variable budget is accu-

TABLE 1–8.

Budget Item	Amount	Percent of Income
Total income	$290,000	100
Food and beverages	$130,000	45
Salaries and wages		
Kitchen	50,000	17
Dining room	32,000	11
Bartender	16,000	6
Supplies, repairs, and maintenance	18,000	6
Total Expenses	$246,000	85

TABLE 1-9.

Budget Item	Actual	Variable Budget	Deviation from Variable Budget	Deviation from Original Budget Shown in Table 1-5
Income	$168,500	$180,000*	$(11,500)	$(11,500)
Expenses (in total)	145,650	143,225†	(2,425)	7,350
Net	$ 22,850	$ 36,775	$(13,925)	$ (4,150)

*Original budget for six months.
†85% of actual income for the six months, based on the relationship of budgeted expenses to budgeted income as shown above.

rate, then the club manager has not been watching his costs carefully enough.

The financial statements would show only the variable expense budget. The original expense budget would not be used. This kind of budget is more difficult to work with because each month the treasurer or bookkeeper has to recalculate the expense figures to be used based on actual income. At the same time by doing so, a meaningful budget comparison can be made. It is very difficult otherwise for the board to judge the restaurant's results.

One final observation about this variable budget. Certain costs are not proportional to income. For example, the club cannot have less than one bartender or one chef. Accordingly, in preparing a variable budget sometimes the relationships that are developed will not be simple percentage relationships. For example, perhaps the relationship of bartender salary will be, say, $5,000 plus 5 per cent of total income over $75,000. If so, then if restaurant income is $350,000, the budget will be $18,750 ($5,000 + 5 per cent of $275,000).

Narrative Report on Deviations from Budget

It will be noted that much of the detail shown in the budget (Table 1-4) has not been shown on the interim financial statement (Table 1-5). If the board felt it appropriate, supporting schedules could be prepared giving as much detail as desired. Care should be taken, however, not to request details that won't be used since it obviously takes time and costs money to prepare detailed supporting schedules.

It may be that a more meaningful supporting schedule would be a narrative summary of the reasons for the deviations from budget for the major income and expense categories. The club manager, in the case of the Valley Country Club, would probably be the one to prepare this summary. The amount of detail and description that he might put in this summary would vary from account to account. Clearly the report should only discuss reasons for the major deviations. This report should accompany the financial statement so that questions raised by the statement are answered immediately. Figure 1–1 shows an example of the type of summary he might prepare to explain the expense deviations from budget (in part).

VALLEY COUNTRY CLUB
CLUB MANAGER'S REPORT TO THE BOARD
EXPENSE DEVIATIONS FROM BUDGET, JUNE 1972

Maintenance of greens and grounds ($2,650)

As you will recall, April and May were fairly wet months. This coupled with other unfavorable soil conditions required that we treat about 25% of the course with a fungicide which had not been budgeted ($1,850). We also had some unexpected repairs to the sprinkler system ($1,500). For the six months to date we have exceeded budget by only $1,650 and I am confident that our annual budget will not be exceeded.

Maintenance of clubhouse ($450)

We had scheduled painting the Clubhouse for May but because of the rains were not able to get it done until this month. Year-to-date expenses are $900 under budget.

Golf activities ($3,500)

After the budget had been approved the Board decided to have an open tournament with a view toward attracting new membership. With promotion and prizes this came to $2,850. So far the membership committee has received thirteen new applications for membership.

FIGURE 1–1. An example of a narrative report prepared by the manager of a country club explaining certain major deviations from the budget

This type of report can be as informal as you want to make it as long as it conveys why there have been deviations from the original budget. But it should be in writing, both to ensure that the board knows the reasons, and to force the club manager to face squarely his responsibility to meet the projected budget. This report is a form of discipline for him.

CONCLUSION

A budget can be an extremely important and effective tool for the board in managing the affairs of the organization. However, to prepare a meaningful budget the organization must know where it is heading and its goals and objectives. Priorities change and this means that many people should be involved in the budget preparation and approval process to insure the resulting budget is fully supported. Once prepared, the budget must be compared to actual results on a timely basis throughout the year to insure that the board knows where deviations are occurring. Equally important, the board must promptly take corrective action if unfavorable deviations occur. The foundations of a sound financial structure are a well-conceived budget, a timely reporting system, and a willingness by the board to take corrective action.

The importance of planning into the future cannot be overemphasized. In this fast-moving age, worthy nonprofit organizations can quickly get out of step with the times, and when this happens contributions and income quickly disappear. A five-year master plan is one technique to help ensure this won't happen.

2

Planning and Budgeting: An Ongoing, Integrated Process

STEPHEN L. WHITE
ANTHONY BROSKOWSKI

Planning is the transformation of ideas into meaningful action, or, to borrow H. L. Mencken's phrase, to progress "from balderdash to excellence." The planning process determines needs and demands for a given service, assesses resource requirements, establishes a specific set of objectives, and designates specific implementation steps.

As soon as implementation begins, so must the process of monitoring progress. Programs expend resources and generate products or services, just as an engine creates movement through the consumption of fuel and air. The part of a program's plan that deals with obtaining and expending resources is the budget. Put in another way, "A budget is really nothing more than a plan of action for one year's duration expressed in the numbers of dollars required to reach the goals the organization has set for itself for that year. A budget answers two basic questions: 'What will it cost to do what we want to do?' and 'From what sources will revenue come to meet these costs?'" (White, 1981, p. 76). Thought of in this way, the planning function and the budgeting function can be combined to form an integrated process, one that follows a series of different phases over an annual period. In this cyclical and integrated planning-budgeting process, each phase of the process is a prerequisite for the phase that follows. Moreover, changes in one phase may affect and be affected by other phases anywhere in the annual cycle.

Many discussions of planning and budgeting begin, logically enough, at the point where the future year's plan and budget is requested by an agency director or a funding agency. Such a view of the planning-budgeting process treats the process as though it were a linear function with a clear beginning, middle, and end. Such a view of planning and budgeting can also minimize the fact that an important aspect of a program is its history. A program's previous commitments, priorities, financial condition, utilization rates, client characteristics, and staffing patterns can all have a profound impact on its future operation. The continuous cyclical and integrated view of planning and budgeting presented in this chapter conveys a better sense of reality than a view of planning and budgeting as two parallel but separate functions.

Given the cyclical, ongoing view of planning-budgeting, we must arbitrarily choose a point at which to begin our discussion. We shall walk through an annual planning-budgeting cycle, artificially breaking into the cycle at a point after a given year's budget is approved and operationalized. Most managers who assume responsibility for an operational program are introduced to a budget at this phase of the annual cycle. For this reason, and because the monitoring of a budget is so often neglected in discussions of budgeting, we shall begin with the monitoring phase. Eight more phases follow (see Figure 2–1).

MONTHLY REPORTS

The task at this point of the cycle is monitoring revenues, expenditures, and progress toward goals. The methods for monitoring these aspects of the program are the monthly financial and budget reports. There are *two* monthly financial reports for a program, one for revenues and one for expenditures. Each report usually lists items of expenditures *or* revenues down the extreme left-hand column. Moving to the right, the information may be divided into values for the current month, the total for the fiscal year to date, and the same month in the prior year. Under each of the columns, "current month" and "year to date," the information is usually divided further into separate columns for what was planned or budgeted, and what was actually earned or expended. In some cases a third column will show the variance between the budget and the actual amounts. At the bottom of the report, totals for all of the above separate lines will be given. Therefore, by looking at a monthly financial report, a manager can clearly see, for the month or the year to date, whether or not the program is spending and/or earning more or less than was planned at the start of the fiscal year. This analysis can look at the program as a whole or focus on particular items of expenditures or sources of revenue.

In addition to the monthly reports on revenues and expenses, each program should have a parallel set of one or more reports about the services provided. This monthly report may take a variety of formats, de-

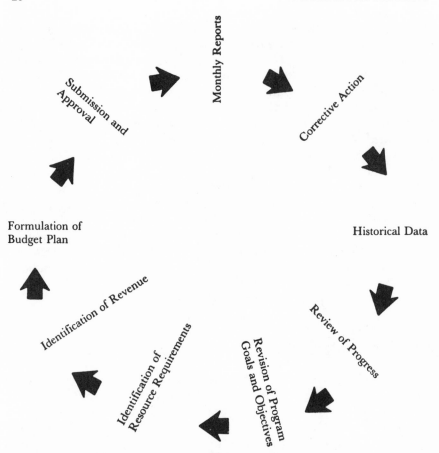

FIGURE 2–1. The annual planning-budgeting cycle

pending on the nature of the program. In some cases, the report may list the number of clients admitted to the program, the number of clients discharged, and the total number of clients remaining at the end of the month. In some cases, the report may list the number of service units provided to these clients, with further breakdowns according to the types of clients. In some cases, the report may itemize separately the productivity for individual staff. In any case, this report reflects actual measures of productivity determined by units of services, numbers of clients, or other types of events that measure productivity. Generally, as in the case of a financial report, these productivity reports should compare actual measures of productivity against planned levels of productivity. For example, the report may show that in a given month 200 units of services were provided and compare that with a goal of 250 units of service for that month. There may be a separate column showing that in this case the program had reached 80 percent of its goal for the month (200 divided by 250).

CORRECTIVE ACTION

Usually, there is some slight variance from month to month between what was planned and what actually happened. A manager may observe that in a given month there was a substantial variance between what was planned and what actually happened in the way of collecting revenues, spending income, or providing services. In that case, it is necessary to determine if a consistent pattern is occurring over a long time period. If a trend develops whereby the program is spending substantially more than it earns and collects, or is producing far less than it planned, then corrective action must be taken.

Corrective action falls into two main categories. The first is the reduction of spending. The manager can examine every facet of the program's spending—rent, utilities, supplies, travel, personnel—to determine if sufficient savings can be achieved to balance expenditures with revenues.

The second type of corrective action is to increase revenues. Assuming staff productivity is not low, the manager can determine whether sufficiently high fees are being charged for services. If so, is there something about the way in which the fees are being collected that could be made more efficient? For example, the greater the delay between rendering the service and billing the client, the lower will be the percentage of funds collected from all amounts billed. Is every attempt being made to capture every type of insurance or other payment for which the program is eligible? Is the mix of clients shifting to the point where discounts based on ability to pay are so great that fewer clients are being billed for services?

Sometimes slight adjustments in spending, revenue generation, or productivity are enough to balance spending with revenues. If a deficit trend continues too long, more drastic corrective action may be necessary. Unless the middle manager is willing to identify areas where action can be taken, top administration is more likely to step in and make the necessary adjustments in ways objectionable to the manager and the staff (White, 1981). For an excellent treatment of this issue, see Sweeny and Wisner (1975).

HISTORICAL DATA

Previous years' budgets, monthly budget reports, and productivity data reflect certain aspects of the program's history. This information is important because it indicates where mistakes may have been made in past budget planning and because it gives the manager a base from which to work in preparing the next year's projections. Even agencies that use a zero-base budgetary approach (Pyhrr, 1973) need historical data about program performance in the areas of productivity, costs, and revenue in order to make reasonable forecasts in these areas for the next year.

REVIEW OF OVERALL PROGRESS

In addition to monthly reviews, the program's progress toward its overall goals should be reviewed in a formal, systematic way. This review should take place quarterly or semiannually, so there is time for corrections to be made. Such a review would compare actual expenditures, revenues, and the quantity and quality of service with what was projected at the beginning of the fiscal year. Goals to serve certain target groups or implement new types of services can be reviewed here. The manager of the program should have the primary responsibility for carrying out this review, but should enlist the assistance of other resource persons in the agency such as the program evaluator and the business manager.

The information gleaned from the review of the program's progress toward its overall goals should be used to correct deficiencies in the program and to develop the following year's budget plan. This information also affords members of the agency's top administration and board of directors an opportunity to understand the achievements and shortcomings of a program.

REVISION OF PROGRAM GOALS AND OBJECTIVES

This is a quarterly or semiannual landmark in the annual planning-budgeting cycle. By now, the manager has an increasingly clear idea of what was right or wrong about the initial fiscal and programmatic projections for the current year. In many cases, the planned projections do not hold up. Perhaps the projections were correct at the time they were made, but the environment of competitive agencies, funding sources, inflationary costs, patterns of client referrals, or a host of other factors has changed so rapidly that projections made a few months ago are obsolete. In any case, at this point the manager must review the entire program's record and revise productivity, cost, and revenue projections for the balance of the year. At times, a manager may even need to change the specific types of services being provided in order to adapt to emerging consumer demands or the shifting priorities of funding agencies.

It is particularly at this point in the planning-budgeting cycle that the manager must begin to make some preliminary guesses about what the future holds in terms of the priorities and resources available through funding sources, the demands of fee-paying clients, or even the future ability of clients to pay fees. These forecasts must also include assumptions about future trends in costs of salaries for professional and support workers, utility rate hikes, rent increases, and essential supplies.

When the forecasting process has generated basic assumptions about the need for the service and the economic scene for the coming year, the manager can engage in discussions with superiors and subordinates to develop general goals and specific, measurable objectives for the coming year.

IDENTIFICATION OF RESOURCE REQUIREMENTS

The next step in the planning-budgeting annual cycle is the identification of future resource requirements for the program. This assumes, of course, that the program for the coming year will be a continuation, albeit modified, of the current year's program. Developing a program involves attention to such matters as initial planning, evaluation, rules and regulations, funding and financing, organizing, external relationships, and program maintenance. A model of program development and management, called PERFORM, is discussed elsewhere (White & Broskowski, 1980; White & Broskowski, 1981).

The nature of the program's goals and objectives identified in the previous phase of this cycle will dictate the types and amounts of resources needed. The single largest category of resources in most human services programs is personnel, usually accounting for 60 to 80 percent of the budget. The manager must match program requirements with specific personnel requirements, not only in terms of the number of people needed, but also in terms of skill and educational requirements for each person and the budgeted salary for each position. In determining resource requirements that pertain to personnel, one must also figure in the cost of fringe benefits (usually calculated as some percentage of the annual salary) and the loss of productivity due to sick time, holidays, and vacations.

The next largest category of resource requirements concerns the program's physical plant. This category includes rent, utilities, maintenance costs, telephone, and insurance costs. Some of these costs, such as rent, might be charged to the program based upon the amount of space occupied or the actual rent charge. Other costs, such as liability insurance, might be charged to the program according to some formula such as a percentage of the total agency's insurance costs in proportion to the program staff's size.

In addition to personnel and physical plant, the manager must identify several other resource categories, such as supplies, travel costs, postage, dues and subscriptions, transportation for clients, and so on. The best indicator of categories needed and costs is the program's line item expenditures for the previous year. These line items and associated costs must be increased or reduced on the basis of planned changes in the program and general inflation.

In the process of preparing this part of the planning-budgeting document for the coming year, the manager should consult with the personnel manager and the business manager in order to get help in deciding upon the quality and cost of each budget category.

IDENTIFICATION OF REVENUE

Expenditures represent only one side of the budget equation. The other side of the equation, of course, is revenue. Revenue can come from a variety of sources. One source could be fees and insurance payments that the program itself generates by providing service. Another source could be grant funds or contract funds specifically earmarked for that program.

A third source of revenue for mental health programs is often federal, state, and municipal or county funds given in lump sums to the program's parent agency. These funds must be further allocated to each of the agency's separate programs by the agency's administration. Therefore, it is important for a program manager to make as compelling a case as possible for the amount of these funds needed for the program.

FORMULATION OF THE BUDGET PLAN

The actual planning-budgeting document, as we have seen, is partly composed of projections regarding expenses and revenues. These projections, in fact, summarize in dollar terms the goals and objectives of the program for the coming year. The planning-budgeting document, therefore, should roughly follow this outline:

1. overview and description of the program,
2. accomplishments of program during past year,
3. goals and specific measurable objectives for coming year,
4. expenses (resource requirements) for coming year by line item,
5. revenues by source projected for coming year.

Appendixes to the planning-budgeting document should include reports of any program evaluation studies done in the past year and an explanation and justification for any significant increases requested in the budget for the coming year. The document should be brief and conform to the format in general use in the agency.

While preparing the planning-budgeting document, it is important for a manager to know as much as possible about the entire agency's future financial situation and programmatic priorities. In some agencies, at the beginning of the budget preparation phase of the year, the executive director will communicate budget guidelines to program managers. These guidelines indicate which programs or client populations will receive priority over others and indicate the nature of future funding assumptions by specific source. If guidelines are not forthcoming, a manager should ask for them. The executive director's guidelines will allow a manager to construct a planning-budgeting proposal that is, within the context of the total agency, realistic and likely to be approved.

SUBMISSION AND APPROVAL

When the planning-budgeting document is completed, it is submitted (usually by a predetermined date) to the executive director. Each program budget is used as a building block in the agency's total budget. At this phase, program proposals may be reduced so that the total budget will balance with revenues.

The total agency budget is then presented to the board of directors or parent organization (hospital, government agency, or other entity) for final approval before the start of the next fiscal year. The decision of the governing body is usually final. Once the decision has been made, the total document becomes the agency's official plan of operation for the coming year, and the process of implementation begins. At this point, the annual planning-budgeting process has come full circle to the phase with which this chapter began: the monitoring of monthly financial and productivity reports. For additional information on budgeting and financial management, see Sweeny and Wisner (1975), and especially Sorensen, Hanbery, and Feldman (1980), and Feldman, Sorensen, and Hanbery (1980).

As we have seen, the annual planning-budgeting process is continuous, and to say that the process begins and ends at any one point is an artificial construction. Every phase affects and is affected by every other phase. Furthermore, program considerations and fiscal considerations are interdependent and must be considered as such.

REFERENCES

Feldman, S., Sorensen, J. E., and Hanbery, G. W. Budgeting and behavior. In S. Feldman (Ed.), *The administration of mental health services.* (2nd ed.) Springfield, Il.: Thomas, 1980.

Pyhrr, P. A. *Zero-based budgeting: A practical management tool for evaluating expenses.* New York: John Wiley & Sons, 1973.

Sorensen, J. E., Hanbery, G. W., and Feldman, S. Financial management. In S. Feldman (Ed.), *The administration of mental health services.* Springfield, Il.: Thomas, 1980.

Sweeny, A., and Wisner, J. N. *Budgeting fundamentals for nonfinancial executives.* New York: AMACOM, 1975.

White, S. L. *Managing health and human services programs.* New York: Free Press, 1981.

White, S. L., and Broskowski, A. PERFORM: A model of program development and management. *Administration in Mental Health 8* (3), Spring 1981.

3

Avoiding Fiscal Management Problems in Human Service Agencies

RICHARD L. HODGES

Scarce economic resources force managers of human service programs to be concerned with financial administration. This concern results from their desire to establish that their agencies have achieved the organizational goals in an efficient manner and in compliance with the specific regulations prescribed by the individuals and/or institutions providing economic resources.

Achieving the goals of fiscal management—effective, efficient use of resources in compliance with restrictions—is difficult under the best of conditions, but program designers and managers may further complicate their lives by several ill-advised practices. This article explores some counterproductive fiscal management practices, concentrating on those that are to a significant degree under the control of the operating manager.

INTEGRATED MANAGEMENT SYSTEM: AN OVERVIEW

The successful operation of a service delivery agency depends on an integrated management system. In a work and training environment that categorizes individuals into various specialties, it is easy to have the management system disintegrate. The need for the integrated system and the general points needed to identify a poor system are described first.

Internal Control

Fiscal management contains the requirement that the planning-action-evaluation elements of the management cycle consider internal control factors. Internal control, simply stated, means that the effort of individuals working within an organization is directed toward meeting the goals and policies of that organization.

Internal control is taking increasing importance in organizations. The increase in emphasis on internal control started in the commercial sector of the economy as a reaction to disclosures that U.S. corporations had made illegal payments to obtain foreign sales. As a result of that the Federal Government passed the Foreign Corrupt Practices Act, 1977, requiring that the management of the applicable organizations have proper fiscal controls in place.

Similar efforts are occurring in the government sector. First, Senator Eagleton introduced legislation in the 96th Congress (2nd sess., 1980) to require agency managers, through the Inspector General's office, to report on the status of their internal control systems. Second, the Comptroller General suggests that auditors, whether inside or outside government, review and comment on a government agency's internal control problems.

> An evaluation is to be made of the system of internal control to assess the extent it can be relied upon to ensure reliable information, to ensure compliance with laws and regulations, and to provide for efficient and effective operations and prevent and discourage fraud, abuse and other illegal and improper acts. [Standards for Audit, 1980, p. 53]

The same GAO report further states that a system of internal control includes:

1. A plan of organization that provides segregation of duties appropriate for properly safeguarding the entity's resources.
2. A system of authorization and record procedures adequate to provide effective accounting control over assets, liabilities, revenues, and expenses.
3. Practices to follow in performing functions of each organizational department.
4. Personnel of a quality commensurate with their responsibilities.
5. An effective system of internal review. [p. 54]

Safeguarding an entity's assets and effective accounting control, listed above, relate primarily to the financial resources of the agency. The third aspect of internal control pertains primarily to the operating management of an agency. The last two deal with personnel and internal review and relate to both the financial and operating elements of management.

> These elements, as important as each is in its own right, are mutually reinforcing and all are so basic to adequate internal control that serious deficiencies in any one normally could preclude effective operation of the system. [p. 54]

The auditor, in examining a human service agency, is going to review both the financial and the operating management elements of the supervisory process on the grounds that one cannot be effective without the other. A well-designed financial management system does not exist unless it relates and supports the operating management. Operating management cannot monitor performance or adequately direct future actions unless it has in place information and communication processes.

Funding

The dissolution of the control system, from a fiscal sense, begins with the process of obtaining monies to operate the service delivery programs. Two aspects of the funding process found in many agencies contribute to the break-up of the management systems.

First is the legislation or grant/donation funding mechanisms. Both of those funding sources are essentially contractual in nature (i.e., the fund providers stipulate the conditions that must be met if monies are to be obtained). The recipient agencies have an ethical if not a legal obligation to comply with these conditions. Compliance can take place in form only, in which case two management structures exist. One structure meets the rules, i.e., "compliance," and is not significantly responsible for actual operations. The budgets, accounting, and reporting aspects of fiscal management are often the components of that compliance in form. Unless a second fiscal information and control system exists, the management structure is weakened.

The second factor that causes the management structure to be weakened occurs if the funding sources have prescribed requirements that required unproductive procedures or are counter to program goals. Short of rejecting funding that carries such restrictions and suffering the obvious consequences, the agency's influence is limited to any persuasion it can exercise during the rule-making processes of the funding source.

An agency with multiple funding sources, each prescribing different procedures, finds the matter of compliance, form, and substance extremely complicated. However, agency personnel may cause compliance problems by their own actions.

Program Design

Nearly all government- or foundation-funded programs require the submission of a document describing the need for the monies and the applicable objectives to meet that need. Weaknesses in the definition of the need, the specific objectives to meet it, and the financial requirements at the program design phase will lead to review problems at a later time.

> An objective of financial statements for governmental and not-for-profit organizations is to provide information useful for evaluating the effectiveness of the management of resources in achieving the organization's goals. Performance measures should be quantified in terms of identified goals. [AICPA, 1973, p. 66]

While recognizing that often the qualitative aspects of service or assistance programs cannot be defined in quantifiable terms, an effort must still be made. The only way an agency can meet its goals is to have defined those goals. The more specific the definitions in terms of the ability to provide objective evidence of achievement, the easier the demonstration of success becomes.

Dismissal of the attempt for specificity, on the ground that it results from a mentality that does not understand the needs of humans or the difficulty of measuring complex social goals, is not defensible for several reasons. First, the program has to be justified on its own merit. Many methods exist to carry out a human service objective, and yet the applicant is arguing for a specific approach. The inability to demonstrate that one approach is better than the alternatives simply means that political power, not merit, will determine social programs, and in the end political power will terminate or continue those programs.

The failure to provide a specific statement of program objectives also makes it impossible to determine whether they are being met. This means that the agency will not be able to demonstrate that monies have been used in accordance with the funding convenant. The agency cannot then demonstrate that it is serving its clients. Therefore, in spite of technological problems relating to the quantification of social goals, it is necessary to use the knowledge and methods available. Hence, as specific a description as possible of the goals and the methods used to meet them should be contained in the program design.

Budgeting

The design phase should recognize that budgeting and accounting are elements in a fiscal management system and not separate processes. A management system consists of planning, action or implementing, and evaluation phases. The fiscal management process also relates to those same three phases (Horngren, 1978). Budgets are a part of the planning phase. As a result, budgeting incorporates not just the monies to be expended but all of the assumptions relating to need, objectives, and ability to deliver services that are found in the planning phase.

The action or implementation element can also be found in the financial records and measurements. Hence, the accounting system should be designed to measure the program's goals. Conversely, the planning and budgeting process should consider the need to measure if accounting is to be successful.

The last management phase mentioned earlier is that of evaluation or feedback. The performance reports prepared from the accounting records are an element of that phase. These reports will be prepared recognizing the budget and the performance objectives stated therein. Hence, if planning is imprecise the action and evaluation phases of operating and fiscal management will reflect that weakness.

Accounting as Part of Management System

An effective accounting system provides information for three broad purposes: (1) Internal reporting to managers, for use in planning and controlling routine operations; (2) internal reporting to managers, for use in strategic planning, that is, the making of special decisions and the formulating of overall policies and long-range plans; and (3) external reporting to stockholders, government, and other outside parties. [Horngren, 1978, p. 4]

For reasons of analysis and learning accounting has divided itself into managerial (found in the first two internal purposes listed above) and financial accounting (external reporting).

Financial accounting is much more tied to form than managerial. However, even financial accounting recognizes the primary concern that reporting the legal and economic substance of a transaction is the objective, and form follows from that goal.

Managerial accounting takes the form desired within the organization, with the constraint that it is expensive to establish and maintain duplicate accounting systems. The single accounting system should, as a result, be designed in a coordinated fashion to minimize cost and effort. The bulk of the information within a system can meet both external reporting and internal management needs simply by designing reports that aggregate the data differently or by adding small sub-units to the main accounting system.

The application of accounting briefly described above is very flexible and if successfully applied will meet both the internal and external requirements. However, it is often applied incorrectly. How? By simply not using the available accounting technology.

Accounting has a theoretical foundation that has developed over several hundred years. This foundation describes what is to be recorded, the reason for recording, and how it is to be recorded.

The flexibility of accounting is often abused by individuals or organizations that deliberately ignore the theoretical foundation. The records look like they comply with the funding requirements. Appearance is not, however, the goal of accounting. The goal, instead, is to record the economic and legal substance of a transaction. The "creative accounting" practiced by some agencies abuses that flexibility with the result being an incorrect, if not inadequate, financial information system.

In addition to causing problems for itself by not using available accounting technology, the agency management can also create difficulties by two other means that tend to interrelate. First, they can make the accounting personnel outsiders within the organization. Second, they leave accounting to the accountants. Both of those practices can lead to significant difficulties for the organization.

Rewarding only the "line" or human service side of the organization is one means of making the support personnel feel like they are not a significant part of the unit. Reward in this context means more than the salaries paid; it also includes respect and the other attributes of recognition. Salary, however, is often a problem since the market demand for skilled accounting personnel may result in their pay being higher than comparable operating personnel. This means that the agency may face a decision between hiring adequate accounting personnel at salaries that other employees feel is inequitable or paying too little relative to the accounting market and obtaining individuals with poor skills. A suggestion to help alleviate that problem is offered in the section on the auditor that follows.

A second means of creating that outside feeling is to use a method often found in other areas where "form" compliance only is the goal. That method is to assign the financial management functions to the least competent member of the agency's top supervisory personnel. Inadequate fiscal control is often accompanied by non-control in other areas of management since information is missing from the decision process. Hence, management is defaulting on its fiscal responsibility and may be handicapping itself in other areas. It is difficult to manage operations unless the financial management is competent and an integral part of the operating structure of the agency.

One aspect of integrating financial information into the operating system is the inclusion on the management team of some ability to use the data being provided. Large agencies should have little difficulty obtaining that skill since they can by design select individuals for management with a variety of training. The small agency, however, is not so fortunate since that variety may not be available and the relatively large cost of obtaining specialized skills makes it prohibitive.

Small business organizations faced with that same problem often subcontract the function to bookkeeping or the Certified Public Accountant (CPA) firms that provide that type of service. This permits them to buy those skills at a fraction of the cost they would face if incorporated into business. The problem of the relative pay of accountants compared with agency personnel may be also be reduced since subcontracting eliminates the comparative inequity in an organizational sense, even if not in a social sense. Management must still have the ability to use financial information, or the outside service will simply complete the forms, and decisions will still lack the fiscal element.

While it may be less expensive, the use of outside services obviously results in the financial processing operating outside the organization. A lack of integration results unless agency management, in consultation with the service provider, overcomes that obstacle.

Since most funding sources require audits, there is also additional assistance available for both large and small agencies, whether they subcontract for the bookkeeping and accounting services or retain them within the organization.

Audit

The auditor at the very least is going to review the financial records, legal compliance, and the processes that support the management of fiscal resources. The review results in identification of weaknesses in financial management. The agency management can either be defensive about any weaknesses, or they can use the auditor as a resource to improve their system.

The agency with well-defined objectives, that has in place a measurement system that records its efforts to meet those objectives, will find the audit to be simply a formality. On the other hand, the agency that is complying in form only will find the audit an unpleasant obligation. The statement of goals in the grant document will be used by the auditor to establish that the goals are not being met. If those goals are poorly stated, inadequately performed, or if the fiscal management system does not record and report the performance, then the resulting audit outcomes will be negative. But, of course, if the audit is accurate, it reflects the operations of the agency.

CONCLUSION

Operating management of a human service agency needs to integrate fiscal information processes with the other data sources if they are going to make considered decisions. Several factors for a lack of integration were suggested. Many of those factors are under the control or at least significant influence of an agency's operating management. The wise use of fiscal information will not solve the problems of an agency, but financial information will provide data for making decisions, highlighting problems, or facilitating feedback and control within the organization. It is a useful tool. The gain or loss depends on the organizational needs and the ability of management to utilize that tool.

REFERENCES

AICPA. *Objectives of financial statements*. Report of the study group on the objectives of financial statements. New York: AICPA, 1973.

Horngren, C. T. *Introduction to management accounting*. 4th edition. Englewood Cliffs, NJ: Prentice-Hall, Inc., 1978.

U.S. General Accounting Office. *Draft standards for audit of governmental organizations, programs, activities, and functions*, 1980.

4

Improving Cash Management in Nonprofit Organizations

CREASIE FINNEY HAIRSTON

A common and recurring problem in many nonprofit organizations is the cash deficit. Although the annual operating budget projects that income for the year will match or even exceed expenses, at some point during the year the agency may find that it is unable to meet its cash obligations. The payroll cannot be met, the plumbing cannot be repaired, or needed purchases cannot be made. For some agencies, this is a one-time problem. For others, it is a recurring crisis which may either be sporadic or follow a predictable pattern.

Cash flow problems occur in all types and sizes of organizations. In fact, Lohmann's (1980) financial management text recognizes cash flow management as one of the most universal financial planning problems facing human services agencies. This author's experiences as a management consultant as well as data from other sources support Lohmann's view. For example, Hartog and Weber's (1978) survey of 141 voluntary health and welfare agencies in the New York metropolitan area revealed that two-thirds of the agencies experienced cash flow problems. A national voluntary association's financial development executive (Becker, 1980) identified cash flow management as a major problem facing the association's local affiliates. Discussions with local executives who participate in management training conducted by the author support the financial development executive's assessment.

In addition to being widespread, cash flow problems are often meshed with other financial problems and are frequently not distinguished from them. A survey by the New York Community Trust (NYCT) demonstrates this point. In 1976, NYCT surveyed over 200

public and voluntary agencies to assess possible cash flow problems resulting from New York City's financial problems (McAdam, 1976). Since
the city provided a large share of the agencies' budgets, delays in city
payments were expected to result in significant cash shortages for the
agencies. The results of the survey were mixed. Although the agencies
contended that cash flow problems were worsening, there was little solid
evidence that the financial problems which the agencies reported could
be attributed to cash flow. Rather, the available data pointed to chronic
budget deficits brought on by the agencies' failure to reduce expenditures to match actual or projected income. The researchers concluded
that most agencies were unable to distinguish between budget reductions and cash flow problems. The ability to distinguish between cash
deficits and budget deficits is also frequently missing in other settings.

Although cash management is an area that all organizations must
address and one with which many experience problems, there are few
resources which the nonprofit manager can draw on to upgrade knowledge and skills. Cash management is a standard feature of financial
management texts in the business sector but the topic is either not
treated at all or is treated superficially at best in most commonly used
nonprofit management materials. This paper is a resource which staff
and board members responsible for agency financial matters can use to
improve financial management practices. It discusses the nature of cash
flow problems in nonprofit organizations and offers practical suggestions to use in planning for and controlling the use of cash. Basic business principles and techniques and the author's managerial experiences
in the nonprofit sector provide background for the information which is
presented.

THE NATURE OF CASH FLOW PROBLEMS

In general, what are cash flow problems? Why do they occur and what
are the implications for the agencies involved? Cash flow refers to the
movement of cash into and out of an organization. Basically a cash flow
problem is a situation wherein the amount of cash which an agency must
pay out exceeds the amount that it has on hand at the time that payment
is due. In other words, the agency has a cash deficit or shortage. Unlike a
budget deficit situation, the agency fully expects to collect the needed
funds and, in fact, may have already provided the income-producing
service. The cash deficit arises because the timing and amounts of cash
disbursements do not coincide with the timing and amounts of cash receipts.

Cash flow problems occur in nonprofit agencies for a variety of reasons. Start-up costs of new programs, irregular payments from funding sources, unexpected expenditures, and time lags between billing dates and payment receipt dates are but a few of the factors which impact on the flow of an agency's cash. Since many agencies do not have long-term funds such as endowment or capital reserves to use as a resource in covering current operating expenses, unexpected deficits are particularly critical.

The fact that an agency's cash receipts do not coincide with its cash disbursements is not reflective of poor management and, in fact, is the norm in many organizations. Failure to plan for irregularities in cash flow and to control the use of cash, however, is generally recognized as an indicator of incompetence. It is possible, of course, for agencies to use last minute, after-the-fact crisis intervention efforts to meet cash obligations. These efforts, however, are frustrating, time-consuming and embarrassing. In addition, they create a negative public image and, at the same time, threaten agency solvency.

The employee who is not paid on time or who is paid but is told by the bank that the agency has "insufficient funds" to cover his or her check is unlikely to have kind words to say about the agency in question. Funders who become aware of cash deficits and an impending financial crisis are forced to assess the wisdom of their continued support of what appears to be a poorly managed operation. In the meantime, those who hold negative views about the agency will not hesitate to seize the opportunity to back their charges.

Fortunately, many cash flow and related problems can be handled by using sound management practices. Several of these are discussed in the following section.

WAYS OF IMPROVING CASH MANAGEMENT

Establish a Minimum Cash Balance for the Agency

The minimum cash balance is the minimum cash amount that the agency desires to have on hand at all times. This amount allows the agency to meet its expected requirements and provides a reasonable margin for the unexpected. Because personnel costs usually represent nonprofit organizations' highest costs, the monthly payroll is a useful guide for determining this amount. The full monthly payroll is used as a realistic amount since this is a major expense that agencies find nonnegotiable in terms of payment due dates.

Prepare a Cash Budget

The cash budget is a written statement of an agency's projected flow of cash. It estimates the agency's expected cash intake, expected cash disbursements, and expected cash balance on pre-established dates. Since the emphasis is on cash alone, the cash budget does not necessarily coincide with the agency's projected statement of income and expenses or operating budget. Expenditures are recognized only when the actual money is expected to be paid out by the agency (a check is actually written) and income is recognized only when the actual money is expected to be received by the agency (a bank deposit is made). Although there are no set rules, most agencies using cash budgeting prepare the cash budget to cover a 1-year period corresponding with the normal fiscal year and divide the yearly period into monthly intervals.

Table 4–1 shows a cash budget which was prepared for Westside Child Development Center (WCDC). Note that the cash budget shows the agency's projected monthly receipts, disbursements, cash excess/deficit, beginning cash balance, and ending cash balance. The budget enables WCDC to predict the months in which the cash balance will fall below a specified minimum, determine the months in which there will be a cash surplus, and assess whether cash deficits are short-term or long-term. Using Table 4–1, one can determine that although WCDC will begin the year with a $2,000 cash balance and end with a $2,300 cash balance, cash deficits are projected for several months. More specifically, if cash inflows and outflows occur in the amounts and at the times projected, the agency will experience cash deficits in every month except August and December.

Use the Cash Budget as a Planning and Control Tool

Preparation of a cash budget does not avert the problem of ongoing cash deficits. Instead, as shown in Table 4–1, it projects when deficits will occur and in what amount if business takes place as usual. With this information in hand, agency leaders can focus on approaches to handling the projected deficits. They would examine areas of leeway with respect to both receipts and disbursements. In the case of WCDC, one might ask if shifting the purchase of supplies or equipment to a later date would alleviate the deficit. A second question might center around the possibility of renegotiating the timing of payments from the funding sources. If change would still result in deficits, the budget would be used to forecast the amount of financing needed to meet cash obligations. In determining this amount, the agency would consider the projected cash deficits plus the minimum cash balance. If WCDC, for example, set $3,500 as a

TABLE 4–1. WCDC Cash Budget Fiscal Year 1980

Cash Categories	January	February	March	April	May	June	July	August	September	October	November	December	Totals
Cash Intake													
Welfare department				12,000				10,000				18,000	40,000
Parent fund-raising						1,500			700		800		3,000
Parent fees	4,500	4,500	4,500	4,500	4,500	3,800	3,800	3,800	4,500	4,500	4,500	4,500	51,900
Foundation grant							18,000						18,000
Total Intake	4,500	4,500	4,500	16,500	4,500	5,300	21,800	13,800	5,200	4,500	5,300	22,500	112,900
Cash disbursements													
Payroll	7,000	7,000	7,000	7,000	7,000	7,300	7,300	7,300	7,000	7,000	7,000	7,000	84,900
Supplies			1,800					1,000					2,800
Equipment						700	700	700					2,100
Rent/utilities	700	700	700	700	700	700	700	700	700	700	700	700	8,400
Food	1,200	1,200	1,200	1,200	1,200	1,200	1,200	1,200	1,200	1,200	1,200	1,200	14,400
Total disbursements	8,900	8,900	10,700	8,900	8,900	9,900	9,900	10,900	8,900	8,900	8,900	8,900	112,600
Excess (Deficit)													
Intake/Disbursements	(4,400)	(4,400)	(6,200)	7,600	(4,400)	(4,600)	11,900	2,900	(3,700)	(4,400)	(3,600)	13,600	
Beginning Cash Balance	2,000	(2,400)	(6,800)	(13,000)	(5,400)	(9,800)	(14,400)	(2,500)	400	(3,300)	(7,700)	(11,300)	
Ending Cash Balance	(2,400)	(6,800)	(13,000)	(5,400)	(9,800)	(14,400)	(2,500)	400	(3,300)	(7,700)	(11,300)	2,300	

minimum cash balance, then the agency would need to borrow $17,900 to cover the first 6 months' cash disbursements.

On an ongoing basis, WCDC would use the revised cash budget to assess the extent of deviation of planned cash flow from actual cash flow. Deviations could indicate the need for budget revisions or might be an indicator of other problems and the need for different actions. For instance, lower amounts from parent fees than those projected might reflect slowness in payments by some parents (a cash flow problem) or may actually be due to decreased enrollments (a budget reduction). Cash flow monitoring is essential; however, emphasis on cash alone, as the above example shows, could be misleading.

Develop a Plan for Repaying Borrowed Funds, and Implement It

The development of a plan which outlines the timing and amounts of repayment to loan sources is useful not only for external purposes but for internal purposes as well. A potential lender will be more inclined to provide funds if the agency can demonstrate that the problem is a cash rather than a budget deficit, that the agency can indeed repay the funds and any interest involved, and that it has a realistic plan for doing so.

Most agencies realize the importance of having a repayment plan for outside sources but many fail to use the same practices with internal sources. Frequently agencies will borrow from capital funds or other reserves to cover cash deficits. They have good intentions of repaying the monies but never seem to get around to it. As a consequence, funds allocated for other purposes dwindle and nobody is able to account for where they went.

Develop Procedures That Facilitate Cash Inflow

Hartog and Weber (1978) found that cash flow problems were frequently caused by agencies' failure to provide timely and appropriate documentation to contractors and third party payers. In some cases, agencies consistently submitted documents after the funders' deadlines and in other cases they submitted incomplete or inappropriately completed documents. In both cases, delayed payments from the funders were virtually assured. The possibility of cash flow problems therefore increased since the agencies' payment due dates for expenditures were not dependent on when they received cash.

A sound accounting and statistical information system is an agency's primary resource for facilitating timely reimbursement for services provided, whether that reimbursement comes from third party payors or the consumers of services themselves. Salsbery (1972) suggests the following as normal records and documents which an agency would be expected to maintain:

1. a file showing a client's financial ability, the person/organization responsible for the account, and the amount of any approved donated service discount;
2. a charge slip prepared when service is rendered showing the type of service and the amount of the charge;
3. a journal in which information from the charge slips is entered in chronological order;
4. an individual client account card summarizing all of the client's charges and payments to date; and
5. a control account showing the balance of all the individual client account cards.

In addition to basic records such as those which Salsbery recommends, the information system should routinely collect all data required by funding sources and should be set up in a manner that enables quick retrieval and compilation for reporting purposes. At any given time, management should be able to tell the due dates, submission amounts and dates, and actual payment receipt amounts and dates by funder. To effectively facilitate cash flow, the entire reimbursement process from initial data collection by line workers to actual receipt of cash payments must be constantly monitored.

Line workers responsible for initial data collection and form completion must know what forms to complete, when and how to complete them, and where to forward them. The same holds true for any staff involved in the collection, retrieval, and compilation process.

Staff training needs to include the proper use of forms, their flow within the agency, and the role and importance of the information system in the agency's continued ability to provide services. Social service workers tend to view paper work negatively since it takes time away from service delivery. However, without adequate and timely funding, and the paperwork that goes with it, there may be no services to deliver.

Management's responsibility is to see that data needed for reimbursement purposes is forwarded to the funder and that payment for services provided is received. This responsibility carries the obligation to identify and correct factors which impede the reimbursement process. Staff training, streamlining paperwork, monitoring and revising information collection and flow, and reviewing guidelines with funders are but a few of the means toward achieving this end.

Explore Ways of Handling Potential Cash Deficits Before They Threaten the Solvency of the Agency

Collaborative efforts with other nonprofit organizations and independent development efforts are methods that agencies can use to plan for and ease the impact of cash flow problems. The NYCT report (McAdam, 1976) suggests the establishment of nonprofit loan corporations which provide short-term loans to ease cash flow problems. The report also discussed the notion of nonprofit agencies' borrowing from commercial financial institutions. Recognizing the problems that such agencies face in obtaining commercial loans, the researchers advocate the use of philanthropic resources to underwrite loan interest, and the development of a certification system acceptable to banks.

Aside from collaborative efforts, nonprofit agencies must develop cash reserves as a component of their long-range financial plans. An agency that barely ekes out the payroll each month is not in a sound financial position. Loans enable agencies to meet immediate cash needs. At the same time, they cost money and further deplete an agency's resources. An agency whose income exactly matches its expenses will find it difficult to repay a loan no matter how small the interest. Along with the development of cash reserves, however, goes the need to invest and use surplus funds wisely. Surplus funds can be easily depleted when the agency fails to establish guidelines such as investment and loan policies, and when funds are used to cover chronic budget (as opposed to cash) deficits.

In conclusion, cash flow management is an area that all nonprofit organizations must address. Although cash deficits are not a sign of incompetent management, failure to plan for and control the use of cash is. Sound management practices such as cash budgeting and utilization of an information and control system can help resolve many cash flow problems. Effective cash management, however, must be part of an overall financial resource development and financial management plan.

REFERENCES

Becker, E. National board of the YWCA of the USA. New York, New York, Interview 17 July 1980, Milwaukee, Wisconsin.

Hartog, N., & Weber, J. *Impact of government funding on the management of voluntary agencies.* New York: Greater New York Fund/United Way, 1978.

Lohmann, R. *Breaking even.* Philadelphia: Temple University Press, 1980.

McAdam, T. *A discussion of the possible cash flow problems of nonprofit voluntary agencies.* New York: New York Community Trust, 1976. (Mimeographed)

Salsbery, D. L. *Accounting guidelines for mental health centers and related facilities.* Rockville, MD: NIMH, 1972.

C. Cost Analysis

5

Costing Nonprofit Services: Developments, Problems, and Issues

CREASIE FINNEY HAIRSTON

What does it cost a nonprofit organization to produce and distribute an educational pamphlet? provide an hour of counseling? screen a child for lead poisoning? prepare and deliver a meal to a homebound individual? provide one day of training for a homemaker reentering the job market? In essence, what are the full costs involved in providing specifically identifiable products and services to individual consumers or consumer groups?

The above questions deal with cost accounting, one of the major emerging fiscal administration issues in the nonprofit sector. This emergence can be attributed to several factors—rising expenditures for human services, changing funding patterns and mechanisms, new service approaches and service systems, and standardized accounting and financial reporting procedures. Individually and collectively these factors have led to a need for cost information previously not considered important in nonprofit management.

Cost data obtained in cost allocation studies provide an information base for more efficient and effective utilization of financial resources. More specifically, cost allocation data can be used to price services and set fees, negotiate contracts with third-party payors, project break-even points for different income and expense levels, and monitor agency spending. The data also allow the organization to demonstrate to funders exactly what is being purchased for given amounts of monies, whether it is ten days of day care, fifty home-delivered meals, or one hundred days of homemaker services.

Despite the potential that cost accounting holds for the nonprofit sector, it is still in a rudimentary stage. Few studies on its use have been conducted, but review and examination of existing materials and observation of agency practices indicate that implementation has been problematic. This chapter reviews the current status of cost accounting in the nonprofit sector. Major conceptual, methodological, and practical problems that impede use are discussed, and approaches for advancing knowledge in nonprofit financial management are presented. Although much of the information applies to nonprofit organizations in general, the focus is on voluntary health and welfare organizations.

DEVELOPMENTS IN NONPROFIT COST ACCOUNTING

Cost accounting, cost finding, cost distribution, and cost allocation are terms used interchangeably to refer to the systematic recording and analysis of the total costs incurred to provide a program service. The process consists of identifying direct and indirect costs and allocating or distributing them to their respective program services. Direct costs are those which can be traced directly to a particular program service. Indirect costs, in contrast, cannot be identified with any specific program service and/or are incurred on behalf of the total organization. The combined total of direct and indirect costs for a program service represents the full or true costs for providing that program service. Unit costs are the full costs of a program service divided by the number of service units produced.

The foundation for cost accounting in the nonprofit sector has been laid. Several developments support this conclusion. First of all, cost accounting principles are clearly reflected in the *Standards of Accounting and Financial Reporting for Voluntary Health and Welfare Organizations* (1975) and in the American Institute of Certified Public Accountants' *Audits of Voluntary Health and Welfare Organizations* (1974). The Standards require that organizations' annual financial statements provide a functional breakdown of expenses into program costs and supporting costs. The audit guidelines that certified public accountants use to render an opinion on an agency's financial practices and statements also call for functional expense reporting. This reporting of expenses by programs and supporting services is a fundamental component of cost accounting.

Secondly, watchdog agencies, regulatory bodies, and major funders require that cost-accounting principles and methodologies be used to develop the funding proposals and financial reports submitted to them. These include the Internal Revenue Service, the National Information Bureau, state agencies that regulate charitable organizations, national and state government agencies that fund human services, and major foundations.

Most of these organizations and groups require that organizations under their auspices report program costs (direct costs) separately from administrative and general and fund-raising costs (indirect costs). They further require that the costs associated with each program service or broad program category be specified. Although most do not require that organizations report unit costs, the major regulatory bodies are exploring the idea.

Third, as Lohmann (1980) notes, the trend toward program funding encouraged by the federal government and the United Way has likewise been instrumental. The development of a program budget requires that an agency be able to identify the direct costs associated with providing the program and to distinguish them from costs incurred for other agency activities.

Fourth, several major organizations have sought to institutionalize cost-accounting principles in their program planning, budgeting, and fiscal-control systems or in the systems of the organizations they fund. Among these are the National Board of the Young Women's Christian Association, the United Way of America, the National Institute of Mental Health, and state departments of human services. These organizations have published manuals, developed and conducted training programs, and established guidelines to facilitate understanding and use of program and unit costs and cost-finding techniques (see, for example, *Accounting and Financial Reporting*, 1974; Sorensen & Phipps, 1975; and Cuenod, 1980). Despite efforts such as these, there are serious impediments to the meaningful use of cost-accounting techniques and to the use of data generated from cost-accounting studies. Major problems are discussed in the following section.

PROBLEMS AND ISSUES

Major problems in nonprofit cost accounting can be grouped into three broad areas. Some problems are conceptual ones. Others arise from the methodologies used to obtain full costs. Still others reflect the current state of financial record-keeping and lack of fiscal controls that plague many nonprofit organizations.

Conceptual problems center on distinctions drawn between program services and supporting services, on distinctions made between one program service and another, and on distinctions made within program services between one service activity and another.

There is general agreement in the nonprofit sector that costs for programs (direct costs) should be separated from those for supporting services (indirect costs). This agreement is reflected in most nonprofit financial reporting requirements, including the *Standards*, the audit guidelines for nonprofit organizations, and the Internal Revenue Service's revised Form 990.

Agreement is not reflected, however, in the conceptual schemes that organizations use to separate program services from supporting services; to distinguish one program service from another; or, within program services, to differentiate one service activity from another. The United Way of America (1975) has developed definitions and examples to distinguish supporting services from program services, and has developed a program classification system as well. The United Way's conceptual scheme is not universally applied, however; even when it is used, varying gradations in meaning and different connotations for major terms abound. What one organization defines as a supporting function, another regards as a program service. For example, Agency A may regard its publications activity as a distinct program. Agency B, though engaging in activities similar in all respects, regards publications as a supporting function. Since treatment of any supporting cost as a separate program-service cost changes the amount of indirect costs distributed to each program, the reported cost data for Agencies A and B, though they engage in similar activities, will be quite different, even if the costs incurred are identical. Cost comparisons between the two agencies will, therefore, be misleading.

The conceptual scheme used to differentiate among program services and service activities will directly affect the accuracy of cost data. The program-service categories used in preparing annual financial statements are usually too broad to use in calculating meaningful unit costs. One program-service category often comprises different service activities that have varying costs. For example, a program service designated as social adjustment on the annual financial statement may actually consist of three major service activities: homemaker services, counseling, and parent education. The unit costs for each of these service activities would probably be quite different.

Comparison of Agency A's unit cost for social adjustment with Agency B's unit cost for social adjustment, though relatively easy to compute, would be of little value. The development of meaningful cost data would necessitate a more detailed grouping of service activities than current annual financial statements provide.

The second major problem area centers on the methodological procedures used to accumulate cost data. These include the identification and measurement of direct costs as well as the methods used to distribute indirect costs.

Typically, organizations assign direct costs to programs on the basis of:

1. actual records of time spent, materials consumed, or space used;
2. estimates based on periodic time or utilization studies;
3. estimates based on the effort managers feel can or ought to be assigned to a given program; or
4. some combination of the above.

If, for example, a staff person is assigned to work in one program, then all of his or her salary and related costs are considered direct costs of that program. If the staff person is assigned to work in two or more programs, then the salary may be assigned as direct costs on the basis of the actual time spent in each program, his or her own estimates of work distribution, or the amount of time he or she is assigned to work in each program. There are no rules for when a particular cost allocation method ought to be used. Observations indicate, however, that when cost data are being used to make budget projections, assigned time takes priority. For financial reporting purposes none of the above methods tends to be used more often than others.

Methods of distributing indirect costs likewise vary. The general practice is, however, to obtain an equitable allocation in an economical and practical manner. Indirect costs are distributed on the basis of:

1. the proportion of total direct costs that a program is responsible for;
2. the proportion of total direct labor-related costs incurred by the service;
3. the proportion of space that the service utilizes;
4. the proportion of total activity that can be attributed to a service; or
5. standard percentages of total costs.

These various accumulation procedures not only yield different cost data but also require varying amounts of time, skill, and effort. Some costing methods are far more complex than others. Sorensen and Phipps (1975), for example, detail fairly elaborate procedures for allocating direct costs; Cuenod (1980) presents a rather complicated approach for conducting a space-utilization study.

In the absence of empirical studies that contrast different cost-accounting approaches it is difficult to say whether more complicated methods produce more accurate and usable results. When consistently applied each method, simple or complex, provides a comparative, though not necessarily accurate, data base. When used haphazardly each produces data of questionable value.

The methodology used to account for changes in the numbers of program services and service units that an organization provides affects unit costs and, subsequently, the uses of the data that are generated. Service volume, for instance, directly affects service-unit costs. The more service units an organization provides for a given budgeted amount, the lower the actual per unit cost. The question then arises as to whether unit costs should be derived by dividing total costs by the actual number of service units provided or by the number of units that could be practically and realistically provided. For financial reporting purposes, actual unit costs seem more appropriate. If fee setting is the main objective, then a fair-share-of-cost basis would appear to dictate the latter approach. An attempt to recover full costs from fees, on the other hand, would lead to the former.

The number of program services that an organization provides also affects unit costs. This occurs because the addition or deletion of a program changes the indirect-costs distribution pattern.

If an organization drops one of its program services but retains all of its administrative and general functions with no decrease in costs, then the full costs of each of the remaining program services increase simply because each must now carry a higher proportion of the indirect costs. Unit costs are also affected if a program service is added. The full costs of the original program services go down since each program service must now cover a smaller portion of the indirect costs. One is again faced with the problem of the most appropriate method to use in calculating unit costs for diverse purposes.

Another methodological problem has to do with the relevance to current programs of cost data collected in prior years. This is particularly problematic for organizations that do not have a stable program structure. If program services and staffing patterns change drastically from year to year, then a previous year's time study cannot serve as a data base for the current year. If an organization relies on these data to project unit costs, it may find that the costs obtained are seriously inflated or deflated.

Practical problems also serve as an impediment to the implementation and use of cost accounting in the nonprofit setting. Many nonprofit organizations still do not have integrated planning, budgeting, and accounting systems. The budget is a group of figures that total correctly but bear little relationship to programs and services. Although an examination of the budget may reveal a breakdown according to specific programs and supporting functions, the figures have been derived without real regard to program activity. Any attempt to use the budget as a data base would be less than fruitful.

Many accounting systems do not provide data that line managers can use in making program decisions. Accounting data are seldom recorded by programs or services. A 1979 study of 271 agencies (Hairston, 1979) found that 41 percent of the agencies did not report expenses according to program and supporting functions. Further investigation of those that did revealed that data were not systematically recorded according to functions during the fiscal year. Often reports were developed at the end of the year, using poorly constructed and outdated time studies or ballpark estimates. This approach to accounting and financial reporting may enable an organization to meet some reporting and accountability requirements, but its managerial uses are limited. The absence of meaningful accounting data on an ongoing basis negates the ability to operationalize effectively the fiscal controls that are integrally related to program and service production. The generation of year-end data with dubious credibility is likewise of limited help in making future projections about programs and related costs.

Another deterrent to cost utilization is the fact that many nonprofit managers have little or no background in financial management. Some prefer to ignore financial matters and leave decision making to the accounting staff. The accounting staff lack preparation in program-services planning and management and often make decisions unrelated to program objectives. In these situations program planning and financial planning and control are distinct rather than integrated activities, and cost data may be little more than additional paperwork.

Nonprofit managers who seek to correct this deficiency often have difficulty obtaining the knowledge and skills needed. Typically, they enroll in a basic accounting course in a university. They learn accounting material, but they find they are not much further along in their grasp of managerial uses of accounting in the nonprofit setting. This outcome should not be unexpected since basic accounting courses are designed to introduce would-be accountants to accounting concepts, principles, and procedures as they apply in the profit sector. The nonprofit managerial uses of accounting data are, appropriately, not the focus of this type of course.

Those managers who choose the route of reviewing nonprofit management literature find a general scarcity of financial-management material. Some financial topics are not treated at all; others are presented at a general or superficial level. Still others provide detailed instructions about a particular technique but only as it may be applied to the management of a particular type of organization. Consequently, nonprofit managers are hampered in their ability to use cost accounting and similar financial tools in organizational management.

From the practical perspective, cost accounting (like many other financial procedures) is threatening. The funding of voluntary health and welfare services is highly political, and managers shun using information that may put their program services in an unfavorable light. Cost data have this potential since the data reveal in black and white not only what is produced in terms of quantity but also the associated costs. In this sense, it is relatively easy to compare one organization with another providing similar services. These comparisons are possible internally, as well, and can generate conflict among different program managers, particularly when the monies generated by one program subsidize the activities of another.

SUMMARY AND CONCLUSIONS

Cost information is needed to manage effectively the finances of any organization, and the nonprofit organization is no exception. Cost accounting, therefore, is a potentially viable financial technique for nonprofit management. As pointed out here, however, several issues must be addressed if the full potential for cost accounting is to be realized.

There are no easy solutions to the problems that have been identified, nor easy answers to the questions that have been raised. Experimentation with different methodological and conceptual approaches is needed, as is exploration of the effects of different responses to practical concerns. There are, however, a few general guidelines that nonprofit organizations can use to facilitate development and use of cost accounting in agency management.

First, organizations must develop integrated program-planning and budget systems that provide cost data related to programs and services. This point cannot be overstated and is timely, given the current move toward computerization of financial and program data. Most nonprofit organizations have not yet computerized their information systems and still have the opportunity to select computer hardware and software that will enable them routinely to collect and retrieve data needed for cost analysis.

Second, organizations should apply the convention of consistency in all cost-accounting procedures. There is no one scientifically defensible way to allocate costs. It is, therefore, important that an organization have a rationale for each cost-accounting decision it makes, that it document and record that rationale and procedure, and that it continue to use that approach in successive cost-accounting studies unless experience dictates that new approaches are in order. This prevents manipulation of figures and data distortion and provides a reliable, comparative data base.

Third, organizations should use the cost data that are collected to understand cost behavior in their own organizations. The reasons behind varying unit costs need to be examined, including the relationship between costs and quality, however quality is defined. This approach constitutes a necessary step in the development of standard rates that can be defended.

The responsibility for the development and use of new financial tools and procedures cannot rest, however, with individual organizations and managers. Professional groups and others responsible for the management of nonprofit organizations must play an active role as well.

Important in this endeavor is the comparison of cost information among organizations offering similar services. The attempt should not be to decide upon a good rate or standard but to examine reasons for variances—whether they be conceptual, methodological, practical, or other—and to use the resulting data to develop techniques that improve management and services delivery in general.

Major attention must be directed toward the educational preparation and ongoing training of nonprofit managers, and the development of financial management expertise should be a priority. The financial knowledge and skills that a nonprofit manager needs must be delineated, and courses of study designed to meet those needs. Curriculum can be designed as part of existing programs, such as the administrative concentrations in schools of social work, special certificate programs, or continuing education activities that provide in-depth instruction in specific aspects of financial management.

Professional groups and educators must work closely with both accountants and computer specialists to see that computer-based accounting systems are designed to generate the financial data needed to meet internal-management and external-accountability needs. Along with this, consultation and technical assistance must be provided to assist managers in making hardware and software purchasing decisions and in using the accounting data that are generated.

Research must be conducted that looks at cost-accounting problems and issues specifically and at nonprofit financial-management developments in general. The dissemination of this information at professional meetings and in published documents is critical to knowledge advancement and further development in this area.

The application of cost accounting in the nonprofit sector is theoretically and technically possible. The foundation has been laid. What awaits now is that broad strategies be developed and specific efforts undertaken to improve the current state of the art.

REFERENCES

Accounting and Financial Reporting. Alexandria, Virginia: United Way of America, 1974.

Audits of Voluntary Health and Welfare Organizations. New York: American Institute of Certified Public Accountants, 1974.

Cuenod, M. *Budgeting guide: YWCA finance manual.* New York: National Board of the YWCA, 1980.

Hairston, C. F. A descriptive study of the financial audit reports of community YWCAs. New York: National Board of the YWCA, 1979. (Mimeographed.)

Lohmann, R. *Breaking even: Financial management in human service organizations.* Philadelphia: Temple University Press, 1980.

Standards of accounting and financial reporting for voluntary health and welfare organizations. New York: National Health Council, Inc.; National Assembly of Voluntary Health and Social Welfare Organizations, Inc.; and United Way of America, 1975.

Sorensen, J. E., and Phipps, D. W. *Cost finding and rate setting for community mental health centers.* Rockville, Maryland: National Institute of Mental Health, 1975.

6

Cost-Benefit Analysis: The Mystique versus the Reality

CARL B. BUXBAUM

It has become difficult to launch new social programs or even maintain the level of existing social services because of restricted government spending for such purposes. Therefore, how resources are allocated to various public enterprises becomes a great concern in the social welfare field. The following discussion reviews the recent effort to allocate resources rationally and objectively through cost-benefit analysis. The discussion examines five key questions:

1. What does cost-benefit analysis presume to accomplish?
2. How does it work?
3. What are its problems?
4. How may it be applied to social services? And most important,
5. What is its relationship to the political context?

SCARCE RESOURCES

In welfare economics it is assumed that resources are always scarce, no matter how abundant they may appear. They are scarce because human desires are very great. As resources increase, so do expectations and, consequently, wants. It follows that human desires will always eventually exceed the resources available to meet them. This assumption incorporates the idea of progress toward an ever-improving human condition. It also implies that we ought to economize. To economize does not simply mean to save money; it also means that we ought not to waste any. Wasted resources mean a lost opportunity to satisfy some human wants or needs and the diminishment of aggregate social welfare.[1]

Based on this kind of reasoning by economists and systems analysts, President Johnson introduced program-planning-budgeting systems (which incorporate cost-benefit analysis) into all departments of the federal government on August 25, 1965.[2] The objective was to promote efficiency in public programs by minimizing the waste of resources. It should be noted that in 1965 the American public was not particularly concerned about scarce resources; resources were thought to be plentiful. The point is that economizing was seen as important even in a political context of social reform. But that context changed at the end of the 1960s, and economizing developed some different implications for social welfare systems.

An Altered Political Context

The Great Society programs led to a perception that public efforts to solve complex social problems were doomed to failure. Ginzberg and Solow described the situation as one in which problems had been permitted to grow and multiply through inaction. A demand for immediate, full-scale action followed because of the extent of these problems. This demand led political leaders and others to make too many promises and build unrealistic public expectations. A skeptical Congress passed high-sounding legislation and then underfunded the programs. Most state and local governments were not staffed or structured in a manner that would allow them to administer innovations. While the Great Society social programs of the 1960s turned out as might reasonably have been expected—a mixture of partial successes and failures—the public had expected more. "A public which has been encouraged to expect great things will become impatient, critical, and alienated if the progress that is achieved falls far short of the rosy promises."[3]

The 1970s began with not only social welfare initiatives but government enterprises themselves in disrepute. The skepticism concerning whether more resources would improve a situation became a rationale for further use of cost-benefit analysis.[4] This state of affairs converged with other related factors. First, there was a clear move toward political conservatism, as manifested in the election of President Nixon. That conservative trend continues. Next, the energy crisis and growing inflation distracted the nation from social welfare concerns.

This altered political context has had a clear effect on reducing government investments in social welfare. In 1950 all government expenditures on social welfare (national, state, and local) were 8.9 percent of the gross national product (GNP) and 37.4 percent of government spending for all purposes. These figures climbed steadily until 1976, when they peaked at 20.4 percent of GNP and 60.2 percent of government expenditures. The figures fell thereafter. The most recent ones available are for 1978: 19.3 and 58.1 percent of GNP and government expenditures, respectively.[5] It must be noted that a good deal of growth in Social Security expenditures is incorporated in these figures; this growth is a result of the aging of the population and legislatively required increases. Therefore, the reduction of investment in social welfare for other portions of the population is understated by the aggregate figures.

The important questions now concern the relationship between cost-benefit analysis and the present context. Will cost-benefit analysis better allocate increasingly scarce resources, or, alternatively, is it used to rationalize reduced social welfare spending?

ALLOCATION OF LIMITED RESOURCES

Setting aside for a moment the issue of political context, it appears that in the mid-1950s there emerged widespread dissatisfaction with the manner in which social policy was being formulated. This dissatisfaction provided the initial impetus for cost-benefit analysis. Policy did not seem to be made by reason: rather, it seemed to consist of a number of small steps which led nowhere in particular and rarely departed much from the status quo. This aimlessness was a result of the diverse values expressed by competing interests in the political process.

Some observers defended this approach to public decision making on a number of grounds: It was realistic rather than utopian, it reflected the values and processes of democracy, and it averted undesirable side effects of social action by adhering to what was known.[6] The critics were clear. If serious problems were to be dealt with, the decisions regarding those problems should be rational, that is, the problem should be defined, goals set, and the means of attaining them put in place. Negative consequences could be minimized by more thorough and comprehensive analyses.[7]

It is difficult to argue against using reason and knowledge in the allocation of resources. Schultze asserts that cost-benefit strategies not only move beyond piecemeal tinkering but can yield better decisions within a political process that results in incremental reform.[8] Others have shown how cost-benefit analysis is a logical next step in the historical development of methods to improve policy decisions.[9]

GOALS OF COST-BENEFIT ANALYSIS

Scarce resources prevent the pursuit of all socially desirable objectives at once. So as not to spread resources too thin and not to waste any on as yet unachievable objectives, priorities must be set. Cost-benefit analysis is a way of making these choices that goes beyond intuition and politics by applying the economist's concept of "investment."

Cost-benefit analysis compares all the programs on the agenda for choice and seeks to determine which are the best investments. The costs and benefits of each program are listed on the assumption that any program in which the benefits are greater than the costs is worth supporting. This method follows the same reasoning as that of private individuals who put money into high-interest savings certificates. When the certificates mature, they do not look at their cost; rather, they look at the return on their investment. Private individuals would not put money into savings plans that paid back less than the original sum. Therefore, any programs in which the costs exceeded the benefits would be dropped from the agenda of choices.

How are resources to be allocated among the number of programs that have passed this investment test? Which of those programs are to get the resources first? The decision is again made in the same manner as is the private citizen's. Individuals faced with a choice of interest rates for savings certificates would select the best return on their investment. Only if they had money left over after having bought all available certificates at the highest interest rate would they purchase some at the next highest rate. The programs for public choice, therefore, are also ranked in order of cost-benefit ratios. Programs that give the greatest increase in benefits for each additional dollar spent come first. Those programs receive each additional dollar that becomes available until the benefits that accrue fall below the benefits that may be attained by placing the same additional dollar in other programs. Investments are then made in the next rung of worthwhile programs and so on down the list.[10]

METHOD

There is no single method of conducting a cost-benefit analysis because it is a tool used in a variety of areas and must be adapted to special circumstances. Regardless of variations in the method, however, there is a set of characteristics that applies to all cost-benefit social welfare decisions. The key characteristics are related to the taking of a broad view that includes all costs and all benefits over time. It does not matter where the costs and benefits fall or whether the costs are incurred now but the benefits accrue in the distant future. All costs and benefits must be identified and valued.

Identification of Costs and Benefits

In order to prevent the inadvertent exclusion of pertinent costs or benefits, they are divided into three categories: direct, indirect, and intangible. Direct costs are those that are incurred in the operation of the program under study; they include necessary facilities, staff, and supplies. Direct benefits are costs that society would avoid by virtue of having the program. For example, a program that prevented abusive parents from further damaging their children would reduce the cost of medically treating abused children in the future. This is a direct benefit to society in the sense that it conserves resources that can then be invested in other contributions to social welfare.

Indirect costs and benefits are those that occur as side effects of the program. These effects are often substantial. They would include, for example, the loss of property tax to a local community because a service was delivered at a tax-exempt voluntary or public agency and the travel expenses of the abusive parent when he or she went to the agency. Indirect benefits can be just as diverse and would include increases in the lifetime earnings of children who otherwise might have been disabled or dead as a result of child abuse.

Intangible costs and benefits include effects on emotions and perceptions that are not readily stated in objective terms. In the case of the child-abuse program, intangible costs would include the fear and discomfort of families living on the same city block as the social agency. They may worry about their children playing on a sidewalk that is shared with adults known to abuse children. Intangible benefits would include the freedom the formerly abused child has from pain and suffering, the reduction of guilt in the parent who no longer hurts the child, and society's knowledge that it has been able to do something about the problem. Intangible does not mean unimportant.

Quantification of Costs and Benefits

Once the costs and benefits have been identified, they must be assigned quantitative values. In order to develop a cost-benefit ratio, all costs must be totaled and all benefits must be totaled. The dollar is taken as the most convenient value, and the stream of costs and the stream of benefits that accrue over time are separately converted to dollars, totaled, and compared.

Accounting for Time

The cost of preventing an additional incident of child abuse occurs in a single time period, but the benefits which follow accrue for the life of the child and perhaps for his or her children. Economists assert that dollars in the present have more value than the same dollar in the future: A dollar today can be used and benefited from in the future, while a dollar in the future provides no present advantage. The reason a private citizen receives interest for the purchase of savings certificates is that someone is willing to pay more for those dollars in order to spend them in the present. Americans purchase homes and automobiles on credit. They pay interest because they want the use of those items during the time it would take to save for them. Thus behavior in the market confirms that present dollars are more valuable than future ones.

Economists have managed to resolve this problem by applying compound-interest formulas to costs and benefits over time so that both streams are reduced to the present value of the dollar. The dollar is discounted at a rate that would make up for the lost opportunity to invest it in the private market.

Conceptually, then, cost-benefit analysis is a straightforward and reasonable approach to allocating resources. By accounting for all costs and benefits, this method achieves an overall sense of the public interest without yielding to special political interests. It selects the optimal program for the resources available and favors neither the "cheapest" nor the "best" program. There is, however, a gap between theory and practice because social decisions are more complex than those of the private citizen in the market.

PROBLEMS OF COST-BENEFIT ANALYSIS

When cost-benefit studies are launched, a number of problems emerge. It is difficult to place dollar values on costs and benefits, especially on intangible benefits. There is no agreement on what the rate of discount should be in adjusting for time preferences, and, because of comprehensiveness, it is difficult to identify and decide what costs and benefits are to be included. Past and recent studies have been severely criticized for presenting distorted findings because of a failure to resolve these issues.[11]

Assigning Dollar Values

Assigning dollar values to direct and indirect costs and benefits is less difficult than assigning them to intangibles. Direct and indirect costs reflect items traded in the market; therefore, they have prices. For example, the tax on agency property and the salaries of staff members can be determined easily. Even the average lifetime earnings for members of particular demographic groups have been worked out fairly well.[12] Nevertheless, it is difficult to determine precise costs for programs conducted by organizations engaged in multiple activities. Joint costs relating to facility space, telephone use, and staff salaries are not easily apportioned to each program conducted by a multifunction agency.[13]

Intangible costs and benefits present a far greater problem because they have no market prices. The literature in economics reflects that discipline's great struggle in trying to find prices that can be imputed or attributed to nontraded items such as feelings. Estimating the value of a human life saved seems to be particularly fascinating to economists.[14] The basic theoretical approach to finding imputed or shadow prices for intangibles has been solved to the satisfaction of most economists. Although there is no market price on anxiety, for example, the economist might ask, What would a person be willing to pay to be free of anxiety? The amount people would be willing to pay would become the assigned price.

Implementation of this approach, however, presents overwhelming problems. If people are asked what they are willing to pay, the results might differ from what would occur if they actually could pay. If people in fact paid a price for intangibles, what they would be willing to pay would reflect *ability* to pay as well as willingness. It has been pointed out that determination of willingness to pay must also take into account possible differences between individual and societal interests. Benefits must measure what society, as well as the individual, is willing to pay.[15] What the abusive parent is willing to pay for social services is an inadequate measure because it does not include what others are willing to pay to stop the abuse of children.

Cost-benefit studies often deal with this problem by treating the service as an intermediate step intended to produce further benefits. Thus contributions to the GNP made by the increased earnings of a child who is saved from further abuse are taken as the social gain. The intangible gain to society, however, has not been dealt with. In most studies, the concept of willingness to pay is lost and is replaced by society's interest, which views the individual's contribution to the GNP as the value of the benefit.

This approach has some strange consequences. It undervalues programs that serve the young and the old, and it perpetuates inequities in the economic system. Future earnings are discounted to find their present value. Children will not have earnings for a number of years to come; therefore, their earnings will be discounted more than will those of young adults who are employed in the present. Older adults will have their earnings discounted less than those of children but will have fewer years left in which to contribute to the GNP. By this calculation younger adults deserve the aid of social programs more than do children or older adults because the benefits to society are greater. Among young adults, programs for whites and males are more beneficial to society because projected salaries are higher for whites than nonwhites and higher for males than for females. As Rhoads points out, cost-benefit studies on lifesaving health programs showed that efforts to encourage the use of motorcycle helmets were a better investment than were programs preventing deaths from cancer of the cervix. The cost of saving a life through each program was nearly the same, but discounted future earnings made young male motorcycle riders more valuable to society than adult women were.[16] Should women be valued less than men because the labor market pays them lower wages for the same work and qualifications and because a method for measuring the real value of a housewife remains difficult to develop?[17] The problem persists because efforts to assign a value to the intangibles have failed.

Titmuss rejects the notion of valuing intangibles in dollar terms. He asserts, on moral grounds, that human life and altruism are priceless and points to the hazard of imposing market structures. He argues that humane values should take precedence over economics.[18] Fuchs suggests that prices are implicitly placed on lives every day.[19] This occurs whenever a decision is made about the coverage of health insurance policies or the postponement of requirements for passive restraints in automobiles. If lives were invaluable, how much would we spend to find a missing child? how many resources would be devoted to the search? over how great a period of time? The limit set represents the price placed on a life. Fuchs does not contend that economics has the answer but asserts that, as long as these decisions are being made anyway, economics can make them more rationally.

This point is arguable. Wildavsky and others have noted that using prices as values assumes that the market allocates values properly. It also assumes a perfect market with full employment and competition. The validity of market-determined values is made questionable by any market imperfections. However, Wildavsky agrees that in an imperfect world a proper mix of economic reasoning and political reasoning can improve decisions.[20]

Discounting Rates and Time Horizons

As noted, the theoretical problem of accounting for the effect of time has been resolved by discounting to find present value. The choice of precise discount rate, however, has not been determined. The rate chosen will have to depend somewhat on expectations of the future. The federal government now uses the same discount rate in all studies it sponsors.[21] This makes the various programs comparable, but it does not make the studies valid.

The fact is that the choice of discount rate can itself determine priorities.[22] This is particularly so when the time stream of benefits is much longer than the stream of costs in only one of the programs being compared. If a case of child abuse is prevented, for example, we might expect benefits to continue into the child's adult life and be felt by his or her children. That is a very long period over which to discount benefits, and a high rate of discount—for example, 15 percent—would reduce those benefits very greatly compared with a rate of 5 percent. It appears that the costs for preventing the case of abuse would occur only during the period of dependent childhood. Those costs then would be relatively unaffected by discounting and would seem large compared with heavily reduced benefits. Now suppose this program is on the same choice agenda as a program in which the benefits accrue early, such as removing plantar warts. This example is not meant to diminish the pain and suffering caused by plantar warts but only to show how the technique can produce odd decisions. The next generation would have a different time preference than that of this generation. This generation does best by imposing high discount rates, and future generations do best with relatively low rates. There is no scientific way to settle this intergenerational dispute.

Implied above is another problem concerning time that lacks a scientific solution. How long a time span is pertinent and practical in such studies? For how many generations should the benefits of preventing a case of child abuse be carried forward?

What Costs and Benefits Should Be Included?

In order to represent the national interest and not just some private interests, all costs and benefits must be included. This objective introduces remarkable complexities in identification and measurement. Yet for cost-benefit studies to be useful, calculations must be simplified,[23] otherwise a large amount of estimation is incorporated into the analysis. Even if all costs and benefits could be identified and valued, should public decision making include "malevolent preferences?"[24] That is, should the intangible costs borne by a racist be calculated in the analysis of an open-housing or school-integration program? The answer to this question will vary, depending on who is conducting the study.

There are so many ripple effects in a complex social world that economists agree not all can be listed. Studies generally exclude trivial effects, but which effects are trivial?[25] A cost-benefit analysis was recently responsible for plans to construct a dam. In the course of the study it was recognized that some wildlife, particularly a fish known as the snail darter, would be adversely affected. The analysts excluded this cost from their calculations as trivial. Reports in the press clearly indicate, however, that some environmentalists thought extinction of the snail darter was an intolerable cost.

Another problem emerges when all costs and benefits are treated equally. This approach reveals an aggregate effect on society, but the individuals who benefit from a program may not be the same ones who bear the costs. The method is indifferent to the fact that each dollar of benefit varies in social value depending on who receives it. Maas points out that in cost benefit analysis, "an extra dollar to a Texas oil man is as desirable socially as one to an Arkansas tenant farmer. . . ."[26] There is no scientific way to determine who should gain and who should lose. Yet this is one of the most central questions of public policy, and it must be determined politically.

Distinguishing Between Costs and Benefits

Public enterprises most often include multiple objectives. Building a new hospital in a depressed urban area, for example, provides not only health services to the community but many jobs as well. The location of the hospital may have been determined by a political interest in stimulating the local economy. A cost-benefit study, however, would list the construction of the hospital and the staff salaries as costs in pursuit of health benefits. Yet given multiple objectives, there are benefits as well, especially salaries to nonprofessional employees which may avert some public assistance payment. The only way to solve this is to assign different weights to dollars associated with various objectives.[27] Such a process, however, is fundamentally judgmental and arbitrary. The analyst is left without scientific knowledge of whether some items are costs or benefits, and studies of similar programs will vary depending on the analyst and the reasons for launching the study.

COST-EFFECTIVENESS ANALYSIS

Economists often retreat to cost-effectiveness analysis in order to escape the major problems of cost-benefit analysis. In this variation benefits need not be measured in dollars. An objective is selected on the basis of a societal willingness to achieve it. Once that is done, intangible and indirect benefits are implicitly valued. Note, however, that this method cannot help establish priorities. Rather, it can help find the most efficient way of attaining priorities established by some other means. Programs seeking the same objective are compared to determine which ones achieve the objective most often for each dollar spent. Benefits are measured as nonmonetary, homogeneous units, such as a reduction in the number of incidents of child abuse.[28]

Although the most difficult problems of cost-benefit analysis have been circumvented, substantial problems remain. It may not be easy to specify the unit of output. In treating heroin abusers, for example, should the benefits be that clients remain drug free, or should only their behavior be modified while they continue in a state of induced dependence on methadone?[29] Should a vocational rehabilitation program for chronic schizophrenics measure benefits as employment for some specified period of time at a specified wage, or is the provision of a structured daily routine a measure of benefits? The issue of multiple objectives has not been resolved.[30]

Nor has the problem of accounting for time been resolved. Watts, Jackson, and LoGerfo point out that when benefits accrue in different periods of time, they must be discounted, and the discount rate chosen makes a great difference.[31] For example, the increased probability of saving a life for an additional year in the present is more valuable to the individual than is the probability of gaining an additional year of life thirty years hence. If a good discount rate could be found, the present value of that future year of life could be determined, but that does not help in deciding between generations. How can the value of an additional year of life saved today for a thirty-year-old be compared with one saved today for an eighty-year-old? There is no ghoulish calculus to answer that question.

Thus far it has been shown that, conceptually, cost-benefit and cost-effectiveness analysis are impressive tools for assisting decisions regarding the allocation of scarce resources. Technical problems, however, prevent these tools from providing convincing guidance to decision making.

CONSIDERATIONS REGARDING SUCCESS

Even if the technical problems were solved, social welfare might not be improved by the use of cost-benefit analysis. The method's prime objective is efficiency. As pointed out, this is an important objective; without it the pie shared by each member of society diminishes and everyone receives a smaller slice. The size of the pie, however, is not our only concern. Quality is also a factor, and, as Okun has powerfully pointed out, society must give up some efficiency in order to attain a certain quality.[32] To highlight his concern about overemphasis on efficiency he says,

> Society refuses to turn itself into a giant vending machine that delivers anything and everything in return for the proper number of coins. When members of my profession sometimes lose sight of this principle, they invite the nastiest definition of an economist: the person who knows the price of everything and the value of nothing. . . . The domain of rights is part of the checks and balances on the market designed to preserve values that are not denominated in dollars. For the same reason that an investor holds many different stocks and bonds in his portfolio, society diversifies its mechanisms for distribution and allocation. . . .[33]

It is not necessary for society always to choose the most efficient approach to allocation.

An additional reason for disputing the power of cost-benefit analysis to improve social welfare is its conservative bias. The method is very complex. Therefore, it is more often applied to small-scale interventions than to major reforms, because the former involve fewer unknown variables. It is difficult to compare innovative programs because of the lack of data. Data are history and can be generated only over time. As a result, many possible alternative programs are neglected.[34] Sloan points out that new projects tend to be inefficient while program administrators are learning from their mistakes. Consequently, their costs are high relative to well-established projects, and there is a tendency for cost-benefit studies to reject innovations.[35] The primary task in social services may be the designing of new programs and systems rather than the comparison of the efficiency of those that exist.

APPLICATIONS OF COST-BENEFIT ANALYSIS IN SOCIAL WELFARE

With all the talk about cost-benefit analysis, it is surprising that a review of published studies reveals very few that meet the test of comparing both costs and benefits over time. Even in cost-effectiveness studies, very few show the causal relationship between costs and outcomes. The paucity of published studies reflects the difficulty and expense of such analyses. Regarding the former, many who have attempted economic analysis in the social services report a series of difficulties in addition to the technical ones associated with the method.[36] Data are often unavailable, the wrong type, or unattainable. There are an overwhelming number of benefits that cannot be adequately valued. Most often there is a missing base of evaluation research which demonstrates that the programs under study are responsible for the benefits attributed to them. Perhaps most important, social services are organized in a manner that discourages the accumulation of data and research opportunities. It also appears that since comprehensive studies are expensive, decision makers tend to commit dollars to demanded services rather than to program evaluation. Of those studies that have been done, most are concentrated on lifesaving health programs. This is the probable result of dramatic appeal, the technical capacity of the discounted future-earnings procedure, and the simple output unit of a year of life saved.

SELECTED STUDIES

A review of some studies reveals the problems involved in conducting them in order to achieve good results.[37] They may be classified by type and quality. Some are simple cost studies, some compare costs and effects, and some compare costs and benefits. Hardly any compare one program with another. In terms of quality they may be classified as partially useful and as useless for policy purposes.

Useless Studies

Studies that measure only program costs are useless in that they report a price but offer no indication of what is purchased. By and large, these studies are technically primitive as well as incomplete.[38] For example, one study identifying the hospital care costs associated with air pollution was technically sound in establishing the increased cost attributed to the pollution. In effect, the analysis revealed some direct benefits of an imaginary pollution control program but said nothing about the nature of the program in terms of either effectiveness or costs.[39] Among the costs might be unemployment, increased welfare payments, and other medical expenses from living in unheated housing and stressful conditions.

Cost-effectiveness studies tend to be technically more sophisticated, but problems remain. One such study is improperly named a cost-benefit analysis.[40] It measures the effects of reimbursing agencies for the full cost of adoptions on the number of adoptions completed. This demonstrates the need for technical analysts to know the field they are studying. The analysts did not, for example, understand that children who were easier to place would be adopted first and that, therefore, the cost of each additional adoption might climb. In general, these studies contain all the weaknesses identified earlier.[41]

Zapka and Averill have unwittingly done an amusing study. They assumed, based on good evidence, that colds were self-limiting and did not require medical attention. They found an acceptable self-treatment procedure that diverted people from seeing a physician.[42] Although this idea is good, a cost-effectiveness study was not necessary: It was clear beforehand that going to a doctor costs more than not going to a doctor. This study exemplifies the problematic tendency to apply methods where they will work rather than where they can make a useful contribution.

Partially Useful Studies

Some studies may suffer the same problems of the Zapka and Averill work but still have practical uses. Bertera and Green, for example, compared the cost effectiveness of a home-visit family planning program for families in which there was a high, moderate, or low risk of pregnancy and birth complications.[43] Their finding that services to the high-risk group were most cost effective was hardly surprising; it costs more to prevent what would not have occurred than to prevent a real problem from developing. This study was useful, however, because the well-meaning staff had to be shown that they could be more humanitarian by being selective and concentrating their efforts.

Where more difficult problems are tackled, the studies tend to be less adequate. Morrall and Olsen, for example, found little difference in the cost effectiveness of various leased public housing programs for low-income families. Some of the dwellings were new, some existing, some rehabilitated. Some were in large public "projects," some in private market apartment buildings, some in private apartment buildings that were not exclusively for subsidized tenants, and some in single-family homes. By their standard, only the single-family homes were not cost effective.[44] *Cost effectiveness* was defined as "the ratio of the total cost of providing a leased public housing unit to its market rent."[45] The "market rent" is estimated to be what the particular dwelling would command in the unsubsidized sector. Thus it met the willingness-to-pay test by assigning values which revealed the desirability of the unit. Housing is not just shelter. It is a bundle of amenities having to do with neighborhood, schools, proximity of parks, safe streets, and the like. Under this concept it is possible to provide good housing for low-income families while accepting the increased cost. The test here is the effectiveness of decent housing, not the cheapest housing. This is clearly useful in improving policy decisions once it is decided that one kind of housing is more desirable than others. How can the failure of the single-family homes to pass the cost-effectiveness test be explained? Americans, on the average, consider such homes more desirable and pay a great deal for them. The explanation may lie in the fact that only undesirable single-family homes in declining neighborhoods were available to the study program.

Two additional and useful studies of high quality are worth mentioning. Muller examined the costs and benefits of motorcycle helmet laws. From a good data base he demonstrated that helmet requirements were cost beneficial. The problems with discounted future earnings and valuing intangibles were circumvented by omission. Comparing only the costs of helmets and law enforcement with the benefit of dollars saved on medical care, the helmets were a good investment.[46] However, a major problem remains. How good an investment are motorcycle helmets compared with something else? The decision makers must handle this on their own. They know the benefits are understated because intangible and indirect benefits are excluded, and they probably consider the intangible cost of discomfort in wearing a helmet trivial—but the magnitude of the understated benefits remains unknown.

In his cost-benefit analysis of a hospital and a community-based mental health program, Weisbrod went further in helping decision makers. He excluded nothing. Whatever could be valued in dollar terms was presented that way. Other costs and benefits were presented in noneconomic units, such as days in the community. Some factors were stated in qualitative terms, and still others were listed but not measured at all. He concluded that, except where hospitalization was required for emergency situations, the community-based program was a better investment.[47] By mixing different quantities and unmeasured intangibles, he moved cost-benefit analysis more in the direction of art than of science. Weisbrod justifies this as an optimal way, if not the ideal way, of making decisions. He suggests that cost-benefit work will never make decisions but that it should be vigorously pursued because it makes decisions more informed.

PITFALLS OF PARTIAL AND IMPERFECT ANALYSIS

Almost every commentator on cost-benefit analysis seems to support Weisbrod's argument. They suggest that the best possible, though imperfect, work is being done in economic analysis and that it be thrown into the hopper of politics. There political rationality will fill the gaps. Political leaders can decide who shall benefit and who shall bear the cost, who is more valuable to society and who is less valuable. They make those decisions now anyway, but with cost-benefit analysis they would make them with more information.

Only Sloan raises some caveats: "Current efforts should not be devoted to obtaining rough estimates of program benefits to be used as a basis for allocating government funds. Partial analysis may lead to less satisfactory policy decisions than no analysis at all."[48] Sloan recognizes that our decision makers are human. Why should their collective minds be able to evaluate each piece of information, weigh it, balance it, and put together a better judgment? It is possible for information to overwhelm decision makers and distort decisions.

Quantified effects tend to dominate considerations: Numbers are something to hold on to, whereas important intangibles are difficult to weigh. It is easier to quantify costs than benefits. Therefore, studies tend to understate the return on investments.

Perhaps more important, there is already a trend toward using cost-benefit analysis in areas where costs and benefits are more easily expressed in pecuniary terms. It seems possible that public resources will be diverted to these areas where the investment function is demonstrated and away from the more important programs where the return on investment is less obvious: highways might be valued over child abuse, for example. The focus on lifesaving programs in health may detract from social services that can make life more worth living because we cannot establish unit values for the quality of life. The real question is, Under what conditions can decision makers be trusted to make desirable use of imperfect economic analysis?

CONCLUSIONS

When cost-benefit analysis was first addressed in the social work literature, many of these problems were recognized, but the technique was
welcomed because its inherent questioning approach and data requirements were believed to point social welfare toward progress.[49] Such a
response seemed appropriate in 1968 and 1970. The political context
suggested that investments in social welfare would be made. Why not try
to make better investments? By 1979 Rothman seemed to be suggesting
that social work embrace this technique and similar ones to conserve
shrinking resources and that we accommodate, at least for the next decade, to disinvestments in social welfare by growing more efficient.[50]

Kogut has argued that, rather than accommodate to disinvestments
in social welfare, coalitions should be formed to alter the political context. Kogut says of Rothman's approach, "It is as though a social worker
writing in 1932 accepted the idea that the depression was inevitable,
and therefore the profession should prepare itself to operate on that assumption without any thought of a 'New Deal' or any other form of intervention."[51] The extent to which resources are scarce, he continues, is
affected by policy. Policies which seek to control inflation by accepting
high rates of unemployment and disinvestments in social welfare are
not the only alternatives. It is possible to support policies of economic
growth, full employment, and investments in social welfare without having to bear unacceptable inflation rates.[52]

The tools for pursuing efficient resource allocation are more artistic
than scientific. For economic analysis to work well, wise decision makers
must fill in where science fails and noneconomic values are present.
They must add reason, judgment, and humanitarian concern. Conditions in the present context are not conducive to such decision making.
Political pressure to limit social welfare expenditures has converted economic analysis into the budget-cutter's rationalization. If the weaknesses
and biases of the methods go unchecked, few social programs will pass
the benefit or effectiveness efficiency test.

At present, it is probably wise to reject economic analysis and pursue political action to alter the political context. When the nation is re-
stored to the pursuit of both efficiency and improved social welfare, rational decision making may be tried again.

NOTES

This article is a revision of a paper presented at the Fifth National Institute
on Social Work in Rural Areas, Burlington, Vermont, July 29, 1980.
   1. For an introduction to economic reasoning, see Robert Haveman and Ken-

yan A. Knopf, *The Market System* (New York: John Wiley & Sons, 1970), pp. 9–12.

2. "Statement by the President to Cabinet Members and and Agency Heads on the New Government-wide Planning and Budgeting System, August 25, 1965," in *Politics, Programs, and Budgets,* ed. James W. Davis, Jr. (Englewood Cliffs, N.J.: Prentice-Hall, Inc., 1969), pp. 149–50.

3. Eli Ginzberg and Robert M. Solow, "Some Lessons of the 1960s," *Public Interest* 34 (Winter 1974): 211–20.

4. John D. Blum, Ann Damsgaard, and Paul R. Sullivan, "Cost-Benefit Analysis," in *Regulating Health Care: The Struggle for Control,* ed. Arthur Levin (New York: Academy of Political Science, 1980), p. 141.

5. Alma W. McMillan and Ann Kallman Bixby, "Social Welfare Expenditures, Fiscal Year 1978," Research and Statistics Note no. 2, Social Security Administration (Washington, D.C.: Department of Health, Education, and Welfare, 1980), pp. 1–3.

6. Charles Lindblom, "The Science of 'Muddling Through,'" *Public Administration Review* 19 (Spring 1959): 79–88.

7. Amitai Etzioni, *The Active Society* (New York: Free Press, 1968), pp. 249–310.

8. Charles L. Schultze, *The Politics and Economics of Public Spending* (Washington, D.C.: Brookings Institution, 1968), pp. 55–76.

9. Claire M. Anderson, Edward E. Schwartz, and Narayan Viswanathan, "Approaches to the Analysis of Social Service Systems," in *Planning, Programming, Budgeting Systems and Social Welfare,* ed. Edward E. Schwartz (Chicago: School of Social Service Administration, University of Chicago, 1970), pp. 42–51.

10. For a thorough review of cost-benefit analysis by economists, see Robert Dorfman, ed., *Measuring Benefits of Government Investments* (Washington, D.C.: Brookings Institution, 1965); Jerome Rothenberg, *Economic Evaluation of Urban Renewal: Conceptual Foundation of Benefits-Cost Analysis* (Washington, D.C.: Brookings Institution, 1967); Alice M. Rivlin, *Systematic Thinking for Social Action* (Washington, D.C.: Brookings Institution, 1971), pp. 46–63; E. J. Mishan, *Cost-Benefit Analysis,* 2d ed. (New York: Praeger Publishers, 1976); Robert H. Haveman and Julius Margolis, eds., *Public Expenditures and Policy Analysis* (Chicago: Markham Publishing Co., 1970).

11. See, e.g., Gene H. Fisher, "Cost Considerations in Policy Analysis," *Policy Analysis* 3 (Winter 1977): 107–14.

12. Dorothy P. Rice, *Estimating the Costs of Illness* (Washington, D.C.: Department of Health, Education, and Welfare, 1976).

13. Anderson et al., pp. 43–44.

14. Jan P. Acton, "Measuring the Monetary Value of Lifesaving Programs," *Law and Contemporary Problems* 15 (Autumn 1976): 46–72; Wenyce H. Brody, "Economic Value of a Housewife," Research and Statistics Note no. 9, Social Security Administration (Washington, D.C.: Department of Health, Education, and Welfare, 1979); Lester B. Lave, "Economic Evaluation of Public Health Programs," in *Annual Reviews of Public Health,* vol. 1, ed. Lester Breslow, Jonathan E. Fielding, and Lester B. Lave (Palo Alto, Calif.: Annual Reviews, Inc., 1980), pp. 262–64; Steven E. Rhoads, "How Much Should We

Spend to Save a Life?" *Public Interest* 51 (Spring 1978): 74–92; Thomas Schelling, "The Life You Save May Be Your Own," in *Problems in Public Expenditure Analysis,* ed. Samuel B. Chase, Jr. (Washington, D.C.: Brookings Institution, 1968), pp. 127–76.

15. Frank A. Sloan, *Planning Public Expenditures on Mental Health Service Delivery* (New York: New York City Rand Institute, 1971), pp. 25–28.
16. Rhoads, pp. 77–79.
17. Richard M. Scheffler and Lynn Pariger, "A Review of the Economic Evidence on Prevention," *Medical Care* 18 (May 1980): 475.
18. Richard M. Titmuss, *The Gift Relationship: From Human Blood to Social Policy* (New York: Pantheon Books, 1971), pp. 198–208.
19. Victor R. Fuchs, *Who Shall Live? Health, Economics, and Social Choice* (New York: Basic Books, 1974), pp. 20–26.
20. Aaron Wildavsky, "The Political Economy of Efficiency: Cost-Benefit Analysis, Systems Analysis, and Program Budgeting," in *Planning, Programming, Budgeting: A Systems Approach to Management,* ed. Freemont J. Lyden and Ernest G. Miller (Chicago: Markham Publishing Co., 1968), p. 373; see also Arthur Maas, "Benefit-Cost Analysis: Its Relevance to Public Investment Decisions," in ibid., pp. 227–28.
21. Scheffler and Pariger, p. 476.
22. Mishan (n. 10 above), pp. 205–24.
23. Wildavsky, pp. 376–77; Rothenberg (n. 10 above), pp. 25–27.
24. Rhoads, p. 80.
25. Lave, p. 260.
26. Maas, pp. 225–26.
27. Herbert E. Klarman, "Application of Cost-Benefit Analysis to Health Systems Technology," in *Technology and Health Care Systems in the 1980s,* ed. Morris F. Collen, DHEW Publication no. (HSM) 73-3016 (Washington, D.C.: Department of Health, Education, and Welfare, 1973), p. 226.
28. Carolyn A. Watts, Morgan Jackson, and James P. LoGerfo, "Cost Effectiveness Analysis: Some Problems of Implementation," *Medical Care* 17 (April 1979): 430–31.
29. Herbert Kleber and Gerald L. Klerman, "Current Issues in Methadone Treatment of Heroin Dependence," *Medical Care* 9 (September–October 1971): 379–81.
30. Scheffler and Pariger, p. 476.
31. Watts et al., pp. 430–34.
32. Arthur M. Okun, *Equality and Efficiency: The Big Tradeoff* (Washington, D.C.: Brookings Institution, 1975).
33. Ibid., p. 13.
34. Blum et al. (n. 4 above), p. 143.
35. Sloan, p. 24.
36. Rivlin, pp. 15–86; Elizabeth B. Drew, "HEW Grapples with PPBS," *Public Interest* 8 (Summer 1967): 9–29; Anita A. Summers and Barbara L. Wolfe, "Improving the Use of Empirical Research as a Policy Tool: An Application to Education," Institute for Research on Poverty, DP no. 580–79 (Madison: University of Wisconsin, November 1979).
37. Social welfare literature from 1970 through 1980 was searched for studies claiming to be economic analyses. For selection here studies had to pass at

least one of two tests: They had to compare both costs and benefits over time or demonstrate a relationship between expenditures and program production. Other studies are mentioned as illustrations of how these tests are most often not met.

38. See, e.g., Coopers & Lybrand, "The Cost of Incarceration in New York City," mimeographed (Hackensack, N.J.: National Council on Crime and Delinquency, 1978); Joseph R. Piasecki, Jane E. Pittinger, and Irvin D. Rutman, *Determining the Costs of Community Residential Services for the Psychosocially Disabled,* National Institute of Mental Health, Series B, no. 13, DHEW Publication no. (ADM)77-504 (Washington, D.C.: Department of Health, Education, and Welfare, 1977).
39. Ben H. Carpenter et al., "Health Costs of Air Pollution: A Study of Hospitalization Costs," *American Journal of Public Health* 69 (December 1979): 1232–41.
40. David W. Young and Brandt Allen, "Benefit-Cost Analysis in the Social Services: The Example of Adoption Reimbursement," *Social Service Review* 51 (June 1977): 249–64.
41. See, e.g., Leo A. McManus, "The Effects of Disability on Lifetime Earnings," Social Security Administration staff paper no. 30, DHEW Publication no. (SSA) 78-11860 (Washington, D.C.: Department of Health, Education, and Welfare, 1978); William Weissert, Thomas Wan, Barbera Livieratos, and Sidney Katz, "Effects and Costs of Day-Care Services for the Chronically Ill: A Randomized Experiment," *Medical Care* 18 (June 1980): 567–84; Michael L. Reid and Jeffrey B. Morris, "Perinatal Care and Cost Effectiveness: Changes in Health Expenditures and Birth Outcome Following the Establishment of a Nurse-Midwife Program," *Medical Care* 17 (May 1979): 491–500.
42. Jane Zapka and Barry W. Averill, "Self Care for Colds: A Cost-Effective Alternative to Upper Respiratory Infection Management," *American Journal of Public Health* 69 (August, 1979): 814–17.
43. Robert L. Bertera and Lawrence W. Green, "Cost-Effectiveness Evaluation of a Home Visiting Triage Program for Family Planning in Turkey," *American Journal of Public Health* 69 (September 1979): 950–53.
44. John F. Morrall III and Edgar O. Olsen, "The Cost-Effectiveness of Leased Public Housing," *Policy Analysis* 6 (Spring 1980): 152–70.
45. Ibid., p. 154.
46. Andreas Muller, "Evaluation of the Costs and Benefits of Motorcycle Helmet Laws," *American Journal of Public Health* 70 (June 1980): 586–92.
47. Burton A. Weisbrod, "A Guide to Benefit-Cost Analysis, as Seen through a Controlled Experiment in Treating the Mentally Ill," Institute for Research on Poverty, DP no. 559-79 (Madison: University of Wisconsin, 1979).
48. Sloan (n. 15 above), p. 40.
49. Abraham S. Levine, "Cost-Benefit Analysis and Social Welfare Program Evaluation," *Social Service Review* 42 (June 1968): 173–83.
50. Jack Rothman, "Macro Social Work in a Tightening Economy", *Social Work* 24 (July 1979): 274–76.
51. Alvin Kogut, "On Macro Social Work," *Social Work* 25 (January 1980): 83.
52. Ibid.

7

Benefit-Cost Analysis and the Social Service Agency: A Model for Decision Making

JOHN A. MORRIS, JR.
MARTHA N. OZAWA

As social work moves increasingly toward what Turem (1974) calls a "management stance," it must perforce expand its technology. More and more often, the ideas, methods, and languages of sister disciplines are finding their way into the social work parlance; nowhere is this more true than in the area of administration and policy development.

This paper addresses one of the more popular economic planning tools, the benefit-cost analysis, with special emphasis on its use in the social service area. Benefit-cost analysis is a product of systems analysis, and finds its heritage in the marriage of economics with management science. It was first used almost exclusively in the design of water projects (for which it is still widely used), but came into its own in the public sector with the adoption of the Planning, Programming, and Budgeting System (PPBS) during the years of the Johnson presidency.

Robert McNamara and other recruits to government service from the nation's think tanks (especially the RAND corporation) emphasized scientific, systematic development of policies. With PPBS adopted by the federal government, and responsibility for its management placed within the Office of the Budget (since renamed the Office for Manage-

Mr. Morris is a specialist in program development and training, Morris Village, 610 Faison Drive, Columbia, South Carolina 29203. Dr. Ozawa is Professor, George Warren Brown School of Social Work, Washington University, Saint Louis.

ment and Budget), the primacy of economic considerations in public policy design was ensured. (For additional information on the history of PPBS and benefit-cost analysis, see Dunlop, 1975; Marvin & Rouse, 1970, pp. 444–460; Merewitz & Sosnick, 1971, pp. 9–12.)

Although economists and others have brought sharp criticism to bear on the benefit-cost analysis (see Tribe, 1973, pp. 3–47; Williams, 1973, pp. 30–62), it has indisputable merits within the context of rational planning and decision making. In this paper we will address both shortcomings and strengths.

First, it seems useful to review briefly the benefit-cost procedure itself (including its theoretical underpinnings). Cost determination, benefit attribution, and data analysis are discussed, all within the context of decision making in the public service field.

A model for adapting benefit-cost analysis to small social service agencies follows, with a simulated application presented to clarify its use.

Having done this, we make the case for increased use of the benefit-cost procedure in the social services.

BENEFIT-COST ANALYSIS

Principles

The basic principle of the benefit-cost analysis is simple: The benefits derived from an undertaking should exceed the costs incurred in its implementation. If the principle is simple, the conduct of the analysis is inversely complex. In the area of public policy analysis, even post hoc studies are difficult: Did Project A achieve its goals in the most efficient way possible? (Did it achieve them at all?) Was Intervention B the most effective in terms of manpower and resources available? And so on. The difficulties multiply severalfold with the use of benefit-cost analysis, as it attempts to answer just such questions a priori.

The principle is usually expressed in terms of a ratio of benefits to costs over a specified time period. According to the most commonly used criterion for evaluating the results of this equation, the Pareto criterion,[1] the ratio must be greater than zero if the project is to be adjudged worthy of investment. As the state of the art advances, more complex formulae and more discrete criteria will continue to emerge. For present purposes, this simple exposition suffices.

Costs

The computation of anticipated costs of an undertaking is the first step in a benefit-cost analysis. In the private sector, a business or industry usually has a fairly clear idea of the market values of the resources needed (manpower, equipment, capital, etc.), already expressed in dollar values. In the production of public goods, however, costs must frequently be approached indirectly. Direct costs for a project (manpower, bricks and mortar, management expenses, etc.) are only the beginning; these so-called internal costs must be added to the costs of spillover effects (also known as "externalities") caused by the project.

To complicate the process further, no market value exists for some resources, and so these must be assigned a phantom or "shadow" price. The determination of shadow prices remains more art than science, and an erroneous figure can radically alter the size of the cost burden (Margolis, 1970, pp. 314–329).

In addition to the explicit costs reviewed above, an additional (implicit) cost factor remains: the opportunity cost. This measure reflects the earning potential of resources (dollars) if left in the private sector. Unfortunately, as the size of the project increases, the reliability of the opportunity cost figure decreases, since resources do not have a constant value throughout a society (Baumol, 1970, pp. 273–290).

Benefits

On the benefit side, there are even more pitfalls for the analyst. For our purposes, benefits are understood as desirable, intended outcomes from a particular course of action; this includes foreseeable spillover benefits, such as redistributive impact (Weisbrod, 1968, pp. 177–209). Traditionally, benefits are given dollar values relevant to the project's intent: welfare dollars saved through a manpower training project, hospital costs saved through a preventive health care service, and so forth. But this belies a fundamental philosophical problem: How are we to assign a dollar value to improved quality of life? How are we to "quantify elements that cannot be quantified" (Merewitz & Sosnick, 1971, p. 279)? At the present time, there are no finally satisfying answers to the questions, and sensitivity to the problem must be maintained in using benefit-cost findings.

The element of benefit attribution that has received the greatest attention from writers and analysts is that of the discount rate. The discount rate is used to formulate benefits in terms of their net present value. A variation of just a few percentage points (e.g., between a discount rate of 10 percent and one of 15 percent) can radically alter the outcome of a benefit-cost analysis, and theorists engage in almost constant combat over what rate should be used, and how it should be chosen (see Baumol, 1970, pp. 273–290; Sandmo, 1973, pp. 177–192; Sandmo & Dreze, 1973, pp. 193–210).

Analysis

If the data available for analysis have successfully weathered all the difficulties mentioned above, a fairly clear picture of the merits of a project or program should emerge. Again we stress that the analysis does not make the decision, but only provides clarity about what is involved in that decision. Other relevant information must round out the decision process.

In most public policy decisions, of course, the other "relevant data" usually include political feasibility. (For discussions of political impact on benefit-cost analysis, see Balutis & Butler, 1975; Peacock, 1973, pp. 17–29; Schultze, 1968.) And all decision making reflects an ethical framework or dominant value set (Boulding, 1969). Even a project that more than satisfies the Pareto criterion may fail to be enacted, and conversely, projects that miserably fail to meet such a standard may be promptly undertaken. This is in the nature of public policy creation, and unlimited advances in benefit-cost technology are not likely to alter the situation radically.

We have said much of the problems associated with benefit-cost analysis; its limitations are real and must be noted. But improvements continue to be made, and on the whole, the procedure's existing and potential merits exceed its problems. Alan Williams (1973) sums it up: "CBA [cost-benefit analysis] is not the way to perfect truth, but the world is not a perfect place, and I regard it as the height of folly to react . . . by shrieking '1984' and putting our heads hopefully back into the sand (or clouds) hoping that things will look better when we look around again in fifteen years' time" (p. 58). The fact of the matter is that there is a paucity of rationally derived tools to assist decision makers; the negative evidence is insufficient to cause us to abandon benefit-cost analysis. We propose, instead, to improve it.

APPLICATIONS OF BENEFIT-COST ANALYSIS

Trends

Even a cursory review of the benefit-cost literature reveals the hegemony of water-use projects alluded to above, but the picture is changing. The procedure is eminently flexible and can be applied to any resource allocation problem, from weapon systems to welfare reform. The creation of the Congressional Budget Office will undoubtedly give further impetus to quantitative analytical techniques in public policy development.

The New Jersey Experiment

The single most important application of benefit-cost technology in the social service area to date is the New Jersey Income Maintenance Experiment (Kershaw & Fair, 1976). In this massive experiment, rigorous scientific methods were used to assess the real costs and benefits of several negative income tax strategies. The designers of this project were concerned not only with cost-efficiency (the cheapest way to accomplish something) but also with real cost-effectiveness (the *best* way to accomplish something with limited resources). Their research included factors beyond mere econometrics, such as the impact on work habits, standard of living, and family functioning.

Robert J. Lampman (1976), who makes explicit the contributions of PPBS technology to the New Jersey Experiment, offers this observation: "The decision to mount a large scale field experiment with negative income taxation may well turn out to be of historic moment in the development of social science" (p. 11).

Social Services

Although the New Jersey Experiment gives testimony of the usefulness of benefit-cost procedures at a broad, national policy level, much sophistication (and money) is necessary to conduct such inquiries. Young and Allen (1977) provide an example of benefit-cost analysis tailored to a specific social service concern on a smaller scale: adoption reimbursement. Their willingness to adapt the basic technique to meet the demands of the target problem is important, and can serve as a useful guidepost to others.

Analysts in the social service area have also explored health service delivery (see Forst, 1973, pp. 393–409; Grosse, 1970, pp. 518–548; Weisbrod, 1975), manpower training (Goldstein, 1973, pp. 338–373), education and training (Johnson & Stafford, 1974, pp. 443–459), and so forth. But at this point, we wish to address the adaptation of benefit-cost procedures to the agency or program level, what Turner (1972, pp. 129–145) calls the mezzosystem level of intervention.

BENEFIT-COST ANALYSIS AT THE PROGRAM LEVEL: A MODEL

David W. Dunlop (1975) states that the chief usefulness of benefit-cost analysis is to provide "a conceptual framework for at least enumerating the possible benefits and costs, in the form of a balance sheet, which can then be used (at least in a qualitative way) in making programmatic decisions" (p. 137). It is within the context of providing a "conceptual framework" for decision making that we propose the following model. We know that a full-scale benefit-cost analysis would be beyond the technical and financial resources of almost all small social service agencies, and yet they are frequently confronted with decisions that demand reliable data. Why should they be denied an analytical tool? As Kast and Rosenzweig (1974, p. 438) suggest, adequate planning (based on sound information) and good decision making are inseparable.

In order to be useful, an analytical tool should be as simple as possible (without sacrificing validity) and should provide maximum flexibility for the user. It should highlight the data, not obscure it in arcane codes and jargon, and should account as clearly as possible for areas of uncertainty. The model presented here has attempted to satisfy these criteria.

The proposed model consists of these five steps:

1. *Clear statement of objectives.* Insofar as possible, objectives should be specific and operationalized.
2. *Determination of costs.* All known or anticipated costs are to be included, including spillover costs if foreseen (expressed in dollar values).
3. *Determination of benefits.* Using criteria given below, a value weight on a 10-point scale (with 10 as the highest value) is assigned to correspond to each objective.
4. *Data analysis.* The average (mean) of all value scores for a given project is divided by the cost per unit of service in that project. This yields a rate of return for that project, which can then be compared to similar scores for other alternatives.
5. *Decision.* Information from the benefit-cost analysis is combined with other relevant data, and a plan of action is selected.

Step 1: Objectives

The most important step in this analytic model is the establishment of clear, concrete objectives. It is impossible to determine in advance the benefits to be derived from an undertaking if goals are fuzzy. In this context, benefits simply do not exist without goals (Merewitz & Sosnick, 1971, p. 179).

Step 2: Costs

All costs for each alternative (which includes the alternative "No change") are computed according to a standardized unit of service delivered (e.g., therapy hour, interview, etc.). Unless the proposal involves capital outlay for new buildings and the like, most social service agencies can restrict their view to personnel and material costs. Personnel costs can be determined simply by arriving at hourly wages, then determining how many hours (or fractions thereof) are involved in the delivery of the service unit.

Step 3: Benefits

It is in the computation of benefits that the model departs from traditional benefit-cost procedures. In the place of dollar values, benefits here are to be determined by the use of scores that reflect perceived value weights. A ten-point scale is used to provide a reasonable range, without excessive complexity; 10 is the highest score. For example, Project A is expected to do much to achieve objective x, and so it might be given a value score of 8, whereas Project B is likely to do little to achieve objective y, and so is assigned a score of 2. When all scores have been assigned, they are averaged, and the mean is the figure used in analysis. (This procedure will become clearer via the simulation below.)

Since this assignment of benefit scores forms a crucial link in the proposed paradigm, we present some normative criteria for assigning these scores. These are by no means exhaustive, and it is expected that they will be revised and expanded in field trials.

First, value weights must be grounded in reality. If there is research information available to suggest that a proposed activity will indeed be effective in meeting a stated goal, it can support a fairly high value score. In the absence of such information, more conservative scores would be used.

Second, value scores must be closely linked to stated objectives. If there is much enthusiasm for a project (perhaps because of its novelty value), and yet its relationship to a stated objective is strained, it would have to be assigned a relatively low score.

Third, value scores should ideally take into account the probability of successful initiation and implementation. If the proposed project would be helpful in achieving stated objectives but stands no chance of approval by a governing administrative body, this necessarily affects the scoring.

Finally, value scores should reflect broad input from those who will be affected. Values assigned by one analyst have less integrity than scores agreed upon by all staff (and clients where feasible).

Step 4: Data Analysis

Once costs and value weights are determined, their relationship must be interpreted. What is sought is a figure that suggests the effectiveness of the investment in terms of objectives desired: a standardized value score. The following simple equation yields such a figure:

$$\frac{\text{Mean value score}}{\text{Cost per unit of service}} = \text{Standardized value score}$$

The standardized value score derived is a qualitative or suggestive number and has no absolute predictive power; its only meaning is in relationship to another standardized value score for an alternative project. No ideal score is posited here.

Step 5: Decision

The decision-making step necessarily reflects the norms of the program or agency engaging in the analysis, and will logically reflect its dominant values. The judgment of the decision maker(s) retains its primacy, as these data "prove" nothing. Hopefully, the decision will reflect an intelligent use of any additional insight that the benefit-cost procedure can provide. We shall return to the role of the decision maker momentarily, but we hope that the following simulation will first help the reader get a clearer idea of the model.

SIMULATION

Setting

The simulation is set in a 150-bed, inpatient treatment facility for alcohol- and other drug-dependent persons. The facility is licensed by the Joint Commission on Accreditation of Hospitals (JCAH) and therefore must prepare individualized treatment plans for all residents (clients). The treatment plan is prepared by an interdisciplinary treatment team, comprised of: one social worker (annual salary of $12,000), one psychologist (annual salary of $14,000), one recreation therapist (annual salary of $13,000), two occupational therapy aides (annual salary of $8,000 each), and a registered nurse (annual salary of $13,500). The team conducts treatment planning sessions (called "staffings") for an average of eight residents per week. At the time the model is investigating, each staffing requires 30 minutes of treatment team time and 1 hour of clerical time. No special supplies are needed, and overhead costs are ignored for this analysis.

Staff have been dissatisfied with treatment planning and feel that the plans are too similar and not genuinely "individualized." There is frequent difficulty with follow-through on the treatment goals. The social worker proposes that the team investigate a new planning technique known as Goal Planning.[2] Because it is known that this method will require more time per staffing, some team members are skeptical but agree to undertake a systematic analysis prior to making their decision.

Step 1

Team members arrive at four objectives for the staffing procedure. (Note that the statements of objectives contain, parenthetically, underlying assumptions.)

1. The creation of a clear, simple, individualized treatment plan that would meet or exceed JCAH standards.
2. The eliciting of maximum input from the resident in identifying issues for treatment. (A consequent increase in commitment to therapy is anticipated.)
3. The assurance of maximum input from all team members in the plan design. (A consequent improvement in follow-through is anticipated.)
4. The assurance of maximum effectiveness of staff time, an already overburdened commodity.

Step 2

Initially, the cost per resident staffing under prevailing conditions was determined to be $20.46.[3] Goal Planning would double the amount of treatment team time but eliminate clerical services, and therefore the cost per staffing would be $32.93.[4] Since consultants will have to be employed, consulting and training costs are also included (prorated over a 1-year period). Including these costs, the new procedure has a per-staffing cost of $38.43.[5]

Step 3

All members of the treatment team next participate in assigning value scores to each condition, contingent upon their perception of how well the method would perform to meet the stated objectives. The present condition obtained a mean value score of 4.75, whereas the proposed condition (Goal Planning) obtained a mean value score of 8 (see Table 7–1).

Step 4

Completing the equation of mean value score divided by cost per unit of service delivered, the standardized value score for the present condition is .232 (viz., 4.75 ÷ 20.46 = .232). The standardized value score for the proposed condition is .207 (viz., 8 ÷ 38.43 = .208). The two conditions, then, offer roughly similar rates of return, with the proposed condition yielding a slightly lower rate.

TABLE 7–1. Value scores by objective desired

Objective	Mean Value Score[a] for Each Objective	
	Present Condition	Proposed Condition
1	6	9
2	2	9
3	6	8
4	5	6
Total	19	32
Grand Mean	4.75	8

[a]Represents average score obtained from all staff involved in rating process.

Step 5

In the example given, the final decision made is to implement the Goal Planning program. Although this may appear paradoxical, it serves to demonstrate the role of benefit-cost analysis in the decision process. The staff involved felt that the slight increase in cost was more than justified in light of the marked increase in ability to achieve stated objectives. The important point is that they were able to make this decision with a fairly clear idea of what was involved. The benefit-cost analysis had provided relevant data.

These same data could have been used to support the opposite decision under different circumstances. The decision makers might have felt that the margin of gain was insufficient to justify undertaking the proposed program (at least at the present time), and so they would have explored other alternatives. Probabilities for successful implementation and initiation might also have been considered at this point, and have contraindicated any change in status. (For a formula designed to compute the probabilities of successful initiation and implementation of a project, see Peterson & Seo, 1975.)

DISCUSSION AND CONCLUSIONS

After reviewing the history of cost-benefit analysis, and having briefly sketched its methodology, we have addressed an area where benefit-cost analysis has been underutilized: the mezzosystem of agencies, projects, and programs. With a view toward responding to Turem's (1974) call for an "increased management stance" in social work, we have proposed a model for using cost-benefit analysis in program planning and decision making. The model makes use of traditional concepts but introduces a value-weighted scoring mechanism for assessing desired benefits.

It has been our intent to offer a heuristic device for the decision maker(s). Whether cost-benefit analysis is used in the Department of Defense or in a small social service agency, it serves the same purpose.

Although we recognize that there are potential weaknesses in a paradigm that introduces a major subjective element such as the value-weighted scores, we also recognize that much value judgments permeate every level of even the most sophisticated analyses (see Baumol, 1970, pp. 273–290; Boulding, 1969; Peacock, 1973, pp. 17–29). A certain advantage is gained, in fact, by having such value choices made explicit and not couched in deceptively "empirical" estimates.

We submit that a foundation tenet of rational management is the acknowledgment of goals and values with maximum clarity and view the paradigm suggested here as an aid to that clarity. (Kast and Rosenzweig, 1974, give an excellent review of the role of goals and values in organizational life.)

Alan Williams (1973, p. 35) raises these three questions about benefit-cost analysis:

1. Is it systematic?
2. Is it objective? and
3. Is it precise?

We answer—as he did—that all of the questions can be answered in the affirmative in principle. In practice, however, an analysis may not be systematic, objective, or precise. The effectiveness of the tool is dependent upon the honesty and skill of the user and the quality of data available for analysis. Like any other device, it can be abused and its conclusions rendered useless by inaccurate or biased inputs.

But used responsibly, benefit-cost analysis has great potential not only in terms of national and regional policy development but also at the agency or program level as well. The critical variable in decision making will remain the judgment of the decision maker(s). This tool can enhance the quality of the decisions made by helping that judgment to resemble more closely an ideal: the *informed* judgment.

NOTES

1. For a discussion of the Pareto criterion (as well as the Kaldor-Hicks and Little criteria), see Merewitz and Sosnick (1971, pp. 78–85). In the case of a one-

time cost and a stream of benefits over time, the benefit-cost ratio can be obtained as follows:

$$\text{Benefit-cost ratio} = \frac{\sum_{j=1}^{m} \frac{Bj}{(1+r)\,m\text{-}j}}{C}$$

where Bj = annual benefits of jth years; r = compounded annual interest rate; j index of years = 1, . . . m; m = number of benefit-receiving years; and C = one-time cost.

2. Goal Planning is a treatment planning strategy developed by Robert A. Scott and Peter S. Houts of the Hershey Medical Center, Hershey, Pennsylvania. References to consulting fees and training expenses are fictitious.

3. This figure is arrived at by dividing the total annual wages (viz., $68,500.00) by 2,080 (i.e., 52 weeks x 40 hours per week), thus obtaining the cost per hour of the whole treatment team: $32.93. One-half hour of treatment time costs $16.46, and 1 hour of clerical time costs $4.00; therefore, the cost per staffing under present conditions is $20.46.

4. This figure is simply the single hour cost for the entire team, as derived above: $32.93.

5. The consulting fee is $1,500.00. Training time needed is 3 full working days (24 hours) for the entire team. The cost for removing these staff members from normal duties is $790.32 (viz., $32.93 x 24 = $790.32). Added to the consulting fee, total costs are $2,290.32 (viz., $1,500.00 + $790.32 = $2,290.32). At eight staffings per week for 52 weeks (8 x 52 = 416), the cost per staffing is $5.50 (viz., $2,290.32 ÷ 416 = $5.50). Added to the basic cost per staffing hour ($32.93), the total cost per staffing under Goal Planning is $38.43 (viz., $32.93 + $5.50 = $38.43).

REFERENCES

Balutis, A. P., & Butler, D. K. (Eds.) *The political pursestrings.* New York: John Wiley & Sons, 1975.

Baumol, W. J. On the discount rate for public projects. In R. H. Haveman & J. Margolis (Eds.), *Public expenditure and policy analysis.* Chicago: Markham, 1970.

Boulding, K. E. Economics as a moral science. *American Economic Review,* March 1969, *59,* 1–12.

Dunlop, D. W. Benefit-cost analysis: A review of its applicability in policy analysis for delivering health services. *Social Science and Medicine,* 1975, *9,* 133–139.

Forst, B. E. An analysis of alternative periodic health examination strategies. In W. A. Niskanen et al. (Eds.), *Benefit-cost and policy analysis, 1972.* Chicago: Aldine, 1973.

Goldstein, J. H. The effectiveness of manpower training programs: A review of research on the impact of the poor. In W. A. Niskanen et al. (Eds.), *Benefit-cost and policy analysis, 1972*. Chicago: Aldine, 1973.

Grosse, R. N. Problems of resource allocation in health. In R. H. Haveman & J. Margolis (Eds.), *Public expenditure and policy analysis*. Chicago: Markham, 1970.

Johnson, G. E., & Stafford, F. P. Social returns to quantity and quality of schooling. In R. H. Haveman & A. C. Harberger, et al. (Eds.), *Benefit-cost and policy analysis, 1973*. Chicago: Aldine, 1974.

Kast, F. E., & Rosenzweig, J. E. *Organization and management*. Saint Louis: McGraw-Hill, 1974.

Kershaw, D., & Fair, J. (Eds.) *The New Jersey Income Maintenance Experiment: Volumu I, Operations, surveys and administration*. New York: Academic Press, 1976.

Lampman, R. J. The decision to undertake the New Jersey Experiment. In D. Kershaw & J. Fair (Eds.), *The New Jersey Income Maintenance Experiment: Volume I, Operations, surveys and administration*. New York: Academic Press, 1976.

Margolis, J. Shadow prices for incorrect or non-existent market values. In R. H. Havema & J. Margolis (Eds.), *Public expenditure and policy analysis*. Chicago: Markham, 1970.

Marvin, K. E., & Rouse, A. M. The status of PPBS in federal agencies: A comparative perspective. In R. H. Haveman & J. Margolis (Eds.), *Public expenditure and policy analysis*. Chicago: Markham, 1970.

Merewitz, L., & Sosnick, S. H. *The budget's new clothes*. Chicago: Markham, 1971.

Peacock, A. Cost-benefit analysis and the political control of public investment. In J. N. Wolfe (Ed.), *Cost benefit and cost effectiveness*. London: George Allen & Unwin, 1973.

Peterson, R. E., & Seo, K. K. Benefit-cost analysis for developing countries: *Economic Development and Cultural Change*, 1975, *24*, 185–197.

Sandmo, A. Discount rates for public investment. In W. A. Niskanen et al. (Eds.), *Benefit-cost and policy analysis, 1972*. Chicago: Aldine, 1973.

Sandmo, A., & Dreze, J. H. Discount rates for public investment in closed and open economics. In W. A. Niskanen et al. (Eds.), *Benefit-cost and policy analysis, 1972*. Chicago: Aldine, 1973.

Schultze, C. L. *The politics and economics of public spending*. Washington, D.C.: Brookings Institution, 1968.

Tribe, L. H. Policy science: Analysis or ideology? In W. A. Niskanen et al. (Eds.), *Benefit-cost and policy analysis, 1972*. Chicago: Aldine, 1973.

Turem, J. E. The call for a management stance. *Social Work*, 1974, *19*, 615–623.

Turner, J. B. Forgotten: Mezzosystem intervention. In E. J. Mullen & J. R. Dumpson (Eds.), *Evaluation of social intervention*. San Francisco: Jossey-Bass, 1972.

Weisbrod, B. A. Income redistribution effects and benefit-cost analysis. In S. B. Chase, Jr. (Ed.), *Problems in public expenditure analysis*. Washington, D.C.: Brookings Institution, 1968.

Weisbrod, B. A. Research in health economics: A survey. *International Journal of Health Sciences*, 1975, *50*, 643–661.

Williams, A. Cost-benefit analysis: Bastard science? And/or insidious poison in the body politick? In J. N. Wolfe (Ed.), *Cost benefit and cost effectiveness.* London: George Allen & Unwin, 1973.

Young, D. W., & Allen, A. Benefit-cost analysis in the social services: The example of adoption reimbursement. *Social Service Review,* June 1977, pp. 249–264.

8

Problems in Evaluating Costs and Benefits of Social Programs

THOMAS V. GREER
JOANNE G. GREER

The wave of domestic social legislation of the 1960s and early 1970s that led to community action programs, measures for reducing racial segregation and sex discrimination, compensatory education, manpower training, and public health initiatives also pushed federal "human services" expenditures to a FY 1980 level of $336.2 billion.[1] The same phenomenon was responsible for the creation of the profession of program evaluation.

Many legislators favor this development, for it offers the possibility of making more rational decisions about social welfare policies and more objective and efficient allocations of public expenditures. On the program management side, the current climate of retrenchment gives a new and additional significance to evaluation. Some program managers now see it as a means of prioritizing spending reductions and protecting the best programs from unwise funding cuts and consolidation into block grants.

The program evaluation discipline, both in government agencies and in the consulting firms performing evaluation work under government contract, developed in a fashion similar to that of operations research during World War II. Like "operations research" in its formative years, "program evaluation" is eclectic, empirical, and welcomes to its ranks researchers of widely varying perspectives and formal training.

Two of the most popular approaches to studying program impact have been adaptations of the pre-treatment vs. post-treatment and/or treatment-versus-control studies of the behavioral scientist and the cost-benefit analyses of the economist.[2] In the "pre-post" study, preprogram data and post-program data are gathered on relevant variables and compared. In the cost-benefit study, program costs and dollar value of program benefits are compared.

Although some fruitful research has been produced, severe "real-world" obstacles have also been encountered. The remainder of this chapter discusses some of these obstacles to effective program evaluation and ways of overcoming them.

OBSTACLE 1: THE NATURAL RESISTANCE TO EVALUATION

The behavioral mechanism involved in resistance to evaluation is fairly straightforward: "Presenting the best possible picture to those who make judgments is a cultural expectation."[3] To be more specific, the lower-level program administrator and his or her staff literally see their bread and butter at risk when the program evaluator arrives on the scene. For example, two researchers who studied interpersonal dynamics in ten applied studies funded by the National Institute of Mental Health commented that "All projects felt they were the target of overt or covert sabotage" by the visiting evaluation team.[4] In addition, program personnel may have a philosophical belief in the program and may have lavished their personal energies on launching it. In fact, in some cases they may have actually lobbied the legislative body, *sub rosa,* in order to establish the program.

The program staff hopes the evaluation staff, whether legislative or executive, will conclude that the new program is excellent, but believes it is better not to take chances. In their thinking, the program evaluator was foisted on the program and cannot be got rid of easily. The next best thing is to make his or her presence as nonthreatening as possible.

It is sometimes suspected that the obstacles discussed below may be created or at least encouraged by program administrators and their staffs. As Scioli states with delightful whimsy, "The marriage of the staff to the program in the sacred church of the bureaucracy is a strong impediment to program evaluation."[5] The proliferation of obstacles is reminiscent of a similar occurrence familiar to private industry, the act of "concealing the audit trail" from the internal management auditor or the outside C.P.A.

OBSTACLE 2: THE QUALITY OF THE MANAGEMENT INFORMATION SYSTEM

The authors have been involved with a number of government computerized information systems and have also exchanged experiences with other researchers. A pattern of obstacles to efficient, inexpensive program evaluation emerges that exhibits some of the classic characteristics of concealing the audit trail. Some of these systems are of such poor quality that a better title, at least from the viewpoint of a program evaluation team, might be the management "misinformation" system. This does not reflect lack of diligence or intelligence. Instead, the state of these information systems is probably a reflection of the low priority given them in top management decisions on staff and funding allocations. Often these systems have one, if not more, of the following troublesome characteristics.

Cost Data Are Taken Over Different Time Periods or Different Service Aggregations Than Utilization Data

For example, cost data are reported by fiscal year, while services rendered (i.e., production units) are reported by calendar year. Particularly on the federal level, the two types of data may also be reported in nonreconcilable semiannual and quarterly figures. More often than not, the data in question are seasonal or cyclical, thus threatening gross error when they are prorated over 12 months in order to make comparisons between cost and utilization. This state of affairs is useful to no one, either evaluator or manager.

Primary Data Are Illogically Aggregated

In any data system that serves multiple users, the levels of aggregation of variables should be kept very low, and the variables should be very simple. Ages of clients and other descriptive data should not be aggregated, and the system should be arranged to provide data for each month or quarter, to be grouped as the user needs. For example, a certain data base on hospital patients grouped all hospital stays after 22 days. The groups were one day, two days, . . . 21 days, 22–45 days, and over 45 days. The inability to compute actual mean length of hospital stay will weaken most conclusions of any evaluation. It also, no doubt, affects the accuracy of the agency's routine management reports.

Variables Are Frequently "Improved" by Redefinition

When a data system is up and running and has been found wanting, there is a tendency to redesign the system. If this is clearly necessary, then variables should be added rather than deleted or redefined. Then studies already underway using the old variable definitions can still be completed. Consider the following example: The first two years of a given data base in a health services agency separately recorded patient encounters with three different types of health care providers: M.D., nurse practitioner, and physician assistant. These types of providers differ widely in years of training, and identifying the most cost-effective mix of the three types is an issue of intense interest to both private sector and public sector health care managers. In examining the first two years of data, some interesting and significant differences were observed in productivity and work patterns for the three groups, and a larger scale study was planned. In the meantime, however, the data division redesigned the raw data collection procedures, and the third year report from clinics pooled all patient encounters for each "health care team," composed of mixtures of the three types of providers. Comparisons by type of provider were no longer possible, and plans for further validation of the evaluation findings from the first two years had to be abandoned.

Low Priority of MIS Personnel and Funds

Some jaundiced program evaluators claim that the contract for setting up a new program's management information system is always awarded to one of the following:

1. a firm that has never set up a management information system,
2. a recently incorporated firm, or
3. a firm with chronic personnel problems.

There appear to be at least some grounds for such complaints. A few years ago, one of the authors witnessed approximately $400,000 spent on a contract to produce a simple MIS intended to generate about 12 tables quarterly using data from a few hundred program sites. After about a year the computer programs still produced tables in which divisions by zero occurred and subtotals were incorrect when checked manually. The project had changed hands so many times that it was very difficult to make progress. Staff assignments to project monitoring were avoided because of top management's disinterest.

A solution seems to be to set up the MIS internally, using agency computer personnel. Again, however, one may see a totally inoperative system for some time if crucial personnel are transferred to related positions periodically, or if overdue staff advancement and recognition are refused until staff transfer to other agencies in the interests of their own careers. Typically, data operations have little glamour, and only if data staff market their services assiduously to program staff do they receive administrative support.

OBSTACLE 3: MISSING ESTIMATES
OF BENEFICIARY POPULATIONS

Conceptualizing useful studies in the area of social interventions and the related costs and benefits is only the first step of a lengthy process. Most evaluators know their assigned program well enough and are knowledgeable enough about research to design studies to address their information needs. Locating the data to carry out a study is more difficult. New programs are typically set up with no explicit plans to study scientifically the impact of the proposed policy. Usually, when the moment to evaluate program impact arrives, a complete set of retrospective data is next to impossible to acquire, making pre-post comparisons weak or totally infeasible. Practically speaking, the enthusiasm of staff to get a new program underway, and the need to act quickly in response to legislative mandates will always oppose the time lag needed to collect baseline data. This may be reasonable and appropriate, since the program exists for other, more urgent reasons than how well it evaluates. But the data problem must be reckoned with when annual report time comes around.

An additional problem which sometimes makes preliminary data infeasible is the potential beneficiary's legal right to privacy. For example, in the case of veteran's widows benefits, identification of future eligibles would require data on such sensitive issues as the veteran's future marital and childbearing intentions. Anonymous surveys on planned family size have been done for years, and have been quite reliable, but current privacy legislation probably makes it impossible to identify directly those respondents who might qualify for benefits in future years. There is also the practical problem of the cost of a fertility survey of adequate size to support such subpopulation estimates.

OBSTACLE 4: INCOMPATIBLE DATA

In evaluation research absolute counts of persons, or population data, are often used directly to measure program growth or projected usage. But in many studies it is just as important to construct relative numbers, such as per capita expenditure, hospital beds per 1,000 population, or deaths per 100,000. These rates and ratios are computed to ensure comparability between time periods, population groups, or geographic areas.[6] Logic demands compatibility between numerator and denominator, however. In a 1979 project conducted by the U.S. Public Health Service,[7] for example, the effect of a pilot medical peer review program on decreasing utilization of hospital days by Medicare patients was studied. A pre-post study was designed, using the year immediately prior to a small-scale program implementation as the "pre" year, and two years after program implementation as the "post" year. The rate computation of interest to the evaluators was "hospital days per 1,000 persons covered by Medicare" for two groups of geographic areas, those areas with and without the new program. In order to generate these rates, one required reliable pre-program and post-program implementation counts of two variables: the numerator, which was the number of Medicare-paid hospital days per geographical area, and the denominator, which was the number of Medicare clients per area. Unfortunately, such a ratio was impossible to compute because the available numerator data was aggregated only by the address of the hospital while the available denominator data was aggregated only by the home address of the client. This problem could have been avoided by recording the patients' counties of residence in all computerized hospital data on usage. In order to calculate rates which could be defended:

1. a separate data analysis had to be done to verify that patient migration, for health care only, was a relatively constant factor; and
2. those areas which experienced large seasonal migration, such as Florida, had to be excluded from the study.

In making plans for an analogous study of Medicaid hospital usage, problems in procuring as denominators accurate counts of eligible persons by area of residence were so severe that no usage rates could be computed and the study had to be abandoned.

In federal programs, sometimes incompatibility of data seems built into the system by the sheer magnitude of operations. For example, when reports originate in over 6,000 hospitals and are collected at 200, 50, or even 10 points for aggregation, only the strictest quality control will produce reconcilable data. Unfortunately, definition of variables is seldom as careful as one would like. A few years ago, in compiling data for budget analysis, it was found, after the fact, that some reporting units included new born babies separately in one of the patient counts while others assumed those newborns and their mothers formed one "patient unit." Fiscal years also vary from hospital to hospital and monthly or even quarterly accounting data are not available for many variables of interest. After the fact, how does one clear up problems like these, and end up with even a small amount of reasonably comparable data for the entire country?

OBSTACLE 5: INAPPROPRIATELY DESIGNED ACCOUNTING SYSTEMS

Accounting systems and reporting requirements are seldom designed with cost-benefit analysis in mind, although the final cost-benefit ratio of a program is usually of high interest. Cost centers should be conceptualized with at least one eye on the future needs of program evaluation. Otherwise, no cost center may exist that relates clearly and directly to the ultimate purpose of the program!

In 1977 one federal evaluation project spent $269,000 to have a team from an accounting firm construct one essential cost center on site for each of a large number of hospitals.[8] The expenditure was necessary in order to evaluate a particular federal health program, but the labor could have been avoided had there been standardized cost centers related to the program among state and local recipients of the program funds. This would also have allowed states to monitor the local program sites more effectively and to compare personnel with neighboring states.

Separation of start-up and operating costs is crucial for a correct cost-benefit analysis of a new program. Normally fixed and variable costs also must be separated. For example, if a program has reduced hospital utilization by one day per 1,000 Medicare beneficiaries, have the costs to the Medicare program been decreased by the hospital's average daily charge? Obviously not, since many fixed costs remain which must be covered whether a particular hospital bed is empty or filled on a given day. Little work has been done to explore the shifts in hospital costs when government "utilization control" programs cause decreasing hospital occupancy rates. It is known that the hospitals will, quite legally, pass on these uncovered fixed costs from a time "t" to patients who occupy the hospital in the following year "t + 1," resulting in a higher per diem charge for the year "t + 1." Typically, the Medicare and Medicaid programs will dictate what they consider their "fair share" of the pass-through for the year "t + 1," insurers such as Blue Cross will negotiate their portion, and the remainder will be allocated to the uninsured patients in the "t + 1" patient population, or will become losses on the operating statement. A multi-stage pricing model, developed from empirical accounting data, is needed to understand the total system and to evaluate the ability of government policy actually to contain health care costs rather than merely shifting them to a lower level of government, to the private sector, or to another fiscal year.

OBSTACLE 6: COMMINGLED FUNDS

Separate funding sources from different government programs are frequently commingled in such a manner as to be untraceable down to the point of expenditure. When one attempts to "evaluate" program A by tracing out the impact of its appropriated funds to the status of its target population, one finds that funds from Appropriation A for Program A have been commingled with those from Appropriations B, C, D, . . . ,

(P. + 1) for Programs B, C, D, . . . , (P + 1) at one or more administrative levels $a_1 a_2, \ldots, a_{m+1}$.

At the local level some publicly funded primary health care centers may have six different funding sources and the center director may not be aware of the exact orchestration of funding from the separate laws. The intent of the person who pooled the funds may have been to simplify everyone's life, from the federal to the regional to the state to the local level. The net effect, however, is that the only evaluation possible is an "all or nothing" evaluation of all the programs simultaneously. This produces maximum safety for the current group of programs, since no legislator will propose giving up all publicly financed programs in health or in education, for instance. Component-wise evaluation, law by separate law, cannot be achieved. If it is attempted the study design will be so poor that the program advocates and the lower level managers will successfully rebut any conclusion from the report.

This problem is compounded by the fact that some city- or county-level managers may solicit extra funds from a multitude of highly original sources when their more usual sources are stingy or slow. For example, in a recent year one small local program for pregnant adolescents procured funds from all of the following: Social Security Title XIX, Social Security Title XX, Law Enforcement Assistance Administration, National Institute of Mental Health, National Institute of Alcohol Abuse and Alcoholism, National Institute of Drug Abuse, Office of Education, State Bureau of Education, State Health Department, United Way, the county commission, the municipal government, and the school board.

OBSTACLE 7:
MULTIPLE TREATMENT INTERFERENCE

This contaminant to studies of program costs and impacts results from the fact that public programs, even at the federal level, are not well coordinated. Usually site selection for piloting a new program takes place without consideration of other federal, state, or local programs for the same beneficiaries which may be introduced during the same time period.[9]

Consider this sample. In Mississippi a demonstration medical peer review program, designed to reduce unnecessary hospital utilization by Medicaid and Medicare patients, was operative during the same period in the same counties as a major demonstration project in maternal and child health care for the poor. This latter program had the effect of increasing necessary hospital utilization. Since "necessary" and "unnecessary" in this context are undefinable, measurement of the true impact of the peer review program on Medicaid clients was impossible. A slight decrease in overall hospital utilization was noted, but not enough to make the peer review program cost-beneficial. This small program success would most probably have been of a greater magnitude in a less confused experimental setting.

Other forms of multiple treatment interference often result from trends and changes in the private sector which either parallel or oppose the purpose of a government policy. For example, length of hospital stays has been decreasing steadily, even in the care of private (not Medicare/Medicaid) patients, for the last decade. This is due partly to a change in styles of medical care, a realization that getting the patient out of bed and on the way home sooner is to his or her benefit. In studying government policy interventions to decrease length of hospital stays of federal (Medicare/Medicaid) patients, then, it is necessary to find comparison areas to control for these general secular trends in medical practice. This is difficult to do effectively.

DIRECTIONS FOR IMPROVEMENT

Cultivating Collaborative Relationships with Program Managers

The program evaluator and the program administrator appear to be natural antagonists, in that the results of program evaluation can be strategic to the survival of the program. It is doubtful that the tension of this adversary relationship can be resolved. It can, however, be minimized by conscientious and ethical behavior on the part of evaluators. To increase long-term credibility with program staff, evaluation staff must produce reports that are balanced and fair and never sensational. Executive summaries and press releases must be written with extreme care, lest important reservations related to "real world" data problems go unnoticed by hurried administrators, legislators, and journalists who stop short of reading the entire report. Moreover, program administrators are justified in regarding evaluators as "hatchet men" if they mention qualifications, reservations, and extenuating circumstances only in the last 10 pages of a 300-page report. It is even more unfair to present "caveats" about poor data quality in statistical jargon which is unintelligible to the average reader.

The evaluator must be particularly careful not to oversell the significance of short-term evaluation data in the case of programs with very long-range intents. For example, in evaluating social programs targeted at children, such as Head Start of Medicaid's EPSDT,[10] it must be pointed out that the evaluator's pre-treatment and post-treatment data are actually only two snapshots in time of a dynamic growth curve. Such data may be less than useful in documenting the program's long-term success or failure in altering the entire growth curve.[11] In dealing with such issues, it is particularly fortuitous when the evaluator is both program specialist and evaluation specialist. Evaluators with dual degrees (e.g., education plus statistics, medicine plus epidemiology) can perhaps more easily integrate program considerations and research design considerations, producing evaluation studies which make sense both to finance experts and to human services experts.

The program evaluator is neither "hatchet man" nor program advocate. In addition, he or she has the humbling responsibility of remembering that "program" is more important to most of the involved parties than "evaluation" can ever be. Consequently evaluators can only negotiate with program officials for reasonable research designs, rather than demanding them. Realistically speaking, if evaluation data are lacking, it is the evaluator who has to solve the problem by personal resourcefulness.

Optimizing Available Data Resources

There are at least two useful strategies for making the best of currently available data. On the one hand, the evaluation team may be able to locate supplementary data from sources extraneous to the program being evaluated. This is particularly likely when it is baseline data or comparison group data which is needed. On the other hand, highly trained and broadly experienced personnel can often extract better mileage from the limited program data which is readily available.

Every evaluation team should include, at least as a consultant, one person who is trained at the graduate level in research design and statistics. Ideally, this team member has experience not only in applying "cook book" statistics to data but also in devising valid approximations and extrapolations to maximize the decision-making power of sparse data. Such team members are optimally useful if they also have solid programmatic knowledge but are not intensely invested in any one program's success.

Cost-benefit studies are difficult to perform without also having an accountant/auditor team member. If ratios are to be formed, the component dollar figures must be computed by standard methods in order to be defensible. The audit function in a cost-benefit analysis must be sophisticated in order to get at "real" costs. Often a cost center can be constructed either to vindicate or condemn a program, and the evaluator will have to be wary of the costing methodology.

Unless one or more team members have recent program experience, a program manager is an essential team member. Otherwise, data interpretations which look technically correct may turn out to be nonsense because of some poorly understood program characteristic. Often it is more effective to utilize someone whose identification with the program is of the recent past, rather than concurrent with the evaluation. This avoids both the fact and the appearance of this team member's serving two masters.

An evaluation team is always fortunate when it has access to a collaborator with a broad interest in data systems and a penchant for collecting documentation on the many federal, state, and special interest data systems. If the study is an important project or a long-term one it may pay to allocate substantial in-house resources to document the existing relevant data held by all reputable sources. This can also be done by contract to a specialized research firm. The Office of Planning, Evaluation, and Legislation in Health Services Administration, which is responsible for national evaluation of Title V (Maternal and Child Health), recently obtained a thoroughly documented catalogue of all existing data bases on developmentally disabled children in this fashion.[12]

Influencing Data System Development

The program evaluation group can often influence the usefulness of data, even if they cannot dictate it. Long-term relationships of mutual respect and collaboration are the goal here. Becoming active in data user groups within one's agency, volunteering for service committees related to data issues, and joining professional associations to which data managers also belong are a few ways of building bridges. The program evaluation group may have specialized types of expertise that other managers need only a few days a year. If such help is forthcoming, it will be remembered when the evaluation group needs custom data runs or an additional variable added to recurring reports.

SUMMARY AND CONCLUSIONS

In the current climate of retrenchment in social programs, there is a possibility that cost-benefit analyses of programs may be inappropriately utilized. Although the concept of cost-benefit is a reasonable decision criterion for social program evaluation, the state of the art in actually performing such analyses is not of a high level. The global nature and long-term goals of many social programs and the poor quality of available data make it inadvisable to use cost-benefit ratios as the sole criterion of program effectiveness. In all fairness, the tentative conclusions reached by cost-benefit analysis must be weighed against other, nonquantitative factors in choosing which programs to cut back or abandon.

On the other hand, when placed in a proper context of the total available programmatic information, cost-benefit analysis is quite useful in weighing alternatives. In order to make this approach more serviceable to the social program evaluator and manager, data quality must be improved. Unavoidable problems with data reliability and validity must be weighed in deciding how much credibility a given cost-benefit ratio is due in the decision-making process.

NOTES

1. "The Budget: 1981," *The Washington Post,* January 29, 1980, p. A15.
2. E. B. Opperman, D. R. Plane, and J. I. Suver, "Applications of Incremental Economic Analysis for Public Sector Decisions," *Interfaces,* Vol. 8, No. 1 (1978), pp. 13–21.
3. N. Cochran, "Cognitive Processes, Social Mores, and the Accumulation of Data: Program Evaluation and the Status Quo," *Evaluation Quarterly,* Vol. 2, No. 2 (1978), pp. 343–358 at p. 347.
4. E. M. Glaser and S. H. Taylor, "Factors Influencing the Success of Applied Research," *American Psychologist,* Vol. 28, No. 2 (1973), pp. 140–146.
5. F. P. Scioli, Jr., "Problems and Prospects for Policy Evaluation," *Public Administration Review,* Vol. 39, No. 1 (1979), pp. 41–45 at p. 42.
6. James Hatten, "Medicare's Common Denominator: The Covered Population," *Health Care Financing Review,* Vol. 2, No. 2 (1980), pp. 53–64.
7. See J. G. Greer and C. M. Dayton, *PSRO: An Evaluation of Professional Standards Review Organizations. Volume III: Some Data on the Medicare Experience* (Washington, D.C.: Health Services Administration, U.S. Public Health Service, 1979).
8. J. G. Greer, R. H. Hamlin, and S. Clemans, *The Costs of Utilization Review Programs in Hospitals and PSROs* (Washington, D.C.: Health Services Administration, U.S. Public Health Service, 1977).
9. In a recent article Boruch et al. present some interesting proposed applications of classic randomized experiments but do not take into account the threat to validity in multiple treatment interference. See: R. F. Boruch, D. Rindskopf, P. S. Anderson, I. R. Amidjaya, and D. M. Jansson, "Randomized Experiments for Evaluating and Planning Local Programs: A Summary on Appropriateness and Feasibility," *Public Administration Review,* Vol. 39, No. 1 (1979), pp. 36–40.
10. EPSDT—Early and Periodic Screening, Diagnosis, and Treatment. This is a program to identify and treat health and developmental problems in children who are eligible for Medicaid.
11. A. S. Bryk and H. I. Weisberg, "Value-Added Analysis: A Dynamic Approach to the Estimation of Treatment Effects," *Journal of Educational Statistics,* Vol. 1, No. 2 (1976), pp. 127–156. Also see T. D. Cook, C. L. Gruder, K. M. Hennigon, and B. R. Flay, "History of the Sleeper Effect: Some Logical Pitfalls in Accepting the Null Hypothesis," *Psychological Bulletin,* Vol. 86, No. 4 (1979), pp. 652–679.

12. *Sourcebook of Extant Data Bases on Developmentally Disabled Children Up to Six Years of Age,* Department of Health and Human Services, Health Services Administration (OPEL), 1980. National Technical Information Service Publication #PB811741187.

9

Management by Objectives in a Family Service Agency

VERNON R. WIEHE

What criteria are used by supervisory personnel in appraising the performance of social workers? How can creativity and enthusiasm in job performance be stimulated? Is it possible to establish short- and long-range service delivery goals in a social agency? Management by objectives, engaged in by administrative and line staff, is one answer to these questions. While management by objectives is not a panacea for management problems, it is a helpful tool in performance appraisal and in program-planning in a social agency.

DEFINITION OF TERMS

The key terms in management by objectives are *mission, objectives, goals,* and *plans.*[1] The mission is the final aim or end of action which an organization wishes to attain. The mission is generally stated in broad terms which set out the general direction the agency is attempting to achieve. The mission describes the purpose of the organization, the reason for its existence. For an agency with family and child welfare services, the mission might be stated as follows:

Middletown Family and Children's Services serves individuals, families, and groups in the community in their attempt to achieve full human potential for themselves and for others.

A sectarian agency or an agency related to a court or school system may add to its statement of mission the unique relationship or channel to the community through which it attempts to achieve its purpose for existence. The mission of such an agency might read as follows:

The Middletown Catholic Family and Children's Services, through its relationship to the parishes and schools of the Catholic community, serves individuals, families, and groups in their attempt to achieve full human potential for themselves and for others.

The objectives are the results the agency wishes to achieve in order to remain a viable organization which is fulfilling its mission. The objectives may be viewed as a further delineation or refinement of the mission of the organization. Objectives for a family and child welfare agency may include the following:

To have a balance in services between prevention and treatment.
To serve individuals and groups in their efforts to become sensitive to social issues.
To incorporate the social action function of the agency as an integral part of all agency functions.
To incorporate research as an agency function toward improving services and expanding social work knowledge.
To maintain a family-focused orientation in all agency services.
To utilize volunteers in the accomplishment of the agency mission.

The goals of a program of management by objectives are the end results to be achieved within a period of time. The period of time will vary according to the nature of the goal. The period for the attainment of a goal may be as brief as one or two months or as long as a year, the latter being equal to the annual appraisal period. In some instances long-range goals may take several years to accomplish. Both short- and long-range goals may be established by a worker, department, or agency depending on the difficulty in achieving the goals, the resources available in the attainment of the goals, and the time necessary to bring a goal to its fruition.

Examples of goals of individual workers in a family service agency may include the following:

During the coming year I intend to improve my skills in leading groups so that I may utilize group methods in working with couples requesting marital counseling.

During the next three months I plan to complete dictation on fifteen cases needing to be closed in my caseload.

During the next four months I will prepare for supervising a field work student in the agency.

The final term used in management by objectives is *plans*. Plans are the means by which goals are achieved. They are the steps, activities, projects, and tasks which must be undertaken by a worker to achieve his goals. The route to the achievement of each goal must be spelled out in terms of the plans the worker has for achieving this goal. Goals are valid and feasible only to the extent that the directions toward their achievement have been carefully thought through and defined. As conditions within an agency may change during any given period of time, plans as well as goals may need to be modified.

The goal which a family service worker may have set for himself and the plans by which to achieve this goal might be stated as follows:

Goal: During the next four months I will prepare for supervising a field work student in the agency.

Plans: Consult with the other staff at next staff meeting on reducing my caseload by 10 percent beginning one month before student's placement in the agency.

Consult with staff during the last month before placement regarding being alert at intake to specific cases for assignment to student.

Review literature in social work journals from the past three years on the supervision of students.

The formulation of plans for attaining a goal is similar to operationalizing a concept in research, wherein the researcher specifies the route he will take in measuring a concept or what he will do to quantify the concept. In management by objectives, the worker spells out in actual practice how he will attempt to reach the goal. Some goals are never accomplished because adequate or realistic plans for their attainment were not carefully developed.

A DEDUCTIVE AND INDUCTIVE PROCESS

Who determines the mission of the agency? From where do the objectives come? Do goals flow out of objectives which have been set, or do objectives arise from the plans and goals of the individual workers or departments within an agency?

In considering these questions it becomes apparent that deductive and inductive processes are involved in implementing a program of management by objectives. It may be necessary for an agency to work down (deductively) from the top (its mission) or at times to build up (inductively) from the bottom (the plans of the workers). Such processes require effort. However, out of such effort can arise a clearer perspective for the agency's board, staff, and constituency of what the agency is about, its purpose for existence, how it is working to reach this purpose, and an evaluation of its efforts.

An agency may already have a statement of mission or purpose for existence in its charter. In instances where such a statement of mission does not exist, a helpful exercise for board and staff is to have each individual formulate an encompassing statement of mission, to compare these statements, and to arrive at a commonly agreed-upon statement. What is the purpose for the existence of this agency? This is the crucial question to answer in the formulation of the statement of mission of the agency.

After a statement of mission has been determined, the objectives of the agency must be formulated. The objectives may be derived from the mission of the agency by delineating more specifically the results the agency wishes to achieve year after year—an example of deducing from the mission of the agency the objectives of the organization.

An inductive process may be used by starting with a statement of the goals and plans of the individual workers or departments of the agency. From these statements of goals the question may be asked: What common objectives are achieved by these goals? Statements of objectives may then be formulated on the basis of the accumulation of goals and plans of workers and departments in the agency. Working still further upward from the numerous objectives which have been written, a capstone statement of mission may be formulated to serve as the final aim or purpose of the organization.

There are disadvantages to using a purely deductive or inductive approach. With the use of the deductive approach of starting with the mission, an individual or the staff of a department can become too ambitious and set more goals than can be accomplished. This may not become obvious until specific plans are formulated for the attainment of the goals. The task of spelling-out in detail the plans the worker must pursue to fulfill a goal assists the individual in determining the reality of the goal in the light of such factors as time, energy, and money. When plans are not specific, goals become even more general and the route a worker must follow in the attainment of a goal becomes lost. If the inductive approach is followed in implementing management by objectives, with the worker first laying the building blocks of plans and goals he or a department wishes to attain during the coming months, the objectives may not reach a very high level of accomplishment. The objectives may only reflect the status quo of the agency rather than challenging the creativity of the organization and its personnel. Experience has shown, however, that when a department gets bogged down in trying to accomplish too much or when it must pull together to handle work because of a staff vancancy or retrenchment, it may be necessary for the department to work from the bottom up by first looking at the number of man-hours available and how intake and other demands the agency must meet can be handled with the time and resources available. After this step is done, the individual can then ask what other goals he might attempt to achieve. Thus, an individual or department may find a combination of the deductive and inductive approaches helpful in implementing management by objectives.

FITTING THE PIECES TOGETHER

Reference has been made to individual or departmental goals and plans. The implementation of management by objectives must occur on the individual, departmental, and agency levels. At this point, the old controversy of which comes first enters the picture.

An individual staff member can not set goals and plans for himself without some understanding and communication with other departmental personnel. The latter are important support systems to him in the attainment of his goals and plans. Likewise, a department can not formulate its goals without knowledge of the goals and plans of staff members whose efforts comprise the building blocks of the department. As workers within a department set goals and plans for themselves, it is necessary that communication occur within the department regarding the effect individual goals and plans will have on other staff members and on the departments as a whole. A process of fitting together into a unit the pieces of the various goals and plans of the workers is necessary in order to arrive at a statement of departmental goals. The same process is necessary on the agency level when the agency is comprised of several departments. The supervisors or departmental heads must coordinate the goals and plans of their respective departments.

The task of attempting to fit together into a mesh or unit the goals and plans of individual staff members and the goals and plans of different departments raises the following questions: Are the goals of a department merely the collection of the goals of the various workers within the department? Also, are the goals of the agency merely the collection of the goals of the various departments? The view that the whole is greater than the sum of its parts is applicable here. The goals of the various workers in a department can not merely be combined to form a departmental statement of goals, but, rather, a system of "best fit" must be achieved, a project which can be accomplished in any of several ways.

The goals of the various workers as expressed in their plans can be examined to determine if they are harmonious or at cross-purposes.

One staff member in a department can not plan to carry out an activity which is directly opposed to the plans of another staff member. (Again, well-stated plans can save the day. It may be impossible to detect the opposition at the goal level.)

In arriving at the goals of an agency comprised of several departments, it is helpful to examine the common objectives under which these goals might fall. The formulation of common objectives from the goals of the various departments within an agency serves as a unifying factor in achieving the best fit possible among these goals.

VALUE OF THE PROGRAM

What is the value of a program of management by objectives? Initially it may seem to be merely a futile exercise of putting together a conceptual jigsaw puzzle. However, with time and experience in working with management by objectives, the effort takes on real meaning. There are several important values to the use of management by objectives in a social agency.

1. The implementation of management by objectives involves the participation of staff members in determining the program and course of direction of an agency. At times staff members may feel they merely respond to the policies and direction of the board and administration. Through the setting of individual and departmental goals, staff members have the opportunity to offer the administration important information from their own perspectives. This information may include the resources available to the agency in terms of staff potential, the need for shifts in service emphasis, and creative thought for new directions.

2. The discipline of writing goals and plans utilizes the initiative of the worker and recognizes his individual contribution to the agency. The worker is confronted with the question: What do I want to do with my skills this coming year within the support system of this agency? In this context workers are not regarded as private practitioners in the framework of the agency, but, rather, individual workers are given the opportunity—and even forced through the writing of goals and plans—to examine what they are contributing to the agency's program, to systematically evaluate their professional development, and to enable the agency to make effective use of their potential contribution. The accomplishment of goals which a worker has set for himself can give the individual satisfaction in job performance.

The above values of management by objectives may be viewed from the perspective of Douglas McGregor's philosophy of management, Theory X and Theory Y.[2] Theory X's assumptions are that people hate to work and that they are not ambitious and do not want to assume responsibility. Theory Y assumes the opposite. Work can be enjoyed; people like to express themselves through their work. Management by objectives allows for the expression of a Theory Y philosophy. Individuals are encouraged to participate in setting goals they themselves wish to pursue and are involved in the setting of goals and objectives for the agency.

3. As staff members within a department are forced to achieve a best fit of their goals and plans, a feeling of cohesion can develop. In this process individual staff members recognize that unless they work together as a team within a department, as well as within the agency, agency and departmental goals cannot be achieved.

4. The use of management by objectives is a tool to assist in the yearly appraisal of performance of workers. The goals and plans which a worker specifies for himself provide a basis on which performance can be appraised. Thus the worker and the supervisor can review performance in a systematic manner. There are variables, however, which are not covered if appraisal of performance is based on the goals and plans of a worker. The quality of performance is such a variable. However, using management by objectives as the framework for the appraisal of performance provides the setting and opportunity for discussion of such variables.

5. Management by objectives assists an agency in setting short- and long-range goals and prevents agency planning, for example in the area of service delivery, from being only a defensive or reactive response to requests for service. Concern for long-range planning in an agency becomes particularly important at the level of setting objectives. The objectives are the results the agency wishes to achieve in order to remain a viable organization which is fulfilling its mission. The dimension of time becomes attached to these objectives as they are delineated further in the goals of the departments. For example, as part of an objective of efficient and effective use of agency resources in the delivery of services, a long-range goal of establishing several outpost offices in parishes or neighborhood centers may be formulated. A time dimension of two, three, or four years may be attached to these objectives, based on the development of population areas in a community, the resources available to the agency, and the needed shifts in present program emphasis.

SUMMARY

Management by objectives is an effective tool for agency planning. The implementation of management by objectives makes it necessary for staff members as individuals, as a department, and as the agency to engage in short- and long-range planning. Such planning occurs through the setting of goals by individual workers, which are carefully specified in plans. Diverse goals are brought together through common objectives of the agency, which in turn are expressed in the mission or statement of purpose of the organization. The use of management by objectives assists an agency in the appraisal of performance of workers, enables staff members to participate in agency planning, and helps an agency determine short- and long-range goals.

NOTES

1. Some writers use the terms *objectives* and *goals* interchangeably.
2. Douglas McGregor, *The Human Side of Enterprise* (New York: McGraw-Hill, 1960).

10

Installing Management by Objectives in Social Agencies

MELVYN C. RAIDER

Although Management by Objectives (MBO) has been used extensively in business and industry during the last twenty years, it is only recently that social agencies have adopted MBO. MBO has been installed in public and voluntary agencies in great numbers and based upon present indications many more agencies are planning to implement MBO in the future. Impetus to use MBO originates from several sources—pressure from boards and funding sources for accountability, for demonstrating program effectiveness, and for increasing efficiency. Regulatory bodies and other governmental agencies have also been eager to see social agencies adopt this system.[1]

MBO is a very simple system in theory. Basically, it is an approach to management in which agency staff participate in the process of specifying long-range goals and short-range objectives to be achieved within an established time period. Success in achieving these agreed upon goals and objectives is evaluated periodically.

Agencies using MBO report mixed results. There have been many successes and too many failures. Based upon the author's experience as a consultant to social work administrators in the use of this technique, it may be observed that there are three primary reasons for failure. First, agencies did not understand what they were getting into and as a consequence did not do adequate preliminary analysis and planning. Second, agencies sought to implement a model of MBO which had not been sufficiently tailored to reflect the unique needs and characteristics of social agencies. Third, a poorly conceived strategy was used to implement the system. This article offers a four-phase approach for installing MBO in social agencies.

PHASE 1—SELF STUDY

Adaptation of MBO requires commitment of agency resources. During the early stages of implementing MBO, when agency personnel are learning the system, substantial expenditures of dollars as well as time must be expected. During this phase, consultants are usually utilized to orient staff to the new system and assist them to develop necessary skills in writing objectives. After the initial learning phase there are ongoing costs and time commitments. Time is usually set aside annually to assess progress relative to goal and objective attainment. Shorter periodic meetings must be held with staff in order to assess interim progress.

To avoid the commitment of such substantial agency resources to MBO only to discover that barriers to its success exist, it is first necessary to enter into a self-study to estimate prospects for success. There are a number of factors which may serve as reasonable indicators of potential difficulties with MBO. These factors are: agency instability, environmental instability, position discontinuity, and unmediated competition.[2]

Agency instability is uncertainty about the expansion or contraction of the agency. Agency instability is usually an outgrowth of funding difficulties especially when funding comes from a variety of sources. If the agency's budget is subject to frequent increases or decreases which could greatly expand or contract major programs, the agency will probably have difficulties with MBO. MBO requires a fair degree of budgetary stability because objectives and plans are usually made a year or more in advance and require accurate forecasts of resources and budgets. Frequent changes in funding require rebudgeting and consequently necessitate the formulation of new objectives and new plans, a condition which will eventually defeat the system.

Environmental instability is uncertainty about the nature of the consumers of the organization's services. It is an outgrowth of changes in the nature of the clientele, either by shifts in the catchment area or population changes within an existing catchment area. Because they require revision of objectives or the priorities assigned to objectives, unplanned changes of this kind hinder MBO. An agency serving a changing community will probably experience difficulties with MBO.

Position discontinuity is the frequent replacement of personnel or changes in duties and responsibilities of existing personnel. Accountability for achieving mutually agreed-upon objectives is an important component of MBO. Large-scale personnel changes or reassignments of job duties significantly interfere with accountability. When this condition exists, especially among administrative staff, MBO becomes almost impossible to carry out.

Unmediated competition is the lack of established channels within the agency for mediating competing goals and objectives. This is evident in an agency where there are several major service programs. Each program is administered by an individual who feels his program is most valuable and who is intent upon enhancing his program at the expense of others. Problems arise where there is no established method within the agency for resolving the competition among programs. In such situations, MBO will probably fail; goals and objectives established will often work at cross-purposes.[3]

The degree to which each of these four factors exist will determine the extent to which MBO is appropriate to an agency. In some instances it may be decided that MBO is inappropriate to an agency. In such instances it would be wise to abandon the notion of installing MBO completely; in other situations, it may be prudent to delay the installation of MBO until some of the difficulties are resolved. If MBO appears appropriate in a particular setting, analysis of the four factors will provide information which can aid in the making of a decision concerning the complexity and comprehensiveness of the MBO system which will ultimately be adopted. (This will be discussed in greater depth in Phase II.)

During the self-study phase it is also wise to collaborate with people from other agencies in which MBO is utilized. It willl be very useful to learn about actual advantages and disadvantages, successes and failures from the perspective of an agency similar to your own. Many costly and frustrating errors can be avoided through such collaboration.[4]

PHASE II—IMPLEMENTATION STRATEGY

It should be recognized that installing MBO is no less than introducing major organizational change. If such change is to be long lasting, a carefully planned strategy must be developed. The first order of business is to gain the commitment of top agency administration and the board. Based upon the author's experience, significant difficulties and delays are experienced because one or both of the above groups were bypassed in the process. An agency executive will often find it easier to gain such commitment when there is a significant external or internal threat to the agency, such as of a major budget cutback. Studies of successful organizational change concluded that an organization under outside pressure is much more open to new ideas and approaches than an organization which is relatively secure.[5]

Once top management commitment is obtained, it is necessary to determine who within the agency will be charged with responsibility for implementing MBO. In many situations in which MBO was installed successfully, responsibility for installing the new system was lodged with the agency director. Lower level people in the organization such as staff development or training specialists charged with responsibility for implementing MBO have had a much more difficult time than top administrators in gaining staff commitment and in demonstrating the significance of the proposed change.[6] When responsibility for the new system is accepted by the top administration, it has been observed that participation and enthusiasm on the part of agency staff is significantly greater. It is also important that administration view MBO as a philosophy of management rather than merely a new technique.[7]

The implementation of MBO, if it is to have a good chance of being accepted, should be initially viewed as an experiment rather than something which is permanent. Staff need to proceed cautiously and to reality test the new system.[8] To feel comfortable with the new approach, they should have the freedom to contribute to modifications of the system as necessary. If MBO proves to be of no value or of negative value, staff need to feel confident that the new system will be discarded. Under these circumstances, the approach to MBO which eventually evolves will be viewed as the product and the property of staff and administration.

Since the initial use of MBO should be viewed as an experiment, it follows that MBO should be *initially* introduced on a modest scale. MBO may be implemented in a single component of the agency or only among middle-level administrators during the first phase. Success on a modest scale will provide participants with a vested interest in seeing MBO introduced on a larger scale.

Administration, the board, the staff should recognize that implementation of MBO is a lengthy process. For most social agencies, implementation of MBO represents a completely new way of doing things. Agency executives and staff members must reorient their styles of operating. A shift to MBO often means a shift from intuitive management to precise, preplanned management. Along with MBO comes a different vocabulary and collection of concepts. For staff members most comfortable with a human behavior frame of reference, such terms as *objective, mission, program,* and *output measures* take significant time to be comprehended and even longer to be fully accepted.

Individuals experienced in training others to use MBO indicate that it takes three successive MBO cycles before expertise in formulating good goals and objectives develops. In most organizations, MBO cycles are usually one year in length; thus, it takes approximately three years to develop requisite expertise.[9]

Training

All individuals who will be using MBO will need appropriate training in writing goals and objectives. Training of this nature usually may be obtained in courses and workshops on MBO offered by most universities and community colleges. For a large agency, however, it is often less expensive to bring an instructor to the agency than to pay tuition fees for a large group of staff members. An in-service training program has the advantage that the presentation may be specifically geared to the agency. Both approaches are equally effective for acquiring the basic skills in writing goals and objectives.

Short-term contracts with management consultants are often entered into by social agencies to implement an entire MBO system. This is very expensive and, unless the consultant is chosen with care, of minimal value. It has been pointed out earlier in this article that the final form of MBO must evolve over time and be specifically tailored to the needs of the agency. If a consultant is to assist in this process he would need to work with the agency in an ongoing capacity perhaps for as long as three years. It is unlikely that a team of consultants can come into the agency for a few weeks, impose a full-blown MBO system, and then depart with expectation that the system will hold up over time. Under such circumstances the agency will most likely be the recipient of a standardized MBO model which may not have been modified to reflect the characteristics of the agency or its environment. Follow-up studies have shown that even a poor model of MBO will have positive results in the short run. These studies have demonstrated that after a year or two the positive results evaporate.[10]

PHASE III—SYSTEM DESIGN

After the self-study is completed, the degree of comprehensiveness of the MBO system to be adopted may be determined. If one or more of the indicators of potential difficulty or failure with MBO are evident to some extent, it is wise to be less ambitious when installing MBO. Under these circumstances a less complex version of MBO may be appropriate. For example, it may be determined that MBO would be used exclusively to enhance planning among administrative personnel. The system, therefore, would not encompass direct-service staff. On the other hand, conditions may be deemed favorable to apply MBO to the entire agency, involving all personnel.

Regardless of the degree of comprehensiveness chosen for the MBO system, the system needs to reflect the characteristics and organizational culture of the individual agency. There is no single model of MBO which will have universal application to all human service agencies. However, the author has identified four general guidelines for tailoring MBO to social service agencies:[11]

Mission Statement Consensus

A process employing consensus is desirable in formulating agency mission statements. The mission statement serves as the foundation or baseline upon which MBO is built. It specifies the reason for existence of the agency and indicates the main purposes of the organization. The mission should reflect services the community expects of the agency if the agency is to survive. Mission statements are long-range in focus and do not have a specific termination point.

In a social agency, mission statements are best developed through a process requiring the attainment of consensus among all relevant interest groups. Consensus is a process involving bargaining, trade-offs, and compromise. Staff members, administration, members of the board, and community representatives must agree upon a mission statement from their own perspectives. Subsequently, representatives from each of these interest groups would meet and attempt to formulate a unitary mission statement which would be satisfactory to all participants. Eventually it is realized that benefits for all can be realized only by mutual commitment to a unitary conception of mission.[12]

Inductive Goal-Setting

Use an inductive process when setting goals. From the mission statement flow several major organizational goals. A goal is a desired state of affairs. Goals are formulated to cover a long time period, usually three to five years.

Goal development should be an inductive process in a social agency. General departmental or unit goals are constructed from many specific individual worker objectives. After compiling individual worker objectives, members of the department would collectively seek to ascertain what common goals could be formulated and what plans could be developed. Advantages of the inductive method of goal formulation may be significant for a social agency. First, such a process respects the individuality of each worker and his unique contribution to the mission of the agency. Second, a more natural or humanistic system for communication and planning is encouraged. Third, participation in the formulation of goals has been shown to be a significant factor in subsequent conformity to them. And fourth, it avoids the risk of proliferation of impractical and unrealistic goals set by administrators who may be somewhat detached from actual service delivery.[13]

Group Objectives

Establish group objectives. Objectives are the heart of MBO. They are desired outcomes to be attained in a specific period of time. Objectives are usually measurable and always expressed in concrete terms. Objectives, to be consistent with the nature of most social agencies and the workers they employ, should be established on a departmental or group basis rather than for individual workers. Emphasis must be placed on establishing a common task to facilitate worker interaction, consultation, and mutual participation.

Establishing individual objectives often results in intense competition which may become destructive to the interests of the client. Establishing departmental objectives rather than individual objectives shifts accountability from the individual to the group; the agency climate will shift from one of competition to one of mutual support. As well as increasing agency productivity, establishing objectives in this manner may help to reduce the shortcuts and expedients which grow out of unchecked competition.[14]

Milestones

Use milestones to approximate objective attainment. Milestones are reasonable indicators for assessing objective attainment. Carefully selected intermediate activities are "milestones" which, in the best judgment of the agency staff, can be utilized to approximate or estimate progress toward the desired final outcome.[15] Some models of MBO require that objectives be expressed in measurable, quantifiable, concrete terms. A good objective is also expected to describe an end result or final outcome rather than an intermediate product or task that will lead to an end result.

When we seek to achieve objectives which affect people, it becomes difficult to quantify and measure objective attainment. It is very difficult to link change in the client's functioning with the service activity. Problems are encountered because "few instruments are available that validly measure before and after impact."[16] Even more significant is the fact that there is no agreement in the profession as to what to measure and how to measure it. Awaiting future development of methods which can attribute change in the client's functioning directly to the service activity (and the service activity alone), intermediate outcomes or activities, rather than end results, will have to suffice for measuring objectives in social agencies.

PHASE IV—DEVELOPING LONG-LASTING COMMITMENT

Flexibility

If MBO is to be installed successfully in a human service setting, it must be applied to each situation in a highly flexible fashion. The process underlying MBO is substantially more important than the form that it ultimately takes. In instances where MBO was installed and great emphasis was placed on forms and procedure, MBO failed to provide the anticipated long-range benefits. Huse cites an example of an installation of MBO in industry in which the individuals charged with the responsibility of implementing MBO encountered great resistance on the part of an individual manager. The manager was strongly resisting the many forms and complex procedures which were being imposed by the installers of the MBO system. Upon closer examination it became obvious to the individuals seeking to install MBO that the resistant manager was in fact effectively using the principles of MBO without its cumbersome forms and procedures.[17]

A consistent finding in studies of MBO installations in a variety of settings is that staff resent and resist the excessive paperwork often required.[18] Unless other reports and procedures are eliminated or kept to a minimum, the paperwork associated with MBO will be regarded as an additional burden. If MBO is to be implemented successfully, care must be taken to avoid creating a paper mill. Forms used should be developed by the agency using them with the input of staff members at all levels. A form which meets the needs of one agency may be grossly inappropriate in another setting. When developing forms to be used in conjunction with MBO, it is far wiser to run the risk of devising fewer forms than too many. In some settings forms developed centrally were suggested only for those who wished to use them. Departments were free to reject or modify forms to meet their particular requirements. A narrative statement is often as effective a device for reporting progress as a series of forms while at the same time avoiding the negative attitudes associated with forms.

Freedom should also be provided to middle-level administrators and staff members with regard to the method they choose to achieve objectives. MBO is most useful in establishing targets. Plans to achieve targets should be those of the work group, not the administrator.[19] Staff should be provided with maximum flexibility to achieve objectives without undue restrictions.

In the process of implementing and using MBO, emphasis must be placed on the process and not on rigid procedures or cumbersome forms.

Personal Growth

If MBO is to be truly accepted and valued by staff, the system must relate directly to the personal growth objectives of staff. Too often MBO becomes a mechanism which facilitates the accomplishment of agency goals while ignoring the individual's need to actualize himself through his employment. Significant attention must be placed on personal and professional aspirations. Opportunities should be structured for individuals to develop on the job. Attempts should be made to make individual career goals consistent and complementary with agency goals. Harry Levinson, a psychologist, takes the position that Management by Objectives can become destructive and self-defeating unless the system emphasizes the importance of the individual's goals. Levinson states: "If a man's most powerful driving force is comprised of his needs, wishes, and personal aspirations, combined with the compelling wish to look good in his own eyes for meeting those deeply held personal goals, then Management-by-Objectives should begin with his objectives."[20]

In a human service setting there is usually a significant meshing of personal growth objectives of staff and organizational goals around the agency's emphasis on delivering quality service. Staff members aspire to a level of competency which will enable them to gain esteem and recognition from colleagues and gain the confidence of administration. Professional staff usually have the need to be reasonably autonomous and creative in their work. Personal growth objectives in social agencies will most probably have a competency focus. It is essential that personal objectives foster a climate for self-actualization.[21]

Provide Frequent Two-Way Feedback

Although the need for feedback is built into MBO, it is particularly important to schedule feedback even more frequently during the implementation phase. Staff members need to feel confident that they can make suggestions and proposals for change. It is only after these suggestions are considered and utilized that staff members begin experiencing a sense of commitment to the system.

Feedback sessions relative to objective attainment should have a problem-solving focus. Assessment of objectives, other than personal growth objectives, should be conducted on a group basis. Furthermore, the group should appraise each individual's contribution to the group effort. Criticism should be avoided. Staff need to identify obstacles which serve as barriers to the achievement of established objectives and determine ways in which these barriers may be overcome.[22]

The feedback sessions should also provide staff with the opportunity to evaluate the extent to which administration has provided input relative to achieving objectives. Here again the focus should not be to criticize but to identify administrative barriers which must be resolved.[23] If feedback and MBO itself are to serve a meaningful purpose in the agency, they must go beyond the one-to-one supervisor-staff member relationship. They must foster a partnership between staff and agency in which influence goes both ways.

NOTES

1. Jason E. Patterson, *Community Mental Health in Social Work Education* (Atlanta, Ga.: Southern Regional Education Board, 1975).
2. These factors which are discussed in a social work context are based upon an assessment of MBO installations in England. Reference may be made to J. D. Wickens, "Management by Objectives: An Appraisal," *Journal of Management Studies* 5 (October 1968):365–79.
3. See Melvyn C. Raider, "An Evaluation of Management-by-Objectives," *Social Casework* 56 (February 1975):79.
4. See Dale D. McConkey, "Implementation—The Guts of MBO," *S.A.M. Advanced Management Journal* 37 (July 1972):13–18.
5. For an interesting discussion of factors facilitating major organization change, see Larry Griener, "Patterns of Organizational Doings," *Harvard Business Review* 45 (May–June 1967):119–130.
6. See Stephen Carroll and Henry L. Tosi, Jr., *Management by Objectives* (New York: MacMillan Company, 1973).
7. Burt Scanlan and Stanley Sloan, "It Doesn't Always Work," *ASTME Vectors* 6 (1969):20.
8. Griener, "Patterns of Organizational Doings," p. 128.
9. George Morrisey, *Management by Objectives and Results* (Reading, Mass.: Addison-Wesley Publishing Co., 1970), p. 155.
10. John M. Ivancevich, "A Longitudinal Assessment of Management by Objectives," *Administrative Science Quarterly* 17 (March 1972):126–38.
11. See Melvyn C. Raider, "A Social Service Model of Management-by-Objectives," *Social Casework* 57 (October 1976):523–28.
12. The use of bargaining in the formation of organizational goals is discussed in John W. Thibalt and Harold Kelley, *The Social Psychology of Groups* (New York: John Wiley and Sons, 1959).
13. The advantages of the inductive method of developing goals are discussed in Vernon R. Wiehe, *Management by Objectives in Mental Health Services* (St. Louis, MO: Monograph, 1974).
14. See Peter M. Blau, "Cooperation and Competition in a Bureaucracy," *American Journal of Sociology* 59 (May 1954):530–35.
15. The use of Milestones in the U.S. Department of Health, Education and Welfare is discussed in Rodney H. Brody, "MBO Goes to Work in the Public Sector," *Harvard Business Review* 51 (March–April 1973):65–74.
16. Edward Newman and Jerry Turem, "The Crisis of Accountability," *Social Work*, 19 (January 1974):5– 16.
17. Edgar F. Huse, *Organizational Development and Change* (St. Paul: West Publishing Co. 1975), p. 189.
18. Carroll and Tosi, *Management by Objectives*, p. 123.
19. Huse, *Organizational Development*, p. 180.
20. Harry Levinson, "Management by Whose Objectives," *Harvard Business Review* 48 (July–August 1970):129.
21. Edgar Huse, "Putting in a Management Development Program That Works," *California Management Review* 9, no. 2 (Winter 1966):78.

22. For a thorough discussion of the dysfunctional effects of criticism in relation to MBO, see Edgar Huse and E. Kay, "Improving Employee Productivity Through Work Planning," in *The Personnel Job in a Changing World,* edited by J. Blood (New York: American Management Association, 1964), pp. 301–02.
23. For an excellent discussion of the group appraisal of objectives, see Levinson, "Management by Whose Objectives," p. 131.

11

Zero-Based Budgeting: Implications for Social Services?

GERARD L. OTTEN

With the election of Jimmy Carter to the presidency of the United States, a substantial portion of the population, especially social service professionals, probably saw renewed opportunities for the expansion and support of social service programs from the federal level. Those associated with the broadly defined field of social services probably felt a rejuvenated vitality and sense of direction for human services programs that had not existed during the preceding Republican administration. Whether reality will meet these expectations remains to be seen. The president's campaign rhetoric, laden with hopes and promises, must now be tested in a demanding political arena of divergent and conflicting interests; the author of "Why Not the Best?" will be hard pressed to make good on all his campaign assurances to the American people.

It is uncertain whether or not the president can achieve all of his stated goals. However, one of these, a commitment to the initiation of Zero-Based Budgeting (ZBB) in all executive departments and agencies, remains firm. President Carter has already directed these organizations to prepare their budget estimates for fiscal year 1979 using a ZBB format (*Federal Register*, 1977).

As part of the president's commitment to efficiency through reorganization and renewed public trust in government, ZBB has rather significant implications for the operation and administration of our government. There appear to be particularly unique implications for the operation of social service programs and the associated stresses that will be placed upon them with the adoption of ZBB.

BUDGETARY REFORM

Author Allen Schick identifies three stages of budgetary reform: expenditure control, management control, and planning control (cited in Lee & Johnson, 1973, p. 101). Although these stages are not rigidly fixed to specific time periods, they do facilitate an understanding of how present budgetary philosophy has evolved. Expenditure control has been identified by a legislative concern for tight control over executive expenditures. The most prevalent means of exerting this type of expenditure control has been to appropriate by line item and by object of expenditures; financial audits are then used to ensure that money has in fact been spent for the items authorized for purchase. This focuses information for budgetary decision making upon the things government buys, such as personnel, travel, and supplies, rather than upon functions performed and the accomplishments of governmental activities. In other words, responsibility is achieved by controlling inputs; outputs are generally ignored.

The second stage is that of management control, which emphasizes the efficiency with which ongoing activities were conducted. Historically, this orientation has been associated with the New Deal through the first Hoover Commission (1949). Emphasis was placed upon holding administrators accountable for the efficiency of their activities through such methods as work performance measurement.

The third and, to the present, final stage of budgetary reform has been for the planning function to be served by budgets. President Lyndon B. Johnson's budget message of 1968 clearly emphasized programs and the relationship between revenues and expenditures in order to accomplish objectives (Lee & Johnson, 1973, p. 10). It was President Johnson who promulgated to federal agencies the adoption of the then heralded Planning, Programming, and Budgeting System (PPBS) that had first been installed in the Defense Department by Robert McNamara.

PPBS had a brief yet significant impact upon the theory of budgeting because of its commitment to the concept of tying planning and budgeting in an analytical framework that focused on programs. However, because of a number of problems associated with PPBS, some political and some practical, the concept met a quiet and unspectacular death; its postmortem has been conducted in a number of professional and scholarly journals (see Mosher, 1969; Schick, 1972; Dougherty, Note 1).

Although PPBS is now considered passé, the impetus for budgetary reform remains. There is, and has been, widespread dissatisfaction with traditional budgeting practices. The stakes are high in any budgeting procedure because "budgeting determines who gets what." Therefore, the crucial aspect of budgeting is whose preferences are to prevail in disputes about which activities are to be carried on and to what degree, in the light of limited resources (Wildavsky, 1974, p. 129). Given those realities, there is little wonder why elected officials, special interest groups, the general public, and agency officials have differing reactions to the cries for a budgetary reform that may produce a more efficient, more effective, and more accountable system.

Critics of the traditional budgetary approach cite a number of significant shortcomings that they feel encourage waste and inefficiency. First, they argue that line item formats prevent the analysis of end products. Thus, ends cannot be easily related to means (Wildavsky, 1974, p. 137). Second, traditional budgeting requires no statement of measurable objectives. For example, a budget request of X dollars will result in the placement of Y number of children in adoptive homes. Last, the traditional approach is incremental—only the increments over the preceding year's budget are analyzed. Consequently, the preceding year's budget, the base, is seldom analyzed. This incremental approach results in budgetary decisions that rarely question the merit of a program or an agency. It also limits the scope of legislative agreement because decisions are based on compromises that have been reached over the few extra dollars requested that are in excess over the previous year's budget. The base is taken as a given—the product of compromises reached in previous years. The budgetary decisions rarely involve basic differences in policy (Wildavsky, 1974, p. 136; for a discussion of the concept of analyzing small changes, or increments as they are called, see Lindblom, 1959).

Given the criticism of the traditional budgeting approach, there has been considerable interest in reform proposals that would address its deficiencies and achieve the goals of efficiency and effectiveness within a rational priority scheme. In the wake of the PPBS failure has risen the most recent hope for reform: Zero-Based Budgeting.

ZBB OVERVIEW

ZBB focuses its activities on answering two basic questions (Phyrr, 1977, p. 1):

1. Are the current activities efficient and effective? and
2. Should current activities be eliminated or reduced to fund higher priority new programs or to reduce the current budget?

In order to address the issues associated with these two questions, the zero-based approach requires each agency systematically to evaluate and review all programs and activities (current as well as new). To do so, the agency must address four basic steps (Phyrr, 1977, pp. 2–7):

1. *Identification of "decision units."* Zero-Based Budgeting attempts to focus an administrator's attention on evaluating activities and making decisions. Decision units are "meaningful elements" that can be isolated for analysis and decision making. In most agencies these may correspond to those budget units defined by traditional budget procedures (i.e., cost center).
2. *Analysis of decision units.* Each decision unit is analyzed in "typically" three decision packages, and more if possible. This enables each decision package to construct a "framework" of performance and funding. The decision package is the building block of the zero-based concept. It is a document that identifies and describes each decision unit in such a manner that management can:
   - evaluate it and rank it against other decision units competing for funding and
   - decide whether to approve it or disapprove it.

   The information contained in the decision package might include: purpose/objective; description of actions ("What are we going to do, and how are we going to do it?"); costs and benefits; work load and performance measures; alternative means of accomplishing objectives; and various levels of effort ("What benefits do we get for various levels of funding?").
3. *The ranking process.* This enables management to allocate its limited resources by making management concentrate on these questions: "How much should we spend?" and "Where should we spend it?"
4. *Preparation of a detailed operating budget.* The budget or appropriation requests prepared by each agency are usually subject to some form of legislative review or modification. Under the zero-based approach, the decision packages and ranking determine specifically the actions required to achieve any budget reductions. If the legislature defines reductions in specific program areas, we can readily identify the corresponding decision packages and reduce the appropriate program and organizational budgets.

The following example briefly illustrates the type of analysis that would be conducted by an administrator to prepare a decision package:

> The decision unit in this case is a hypothetical Adoptions Division in a large state social service agency. The division's responsibility is to find suitable adoptive homes for children. The administrative head of

this unit would (a) identify different ways of performing the function and (b) identify different levels of effort for the recommended decision package.

1. Different ways of performing the same function.
   a) Recommended decision package: Use the agency's county-based staff to complete all adoptions. This expenditure would permit the adoption of 500 children at a total cost of $250,000.
   b) Alternatives not recommended (for same number of adoptions):
      (1) Contract with private agency XYZ. Cost: $310,000. The cost per adoption exceeds the projected cost for completing the adoptions using the county-based staff. Also, the administrative cost of administering the contract with agency XYZ is a factor.
      (2) Contract with public agency ABC which would operate from a central location. Cost: $290,000. Rejection is based on the same rationale as in the preceding alternative.
      (3) Use the agency's county-based staff to complete all adoptions. This expenditure would permit the adoption of 500 children at a total cost of $225,000. Although this alternative is clearly more economical than the recommended decision package, it incorporates the idea of reducing the depth and detail of the home study required to complete each adoption. A commensurate reduction in the staff resources necessary to perform home studies is responsible for a cost projection that is $25,000 less than the recommended decision package. The administrator has not recommended this alternative because of concern that the quality of adoption services would be reduced to a professionally unacceptable level.

In this example the recommended way of performing the adoption function would be chosen because the alternatives are either more expensive or offer no compensating advantages.

2. Different levels of effort for operation.
   a) Adoptions Division (1 of 3), cost = $150,000. Minimum package: Complete adoptions on 300 children, and leave an approximate 1-year backlog of cases.
   b) Adoptions Division (2 of 3), cost = $50,000 (levels 1 + 2 = $200,000). Complete adoptions on an additional 100 children, and reduce the case backlog to 6 months.
   c) Adoptions Division (3 of 3), cost = $50,000 (levels 1 + 2 + 3 = $250,000). Complete adoptions on an additional 100 children, all of whom are so-called hard-to-place (older children, handicapped, ethnic minority) children.

The chief administrator has thus prepared three decision packages (levels 1 of 3, 2 of 3, and 3 of 3). These three packages are then submitted to higher level agency administrators who must incorporate them into the overall ranking scheme for the agency.

The ranking process establishes priorities among the incremental levels of each decision unit (i.e., decision package). The rankings therefore display a marginal analysis (Phyrr, 1973, pp. 130–135). An example of how the agency would rank its decision packages is shown in Table 11–1. This type of ranking would be completed for the entire agency. Once the agency's budget is approved, the total amount of funds would be matched with the corresponding cumulative cost, thereby identifying the decision packages that can be operationalized. For instance, if the agency were appropriated $3,200,000, only packages 1 through 3 could be afforded.

The above example can be used to highlight a significant shortcoming of the applicability of ZBB to the social services. Whereas an adoption service is a relatively easy service to understand and conceptualize in terms of goals and objectives (it is also politically "acceptable" and serves a deserving clientele), other social services are not. In contrast, for example, what constitutes the effectiveness of a substance abuse counseling service? Can the goals and objectives of such a service be stated in ways that lend themselves to statements about accomplishments or effectiveness? Can the social work administrator successfully argue that factors other than cost must be considered?

EXPERIENCES WITH ZBB

In looking at governmental experiences with Zero-Based Budgeting, one would logically place a primary focus on the Georgia experience. Georgia was the first state to fully implement the concept; since this innovation occurred under the direction of Governor Carter's administration, inferences may be drawn about what might be expected when the

TABLE 11–1. Agency's Ranking of Decision Packages

Rank	Decision Package	Incremental Cost	Cumulative Cost
1	Child day care (1 of 2)	$1,000,000	$1,000,000
2	Protective services (1 of 2)	2,000,000	3,000,000
3	Adoptions (1 of 3)	150,000	3,150,000
4	Child day care (2 of 2)	500,000	3,650,000
5	Adoptions (2 of 3)	50,000	3,700,000

federal government adopts Zero-Based Budgeting. Additionally, there is a reasonable probability that states will rush (as many did with PPBS) to implement Zero-Based Budgeting at the state level.

Were there to be a general transfer and application of the ZBB concept, as employed in Georgia with its associated strengths and difficulties, there might be a number of similar observations. Among the more noteworthy were those offered by Peter Phyrr, ZBB innovator and consultant to Carter's budget director, after Georgia's first year of zero-based experience (Phyrr, 1977, p. 8):

1. Zero-Based Budgeting can be effective and should be continued.
2. The quality of decision packages was poor but may improve with experience.
3. There is little incentive in government to be cost-effective.
4. Cost information was poor due to:
● the large number of discrete activities encompassed in budget units and,
● the fact that many managers/administrators who prepared packages generally never saw budgets or actual costs.
5. Agencies with large numbers of packages (exceeding 250–300) had difficulties in producing a single agency ranking.

Phyrr (1973) presents a much more detailed critique in his book *Zero-Based Budgeting: A Practical Management Tool for Evaluating Expenses*. In a recent article Phyrr (1977) suggests some significant strengths, which he argues are four overriding reasons that make the zero-based approach worthwhile:

1. low-priority programs can be eliminated or reduced;
2. program effectiveness can be dramatically improved;
3. high-impact programs can obtain increased funding by shifting resources within an agency, whereas the increased funding might not have been made available had the agency merely requested an increase in total funding; and
4. tax increases can be retarded.

Phyrr observes that there may be bureaucratic resistance to an approach that involves an evaluation of program effectiveness. He also speculates that it would be politically naive and unrealistic to assume that any one major agency will be significantly defunded for the benefit of another. Nevertheless, Phyrr believes that ZBB should be considered a management and budgetary improvement effort that may require several years to reach full utilization and effectiveness. He encourages patience and perseverance.

It is quite interesting to contrast Phyrr's comments about the Georgia zero-based experience after its first year with the more recent comments of Minmier and Herman. These two authors recently researched Georgia's budgeting systems and surmised that few financial resources were reallocated directly due to the use of ZBB. They concluded that any substantial reallocation of financial resources within state government during Mr. Carter's administration was due primarily to Georgia's Executive Reorganization Act of 1972—not to Zero-Based Budgeting. Mr. Carter has argued that the Executive Reorganization was the primary force behind allocation of financial resources, but added that success would have been impossible without Zero-Based Budgeting (Minmier, 1975, p. 11). Minmier and Herman conclude that ZBB appears to have served the best interests of the state of Georgia. They see great advantages accruing from the involvement of personnel at "activity" levels within the increased time and effort required for budget preparation (Minmier, 1975, p. 11).

Other state level experiences with ZBB have been somewhat limited—Texas and New Jersey have installed ZBB-type systems only recently, and evaluative reports are rather sketchy. However, it is interesting to note that New Mexico, because of dissatisfaction with the traditional budgeting process, conducted a limited experiment with ZBB in 1971. The conclusion of the author describing the zero-based program in New Mexico was that pure Zero-Based Budgeting was probably a normative concept that needed modifications given the institutional nature of the traditional incremental approach. It was also felt that true reform cannot be realistically accomplished without the full cooperation and support of the legislature—it must be willing to learn and embrace fully the approach embodied in ZBB (LaFaver, 1974, p. 109).

PPBS RENAISSANCE?

Regardless of the depth of the analysis, it appears that the application of ZBB has been too limited to draw any definitive conclusions about its efficacy. Certainly, there appears to be no specific reference to the possible effects of such a reform on the "softest" of the generally soft governmental services—social services. Therefore, this author suggests that there are certain political, practical, and technical similarities between the now disfavored PPBS and ZBB that permit comparisons between the two and inferences about ZBB's potential for success. Consequently, it is suggested that ZBB must overcome significant barriers in order to preempt the publication of its obituary in scholarly and professional journals at some point in the future.

The first barrier that ZBB must surmount lies in the political arena. It is not sufficient for a governor or agency executive, or any one individual or group, to support and espouse the virtues of the concept. These endorsements must be accompanied by well-planned, coordinated efforts that are designed to garner broad support for change. Although there was a measure of support for PPBS, such support was not upheld by coordinated planning efforts. Consequently, with a few notable exceptions, it was never incorporated into the central budget and decision-making processes of state government (Schick, 1972, p. 13).

An associated issue in dealing with the problem of obtaining more than just nominal support is related to encouraging elected officials to move away from their bargaining-incremental tendencies of decision making. The difficulties of this task cannot be understated; considerable ramifications for our political system are inherent in this task. It is therefore unclear whether or not such a goal can be realistically achieved. The fundamental issue related to this political difficulty lies with the concept of politics as the "art of compromise." Virtually all legislative decisions, especially those involving the appropriation of tax dollars, are the products of give and take (i.e., bargaining). Consequently, our country's current political institutions are built on historically based compromises. A transition to ZBB would require the rejection of a familiar, traditional *modus operandi* and the adoption of what is considered by public administrators to be a more rational decision-making process.

If the political problems can be dispatched, there remain both practical and technical difficulties. In the practical vein, ZBB, like its precursor PPBS, requires additional staff involvement and the completion of a considerable amount of paperwork. It appears that:

1. personnel resistance could subvert any transition to ZBB, and
2. additional paperwork might be unduly burdensome.

Furthermore, ZBB, like PPBS, requires a statement of objectives—an alien activity for most public servants. Surely technical problems are associated with such a requirement; there are certainly dilemmas when decision packages may have several possible objectives. Which one is chosen? For example, what is the objective of a penal institution? Punishment? Societal protection? Crime deterrence? Correction? Who decides? If the function of a penal institution is to attain all four of these objectives, what criteria are used to allocate the cost among them (Mosher, 1969, p. 163)?

It appears that all suggested budgetary reforms have strongly advocated the collection and application of more and better data. The empirical logic supporting such a feature is an obvious and quite justifiable effort to rationalize the entire budgetary process. In principle, there are probably few who would argue with such proposals. Unfortunately, the technical demands for such data are in many cases beyond the system's (or individual's) ability to deliver. In the first place, it appears that many governmental agencies collect voluminous data in formats that render them useless for budgetary processes like ZBB. Data are often collected so that certain local, state, or federal reporting requirements can be met; these are rarely uniform (this poses certain unique intergovernmental problems associated with federalism). Second, it is difficult to quantify many of the activities of governmental agencies. Certainly, this is true for social services as it is generally true for governmental operations. Given the inability to state objectives in any meaningful and quantifiable manner, it is obvious that these objectives cannot be evaluated and ranked in a way that facilitates budgetary decision making. Consequently, the adoption of ZBB would, in a sense, be dependent upon:

1. the development and adherence to a set of objectives for use in decision making,
2. the ability to develop meaningful objective criteria to incorporate in decision packages,
3. the collection of appropriate data, and
4. the ability to train administrators to think in nontraditional ways so they will use the data to develop these packages.

IMPLICATIONS FOR SOCIAL SERVICES

Certainly, any accelerated move for broad implementation of ZBB in governmental agencies will have significant and far-reaching implications for those agencies and the political environment in which they must function. This will be especially true for social service agencies and the programs they administer. It will undoubtedly create conflicts which will be most severe for lower echelon supervisors (many of whom identify with the social work profession) who will be forced to apply quantitative and cost data in the development of budgets. Such activities are foreign to such persons who have had little training in budgetary processes and who are often philosophically opposed to using cost concepts in the social services.

Prior to any attempts at operationalizing ZBB, it will become necessary to develop greater conceptual clarity about what social services are intended to accomplish; the adoption of the new language of goals, objectives, and measurement of outcomes may appear too mechanical and resemble the nonhumanistic efficiency identified with the previous administration and its budget cuts. However, the social work profession should, and must, move in this direction if it does not want its managerial role usurped by "pure" management types. Management technology, systems, concepts, and information science can be important means for improving services even if they are not viewed as ends in themselves. The core values of social work and its concern for people must still be the base from which to use these concepts (Rosenberg & Brody, 1974, p. 346). Zero-Based Budgeting may have the potential to help us serve our clients more efficiently, effectively, and comprehensively than heretofore.

CONCLUSION

The preceding discussion does not present an exhaustive analysis of ZBB and the possible implementation difficulties it may present and encounter if adopted on a large-scale basis. The discussion has attempted to suggest to the reader what may be some of the more salient issues. Specific effects upon the social services have been, in most cases, left for the reader's inference.

One must not be too harsh in rendering premature judgment on ZBB. The concept squarely addresses many of the shortcomings of the traditional budgeting approach. That alone should provide an impetus for its consideration. Certainly, it presents a unique challenge for those who advocate accountability, and it offers an even greater challenge to those committed to delivering more effective services to the impoverished and disadvantaged of our nation.

REFERENCES

Dougherty, L. A. *Planning-Programming-Budgeting in state government—Some lessons learned* (R-784-RC). Rand Corporation, August 1971.
Federal Register, May 2, 1977, *42*(84), 22341–22353.
LaFaver, J. Zero-Based Budgeting in New Mexico (by the Legislative Finance Committee). *State Government*, Spring 1974.
Lee, R. D., Jr., & Johnson, R. W. *Public budgeting systems*. Baltimore: University Park Press, 1973.
Lindblom, C. E. The science of muddling through. *Public Administration Review*, Spring 1959.
Minmier, G. S. *An evaluation of Zero-Based Budgeting systems in government institutions*. Atlanta: Georgia State University School of Business Administration, Publishing Services Division, 1975.
Mosher, F. C. Limitations and problems of PPBS in the states. *Public Administration Review*, March–April, 1969.
Phyrr, P. A. *Zero-Based Budgeting: A practical management tool for evaluating expenses*. New York: Wiley Publications, 1973.
Phyrr, P. A. The zero-base approach to government budgeting. *Public Administration Review*, January–February 1977.

Rosenberg, M. L., & Brody, R. The threat or challenge of accountability. *Social Work,* May 1974.

Schick, A. PPB—A view from the states. *State Government,* Winter 1972.

Wildavsky, A. *The politics of the budgetary process* (2nd ed.). Canada: Little, Brown, 1974.

12

Paying the Piper and Calling the Tune: Accountability in the Human Services

ROBERT ELKIN

Although human services may be provided under proprietary auspices (Born, 1983), they are provided in nonprofit organizations for the most part—either under governmental or voluntary auspices. These nonprofit organizations typically are dependent for a portion of their revenues on resource providers other than the clients who directly receive the services. These resource providers represent a wide variety of organizations: federal, state, and local governments; federations for fund raising; foundations; and corporations. In addition, these nonprofit organizations pay for their services with an increasingly wide array of funds from their own operations, from endowments, and from commercial ventures.

These resource providers, because of pressures upon them to be accountable, promulgate requirements upon human service agencies to report on both financial and nonfinancial aspects of their service delivery operations. The very multiplicity of funding sources that human service organizations have creatively developed presents a problem for them because different resource providers have different reporting requirements. These differences are based upon different concepts of accountability, historical patterns, and relationships between resource providers and service providers that will be discussed in this chapter. In addition, other constituency groups and organizations demand information about the performance of nonprofit organizations. These include better business bureaus, chambers of commerce, charities regulatory agencies, and contributor information bodies.

The seriousness of the issue of accountability was viewed by Newman and Turem (1978) as follows:

> The current crisis in social services is a crisis of credibility based on an inadequate system of accountability. Social programs are in trouble because they focus on processes and not results. . . . When the market mechanism is weak or missing and the support of social institutions is necessary, then political interplay influences preferences and those providing services are required to show that available resources are spent on the most pressing problems with maximum effectiveness and efficiency (p. 324).

This chapter reexamines the issue of accountability from the perspective of its administrative implications for human service organizations. This is a complex issue involving government as well as the voluntary and foundation sectors, and both financial and nonfinancial measures of organizational activity. In addition, a series of political and pragmatic considerations are explored from the viewpoint of managers of human service organizations. One of the major tasks for these managers is to reconceptualize and define the concepts of effectiveness and efficiency of their programs.

UNIQUENESS OF NONPROFIT ORGANIZATIONS

Absence of Profit Measure

From the perspectives of both accountability and management control, the absence of a satisfactory, single, overall *measure* of performance is the most serious management problem in nonprofit organizations. Anthony and Herzlinger (1980), in discussing the characteristics of nonprofit organizations, point out that the profit measure (not motive) is the most significant differing factor. This gap is particularly important for this discussion of accountability. Profitability provides a measure that incorporates a great many separate aspects of performance within it. Although many aspects of a profit organization's performance may be important, it is the "bottom line," profit, that incorporates these separate elements. This measure is valuable both to the managers themselves and to those who judge their performance (usually stockholders and boards of directors).

The dual goals of service and financial performance lie at the heart of the challenges of internal management and external accountability of nonprofit organizations. Although financial performance can be measured through financial statements, the amount and quality of service rendered is not measured by these statements. It is also noteworthy that most nonprofit organizations are service providers rather than producers of tangible goods and products. As compared with production of goods, service production has a number of characteristics that complicate its management as well as measurement:

1. Services cannot be produced according to convenient or efficient schedules and stored in inventory.
2. Service organizations are labor intensive, thereby reducing potential efficiencies of machinery and automation.
3. It is difficult to measure the quantity of some services.
4. The quality of services cannot be inspected in advance and controlled.
5. Judgments as to the quality of most services are difficult and complex.

Revenue from Resource Providers vs. the Marketplace

Nonprofit organizations also differ in that most recieve a significant amount of financial support from resource providers rather than from revenues from services rendered. Accordingly, they are not subject to the forces of the marketplace as are profit-oriented organizations in the same industry such as proprietary hospitals, colleges, children's institutions, and nursing homes. While it appears that nonprofit organizations are moving more into a mode in which they increasingly generate revenues from operations through the marketplace, during the current period, these market resources account for only a small part of the resources of the human service organizations with which we are concerned. Therefore, these organizations will, for some time, continue to be dependent upon other resource providers.

Within the governmental sector, almost all financial sources come from government itself, through tax revenues at federal, state, and local levels. Although each level of government is accountable to its legislative body (and, through them, to the taxpayers), there is also a major resource flow downward from federal to state and local levels and from state to local levels. At each level, the resource providers exercise their accountability responsibilities and options by imposing reporting requirements. Because of the significance of federal funds and accompanying regulations and reporting requirements, the federal attitude toward accountability strongly influences the entire chain of accountability for governmental funds as they flow to different levels of government and to the voluntary sector through grants and purchase of service.

Within the voluntary sector, financial sources are more diversified and differ according to types of services. Because of this diversity of finance sources, voluntary human service organizations have multiple requirements for accountability. A current (1984) project of the National Charities Information Bureau is studying the problem with the purpose of developing some consensus among corporate and foundation grant makers about reporting requirements of quantity, efficiency, and effectiveness of services of grantees.

Defining Resource Provider and Service Provider

In this chapter, the terms "resource provider" and "service provider" are used to describe organizations that provide funds to service providers or that provide services to clients or the community. In many instances, however, these terms actually describe two functions that may be conducted by the same organization. For example, the following types of organizations are both service providers to a defined group of clients and are also resource providers to other service providers through grants and purchase of service: state and local departments of social services or mental health, area agencies on aging, and community mental health centers.

FINANCIAL MEASURES OF ACCOUNTABILITY

Historically, the concept of accountability of government and voluntary nonprofit organizations developed around concerns for how these organizations spent funds entrusted to them. Basically, responsibility in a democratic society entails holding elected officials answerable to their constituents (Lee & Johnson, 1977). The concept of stewardship of funds is central to nonprofit or fund accounting principles as they have evolved in both the government and voluntary sectors. Although there are pressures to shift to measures of effectiveness—a nonfinancial measurement—the demands for financial accountability continue and require the informed attention of managers of nonprofit organizations.

Financial Accountability in the Voluntary Sector

Within the voluntary health and welfare sector, dissatisfaction with the lack of full disclosure and uniform financial reporting led to the publication in the mid-1960s of standards of accounting and financial reporting. Those standards were developed over a period of several years with considerable stress because of honest differences of professional accounting opinion on how best to record and report certain elements (such as depreciation) as well as differences of opinion between charities regulators and major voluntary agencies over other elements (such as how to define and report fund raising costs—an issue that is still not fully resolved). After the *Standards* were published by the National Health Council and the National Assembly for Social Policy and Development, these two organizations, fifty-four of their member national organizations, and others made major investments of time and money in implementing them.

In 1975, the two sponsors of the earlier *Standards* were joined by United Way of America and published a revised edition (National Health Council et al., 1975) that achieved compatibility with the recently revised guide *Audits of Voluntary Health and Welfare Organizations*, published by the American Institute of Certified Public Accountants (1974). The revised audit guide describes generally accepted accounting principles applicable to voluntary health and welfare organizations. At the same time, United Way of America published a guide for United Ways and not-for-profit human service organizations that was compatible with the other two publications (United Way of America, 1974). The compatibility of these three guides provides a significant base for communication of financial information from service providers to their diverse audiences. By following the revised *Standards*, voluntary health and welfare organizations are better able to comply with the requirements of their independent public accountants and will be in conformity with the revised audit guide. The result should be greater uniformity and a higher degree of responsibility in accounting and financial reporting in the field.

Financial Accountability in Government

Within the government sector, variations in the types of accounting practices are widespread among governments and within larger governments. State departments of urban affairs have tended to encourage local governments to adopt "model" systems, as has the National Council on Governmental Accounting. A standard accounting system for local governments would allow greater exchange of information among these governments. State governments and the federal government do not have standardized government-wide accounting systems. Each agency may have one or more system. At the federal level, there are approximately 160 civilian agency systems and 125 systems in the Department of Defense. The Comptroller General of the General Accounting Office is responsible for approving first the principles and standards of each system and then the system design (Lee & Johnson, 1977).

Against this background of variations in government accounting practices, many of the federal agencies have developed specialized reporting procedures for the governments and voluntary and proprietary organizations that receive federal funds. These reporting requirements are designed to fit in with the unique accounting systems of the various departments and with differing concepts of reporting content and format as well as differing regulations and guidelines for many critical aspects of reporting, such as allocation of indirect costs and measuring performance.

Because the audit is an integral element of accountability, audit standards for governmental organizations are of particular interest. The Comptroller General of the United States (1981), after noting the substantial growth of both the number and dollar amounts of government programs in the 1960s and 1970s, observes that this increase has brought with it an increased demand for full accountability. Several state and local audit organizations have also officially adopted these standards, and in 1978 the Institute of Internal Auditors issued standards that were compatible with these.

The standards issued by the Comptroller General provide for an expanded scope of audit to help ensure full accountability and include three elements, all of which are of particular concern to human service managers:

1. *Financial and compliance*
2. *Economy and efficiency*
3. *Program results*

Future Trends in Financial Accountability

This move of government auditors to examination of nonfinancial measures has a somewhat parallel effort in the voluntary sector. The potential is being explored of extending the work of auditors into an examination of the reporting of service efforts and accomplishments (Brace et al., 1980). This issue is discussed in the next section.

Because the financial statements of nonprofit organizations include substantial detail, in accordance with generally accepted principles of fund accounting and the various relevant standards, they may be difficult to understand for many users of the statements. This is especially true for board members, constituent groups, and may even be true for resource providers or regulators to whom the statements are sent or for administrators of the organizations. In order to improve communication there is clearly a need for additional financial analysis and planned presentation as well as some selectivity in what indicators are chosen (Elkin & Molitor, 1984). Ratio analysis is one analytical technique used by accountants to facilitate and enhance the user's understanding of the reporting organization's financial statements (Peat, Marwick, Mitchell & Co., undated). Ratio analysis is an analytical technique that employs summary indicators to formulate fundamental questions about the organization's financial status and performance. Ratios developed from the financial statements provide a general answer to these fundamental questions. The result of the analyses will suggest other questions to be examined to better understand the causes of a particular positive or negative ratio. This concept of a few selected ratios provides the basis of measurement of adequacy of finances in the development of management indicators illustrated below in Figure 12–1 (Elkin & Molitor, 1984). These ratios, based on the work of Peat, Marwick, Mitchell & Co. (undated), assess the status of an organization in terms of its net resources (financial condition ratios), indicate whether an organization has lived within its means (net operating ratio), assess the contribution of various sources of support and revenue to fund programs (contribution ratios), and determine what share of total resources are devoted to a particular program or administrative category (program demand ratios).

NONFINANCIAL MEASURES OF ACCOUNTABILITY

The dual goals of nonprofit organizations—efficient and effective delivery of services and financial breakeven—emphasize the need to examine nonfinancial measures of organizational performance in order to have a full understanding of the organization. At both the policy as well as the auditing levels of the federal government, concern has been expressed and implemented into accountability requirements. The expression of the Comptroller General is clear: the interests of many users of reports on government audits are broader than those that can be satisfied by financial information alone.

In addition, The Financial Accounting Standards Board, the standard setter for the accounting profession, is studying the problem of financial reporting of "nonbusiness" organizations with a view toward establishing standards. In its one publication to date directed toward nonbusiness organizations, FASB endorsed the concept of reporting information about service efforts and accomplishments as an objective of general purpose financial reporting (FASB, 1980).

A study of the issue that examined the status of reporting information about service efforts and accomplishments found that the state of the art in reporting inputs, processes, outputs and efficiency is probably now adequate for enhancement of financial reporting. However, information about program results and, therefore, effectiveness has not reached this level. If such nonfinancial information on service efforts and accomplishments were to become part of financial accounting reports, the study concluded, there is much work to be done in developing these measures to improve their relevance and reliability to a point where they come close to the quality of current financial accounting information. They also concluded that information about service efforts and accomplishments may lie beyond the capabilities of financial accounting and belong to some other field of accounting (Brace et al., 1980).

Effectiveness and Efficiency

The brief look at recent developments in accountability above demonstrates that a base has been established in financial reporting, with standards set in both governmental and voluntary sectors. In addition, there appears to be a need to develop improved analytic and presentation techniques to make financial information more understandable and meaningful for the users. Such techniques as financial ratios and use of computer graphics are seen as future trends.

However, a major concern of those involved in financial accountability is the question of how to elicit the nonfinancial information that is generally recognized to measure the major service goals of nonprofit organizations. In a recent research effort to develop a conceptual framework for selecting management indicators, an attempt was made to place financial and nonfinancial measures within an integrated framework (Elkin & Molitor, 1984). A study of the literature and of practice led to the identification of three major management concerns, which are reproduced from the report in Figure 12–1: effectiveness, efficiency, and adequacy of finances.

Effectiveness

Although some concept of effectiveness is generally recognized as a major management concern, this consensus is not manifested in a general agreement on the meaning of effectiveness nor in ways to measure it (Kanter, 1979; Hatry, 1982). An examination of the varying approaches to measuring effectiveness suggests that no one perspective can be applicable to all situations. There are wide variations in settings; in the value systems of managers as well as resource providers, standard setters, and regulators; and in the availability of and relative difficulty of securing data. Therefore, Elkin and Molitor (1984) conclude that their conceptual framework should include a number of dimensions for measuring effectiveness so that managers can see the range and can select those dimensions that make the most sense for them at a particular time.

This approach raises an important question for the issue of accountability where a resource provider may define effectiveness strictly in

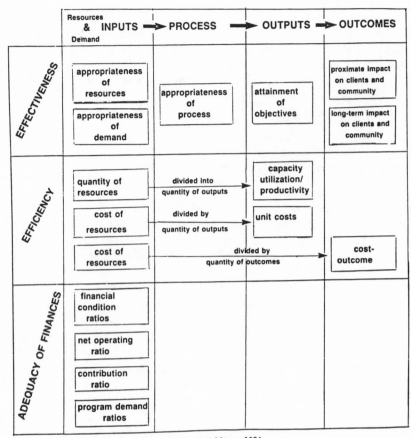

Excerpted from Elkin and Molitor, 1984

FIGURE 12–1. Conceptual framework for selecting management indicators in nonprofit organizations

terms of long-term impact on clients and community, as suggested by Newman and Turem (1978). Some ideas for dealing with this issue within the constraints of an ongoing information and accountability system are discussed below.

The six dimensions for measuring effectiveness are related to an expanded concept of the general systems approach. Although each dimension is important in its own right, it may not be sufficient by itself to measure overall effectiveness, or it may not be pertinent or measurable in a particular setting. Rather, the dimensions complement one another and together may form a more complete assessment of effectiveness.

1. *Appropriateness of resources* builds on the premise that higher-quality inputs will tend to produce higher-quality results. Actual resources are assessed against agency objectives or standards.

2. *Appropriateness of demand* may be viewed as market information as these data quantify the responses of the target population to the organization's mission and its service package.
3. *Appropriateness of process* measures the ways in which resources are arranged to meet the demands for service and are then compared with agency objectives or standards.
4. *Attainment of objectives* measures quantities of outputs as compared to objectives to measure the degree to which an organization reaches its service or managerial objectives.
5. *Proximate impact on clients and community* measures near-term or immediate changes in those served, typically when service is terminated or at intervals during service delivery.
6. *Long-term impact on clients and community* examines changes in level of functioning or attainment of outcome objectives over a period of time after service is completed.

Efficiency

Efficiency is a concept that is broadly accepted in both the literature and practice, although there is some tendency for nonprofit organizations to give it a lower priority than effectiveness. Efficiency describes the relationship between inputs and outputs. Three dimensions of efficiency are identified in the conceptual framework. Even more than with other indicators, efficiency measures must be compared to a standard or another measure of efficiency that provides a base line of experience.

1. *Capacity utilization/productivity* are two measures of the efficient use of available resources.
2. *Unit costs* describe the same ratios of outputs to inputs as do capacity utilization and productivity, but a variety or range of inputs is measured in dollars.
3. *Cost outcome* measures indicate what impact is achieved per dollar spent for optional service modes to accomplish a similar goal or to evaluate the costs of accomplishing outcomes over a period of years.

IMPLICATIONS FOR INTERNAL MANAGEMENT

Because nonprofit organizations must meet their accountability responsibilities in order to assure resources and continued compliance with regulations, managers of these organizations must give priority to setting up appropriate administrative mechanisms to produce the information and reports in a timely fashion. In addition, managers need in-depth knowledge of the implications of accountability requirements so that they can negotiate realistic requirements and influence resource provider requirements.

In many ways, fulfilling accountability responsibilities may be thought of as a subgroup of activities related to a cycle of more general management functions: planning and budgeting; obtaining funds; allocating resources; recording financial and program information; monitoring, controlling, and evaluating service delivery; reporting; and auditing.

Planning and Budgeting

Although accountability is typically associated with evaluating and reporting, Lee and Johnson (1977) report that the emergence and reform of formal government budgeting can be traced to a concern for holding public officials responsible or accountable for their actions. In a democracy, budgeting is a device for limiting the powers of government. Thus, accountability, budgeting, and to some extent, the struggle for control of program is involved in these early planning steps in the management process. The budget process in both government and voluntary sectors establishes the parameters within which the organization will function for some period of time. In addition, the budget will identify the multiple sources of funds and the need for meeting the multiple accountability demands.

Obtaining Funds

In the process of proposing and negotiating for funds from multiple sources, managers will find themselves committing to a variety of accountability demands. All resource providers will request reports of financial data, usually in different formats and for different fiscal periods. In addition, most resource providers will at least require output data on service programs, while others will require conformance with special regulations for handling finances as well as program arrangements. Increasingly, resource providers are asking for efficiency and effectiveness evaluative information—many times in terms of long-range impact on clients. These varying accountability requirements must be recognized early so that appropriate procedures can be established to comply, although early negotiations may reduce accountability requirements that would be impossible or too costly to implement.

Allocating Resources

Once funds are secured, they must be allocated to both program and administrative functions. Accountability requirements may be met simply, with no material costs, by minor adaptations to an existing information system. However, there may be some demands that will require special assignment of staff to establish effectiveness or efficiency measures or to develop special fiscal reports, perhaps based on special staff time studies.

Recording Financial and Program Information

The first and crucial step in recording is to define financial and program activities for each of the special reports to be made. These definitions must serve as the guide to collecting data from diverse sources and then linking them back together. Within the financial accounting area, records must be kept in conformance with appropriate, generally accepted accounting principles as well as in recognition of special breakouts of funds for special purposes for the different resource providers. The organization may find that two providers require different standards of accounting (e.g., a special state requirement vs. general voluntary standards). In such instances, the organization's auditor may have to be consulted to devise special recording procedures. Most information must be kept on an accrual basis by month or quarter so that information can be aggregated to different fiscal reporting periods.

Program information may be quite simple—such as numbers of clients seen in a period—or it can be very complex, especially if outcome evaluation data is required. In addition, nonprofit organizations increasingly need accurate service activity data for billing clients or third-party payers. Securing all these data may mean major changes in internal data collection systems and an increasing amount of direct service time going into such activities. Accountability can be costly—from the points of view of the administrative staff involved as well as of direct service staff.

Computer support for the collection, storage, manipulation, and reporting of data may also be necessary, especially as an organization grows and increases its number of resource providers.

Monitoring, Controlling, and Evaluating Service Delivery

In addition to the procedures that managers would normally establish to monitor and evaluate service delivery, additional accountability requirements of resource providers may significantly increase a manager's responsibilities. The importance of internal controls is emphasized by the Comptroller General (1981) because of the lack of administrative continuity in government units due to continuing changes in elected legislative bodies and in administrative organizations. Accordingly, both accounting and administrative controls must be established and systematically documented to provide an audit trail to demonstrate those policies, procedures, practices, and controls that assure that the entity is managing its resources economically and efficiently, and that they have a specific bearing on the attainment of the goals and objectives specified by the law or regulations for the organization.

In some instances, internal auditing must be established to assure the soundness of internal controls. For the most part, such internal auditing practices are considered by external auditors.

The most difficult of the accountability requirements may be related to providing measures of effectiveness or program results, especially if the resource provider has a narrow definition of effectiveness.

Reporting

Special reports to resource providers must be made. As noted earlier, the content and format of these reports must be determined early in the period of interest. That will allow for special records to be made, special procedures to be followed, and special research efforts to be initiated to fulfill accountability requirements.

Auditing

The cycle of accountability is completed with an audit made by an agent of the resource provider or by an independent auditor working within regulations and generally accepted accounting principles. The scope of the audit should be identified in the initial agreement between the resource provider and the service provider. Although audits may be completed within a few weeks of a fiscal period, there are often delays up to two or three years before such audits are completed and the service provider can be assured that all requirements have been met.

POLITICAL AND PRAGMATIC CONSIDERATIONS

In this chapter, accountability has been treated as a technical requirement that has significant administrative requirements, but it must also be viewed within a broader context of political and pragmatic concerns. In many ways, the pressure for reelection of government officials as well as the public exposure of elected officials to multiple influences plays a strong role in resource allocation decisions.

However, the success of a public-supported organization depends on its ability to satisfy those who provide resources, and it is an essential part of the nonprofit organization manager's role to make sure that his or her organization fulfills that responsibility. Because the nonprofit organization can function best with a reasonable level of independence in program, administration, and communications, one can expect a continuing level of stress to exist between resource providers and service providers. In addition to traditional responses of developing constituency groups and advocating in the public arena, a number of options appear to be available to service providers when faced with unreasonable accountability requirements.

The first step toward negotiating a more sound relationship is to confirm the need for the service. This is especially important in government purchase-of-service contracts with voluntary service providers, but it also holds for government services and in dealing with fund-raising federations and other granting organizations such as foundations.

Another option is to move away from major support from a single source of funds. Experience suggests that the greater the funding from a single source, the greater the control that source can wield. Moving toward multiple sources of funds may mean that new services must be developed or that current service delivery patterns may have to be altered. Such an action may require marketing skills to define new target populations and new service packages. Funding from additional resource providers will also add to the diversity of accountability requirements.

Rosenbaum and Smith (1984) report that an increasing proportion of funds come to voluntary agencies from revenues from operations. Considering such an option could move a service provider to act more like a business enterprise in marketing its services and improving its billing and collection capabilities.

CONCLUSIONS

Resource providers and others with authority to require accountability are moving increasingly to concern for efficiency and effectiveness at the same time as they retain requirements for financial, compliance, and quantity reporting.

Accountability must be viewed in part as an attempt to control the way that resources are expended. Excessive controls that are exercised through accountability reduce the freedom of action of organizations and may work against the intent of the resource provider to increase efficiency and effectiveness of service delivery.

Two essential things for managers of nonprofit organizations to keep in mind are basic to negotiating for some different approach to accountability:

1. Accountability is an integral part of the relationships of resource providers and those organizations that receive their funds. These resource providers are accountable to the taxpayers and contributors, who, in turn, make the funds available

2. Service providers need to be well informed on optional ways to meet accountability requirements, especially when unreasonable requirements are being made. There is a need to conceptualize ways of measuring efficiency and effectiveness in terms that can be built into ongoing reporting systems.

As the financial pressures upon the voluntary sector continue, it appears that an increasing number of agencies will shift to the marketplace to derive their resources from sale of services. Because these trends have already been identified (Rosenbaum & Smith, 1984), it can be concluded that institutions of the voluntary sector face a period of profound readjustment in their role in American society.

REFERENCES

American Institute of Certified Public Accountants. *Audits of Voluntary Health and Welfare Organizations*. New York City: AICPA, 1974.

Anthony, Robert N., and Herzlinger, Regina E. *Management Control in Nonprofit Organizations*. Homewood, IL.: Richard D. Irwin, 1980.

Born, Catherine E. Proprietary Firms and Child Welfare Services: Patterns and Implications. *Child Welfare*, 1983, *LXII*, 109–118.

Brace, Paul K., Elkin, Robert, Robinson, Daniel, and Steinberg, Harold I. *Reporting of Service Efforts and Accomplishments*. Stamford, CT: Financial Accounting Standards Board, 1980.

Comptroller General of the United States. *Standards for Audit of Governmental Organizations, Programs, Activities, and Functions*. (General Accounting Office publication, #020–000–00205–1). Washington, D.C.: U.S. Government Printing Office, 1981.

Elkin, Robert, and Molitor, Mark. *Management Indicators in Nonprofit Organizations: Guidelines to Selection and Implementation*. New York City: Peat, Marwick, Mitchell & Co., 1984.

Financial Accounting Standards Board (FASB). *Exposure Draft, Objectives of Financial Reporting by Non-business Organizations*. Stamford, CT.: FASB, March 14, 1980.

Gummer, Burton. Organization Theory for Social Administration. In Felice Davidson Perlmutter and Simon Slavin (Eds.), *Leadership in Social Administration*. Philadelphia: Temple University Press, 1980.

Hatry, Harry P. *Performance Measurement Principles and Techniques; An Overview for Local Governments*. Washington, D.C.: The Urban Institute, 1982.

Kanter, Rosabeth Moss. *The Measurement of Organizational Effectiveness, Productivity, Performance, and Success: Issues and Dilemmas in Service and Non-Profit Organizations*. New Haven, CT: Yale University Program on Non-Profit Organizations, Institution for Social and Policy Studies, 1979.

Lee, Robert D., Jr., and Johnson, Ronald W. *Public Budgeting Systems*. Baltimore: University Park Press, 1977.

National Health Council, National Assembly of National Voluntary Health and Social Welfare Organizations, and United Way of America. *Standards of Accounting and Financial Reporting for Voluntary Health and Welfare Organizations.* New York City: National Health Council, 1975.

Newman, Edward, and Turem, Jerry. The Crisis of Accountability. In Simon Slavin (Ed), *Social Administration.* New York City: The Haworth Press, 1978.

Peat, Marwick, Mitchell & Co. *Ratio Analysis in Voluntary Health and Welfare Organizations.* New York City: PMM&Co., Undated.

Pifer, Alan. *The Quasi Nongovernmental Organization.* Reprinted from the 1967 Annual Report of Carnegie Corporation of New York.

Rosenbaum, Nelson, and Smith, L. R. *The State of the Voluntary Sector.* Washington, D.C.: C. R. G. Press, 1984.

United Way of America. *Accounting & Financial Reporting, A Guide for United Ways and Not-For-Profit Human Service Organizations.* Alexandria, VA: UWA, 1974.

13
The Crisis of Accountability

EDWARD NEWMAN
JERRY TUREM

Accountability is an elusive concept. As addressed in this article, its terms of reference are personal social services in the broad spectrum of human services, concentrating in the main on social services available in either the public or private sector under the Social Security Act. The problems of social services that are publicly delivered or publicly supported are not necessarily different from those of services funded through other sources. However, in the case of services having governmental assistance, the problems of accountability—problems that are related to political action, ideology, policy-making, program effectiveness, and professional responsibility—are today more striking and visible. They are therefore more symptomatic of the current crisis of accountability.

This article will focus on issues that go beneath the surface of political polemics, administrative style, or intergovernmental issues to the raison d'etre of the social service profession—the problems, the goals, the means of achieving these goals, and the value of the profession's efforts according to the extent to which tasks are accomplished. Implications of accountability in social services will then be considered from the vantage point of public responsibility.

Finally, a perspective on accountability will be presented that explores why, in publicly supported programs, accountability does not simply involve accounting for the "quality of service delivery," as stated by Austin and Caulk in a paper prepared for the 1973 Delegate Assembly of the National Association of Social Workers (NASW).[1]

Indeed, that view largely misses the point that accountability comprises a series of elements ranging from problem identification to goal formulation, and it raises the central questions of efficiency and effectiveness in reducing social problems. To be accountable, in this sense, means addressing a real problem that can be remedied. It means that professional and technical work can be provided if society makes the resources available, that this work will be provided in the manner promised, and that the problem may then be effectively minimized at the least possible social cost.

Accountability is an emotionally laden issue for social workers. The profession naturally reacted vigorously when news reports of the president's former chief domestic adviser stated:

> There seems to be a folk tradition around this town that it's somehow indecent to cut any social program. I don't think the second administration will be a believer in that folk tale. I think a President with a substantial mandate, who feels that the majority of the people are behind him, will feel very comfortable in saying to a vested interest group, such as the social workers, "Look, your social program of the 1960s isn't working, and we're going to dismantle it so you'll just have to go out and find honest labor somewhere else."[2]

In March 1973, Mitchell I. Ginsberg, then president of NASW, pointed out to members the unprecedented challenge presented by "program and fiscal cutbacks at all levels of government, which presage fewer services for those in need." Ginsberg called on NASW "to see to it that social services are not decimated, that government does not abdicate its responsibility" and to focus its efforts "on a program of professional action which will counter the erosion of services to people and the assaults on social work."[3]

Austin and Caulk recommended to the NASW Delegate Assembly program objectives and actions concentrating on political, governmental, administrative, and fiscal strategies.[4] They outlined the following roles for the federal government and the states:

- The states rather than the federal government should set priorities for social services.
- The federal government should not set forth detailed regulations and rules and keep changing them.
- The states should develop machinery to maximize rational, technically sound programs that include full participation by consumers, providers, and other individuals and groups.
- The federal government should finance the system and distribute funds to states through relatively unencumbered procedures.

These proposals reflect a concept closely allied to issues of public responsibility. Austin and Caulk seem to suggest that politically the federal government is either untrustworthy or unresponsive. Ideologically, they find a federally directed public social service strategy repugnant. Administratively, they consider federal priority-setting more aloof from the public interest than state and local priority- setting would be. Their view slides over some critical factors as to why the crisis of accountability exists.

POLITICAL AND ADMINISTRATIVE ACCOUNTABILITY

One often hears complaints that political influence is diverting the good intentions of planners and practitioners. This sounds as if planners and practitioners have a rational and comprehensive approach to developing goals—and the means to achieve them—which politicians distort or pervert. Planners tend to ignore or underrate political considerations, that is to say, the roles of power and influence. They do not realize the extent to which the political process is a means for identifying and allocating social values and for legitimating the means and resources to achieve the ends that those values define. It is in this sense that politics inevitably influences the outcome of any planning process. More strongly stated, effective planning in the public sector is always politicized.

The pluralistic American approach to services will, for the foreseeable future, be based on choices made by providers representing disparate interests who may choose to be "in" or "out" of any national scheme. So far, no interest group or coalition of like-minded interests (including the organized social work profession) has brought together sufficient influence to interest the Administration, the Congress, or other important elements of the American public in a plan to organize social services. It is particularly disconcerting that neither NASW nor professional social workers acting independently or under other auspices have successfully influenced recent decisions in more appealing directions.

A strategy that posits the states as priority-setters and orchestrators for the services within their domain moves away from a national, unified, comprehensive approach. The federal executive branch does have a point of view about services (even though social workers may not like many of its components) and has the potential power to impose decisions and make binding proposals (about which many social workers may raise questions). But the federal government is the only source from which both significant funding and comprehensive programs can develop.

The question of accountability is raised at this time because of recent events in Washington. Congress approved a ceiling of $2.5 billion on formerly open-ended public social services and narrowed the range of clients who could be served. The Administration proposed regulations that narrowed the range even further. Why has this happened and why now? What does it portend? A few years ago most social workers would have thought $2.5 billion for social services was unattainable. Now it is considered inhibiting. Why? What impelled the growth? Is there a real "crisis" in services, or are social workers reacting without even a moment's reflection? Could it be a return to normal growth after an aberrant spurt?

THE BUDGET CRISIS

When the president delivers his annual budget message some time in January, the major newspapers of the country usually greet it with a "canned" description of his recommendations for the ensuing fiscal year. Their descriptions contain summaries of the budget's major sectors—national defense, human resources, natural resources, the national interest, and "other." Their source material is provided annually in a prereleased pamphlet. The real news related to the budget announcement usually revolves around its total magnitude and legislative initiatives. Within a day or so after the president presents the message, the budget no longer is news.

In 1973, however, the budget, especially its recommendations in the human resources sector, was big news for those interested in the progress of social services.[5] Reaction to this budget generated the crisis in human services. Various groups interested in human resources agitated and formed coalitions spanning previously autonomous fields.

In most years the presentation of the budget and its appropriations processes have resulted in incremental changes in the existing budget authority and have given a slight leeway for substantial starts in any new program. As Newman and March have noted:

> The complexities of institutional arrangements guard against radical departures. These complexities also make it very difficult to adjust priorities on a major scale to adjust to changing social needs.[6]

In 1973 actions on the president's budget in the human services sector involved more than incrementalism. A number of economic and administrative premises incorporated in the executive budget are difficult to attack, others go beyond substantive differences and relate to more basic political and constitutional questions of the separation of powers. The serious questions are the choices that must be made about the human services, given a relatively limited level of federal funds.

One may agree or disagree with an overall $268.7 billion maximum for fiscal year 1974. Most people would agree, though, that a budget of this magnitude will have a significant impact on prices, wages, and employment. Social workers and others may disagree with the distribution among national defense, human resources, and natural resources. Many would agree, however, that some level for defense expenditures should be preserved. They may disagree with the rise in expenditures for natural resources, although most are sympathetic to efforts to reduce air and water pollution, preserve the physical environment, and deal with the energy crisis.

The rhetoric supporting the federal government's role in promoting national priorities, while decentralizing authority and decision-making to states and local governments and moving away from central control in Washington, appeals to some social workers but not to others. Traditionally, social work support was often directed to the centralist programs of the New Deal and the Great Society. It is indeed difficult now to counteract a rationale that professes to maximize economic well-being, stresses concentration on national priorities "which really work," and justifies its humaneness on grounds that the comparative levels of defense expenditures will have decreased from 41 percent in fiscal year 1969 to a projected 30.2 percent in fiscal year 1974, while human resources will have risen from 39 percent to 46.7 percent during the same period.

In examining the human resources sector we find that of an estimated $93.9 billion proposed for fiscal year 1974, over $80 billion are tabbed for income security (mostly social security and income maintenance). These resources are allocated without regard to congressional authority to make annual appropriations and are expended from trust funds and from ostensibly uncontrollable matching funds disbursed through state and local authorities.

Responsible groups cannot ignore the implications of extending all programs under the Department of Health, Education, and Welfare (HEW) to all potential recipients. In December 1972 the secretary of HEW estimated that the department's service delivery programs, which then cost $9 billion, would cost $250 billion (about the total of the federal budget) if they were actually extended to all who could be covered.[7] Also, a recent study estimated that meeting the objectives of two major programs in compensatory education and four in social service would require the recruitment and training of an additional 6 million professionals, paraprofessionals, and volunteers.[8]

This recounting is presented neither to defend nor to scare those who may be incensed by current efforts to roll back commitments to social programs. It is meant, rather, to remind social workers that fiscal and human resources are not unlimited even in this affluent nation and that choices must be made among goals for programs.

SERVICES UNDER SOCIAL SECURITY

The treatment of the social services under the Social Security Act presents a special case of gross inconsistency between the rhetoric of decentralization and the reality of Administration proposals. Detailed federal regulations set priorities and limit eligibility and allowable services. Financial penalties for noncompliance place the states in an advocacy relationship to the federal bureaucracy. Yet Nixon's New Federalism affirms that state and local governments should have discretion in setting priorities for social programs and that the federal bureaucracy should disengage itself from handling problems that are state or local.

How closely do specific public benefits or services approximate generally accepted "rights?" For example, in the field of education, the idea that elementary and secondary education should be available to all has wide acceptability. But no such broad consensus has developed for social services, either on their parameters or on their separate components.

Services available under the Social Security Act are still generally associated with actual provision of or at least control by public welfare agencies, even though advocates of a comprehensive social service system would like it otherwise. The great growth in expenditures for social services, which some thought would reduce welfare, parallels growth in case loads and payments. Finally, and perhaps most significantly, a basic income floor under all Americans has given way as a major public issue to questions of how much income, for what categories of people, under what conditions. Some programs still include maintenance benefits as an ingredient in a plan for training or treatment. In these instances, maintenance payments may be used as incentives to continue participation in such programs.

Given lack of consensus on the scope and effectiveness of social services, along with the growth of expenditures in public assistance, changes at the federal level over the past few months are best explained as attempts to control the anticipated overall expenditures available for welfare-related services, to reduce the numbers eligible to receive such services, and to circumscribe the categories in which available resources may be expended.

Observers both within and outside the field warned, even during the early 1960s, that tying services to the goal of reducing dependence on public assistance would weaken their public credibility. At least three developments can be cited for the unhappy consequences of not heeding these warnings—all dealing with the central theme of accountability.

First, studies of service effectiveness do not convincingly show that direct service intervention, especially casework, leads to client improvement.[9] Second, federal, state, and local welfare agencies have failed to find adequate monitoring or reporting devices for separating administrative from service costs or to account adequately for the use of purchased services under the 1967 amendments to the Social Security Act. Third, state and local governments were caught short fiscally in the last few years and abused the purposes of the services amendments by replacing at least some state and local funds with federal moneys probably illegally in some instances, such as charging for social services activities properly reimbursed at the lower administrative rate authorized by the Social Security Act. Accountability was therefore increasingly challenged on grounds of effectiveness as well as evidence of inadequate responsibility to the taxpayer and intended recipients.

No one is convinced that the building blocks for social services that are clearly accountable to the public are yet available. Existing programs become exceedingly vulnerable to a cost-conscious leadership unsympathetic to unsupported claims.

What are the first steps that go beyond the political awareness necessary to make any profession responsive to societal needs? Can social workers meet the following challenge Eulau recently threw to all the humanistic professions?

> . . . the professionals must bring to the treatment of public issues professionally pertinent criteria of substance and conduct that warrant their being respected for their knowledge and skills rather than for the particular ideological predilections that may be the fashion of the moment. The winds of politics are moody and have a way of changing faster than professional responses to these winds.[10]

As indicated, budget restrictions are symptomatic of a more deep-seated problem: lack of recognition of the effectiveness of social service programs. In large measure, this is because social work has not sustained the burden of proof of cost effectiveness and because service programs often operate without regard for basic accounting and the requirements of program data collection. Also, the squeeze on social service programs is part of an overall program of resource allocation within a given budget.

THE VALUE OF SERVICES

Are social work services valued? This is a question central to the concern of social workers. If services are valued, the problem of demonstrating effectiveness is easier. This is not the same as asking if they *are* effective. The term "valued" is used in the sense that someone believes services are worth spending money on them. Worth could be established by a given individual who elects to spend some of his income to purchase a service. Or it could be established by society wishing to buy a set of activities from which it gains satisfaction. This latter is a bit tricky since society may gain satisfaction from results other than what practitioners actually attain. Thus, society may indicate that it values social services by making donations to support philanthropic institutions or by providing direct tax subsidies. However, such actions may be taken primarily because they reduce social guilt rather than because they bring about change in individuals or conditions.

Consider the legal profession by analogy. The fact that people are willing to purchase unsubsidized legal services from lawyers is evidence that these services are valued in the private sector. To the extent an attorney is effective he will usually prosper. If he is ineffective, then his income will likely be less than that of his successful colleagues.

When publicly subsidized programs of legal services for the poor were established, lawyers held that the subsidies were required only for those incapable of paying. Some lawyers claimed that no such programs were necessary since there are existing societies that provide services and since many lawyers reduced their fees to the poor. The recent attack on programs of legal services for the poor did not occur because of lack of demonstrated effectiveness but because of the alleged practice of too little "personal service" law and too much "social action" law. But these are questions of emphasis and arguments as to whether government should sponsor litigation against itself, not whether people value the legal profession.

In the social services there are some, but few, comparable programs so valued. Child care, for example, can be shown to be valued; that is, one can point to programs of child care operated solely by parent subscription. Child care becomes controversial when, with government subsidy, program operators and planners develop standards that tend to price the services higher than people are willing or able to pay. The wish to subsidize, then, all "extras" for all users becomes subject to the question: What differences, if any, do these extras make?

If social work was an essentially private profession supported in the marketplace by persons willing to purchase whatever they thought gave them satisfaction, then the question of public accountability and the question of effectiveness would be less compelling. Since professional social work activities largely depend on public sources of funding, society requires some accounting. And alternative uses of limited resources will always be a major issue.

It is a simple fact, although often unappreciated by professionals, that resources expended on one person are unavailable for another—

and this is true of money, time, or talent. Thus resources used for a person with a long-term, intractable problem are not available for one or two or three other persons with serious, tractable problems.

If left up to the marketplace, the problem works itself out to some extent, although one might quarrel with the distribution that results. To the extent that people perceive that they need something badly enough to spend their scarce resources to demand it, and to the extent that other people will agree to supply that amount of resources, then the allocation of resources becomes efficient. If a provider does not meet the individual's needs, a new provider is sought. To the extent that the individual is unwilling, rather than unable, to meet the provider's price, then his need cannot be said to be great in relation to other things he wants to spend his resources on. If this was the way social work operated, and if the main problem was to extend services to persons unable, rather than unwilling, to pay a price, then it would be easier to defend programs and budgets.

In the absence of a market mechanism by which individual tastes can be expressed and individual offerings may be accepted or rejected, some other way of expressing value must be developed. When the government subsidizes a program, the effect is to reduce the price to the user, thus encouraging use even by those who would not value the service enough to pay full price. When services are provided without charge, the maximum number of potential users would be expected. Without a pricing mechanism, inefficiency and ineffectiveness can be masked. Without competition among providers, there is little incentive for innovation and efficiency.

Thus, in a market context, the allocation of resources occurs through the expression of individual tastes with demanders offering a certain amount of money and suppliers offering services if an acceptable amount of money is offered. Once an equilibrium price is reached, then the exchange occurs. Without this mechanism, conscious decisions regarding allocation must be made since too few resources are available to serve everyone, especially at zero price.

One way to handle the problem of persons with low income is to have a price that varies with income. This is usually called a sliding fee. It tends to reduce the price for users, but not to zero. It requires that persons pay for some portion of their services, thereby giving an indication of how much they value them. However, with sliding fees there must either be a third-party subsidy to the provider, or else persons with higher incomes must pay enough to offset the deficit created by persons paying less than full cost. Any private practitioner realizes that, to maintain a solvent practice, full costs must be paid by someone for all clients. Charging a fee affects a program by (1) showing how those most willing to pay—presumably those in greatest need—line up for the service and

(2) making additional funds available, which may permit extending the program.

The concept of pricing social services in the open market without subsidy is abhorrent to some social workers. Often, they point out, persons need services but cannot afford them. In addition, they say, "Anything that helps a person is worth the price." However, definitions of need are elusive. People have many needs they would not be willing to transform into effective demands. And not everything is "worth the price."

SCREENING AND ELIGIBILITY

It is virtually in the nature of the social work profession to try to assist an individual who lays claim to assistance, regardless of whether anything can actually be done to help. Of course a specific agency may turn away some persons seeking help because it does not provide that range of services usually identified as meeting their needs. For example, some agencies specializing in counseling may turn away persons presenting problems that require tangible resources. Some studies have indicated that the poor and minority groups are often turned away or dropped without assistance.[11] However, once a person is labeled client, there seem to be few bounds of the investment to which he can lay claim. Thus a clear conflict is evident between a professional ideology of full services to all persons in need and the practical necessity to ration scarce resources.

Suppose one thought that services should be targeted to certain individuals or that society would be better off if certain persons were required to have services. Price screening would not be an appropriate first step, although it could be used at some point. The problem would be that all people cannot be served, either because resources are limited or because limited technology prevents help being given to some.

The usual step is to provide screening according to eligibility criteria. These may be based on income or capital resources, demographic or geographic characteristics, type of problem, or other such variables. Basically, eligibility requirements tend merely to reduce the universe of potential users rather than select among potential clients those whose utilization does most to accomplish the program's ends. Once the eligibility hurdle has been cleared, the individual is usually put on a waiting list or accepted for service and carried until closed. The first-come, first-served technique tends to be inefficient in that it does not identify the range of clients from whom those who would use the service resource most efficiently might be selected.

One can view eligibility screening as a form of tax or a price people pay to get services. For example, when government-sponsored services are free to those in the population who meet certain criteria, then persons who do not meet the criteria must pay for the services, assuming they are available in the market. Thus some people pay the total costs of such services while others pay nothing. This example is not intended to support the position that all services should be free to all people but to point out that eligibility requirements provide a way to ration scarce resources. The case has already been made against providing all things to all people. There just is not enough to go around.

If the profession operated in the marketplace, individuals could translate their preferences into demands by bidding dollars for services. Many services, such as homemaking, child care, and marital counseling, are provided in this way. When there is no market mechanism, society defines its preferences by processes that are essentially political. The rules then change drastically.

When individuals make their own way in the private sector of our society, they are accountable only to their customers, their professions, and themselves—except for certain requirements to keep fraud and dishonesty to a minimum and licensing requirements to assure some minimal level of standards. When one turns to philanthropy or taxes, then stricter requirements for accountability are imposed. Since this involves society's money, administered through its public agents (whatever one may think of them at the time), supplicants are bound to accept certain limitations as well as responsibility for their own actions. Their alternative is to abandon this source of funds or seek to change the rules by the political clout.

Accountability, at a minimum, is utilized to assure the criterion of honesty. Honesty is a necessary but not sufficient condition for a fully accountable system. When funds are misappropriated for personal use, that is clearly dishonest. When those operating programs act in capricious and discriminatory ways—that is, when they are lawless in the literal sense of having no authority to behave as they do—they are socially irresponsible. When evidence of ineffectiveness and waste is neglected or covered up, then too there is a lack of accountability. The requirements for full accountability protect everyone, in the social services, defense contracting, or whatever area. Such a system of accountability presumes having ethical persons at the top who recognize that society's resources are never adequate to meet all needs and who insist therefore that these resources should at least be expended honestly and legally.

THE CRITERION OF RESULTS

A sound system of accountability goes beyond honesty and is based on results. The techniques oriented to relationships and processes, which are the heart of the social work profession, are the most "soft" and most in need of being put in proper perspective. If credible professional accountability is to occur, casework and group work must be viewed as inputs that may or may not reduce the incidence of definable social problems, and the profession must develop a new orientation based on outputs that can be measured objectively.

Accountability, in a political system, requires a reasonable expectation that the purposes for which dollars were raised have been or could be achieved with maximum efficiency and effectiveness.

Social workers worry about accountability to clients, but there are no fiscal incentives to assure it, since clients have no market mechanism for expressing their preferences. Other mechanisms, such as having users participate on boards, are required. But to the extent that clients do not pay the bill, the focus is on the social institutions that do.

The authors are concerned with the type of accountability that argues it is wrong to continue to demand pay from society for an elegant surgical operation that impresses the interns but never saves a patient's life. The resources required might well have been used for many other untreated patients who could benefit from known procedures.

Not all outputs have to be successful nor must all interventions be measured and be statistically and methodologically precise. The concern is with accountability in a political environment in which reasonable men do not require anything resembling perfection. In vocational rehabilitation, for example, many cases are closed without attaining success. Yet a preponderance of cases are closed with a claim that clients were rehabilitated since many can be accounted for in addition to those able to meet program objectives. But these are questions of efficiency, which is but one component of accountability. In governmental policy-making it is recognized that reasonable levels of success and a reporting system that retrieves most of what actually occurs are "good enough."

GOALS AS OUTPUTS

Mogulof has noted the following with respect to goals of social work:

> Our goals are couched in the kind of generalities which are unable to inform action. The actions we take are not subject to measurement, and are not conceived of as leading to goals larger than the actions themselves. In effect the instrument (Family Planning, Day Care, Counseling, etc.) becomes the ends, and our administrative energies go toward the preservation of instruments. In a sense, it is a remarkable performance by a society whose great technical achievements have come through the employment of the scientific method, where all action is potentially subject to test. We seem uninterested in viewing our social services as action probes which may or may not achieve desired states. Is it because we really don't know what these desired states are? Or is it ev-

idence of a misguided professionalism, which develops a stake in a particular probe (e.g., Headstart) and pushes all of us (the Congress included) to see the probe as an end in itself?[12]

Characteristically, the social work profession does not define goals in terms of output, but rather input (for example, casework hours, number of persons served). One reason for emphasizing new output conventions is that better program analysts are advising decision-makers who are more sophisticated. Future decision-makers will increasingly include state and local elected officials and superagency manager-budget types. The categorical program managers at both federal and state levels will no longer define the scope of the problem and the resources needed through the traditional device of continuing to expand the programs. Tougher questions will be asked. To a greater extent, demonstrated results will be demanded because of greater exposure to a more open political process.

Social work needs an improved technology for defining goals in terms that entail not only measures of effectiveness but also measures of efficiency. There may have been a time when it was sufficient to state objectives in obscure terms, but this is no longer the case.

Seemingly, the profession is in a poor position to claim it knows best. In principle, it might be said that those providing the funds to pay the piper should call the tune, but social workers should try to be included in that essentially political process. It might also be argued that the means of achievement should be in the hands of professionals—but only as long as they are effective and do not displace or obscure the achievement of goals.

Defining goals more rigorously is so large a first step for social work practitioners and supporting scholars to develop that a concerted effort to do so would probably satisfy critics for a while. Merely redefining one set of abstractions with another may give the illusion of movement, but in fact goes nowhere. The day of reckoning comes closer with each attempt. Devising new catchwords or slogans or grasping for the latest fad in rhetoric can no longer suffice. Nor are fancy new delivery systems required. Social workers must simply define what they already do best.

Those active in the social work profession must learn to focus on the few, perhaps narrow, areas in which they can demonstrate that what they do makes a difference, a difference not possible by other means for fewer resources. They cannot afford to make promises that, given the resources, they will reduce welfare rolls, eliminate delinquency, cure the mentally ill, or educate the poor. They must learn to talk about which of how many, at what price, with what expected success, and why this is the way society should do it.

Knowledge bases and the role of schools of social work in relation to accountability have been covered by Briar.[13] To echo his views, truth, beauty, justice, and mental health are goals, but they are not useful for stimulating specific actions, and it is difficult to know when one has such a goal in hand. Systematic evaluation requires ability to state goals in objective, measurable terms. Evading such a statement leaves one open to the accusation of masking ineffectiveness or of committing a form of fraud and leads to a discounting of claims of credibility that may be sound.

If, for example, social workers claim that working with juvenile delinquents can reduce recidivism, and then recidivism is not reduced, they have demonstrated that what they were doing could not achieve the end promised. They have not made the case for the total ineffectiveness of what they were doing or denied that it accomplished some things for some people. (For example, it may have reduced the severity if not the incidence of offenses.) Nevertheless, they may have shown that it is not the best tool for reducing juvenile recidivism in general. The argument that some good was done anyway, even if it was not what was primarily intended, saves little face in the budget shop.

Delinquency has many roots: economic conditions, community and neighborhood influences, social class, the educational system, the local police and court systems, and the like. Social work cannot influence many of these factors. Therefore, the objectives should be expressed in terms of whether, for some subset of juveniles who have certain characteristics and whose offenses stem from, say, inadequate parental supervision, social work can help reduce recidivism by a specified percent through working with the parents. Casting objectives in such a fashion makes headway in defining credible goals.

This approach, however, would only help determine whether the intervention worked at all. The vital questions are: Does it offer the best way? Are there alternatives that, with the same resources, would have further reduced recidivism? Or are there alternatives that would have reduced it to the same extent at less expense? Together these questions define the effectiveness and efficiency of the system of accountability.

What should be measured and how it should be measured involve a mixture of technical and political concerns. How precise the measurement should be depends on its purpose and on the person prompting it, who may be a cost-benefit expert concerned with the discount rate on future income, a politician who wants to make sure someone is really being "helped," or a program operator who wants to stay in business. The system should produce sufficient information to provide a record for audit showing that the funds were spent honestly. After that the question of how much one wishes to know to evaluate the program can vary widely. The minimum, then, is an acceptable fiscal reporting system and a management-information system covering program data.

EFFECTIVENESS AND EFFICIENCY

Briar has discussed many factors involved in the inability of social work to show effectiveness—its sliding from theory to theory, from technique to technique, but seldom grappling with the question of whether what was accomplished did the clients any good.[14] Effectiveness may be the heart of the truly legitimate question of what benefit professionals, or the profession as a whole, may be bringing clients.

If social services help people, and social workers think many of them do, then it behooves the profession to demonstrate how. Again, the authors take the hard line that case studies and case histories do not constitute evidence since they do not show controlled conditions, the influence of the intervention, the relative overall numbers of successes and failures, and the long-term effects and costs. Nor do they control for enough variables. Who asks what percentage of his clients improved? Further, how would one show it, and at what cost was the client improved? Could more have been done for others at the same cost?

As for efficiency, it would be monumental to show that any intervention worked. Before the cheers died down, one should look at the problems facing those who want to find out whether this intervention works better than another, or if the same result could be attained for less money. Efficiency in this instance does not mean that what is done is done for the lowest cost but that the ends achieved cannot be brought about in another way or at an even lower cost.

Efficiency involves weighing alternatives against costs. To a large degree, many trade-offs are not precisely comparable. For example, looking at trade-offs—say, between two techniques for reducing recidivism among inner-city delinquents—is only one way of judging efficiency. The comparisons could be between casework and group work or between counseling and manpower programs and compensatory education. Each has a different approach and different techniques, but the comparison should be with regard to degree of impact on the same measure of outcome.

Another set of issues related to efficiency deals with normative judgments as to the choice of what to do at given levels of expenditures to make society better off. Should the money go, for example, to nursing homes for the aged, foster homes for neglected children, rehabilitation of the handicapped, or services to reduce delinquency? If all are worthy, what should the mix be? When a program is fully accountable, those responsible for it can show not only that what it accomplishes is done with fiscal economy and that it is effective, but also that it does what it does better and less expensively—given quality and quantity levels—than any other program could.

SUMMARY AND CONCLUSION

The current crisis in social services is a crisis of credibility based on an inadequate system of accountability. Social programs are in trouble because they focus on processes and not results. A society with limited resources can agree on an endless catalog of needs, but its needs must be ranked to concentrate enough resources to do some good. An analogy to the marketplace indicates that when individuals translate their needs into demands by showing how much they are willing to pay, then many of the issues surrounding accountability recede. When the market mechanism is weak or missing and the support of social institutions is necessary, then political interplay influences preferences and those providing services are required to show that available resources are spent on the most pressing problems with maximum effectiveness and efficiency.

With respect to the "soft" services—those that primarily involve relationships, counseling, and process technologies—it is difficult to attribute changes in the individual's status to the service activity. Testimonials are suspect, and few instruments are available that validly measure before-and-after impact. When the bulk of activity is based on individual or group processes, changes take a long time. Experimenters and practitioners experience difficulties when they try to isolate the intervention as the key to change over time. In most cases, however, claims that the successful outcome was based on the intervention would be given benefit of doubt if the intended outcomes had been clearly specified and believable.

Occasionally one hears that programs of social work produce outcomes so subtle they cannot be measured but that somehow without them society would be worse off. When the outcome is not measurable, social workers are probably engaging in self-delusion.

At the end, these are the paramount questions: Are social workers useful? Do the programs in which they work leave society better off than it would be if the programs were abolished? In general, the authors think many aspects of society would be worse off were there no social workers and no social programs, but they hold no brief for the sacredness of any one program or any one intervention technique. It is cause for despair, however, that social workers, while indulging in rhetoric about their social responsibilities, often do not have even the most elementary regard for the mechanics of social accountability.

Many programs or specific aspects of services are in a favorable position for sophisticated defense on a limited scale, with modest claims for accomplishment. Family planning, rehabilitation, day care, homemaking, protective services, and the like, should be able to prove their worth if the necessary rigor were applied. It could be shown that other services can accomplish desired ends less expensively than alternative techniques—for example, in-home care for the retarded, the elderly, and the severely handicapped.

This article has tried to show what accountability is about, where the profession falls short, and what might be done. The rest is up to all of us in the social work profession—and time may be short.

NOTES

1. David M. Austin and Robert S. Caulk, "Issues in Social Services: A Program for NASW," *New Directions for the Seventies* (Washington, D.C.: National Association of Social Workers, 1973), p. 16.
2. John D. Erlichmann, cited in James P. Gannon, "If President Wins Again, the Nation May Have a Do-Less Government," *Wall Street Journal*, October 18, 1972, pp. 1, 20.
3. Mitchell I. Ginsberg, "A Letter from Our President," *New Directions for the Seventies*, p. 1.
4. Austin and Caulk, op. cit., pp. 7–18.
5. "The United States Budget in Brief, Fiscal Year 1974" (Washington, D.C.: U.S. Government Printing Office, 1973).
6. Edward Newman and Michael S. March, "Financing Social Welfare: Governmental Allocation Procedures," *Encyclopedia of Social Work, 1971* (New York: National Association of Social Workers, 1971), p. 433.
7. Internal HEW memo.
8. Elliot L. Richardson, "Responsibility and Responsiveness," Monograph on the HEW Potential for the Seventies (Washington, D.C.: U.S. Department of Health, Education & Welfare, 1972), p. 3. (Mimeographed.)
9. *See*, for example, Joel Fischer, "Is Casework Effective?" *Social Work*, 18 (January 1973), pp. 5–20.
10. Heinz Eulau, "Skill Revolution and Consultive Commonwealth," *American Political Science Review*, 67 (March 1973), p. 188.
11. For a review of studies, *see* Richard A. Cloward and Irwin Epstein, "Private Social Welfare's Disengagement from the Poor: The Case of Family Adjustment Agencies," in Mayer Zald, ed., *Social Welfare Institutions* (New York: John Wiley & Sons, 1965), pp. 623–643; and Cloward and Frances Fox Piven, *Regulating the Poor: The Functions of Public Welfare* (New York: Pantheon Books, 1971).
12. Melvin Mogulof, "Special Revenue Sharing in Support of the Public Social Services" (Washington, D.C.: Urban Institute, March 1973). (Mimeographed.)
13. Scott Briar, "Effective Social Work Intervention in Direct Practice: Implications for Education." Paper presented at the annual meeting of the Council on Social Work Education, San Francisco, California, February 1973.
14. Ibid.

14

Social Equity and Social Service Productivity

STEPHEN R. CHITWOOD

Government spending for federal, state, and local activities currently accounts for approximately 30 percent of the Gross National Product of the United States.[1] Public decision making, therefore, controls almost a third of the monetary resources of the country and thereby determines a major portion of the goods and services provided in the economy. As government has assumed this enlarging role in American life, various managerial techniques have been promoted with the purported intent of increasing the value or benefits flowing from public expenditures. The Hoover Commissions offered performance budgeting and accrual accounting.[2] The Kennedy and Johnson Administrations promoted planning, programming, and budgeting systems (PPBS).[3] And since 1969, the Nixon Administration has emphasized program evaluation and the measurement of government productivity.[4]

This essay examines the current emphasis on increasing the productivity of government activities and briefly assesses its historical relation to earlier government management movements. This assessment illustrates how productivity measures have traditionally neglected a basic element in providing public services—the social equity accompanying the distribution of those services. Having identified this area of neglect, the important relationships between productivity measures and the determination of social equity in supplying government services are identified. This is followed by a categorization of distribution patterns and standards which may be used in measuring the social equity with which public services are provided.

PRODUCTIVITY MEASUREMENT IN GOVERNMENT

According to Harry P. Hatry of the Urban Institute:

> Productivity measurement essentially means relating the amount of inputs of a service or product to the amount of outputs. Traditionally this has been expressed as a ratio such as number of units produced per man hour.[5]

Productivity measurement in government is not new. In an effort to increase the productivity of federal employees in U.S. Army arsenals in the early 1900s, managers sought to use F. W. Taylor's stopwatch, scientific management procedures—with the result that a special committee of the House of Representatives was formed to investigate the Taylor and other systems of shop management.[6] During the "good government" movement days, Herbert Simon, working with the International City Managers Association, sought procedures for measuring the unit costs of various municipal services, e.g., street cleaning, sanitation activities, etc., with the intent of designing means to reduce those costs.[7] Since 1902, the army Corps of Engineers has had to justify proposed water resource projects with data relating benefits to costs, a measure of dollar output per dollar input.[8]

Productivity measures offer potentially valuable information to all government officials, i.e., political executives, legislators, and career public administrators. As measures of efficiency, such as work measurements or unit costs, productivity measures furnish standards for assessing actual performance and taking corresponding actions in view of the efficiency demonstrated. When productivity measures incorporate effectiveness indicators, information is also given on results achieved versus objectives stated. These data may lead to changes in objectives, alterations in program activities, or shifts in expectations of results achievable. Trend measures illustrate relative performance over time. Productivity indices provide trend information that can:

- reveal the cumulative effects of all factors which have influenced efficiency of the organization measured.
- flag the need for management action, such as plant modernization, when the trend shows signs of slowing.
- help in the determination of rational, attainable productivity improvement objectives.
- provide a means of evaluating management actions, such as the effects of installing capital improvements.[9]

From the preceding list of uses, productivity measures may be seen to offer a variety of beneficial information to participants in the governmental process. There is, however, one important dimension of government services which seldom is reflected in productivity measures. This excluded element is the distribution of services among the population, and the social equity associated with that distribution.

PRODUCTIVITY AND SOCIAL EQUITY COMPARED

Social equity and government productivity are both concerned with the final outputs of public activities. Questions of social equity, however, center upon the distribution of services and the distribution of their effects. Government productivity measures, on the other hand, focus upon the quantity or quality of output. (The distribution of services and their effects could be incorporated in productivity measures by including effectiveness indicators, but this is seldom done.) Similarly, social equity and government productivity are each concerned with accounting for resource inputs. Once again, though, social equity examines inputs in terms of the sources from which they were derived, e.g., income classes, socioeconomic groups, geographic groups; whereas government productivity measures look merely at the amount of dollar value of inputs utilized.

The magnitude of resources now under federal, state, and local government control allow these governments to bestow increasingly significant benefits or penalties on their citizenry. These benefits or penalties arise primarily from the governments' distribution of public goods and services (hereafter referred to only as public services). Thus, while expenditure accountability and efficiency of operation will continue to be prime considerations of government officials, the distribution pattern of public services must also be viewed as a basic criterion for public decision making. As a result, measures of social equity must increasingly accompany measures of productivity in order to assess the adequacy of public services.

SOCIAL EQUITY AND PUBLIC SERVICES

Proponents of the new public administration take the normative position that social equity should have a significant role in public decision making.[10] While many people share this normative orientation, recent court cases have caused the consideration of social equity to become a pragmatic as well as a philosophic and ethical matter. In the case of

Hawkins v. *Town of Shaw* (427 F. 2d 1286 (5th Cir. 1971) *aff'd* 461 F. 2d
1171 (1972) (en banc)), evidence showed that although a range of public
services in the Mississippi town was financed out of general tax revenue
(without regard to assessment or property ownership), black residential
areas were manifestly underserviced. The court found no constitutional
justification for residents who were similarly taxed to have fewer paved
streets, less sewerage service, poorer street lighting, and less police protection. The court in *Hawkins* did not consider the prevailing municipal
finance scheme as such; it held only that the distribution of the services
financed by that scheme was discriminatory. The facts of the case presented a clear example of discrimination, because services were distributed to the "suspect classification" of race. The Town of Shaw was therefore ordered to develop and present to the court an equitable plan for
delivering public services to all the town's citizens.[11]

Reasoning similar to that in the *Hawkins* case has resulted in other
local jurisdictions being required to examine the distribution pattern of
their services.[12] If suits of a similar nature are upheld by future court
rulings, public officials will have to consider questions of social equity for
legal, if not moral, reasons. Even if the courts fail to support these earlier decisions, as the United States Supreme Court refused to sustain
lower court rulings relating to inequities resulting from financing education through property taxation, political activism by various public
groups will require public officials to give growing attention to matters
of distributing public services.

While the movement toward considering the distribution of public
services appears to be acquiring momentum, a severe hindrance to this
effort lies in the vagueness of the notion of social equity.

Without criteria for measuring social equity, public officials will be
unable to use this criterion for decision making. To date, no single definition of social equity has been developed. Nevertheless, several aspects
or interpretations of social equity have been identified and articulated.
To facilitate a clearer, and possibly more productive discussion of social
equity, the more prominent aspects of this term are described in the following pages. These dimensions of social equity were deduced from past
legislative, administrative, and court decisions and actions.

DIMENSIONS OF SOCIAL EQUITY

An infinite number of patterns might be used to distribute public services. Fortunately, this vast variety may be reduced to three basic distribution patterns:

1. equal services to all,
2. proportionally equal services to all, and
3. unequal services to individuals corresponding to relevant differences.[13]

Each of these patterns has at some time been advocated as the only socially equitable way to distribute government services. A brief examination of each of these patterns will quickly suggest their potential usefulness for assessing the social equity of services provided by federal, state,
and local governments.

Equal services to all as a measure of social equity of allocating public
services has limited applicability. Most government services cannot be
equally utilized by all citizens, either because insufficient funds exist to
provide them on such a broad scale or because the services are initially
designed to serve the needs of a restricted clientele. Certain government
services, termed pure public goods by economists, may have some limited potential for providing equal benefits to all citizens.[14] Nevertheless,
the restricted range of pure public goods renders equal services to all an
inadequate basis for measuring the social equity of the distribution of
public services.

Proportional equality in providing public services consists of delivering services in amounts that reflect a monotonically increasing function
of a specified characteristic(s). For example, the number of uniformed
policemen (public service) assigned to patrol a particular city precinct
may vary in direct proportion to the crime rate (specified characteristic)
of that precinct. Or the total public assistance payment (public service)
made to an unemployed single head of household may increase directly
with each dependent (specified characteristic) that is supported. In each
instance, the quantity of service provided varies directly with changes in
the amount of specified characteristic possessed by the client.

Providing public services on a proportionally equal basis seems both
pragmatically and humanistically appealing. On pragmatic grounds,
it provides apparently concrete, objective bases for allocating services
among the populace; and on the humanistic side, it allows more services
to be provided as their perceived need increases. Regardless of these
aparent virtues, social equity measured on the proportionally equal basis
of providing government services has several difficulties. Once a policy
decision is made to provide a public service, the complex task arises of
selecting the specified characteristic(s) whose magnitude determines the
amount of service to be delivered. Another problem involves the proportional amount of service to be given in relation to the specified characteristic. Even when these problems have been resolved, there are the
administrative difficulties of assessing the extent to which potential re-

cipients of a service possess the specified characteristic and then providing the corresponding quantity of services. In addition, as with the equal
services to all approach, this concept of social equity may also be un-
workable because of insufficient funds to provide services to all eligible
recipients.[15]

Unequal public services corresponding to relevant differences represents a third approach to defining social equity as it relates to delivering
public services. With this concept, social equity in distributing public
services is achieved if individuals receive services in amounts corresponding to relevant differences in some characteristic possessed by those recipients. The total services received need not be proportionate to the
amount of the relevant differences present in each recipient, thus differ-
entiating this concept of social equity from that of proportional equity.

The critical aspect of this approach to social equity is identifying the
characteristic whose relevant difference among the client group will determine the quantity of services each person will receive. Two frequently
used characteristics are the willingness and ability to pay for public services and the results to be achieved through those services. City libraries,
parks, and other public facilities may be placed in more affluent sections
of a city with the justification, usually unarticulated, that the affluent citizens have paid the most taxes and therefore deserved more service.
Similarly, where public services are provided on a user charge basis, e.g.,
airports, cemeteries, sewer service, or sanitation collection, the relevant
difference in their distribution may well be the willingness and ability of
recipients to pay their costs.

Where the distribution of services depends upon individuals meeting certain minimum qualifications, criteria, or standards (other than
willingness or ability to pay), each criterion represents a relevant difference which has been deemed appropriate to the receipt of the particular
service. Numerous reasons exist for requiring that minimum relevant
differences in characteristics or qualifications criteria, however, relate
directly to the results which are to be achieved by those services.

Among the most important results sought by public services are:

1. providing services to individuals who are unable to obtain them
   through the free market mechanisms in the quantity or quality
   deemed essential by society, e.g., adequate education, police and fire
   protection;
2. providing services to individuals which will give them an equal opportunity to compete for and occupy all positions in society, including the most attractive ones, e.g., compensatory education, job training, physical rehabilitation;
3. providing services which insure that people will receive the benefits
   they are entitled to under law, e.g., public defender services, out-

reach activities to notify people of their rights to program benefits; and

4. providing services which allow individuals to meet approximately minimum survival needs, e.g., food stamps, public housing, cash payments.[16]

Determining the criteria for distributing the services necessary to achieve the preceding results is an extremely precarious and judgmental process. For example, what standards should be used to distribute limited, available police protection throughout a city? Should the criterion be an area's existing crime rate, with the desired results being to reduce areas of high crime? Or should the criterion be to maintain existing low crime rates in selected areas of the city by keeping those areas heavily policed? Depending on the results sought, either distribution of services could be justified as socially equitable under the unequal distribution concept.

What criteria should be used to determine the amount of services to provide individuals so they might achieve an equal opportunity to compete for and occupy all positions in society? The initial problem is to identify the different characteristics which currently exist and inhibit equal competitive opportunity among all citizens. Even when these differences are identified, and experience suggests we have often selected unimportant differences, two additional difficulties arise. First, how do you identify the level of the characteristic to which people must rise in order to have an equal opportunity? For example, if attaining a particular level of literacy is seen as necessary for equal opportunity, how is that level identified? Second, even if specific goals are established to which characteristics should be raised, how will the amount of services necessary to raise each individual to that level be determined? For example, since each individual below a set standard of literacy may have varying deficiencies, what criteria, e.g., intelligence quotient, current reading level, age, etc., should be used to determine the appropriate amount of educational services needed for each person to reach the desired level? If these problems are not solved, services will tend to be provided on an unequal basis. But to the extent the goals of equal opportunity are achieved, the initial provision of services, though unequal, will have been equitably distributed.[17]

Distribution of services so that people might meet approximate minimum living standards is another approach to social equity and shares some of the problems associated with fostering equal opportunity. The designation of the minimum living standards to be sustained is itself a relative decision, since the quality of average living standards varies even among sections of the same country. Such standards are particularly difficult to develop, since they include such a wide range of elements, e.g., diet, shelter, clothing, health care, etc. Attempting to establish minimally acceptable levels for each of these elements, assessing individuals to determine where they are in relation to these standards, and then developing programs to provide services to bring all individuals exactly to these minimal levels represent enormously complex tasks. Nevertheless, where this is done and unequal services are provided to achieve these minimal standards, a socially equitable distribution of services may be said to have occurred.

Providing services to clients to insure they will receive public benefits entitled to them by law requires: first, a delineation of the characteristics of citizens making them eligible for those benefits; second, an identification of those specific persons who meet the eligibility criteria; and third, an evaluation of what services will have to be provided to each eligible person to insure he will receive his benefits if he wants them. While the first activity is relatively simple to complete, activities two and three are more difficult and potentially quite expensive to the government. Nonetheless, if unequal services are provided in such a manner that each person entitled to and desiring public services does obtain them, the services will have been equitably distributed.

Not all qualification standards for distributing public services, however, are based on the results to be achieved by the program. Some criteria, such as residence requirements in the jurisdiction, may be designed to reduce the migration of people to that jurisdiction merely to receive public services. Other criteria, e.g., having a farm of particular size in order to receive various subsidies, may be established to reduce the administrative burden of handling numerous minor clients. Still other requirements, such as having to apply formally for benefits, may be designed to reduce the number of people who will receive them. In these cases, the criteria justifying unequal services rest not on the intrinsic results sought from the program but on obtaining or avoiding external or spillover effects related to the program.

SOCIAL EQUITY AND
PUBLIC DECISION MAKING

Social equity based upon equal, proportional, or unequal distributions of public services is in each instance justified on the grounds of how services and their benefits are ultimately apportioned among a jurisdiction's populace. Another approach to judging the social equity of a distribution of services, however, stresses the process of determining that distribution rather than the distribution pattern itself. When social equity focuses on process, any distribution pattern determined by the legitimate public decision-making process is deemed socially equitable. Any distribution pattern in conflict with that prescribed by the legitimate public decision-making process is socially inequitable.

When the process criterion is used to assess the social equity of a distribution of public services, an underlying assumption is that social equity (much as the concept of public interest) is reflected in the judgments of those groups and individuals who have access to the public decision-making process. For the pluralist school of political science, this means that whatever distributions of services emerge from the legal political processes of federal, state, and local governments, they are by definition socially equitable.[18]

In contrast to and in conflict with the pluralists are those persons who believe that social equity in providing public services requires a major, and possibly controlling, influence from those receiving the services. Proponents of the citizen or client participation school of political science emphasize that social equity in providing public services requires the development of a type of relationship between the recipient of a service and the administering agency which reflects mutual trust and respect, two-way communication, and participation. Only when such a relationship is established can the provision of those public services be classified as socially equitable.[19]

VERTICAL VS. HORIZONTAL EQUITY

Assessing social equity in providing public services, therefore, may include both an examination of the process for establishing a distribution pattern for services and an analysis of the pattern ultimately selected. Each of the three patterns discussed earlier addressed the problem of allocating services among citizens differing in numerous characteristics, e.g., sex, age, geographic location, health, wealth, etc. These criteria for distributing services among heterogeneous people represent an attempt to achieve what might be termed vertical social equity. This term connotes the effort to devise a rationale for allocating services among individuals who possess greater and lesser degrees of various personal attributes or characteristics. To the extent such a rationale is developed and widely agreed to, vertical social equity will be thought to have been achieved. Where no rationale can be developed for apportioning services among different individuals, or where the rationale is not broadly accepted, vertical social equity will be held in question.

Accompanying vertical social equity is the idea of horizontal social equity. Horizontal equity refers to the equal treatment of equals.[20] It requires that all people possessing like amounts of a characteristic determining the provision of a particular public service should receive the same quantity of that service. A recent study by the U.S. General Accounting Office dramatized the horizontal inequities of the present welfare system. Numerous recipients who shared a similar dependency status often received quite varied dollar value benefits from several federal programs. While these individuals were basically similar in their degree of need, the qualification standards for different programs might summarily bestow benefits on one person but not another.[21] Thus, assessing social equity in providing government services must include the examination of horizontal equity as well as vertical equity and the process whereby service distribution patterns are established.

STANDARDS FOR MEASURING SOCIAL EQUITY

Even when participants in the political process can agree on a definition or criterion for identifying a socially equitable distribution of services, they often fail to use similar standards when comparing and evaluating the social equity that exists with the social equity they believe should prevail. Regardless of the criterion selected to define social equity in providing government services, each criterion may be compared to one of the following standards.[22]

First, any criterion of social equity, e.g., equal services, may be applied to the distribution of a service, and existing equity may be compared with the standard of past equity to see whether changes have occurred from previous years. Thus, as with productivity measures which compute changes in output per unit of input over time, social equity measures may also generate time series data reflecting changes in social equity in the distribution of services. A second standard is the social equity with which other governmental jurisdictions distribute their services. A third standard is a comparison of planned equity in the distribution of services with the actual equity that is finally achieved. A fourth standard is the satisfactory or satisfying level of social equity. Does the existing pattern of service distribution meet a satisfactory level of social equity as perceived by the citizenry?[23]

Numerous problems may arise when political participants cannot agree on the standards they will use to appraise existing social equity. Certain protagonists of social welfare services, e.g., aid to families with dependent children, will say that the existing social equity in the distribution of services is better than in the past and is therefore good enough. Proponents of more aid or a different distribution of services will say that the social equity of the existing distribution is inadequate compared to the services distributed by other government jurisdictions.

CONCLUSIONS

In future years, measuring the productivity of government services will continue to have high priority among the activities of public administrators. Of ascending importance, and probably of equal or greater importance, is the public administrator's responsibility for identifying the social equity with which government services are provided. As more and more benefits are generated by government programs, administrators will increasingly need to articulate their personal version of a socially equitable distribution of services. To insure that social equity considerations ultimately become as visible as matters of productivity in providing government services, a common ground for discussion of this concept is required. The preceding pages have attempted to provide a beginning for such a common ground by describing several dimensions of social equity. In addition, a suggestive set of standards is proposed which would allow a comparison and evaluation of the degree of social equity associated with different distributions of government services.

These dimensions and standards for assessing social equity should provide a theoretical departure point for students of public administration interested in investigating the social equity of existing government services. At the same time, these concepts may serve elected and appointed public officials and career administrators as a specific and concrete basis from which to legislate and administer public programs with a clear understanding of their social equity implications.

NOTES

1. "Empty Pockets on a Trillion Dollars a Year," *Time*, March 13, 1972, p. 72.
2. Arthur Smithies, "Conceptual Framework for the Program Budget," in David Novick (ed.), *Program Budgeting* (Washington, D.C.: U.S. Government Printing Office, 1964), p. 7, and Second Hoover Commission, *Budget and Accounting* (Washington, D.C.: U.S. Government Printing Office, 1955).
3. For a general description and critique of the PPB system, see Leonard Merewitz and Stephen H. Sosnick, *The Budget's New Clothes* (Chicago: Markham Publishing Company, 1971), especially chapters 1–6.
4. See Allen Schick, "From Analysis to Evaluation," *The Annals*, Vol. 394 (March 1971), p. 50; and Thomas D. Morris, William H. Corbett, and Brian L. Usilaner, "Productivity Measures in the Federal Government," *Public Administration Review*, Vol. 32 (November/December 1972), pp. 753–763.
5. Harry P. Hatry, "Issues in Productivity Measurement for Local Government," *Public Administration Review*, Vol. 32 (November/December 1972), p. 777.

6. Harwood F. Merrill (ed.), *Classics in Management* (New York: American Management Association, 1960), p. 66.
7. C. E. Ridley and Herbert A. Simon, *Measuring Municipal Activities* (Chicago: The International City Managers' Association, 1938).
8. U.S. Congress, Senate, Subcommittee on National Security and International Operations, *Hearings, Planning–Programming–Budgeting*, 90th Congress, 2nd Session, 1968, Part 3, p. 168.
9. Thomas D. Morris, et al., *op. cit.*, p. 757.
10. H. George Frederickson, "Toward a New Public Administration," in Frank Marini (ed.), *Toward a New Public Administration* (Scranton: Chandler Publishing Company, 1971), p. 311.
11. Peter Jaszi, unpublished memorandum to Howard Hallman, Center for Governmental Studies, Washington, D.C., December 13, 1972, pp. 9–10.
12. *Ibid.*, pp. 10–11.
13. Felix E. Oppenheim, "The Concept of Equality," in David L. Sills (ed.), *International Encyclopedia of The Social Sciences*, Vol. 5 (The Macmillan Co. and The Free Press), pp. 102–107. While not specifically phrased in terms of social equity, this article provides a useful theoretical basis from which to begin an analysis of this topic.
14. Charles L. Schultze, *The Politics and Economics of Public Spending* (Washington, D.C.: The Brookings Institution, 1968), p. 83.
15. The financial problem encountered in supplying services to clients in the amounts necessary to achieve equity and the desired effects was articulated by former Secretary of HEW Elliot L. Richardson. Secretary Richardson noted that his studies indicated that HEW's $9 billion in service programs would cost roughly $250 billion if they were "extended equitably" to all those similarly situated citizens who need them. William Greider and Nick Kotz, "Harvard Abstraction Becomes Reality," *Washington Post*, April 9, 1973, p. A–14.
16. These objectives of public expenditures are discussed in the following sources: Peter O. Steiner, "The Public Sector and The Public Interest," in Robert H. Haveman and Julius Margolis (eds.), *Public Expenditures and Policy Analysis* (Chicago: Markham Publishing Company, 1970), pp. 21–33, and Felix E. Oppenheim, *op. cit.*
17. Felix E. Oppenheim, *op. cit.*
18. The emphasis of the pluralist school is primarily on process rather than outcomes of political activities. The inference is therefore made, in a recognizably general manner, that for this school of political analysis, social equity is reflected not in political outcomes but in the nature of the political process itself. For a related critique of the process approach to political science, see Allen Schick, "Systems Politics and Systems Budgeting," *Public Administration Review*. Vol. 29 (March/April 1969), pp. 137–151.
19. Comments of Orion White as interpreted and recorded by the author during a panel discussion on "Social Equity and New Public Administration" at the ASPA 1973 National Conference on Public Administration, Los Angeles, California, April 4, 1973. See also the special issue of the *Public Administration Review* on "Curriculum Essays on Politics, Administration, and Citizen Participation," Vol. 32 (October 1972).

20. The concepts of vertical and horizontal equity have traditionally been used in relationship to governmental tax structures. These terms, however, appear equally valid for use in appraising the equity accompanying the distribution of public services. For a short discussion of vertical and horizontal equity applied to tax structures, see Otto Eckstein, *Public Finance* (Englewood Cliffs, N.J.: Prentice-Hall, Inc., 1967), p. 60.

21. George Lardner, Jr., "Hill Welfare Study Shows Inequities," *Washington Post,* March 26, 1973, p. A–1.

22. These standards are identical to several standards prescribed by Yehezkel Dror for appraising the efficacy of public policy making in *Public Policy-making Reexamined* (San Francisco: Chandler Publishing Co., 1968), pp. 58–69.

23. *Ibid.*

15

The New Scientific Management: Systems Management for Social Welfare

RINO J. PATTI

INTRODUCTION

In the mid-1960s when the administration was attempting to give birth to the War on Poverty, another less dramatic and seemingly innocent presidential initiative was being launched which would have far more staying power than the poverty program, and may, in the long light of history, have an even greater impact on the nature of social services in the United States. This initiative was President Johnson's order that a new management approach called the Planning, Programming and Budgeting System (PPBS) be put into general usage throughout the federal bureaucracy. This system, in the president's words, had "proved its worth many times over in the Department of Defense," and would now bring to other departments and agencies of the federal government the "most advanced techniques of modern business management."[1] The optimistic rhetoric that accompanied the introduction of PPBS reflected a conviction that at long last a management technology had become available that would bring order and precision to the processes of program planning, implementation, and evaluation. It promised a set of tools that could be used with equal facility whether one was dealing with missile systems or welfare systems, and provided the advantage of imposing a common analytic framework that would enable policy makers to comparatively assess the costs and effectiveness of various programs.

A decade later, the glitter and promise that surrounded PPBS at its inception has dimmed somewhat, but the managerial ideology, the mind set that gave rise to it, has, if anything, become more pervasive. For purposes of this discussion, I shall refer to this ideology as the "New Scientific Management." I specifically use the term "ideology" to convey the assertion that the new scientific management is not distinguished as much by its technology as it is by a particular socio-political world view, characterized by certain definite (albeit often implicit) assumptions about how best to understand, control, and change organizational behavior.

In its practical expression, the new scientific management is more familiarly associated with terms like systems management, systems analysis, operations research, and systems engineering: that collection of methodologies that now enjoy increasing currency and favor in social welfare bureaucracies at every level of government. It is to this ideological and technical phenomenon, its definition, emergence, and limitations, and its implications for the social welfare enterprise, that this paper is addressed. The position I intend to argue is that the indiscriminate application of this approach in social welfare can generate negative consequencs for human services agencies and the clients they serve.[2]

THE NEW SCIENTIFIC MANAGEMENT: WHAT IS IT?

It is difficult to crisply define and characterize the new scientific management without doing injustice to someone's conception of what it means. Like all management approaches, its adherents and practitioners differ markedly among themselves as to how much weight should be attached to which tenets or principles, how dogmatic or selective one should be in implementing certain strategies, and so on. Despite these variations, however, it is important to attempt a definition of this managerial phenomenon so that there can be a common referent.

Practitioners of the new scientific management, or what we shall refer to here as systems managers, are a diverse lot that come from many different academic and experiential backgrounds, including engineering, computer sciences, economics, business, the behavioral sciences, and public administration. Here and there, one even finds a social worker or a lawyer, who by virtue of personal predisposition or on-the-job training has gained entry to this coveted circle of "management scientists." What makes it possible to treat this collection of practitioners as a group, however, is not a common occupational or academic identity, but rather their adherence to a certain belief system. Committed as they are to objectifying management practices based on rigorous quantitative analysis, the belief system that directs and influences their activities tends often to be quite implicit. In day-to-day interaction it is, in fact, often difficult to discern the assumptions and values which underlie their activities, because they appear as ultimate pragmatists prepared to move in whatever direction data and logic suggest. Nevertheless, lurking below this formidable objective facade is a belief system that bears identification; among its central tenets are these:

1. *All organization systems, notwithstanding their particular histories, cultures, language, and programmatic content, can be analyzed and understood in terms of the logical relationship between means and ends.* With adequate expertise and computer hardware, information systems can ultimately be devised that will isolate and quantify all, or at least most, of the variables that are salient to an effective decision-making process.[3]
2. *The essential similarity of organizational processes, regardless of substantive content, makes it possible for the systems manager to be a paninstitutional generalist, who can apply theoretical knowledge and analytic skills with equal value in any situational context.*
3. *With adequate research technology, it is possible to define situations such that all "action relevant to environmental conditions are specifiable and predictable; and all relevant states of a system are specifiable and predictable."*[4] Organizational processes can, in short, be defined as established situations.
4. *The efficient use of material and human resources is a paramount value.* One of the major problems to contend with in this respect is the tendency for the components of a system to displace organizational goals with selfish and parochial interests. In terms of overall organizational objectives, this is defined as waste and error. To minimize these factors, the systems manager must specify activity elements and output criteria and construct an information system that allows him to monitor performance and to detect deviations so that these can be brought under control.[5]
5. *Impatience with human error motivates a constant search for ways to structure, and where possible reduce, the exercise of judgment and discretion.* The preferred approach to increasing predictability and reliability of performance is reducing the complexity of tasks performed so that activities can be routinely and consistently carried out. Human motivation and social and cultural conditioning are not considered problematic in this regard and tend to be treated as constants. The atomization of work, however, is only practicable when accompanied by well articulated systems for control and coordination.[6] Only in this way is it possible to orchestrate the universe of tasks in the service of centrally defined objectives.

6. *Consensus, bargaining, and negotiation are suspect as processes for decision making and should be replaced where possible by choices that are informed by comprehensive, rational analysis of alternatives in terms of their relative costs, effectiveness, and risks in achieving specified objectives.*[7] Organizational or subsystem survival should not be a major decision variable, nor should socio-political criteria of success.

This set of values and assumptions, as we shall see in a moment, is open to serious questions. Were these the primary tools of a systems manager, he would be vulnerable indeed. However, what makes the new scientific management such a formidable force in contemporary organizational life is not the tenets of its ideology alone, but the technology which buttresses and justifies it. The systems manager is himself skilled in, or can mobilize experts with such esoteric specialties as, cost-benefit analysis, operations research, program budgeting, network analysis, and the program evaluation review technique. This arsenal of systems analytic technologies grew out of the space and defense efforts in the post-World War II era and were collectively credited with no less lofty achievements than putting a man on the moon and bringing rationality to the Byzantine decision processes of the Department of Defense. A systems manager brings with him the credibility gained from these ventures, plus more than a little arrogance rooted in the belief that if his technology can harness problems like space travel, it should be more than equal to the task of improving the effectiveness of social welfare organizations.[8]

Thus, the new scientific management is no passing fashion that we can expect to recede quickly from the scene. It is, rather, a well articulated ideology practiced by professionals who enjoy considerable stature by virtue of a technological know-how that gives them the image of being hard-headed realists with the ability to produce. That they should be chosen to bring some order and rationality to the muddled social welfare bureaucracy is not surprising. We turn now to how the diffusion of the new scientific management occurred in social welfare.

EMERGENCE AND DIFFUSION OF SCIENTIFIC MANAGEMENT IN SOCIAL WELFARE

The spread of the new scientific management across institutional boundaries into domestic and, specifically for our purposes, social welfare governmental areas should first of all be placed in the economic context of the 1960s. The decade of the 1960s witnessed a growth in social welfare expenditures unparalleled in this country's history. New programs, expanded eligibility, and increased benefits, while insufficient to meet rising expectations, nevertheless resulted in a mushrooming of governmental responsibility. Between 1960 and 1973, for example, social welfare expenditures, encompassing income maintenance, health, housing, education, and social services at federal, state, and local levels increased from $52.3 to $215 billion, an increase of over 400 percent. During roughly this same period, social welfare expenditures as a percentage of the gross national product also increased dramatically, from 10.6 percent to 17.6 percent. Similarly, while federal, state, and local governments had expended 38 percent of their budgets for welfare purposes in 1960, this proportion had risen to 53 percent by 1973.[9] Thus, in both absolute and relative terms, the social welfare enterprise had expanded at a phenomenal rate. By the end of the decade it had become not only a major governmental activity but a central preoccupation of the American people and their elected officials as well.

Throughout this decade a subtle but important phenomenon was occurring, namely, a gradual shrinking of the fiscal dividend. In the early 1960s it had been assumed that a continued rate of economic growth would generate a fiscal dividend sufficient to support an expanding effort to combat social problems. However, the combined effect of several tax cuts, the Viet Nam War, increased social welfare expenditures, and, more recently, inflation and a reduced rate of economic growth has served to seriously erode the surplus that might have underwritten the continued expansion of social welfare programs. It is now clear, as the Brookings Institution studies have pointed out, that there will not be sufficient resources to support all the social welfare initiatives that seemed worthwhile on their face. This will be true, one should add, even if defense expenditures are substantially cut back.[10]

The net effect of these developments has been to create a politics of scarcity where emphasis is increasingly placed on choosing from among program alternatives those that produced the greatest increment of desired social and behavioral change for the dollar expended. In this context, decision makers, both executive and legislative, increasingly look to experts who can provide them with hard information on which to base the difficult choices.

The politics of scarcity has had, and will continue to have, a profound effect on management technology and social welfare organizations. Where once the administrators of these programs had the relatively simple tasks of advocating program expansion and justifying the need for additional allocations of money and resources, by the latter part of the 1960s, they were being asked to provide detailed information about what was being done, at what cost, and with what results. Management was forced, in short, to shift from a preoccupation with program maintenance and expansion, to a concern with program description, control, and evaluation. In making this shift, social welfare organizations found themselves confronted with a gigantic skill and knowledge vacuum. The pool of career professionals and program experts that had traditionally been recruited to middle and upper management did not possess the technical know-how needed to fill this vacuum, so social welfare organizations began to import, or have imposed upon them, the technology that the new age required.

Like the social scientists who had preceded them during the early 1960s, and the psychiatrists before them, each of whom were sought to fill different vacuums, the systems analysis technicians came marching into the social welfare sector as teachers, consultants, and researchers. On the placards they carried was a new lexicon bristling with the sound of rigor and precision: management information systems (MIS); program financial plan (PFP); management by objectives (MBO); and so on. As in previous eras, social welfare professionals embraced these prophets warmly, attending endless workshops, institutes, and management seminars to learn more of this new wisdom so that it might be incorporated into their own practice repertoires.

Before long, however, it became clear that the implementation of the new management technology would require not only the infusion of knowledge but the infusion of systems managers themselves. Retraining the program-oriented, career professional was proving too difficult. The process by which this personnel succession began to occur is reflected in the study jointly conducted by the General Accounting Office and the Bureau of the Budget in 1969 to determine those factors that influenced whether sixteen federal agencies had successfully implemented PPBS. The major finding of this survey was that the attitudes of the agency head was the single most important factor in development of an agency-wide PPB system. Departments with executives who were considered indifferent to "the development of systematic analysis and planning processes . . . made less substantial progress," according to this study.[11] Note the implicit assumption here that an executive's failure to embrace PPBS was the equivalent of an indifference to systematic analysis. Perhaps more revealing is what the study concluded about the reasons for executive indifference:

> . . . Wide experience in the agency's program areas: professional background which leaned toward bargaining or argument as issue resolving techniques; and finally, strong agency constituencies, whose interests would not be served by the kind of policy analysis contemplated by the PPB system.[12]

The not-so-implicit image of the PPBS resistant administrator that emerges from these "findings" is someone who is not committed to rational planning, whose vested interests in the existing program of the agency make him impervious to data suggesting the need for changes, who prefers compromise to logic as a basis for decision, and finally, one whose consideration of alternatives is constrained by the biases and interests of groups upon whom he relies for support. One could easily come away from this characterization feeling that this group of administrators is an unprogressive, recalcitrant lot. Only a short jump in logic is necessary to conclude that if systematic analysis and planning are to be incorporated, then these administrators must be replaced by those who support PPB.

Yet looked at from another perspective, the characteristics attributed to PPB-resistant executives might well be those that are often associated with the effective administrator—i.e., an intimate acquaintance with program; an appreciation of, and ability to use, political processes in decision making; and an awareness of, and sensitivity to, agency constituencies. Needless to say, this was not the interpretation given in the study just alluded to.

The point is that once the new scientific management gained a foothold in social welfare, the program-oriented manager became a proverbial sitting duck. The process of succession was virtually assured. The mismatch between these contending forces is aptly summarized by Hoos:

> Is it conceivable that anyone would logically opt for anachronistic inefficiency through horse-and- buggy means, when instead, he can invoke an arsenal of sophisticated tools that will bring efficiency? The answer to this almost rhetorical question draws strength from and strengthens the already existing ethos of efficiency, automatically accredits efficiency as a social good, and practically assures easement into the next step of the syllogism, that [social problems] need better mangement. It is through this logic that systems analysis has been transplanted from the realm of the military and the moon-bound to the social scene.[13]

PROBLEMS AND PITFALLS

Having asserted that the new scientific management is, and will continue to be, a potent force in social welfare, I would now like to discuss several of the problems in, and consequences of, this development. Basically, the discussion will revolve around two major points: the applicability of systems management and kindred technologies to the social welfare sector; and some of the organizational problems that will be attendant to a full-scale implementation of this management style.

On the face of it, the new scientific management and the technology it employs would seem to provide an ideal approach to solving social problems. Among other things, it suggests exhaustive fact finding regarding the problem at hand; a detailed specification of desirable goals and objectives; a comprehensive evaluation of the alternative means for achieving the desired outcomes, together with the anticipated costs and consequences of each; and, finally, the selection of those means that seem optimal for achieving goals sought. The implementation of the entire program is carefully monitored so that the decision maker is aware of how each program component is progressing toward the achievement of its subobjectives, and how its activities articulate with those of other components. Feedback is provided at periodic intervals to allow the administrator to make the necessary adjustments in the nature of the program activities, the goals, or both. At the end of a planning or budget period, the decision maker is presumably in a position to quantitatively determine the extent to which the goals set were in fact achieved.

What concerns us here is whether, in fact, this appealing scenario can be effectively applied to most social welfare organizations whose tasks and functions are influenced by a whole host of rapidly changing and difficult-to-anticipate contingencies. Systems managers argue that there is no reason why it cannot. For example, these PPB enthusiasts state:

> Nothing inherent in the subject content of *any agency's program mix* [emphasis added] should impede PPB analysis. . . . It should be possible to define the benefits of a program in ways that make them susceptible to measurement.[14]

Despite this optimism, there is a growing body of opinion which suggests that the transferability of the systems management model to people serving organizations is not as simple as the advocate of PPB would lead us to believe. There are several reasons for this.

First of all, the application of systems management technology assumes certain organizational and environmental preconditions, which on examination, are found to be largely lacking in the social welfare sector. Wildavsky, for example, in his analysis of factors that facilitated the implementation of PPB in the Department of Defense, found the following factors to be essential:

1. A rising level of appropriations and program expansion which makes it possible to hire large numbers of new people who are thoroughly immersed in the new management technology.
2. A highly centralized decision-making process and a corresponding ability of those in power to control the processes of implementation.
3. Organizations that enjoy relative autonomy from their environments in the sense that they are not constrained by well-entrenched constituent groups that are likely to oppose policy decisions.

4. A situation in which a rather large margin of error is allowable—that is, where policy-making and funding bodies are willing to tolerate a substantially larger expenditure than was originally anticipated in order to solve the problem at hand.
5. A situation in which the cost of a contemplated policy or program development justifies a rather large expenditure on the implementation of systems management technology.
6. A small group of experts who have devoted to the substantive problems confronting an organization using the tools of systems management.[15]

We need not discuss each of these criteria as they apply to social welfare, since those who are familiar with human services organizations are aware that these conditions generally do not obtain in this field. Moreover, the absence of these facilitating factors becomes more marked as one considers those social welfare organizations that operate under state and local jurisdictions. What interests us here is that so little attention has been given to these preconditions that experience would indicate are necesssary to properly install systems management technology. One wonders if in their eagerness to gain access to a new organizational territory, the systems technicians and managers engaged in a bit of oversell much like social workers did in the early 1960s. In any case, it appears that without adequate support, the systems management approach will find it difficult to actualize its potential.

A second and perhaps more fundamental reason for questioning the transferability of the systems management approach to social welfare is that it has proven to be most effective in situations of moderate complexity where goals are relatively clear and easily measured and the performance characteristics of the systems components are known. It deals, in other words, most effectively with those organizational processes concerned with established, routine situations.

When, however, the phenomena with which a system deals are highly complex, and influenced by an array of largely unknown and subtly independent variables, many of which cannot be observed, let alone controlled, the utility of systems management techniques declines considerably. Add to this the fact that unlike man-machine interaction, where the behavior of the worker and the responses of the machine can be specified and within limits predicted, no corresponding claim can be made for client-worker interactions in human services organizations.

Our concern, of course, is not that systems management technology cannot deal with this order of complexity, but *rather that its practitioners are likely to act as though it can.* After all, the claim of the new scientific management is based on its presumed ability to bring order and logic where disorder and confusion have previously existed. To make good on this claim, there will be a compelling tendency for systems managers to impose an artificial precision on client-worker interactions, by either selectively screening out those variables that are not amenable to measurement, or by assigning numerical values to variables no matter how imprecise or arbitrary such assignments might be.[16] The temptation will be to fill in the "black box" in the systems flow chart, impose definition where none is called for. Some will argue that such efforts, while more form than substance, are necessary at the outset in order to move toward increasingly refined measures. However, the danger is that once these data have been set into the computer and subjected to impeccable mathematical calculation, the decision makers, in their quest for hard information, will come to forget that they are dealing with the "illusion of certainty" and not the real thing.[17] Ultimately, this process has the potential for masking vast areas of ignorance and obscuring the need for real knowledge development.

Finally, the utility of systems management technology for social welfare should be questioned because of its generally simplistic view of the relationship between the organization and its environment. It is clear that policy and program development in social welfare is more characterized by its incremental and consensual nature than by its emphasis on purely rationalistic planning. In no sector of public service are there more diverse experts and interest groups who have a say in, or the ability to block, policy developments. Client groups, unions, professional associations, state and federal legislative bodies, groups of administrators, and a host of other interest factions must be considered in the development of policy and program. The potential of these groups for confounding a welfare program is substantial no matter how impeccable its design may be.[18] Because of this, it is imperative that management and social welfare organizations be sensitive to, and capable of compromising with, elements of the support environment that surround virtually all such organizations. This process may result in less than ideal programs, but it is essential to maintaining a modicum of community support. To the extent that systems managers consider these groups to be impediments in the policy development process and/or attempt to centralize decision making in the interest of gaining greater effectiveness, one would expect there to be not only a reduction of input from these groups, but an increase in resistances to proposed changes not only from those that are traditional antagonists of welfare programs, but from friends and allies as well.

In addition to those problems mentioned above, there are other limitations to the systems management approach that are likely to impede the service delivery capability of social welfare organizations. Central among these is that the assumptions and techniques which make up the new scientific management are by their nature likely to accentuate the

trend to centralized decision making and control that are already pronounced in many welfare bureaucracies.[19] There are several reasons
for this assertion. First of all, as we have previously pointed out, systems
management tends to abhor error, uncertainty, and unreliability—i.e.,
those phenomena that attend the exercise of discretion and judgment by
workers. To minimize these factors, the systems manager tends to divide
the tasks to be performed in the organization so that each is reduced to
its simplest and most routine dimension. In this way it is possible to simultaneously define and specify the nature of the work performed and
to maintain better control. But the process of achieving more predictable worker performance cannot stop here because in order to avoid
chaos, the atomization of tasks must be accompanied by an elaborate
data retrieval and monitoring mechanism. This in turn compels the
need for increasingly complex and comprehensive information systems,
a sophisticated data processing capability and a sizable cadre of middle
management experts who can man the hardware, analyze and interpret
its output, and make the findings available to top management. The net
effect of this process is that while the purview of the personnel in the
lower echelons is more and more constricted, the data they generate
tends increasingly to aggregate at the top. Central management comes to
have a virtual monopoly on the information necessary for decisions.
From the perspective of the systems manager, this may be desirable because it affords the comprehensive, holistic view that is deemed necessary to evaluate the overall performance of the organization. On the
other hand, there is considerable evidence suggesting that the organizational structure and processes necessary to sustain centralized decision
making generate significant undesirable consequences for staff and clients. Included among these are: stereotyped and procedure-bound staff
behaviors; poor staff morale; and alienation.[20] Moreover, in a work
environment which emphasizes routine and narrowly defined work
parameters, one can expect that the search for innovative solutions to
problematic situations will be diminished considerably.[21]

    In the utopian world of the new scientific management, it is as-
sumed that a rationally derived decision clearly communicated to subordinates will be complied with. Drawing upon experience with mechanical models, the systems manager looks upon compliance as a relatively
simple process in which the component, in this case the worker, receives
a message, acknowledges receipt, and proceeds to behave in a specified
manner. It is true that all but the most obtuse systems technologists observe the difficulties that occur in this process, but those factors that interfere with machine-like responses tend to be lumped together as "external rational" annoyances, that cannot be understood or systematically
dealt with. This kind of intellectual sleight of hand is an expensive luxury in social welfare bureaucracies, even the most elementary observa-

tions will suggest that workers have an infinite variety of ways of filtering and selectively interpreting messages from superiors, and even of undermining orders they receive. The limitation of the systems management perspective is that is is predicated on the notion that the most compelling factor motivating worker action is the rational, authoritative message. Yet rather extensive research in organizations employing well-educated, professional personnel indicates that an overreliance on the use of authority to obtain compliance and exact obedience is likely to produce not more, but less efficient and effective worker performance.[22] The systems manager is, of course, likely to interpret this as a problem requiring yet a further set of rules, procedures, and controls.

CONCLUSIONS AND RECOMMENDATIONS

Criticism serves a useful purpose, and the new scientific management, like any major movement, deserves to receive its share. But it is one thing to criticize and quite another to suggest constructive alternatives. So, in conclusion let me suggest several ideas that I believe may be useful to the long-term development of management capability in the social welfare sector.

In the short run there seems to be no clear alternatives to the infusion of systems management perspectives and technology into social welfare. This approach is riding a crest of popularity compounded of the status borrowed from other fields of endeavor, its own salesmanship and soaring rhetoric, and the public's desperate quest for solutions to the "welfare problem." The new scientific management has promised to deliver more effective programs at less cost, and notwithstanding this assessment of its limitations, the final returns are not yet in. One suspects that the glitter of the new scientific management will begin to dim when there has been time to measure the payoff against the promise. In the meantime, the social welfare sector should actively proceed to design and implement management training programs that are specifically tailored to the distinctive organizational and political conditions that obtain in this field.

The argument for the development of specialized professional training programs in social welfare management is based primarily on the recognition that human services organizations can no longer afford to find their leadership in technicians who have developed their administrative skill through on-the-job training, nor from those trained in management skills that were developed in, and are better suited to, other substantive program areas. Social welfare is a gigantic enterprise, whose complexity, cost, and significance to the political economy of this country is such that it requires the specialized management expertise of persons whose basic educational preparation and subsequent career development occurs in the context of social welfare proper. Such persons must be identified early in their college years and groomed for a career in social welfare management, because only with lengthy, continuous, and intensive training will they be adequate to the task that confronts them. The idea that someone can spend ten years working in a direct service capacity and then be recruited to and retrained for management is an anachronism that grew out of the early days of social welfare when the nature of administration was much less well understood and the programs and policies to be administered were less complicated. Some people were able to make this transition effectively, but the vast majority were not, as evidenced by the gigantic skill vacuum that became evident in social welfare in the 1960s.

There are some who cling to the notion that the best administrators are bred in the ranks of direct practice. But if nothing else, the new scientific management has jolted most career professionals into a recognition that the task of managing an organization requires a distinctive and rigorous preparation. The persons specially trained in social welfare management should be no less sensitive to client needs, and no less steeped in social values than front-line practioners, but they must have specialized training in the broad range of theoretical, empirical, and practical skills required of today's administrator. To detail the nature of such a training program would require yet another paper, but let me suggest some of its general dimensions.

1. *Social program managers should have substantial grounding in the cluster of technologies that we have lumped together under the phrase "systems management."* These tools have considerable value when not tied to some of the assumptions of the new scientific management and when they are selectively utilized to accomplish limited purposes. Social welfare managers should be sufficiently familiar with these technologies to know when and where they can be appropriately utilized.

2. *Social welfare managers should have substantive grounding in some problem-policy area within social welfare*—e.g., criminal justice, poverty and income maintenance, development disabilities, or child welfare. They should be intimately familiar with the empirical and theoretical evidence pertaining to the causes and effective treatment of the problem; the community organizations and constituencies that are concerned with the problem; the legislative and administrative policy context of program delivery; the policy development processes and economic factors that contribute to and result from the particular problem phenomena.

3. *Social welfare managers should have a repertoire of interpersonal skills relevant to task group development and leadership, in-service training and*

staff development, and personnel management. They should be familiar with organizational development strategies and techniques and know when they can be appropriately utilized. They should have a thorough comprehension of organizational research that suggests the interpersonal and structural conditions necessary to develop and maintain worker commitment to organizational goals.

4. *Social welfare managers should have a substantial grounding in research design and quantitative methods, especially as they relate to policy analysis and program evaluation.*

This is, of course, only the barest outline, but it is enough to suggest that the range of knowledge and skill required for the management of today's social welfare organization cannot generally be found in professional schools of engineering, business, or public administration that are currently providing much of the systems management manpower for the field of social welfare. Each has its contribution to make to the preparation of the social welfare manager, but none provides the breadth and flexibility that is required.

I believe that schools of social work should provide the leadership for this kind of training in the next decade. Significant developments in this area have been initiated in a number of schools, and enrollment in administration programs has grown substantially in the last few years.[23] While the number of graduates is still infinitesimal in relation to the need, it seems likely that these programs will continue to develop and expand. The success of such programs, if indeed they are to succeed, will depend crucially on the guidance, support, and cooperation of career professionals in social welfare who know best the urgent need for effective social welfare management and the consequences that will follow if we fail to meet this challenge.

NOTES

1. Ida Hoos, *Systems Analysis in Public Policy: A Critique* (Berkeley: University of California Press, 1972), p. 65.
2. This is not to deny the value of systems analytic technology when it is selectively utilized for specific administrative tasks. My concern here is with those situations in which this technology and the assumptions on which it is based become the dominant management strategy in an organization.
3. See, for example, Robert J. Wolfson, "In the Hawk's Nest," *Society* 9 (April 1972):24, 69; Hoos, *Systems Analysis in Public Policy,* p. 86–96.
4. Robert Boguslaw, *The New Utopians: A Study of System Design and Social Change* (Englewood Cliffs, N.J.: Prentice-Hall, 1965), p. 7.
5. David Clelland and William King, *Management: A Systems Approach* (New York: McGraw-Hill, 1972), pp. 395–411.

6. Boguslaw, *The New Utopians*, p. 2.
7. See, for example, discussions by Kate Archibald, "Three Views of the Experts' Role in Policy Making: Systems Analysis, Incrementation, and the Clinical Approach," *Policy Sciences* 1 (1970):77–78; and Jean Millar, "Selective Adaptations," *Policy Sciences* 3 (1972): 130–131; and Victor Thompson, *Bureaucracy and Innovation* (University: University of Alabama Press, 1969), pp. 54–55.
8. Wolfson, "In the Hawk's Nest," p. 58.
9. Alfred Skolnik and Sophie Doles, "Social Welfare Expenditures, 1970–1971," *Social Security Bulletin* 37 (January 1974):3–5.
10. Charles Schultz et al., *Setting National Priorities: The 1973 Budget* (Washington, D.C.: The Brookings Institution, 1973), pp. 394–409.
11. Keith Marvin and Andrew Rouse, "The Status of PPB in Federal Agencies: A Comparative Perspective," in *The Analysis and Evaluation of Public Expenditures: The PPBS System*, vol. 3 (Washington, D.C.: Government Printing Office, 1969), p. 808.
12. Ibid.
13. Hoos, *Systems Analysis in Public Policy*, p. 90.
14. Marvin and Rouse, "The Status of PPB in Federal Agencies," p. 814.
15. Aaron Wildavsky, "Rescuing Policy Analysis from PPBS," in *The Analysis and Evaluation of Public Expenditures: The PPB System* (Washington, D.C.: Government Printing Office, 1969), pp. 838–840.
16. Hoos, *Systems Analysis in Public Policy*, p. 70.
17. Thompson, *Bureaucracy and Innovation*, p. 57.
18. The experience with the Goal Oriented Social Services approach (GOSS), an information and evaluation system proposed by HEW for implementation on a national basis several years ago, is a good example of this. After a substantial investment in designing the system, HEW was forced to postpone implementation in the face of substantial opposition from many groups and individuals.
19. See Archibald, "Three Views of the Experts' Role in Policy Making," pp. 74–75; and Thompson, *Bureaucracy and Innovation*, pp. 29–60.
20. Gerald Hage and Michael Aiken, "Organizational Alienation: A Comparative Analysis," in *The Sociology of Formal Organizations: Basic Studies*, ed. Oscar Gursky and George Miller (New York: Free Press, 1970), pp. 517– 526.
21. Thompson, *Bureaucracy and Innovation*, pp. 9–28.
22. See, for example, Rensis Likert, *The Human Organization: Its Management and Value* (New York: McGraw-Hill, 1967), pp. 3–40.
23. Statistics available from CSWE indicate that between 1968 and 1973 the number of graduate students enrolled in programs of administration, management, and social policy in schools of social work increased approximately five-fold. *Statistics on Social Work Education, 1974*, Council on Social Work Education.

PART II

Administering Human Service Personnel

Editor's Introduction

Social agencies are labor-intensive organizational systems investing most of their financial resources in personnel who are engaged in the process of delivering social services. Administration is centrally concerned with making this factor productive. To do so it organizes, allocates roles, and monitors the activities of the staff responsible for achieving the agency's objectives.

An organization's approach to staffing involves an elaborate personnel process. Once the need for a staff member is declared and articulated, the search begins, often guided by a search committee. *Identification* of a personnel pool in which a candidate might be found and *recruitment* are the first steps. Much depends upon the way the agency establishes the criteria of choice—setting forth requirements and qualifications—and the actual availability of potential candidates. *Selection* follows in which the candidate's education, experience, and recommendations are assessed. Either the executive, executive surrogate, or a personnel committee interviews the candidate and engages him or her, having detailed the job expectations and terms of employment. Once chosen, the new employee is then *inducted* into the position, care having been taken to arrange an appropriate orientation and to provide a helpful initial experience, to clarify responsibilities, to clear up ambiguities, and to set the stage for a satisfactory assumption of the position. *Supervision* and *training* ensue, both intended to maximize the employee's performance, insure professional growth, and guide the worker's activity in accordance with the organization's policies and procedures. Periodically the staff member's work is *evaluated,* in the course of which agreed-upon expectations and actual performance are matched and areas of further development are probed. The process concludes with the ultimate *termination* of the work agreement either through retirement, resignation, separation, or death.

Each phase of this process includes multiple considerations and conditions that require thought and action. The selections in this section probe many of these aspects of personnel work. They are drawn from the available literature and stress those aspects of human resources management that have figured prominently in the current personnel environment.

A. PERSONNEL PRACTICES

As the professional association in the field, the National Association of Social Workers was from its inception concerned with developing acceptable standards for professional practice. Successive statements of desirable personnel practices appeared through the years, the current document having been adopted in 1975. The assumptions behind these activities were that qualified staff was essential for the effective delivery of social services, and that personnel performed most adequately when they worked under favorable conditions of employment. From time to time new standards have been added and traditional practices upgraded. The document that follows covers a multitude of circumstances and contingencies, and represents a fairly exhaustive listing of significant considerations affecting the working environment of practitioners. The statements included in the standards represent guidelines for the development of personnel policies of social agencies that employ social workers. A quick reading will suggest the similarity between items included in the *Standards* and those that tend to appear in union contracts.

Having established these standards of personnel practices, the profession now has a well-defined procedure for dealing with violations of the stated practices. These are incorporated in the NASW "Procedures for Adjudication of Grievances," according to which professional practitioners who feel aggrieved because of substantial defiance of proper personnel practices can seek relief.

B. AFFIRMATIVE ACTION

An increasingly important consideration in the administration of personnel concerns the ways in which affirmative action requirements are met by social agencies. This is particularly true where public resources are made available for social programs. Objectives of equal opportunity in employment are mandated by statutes and administrative regulations, and organizations are required to adhere to designated standards and procedures.

Few issues in personnel management have engendered as much discussion and anxiety as affirmative action policies, and few have occasioned more political activity and public debate. Most recently, issues defined as reverse discrimination have come to the fore as goals and timetables for action have been implemented. The policy context of equality of opportunity versus equality of results is frequently at the heart of the controversy.

Buttrick reviews the legislative history of affirmative action and examines the relationship between efforts to guarantee equal employment opportunity, unionization, and seniority. A social economy of contradiction and scarcity exacerbates competition between minority and majority and poses severe problems in achieving intergroup parity. Policy issues and dilemmas are identified and partial solutions suggested in what is surely to become an increasing preoccupation of even-handed administration.

Lovell deals with three issues that surround some of the controversial areas of affirmative action. She indicates why she feels that preferential hiring, active antidiscrimination efforts, and the reexamination of conventional quality standards and measures are necessary to overcome the apparent exclusion of women and minorities from many areas of professional employment, and particularly in advanced positions of authority.

C. LABOR RELATIONS AND COLLECTIVE BARGAINING

Social workers have been organized in labor unions for more than four decades. The history of this movement is dotted with conflict both within professional ranks and between workers and employers. Questions have periodically been raised about the applicability of the industrial model of unionism to social service institutions. Similarly, ethical considerations have been directed to the right to strike, particularly where matters of safety and client survival were at stake.

The profession has rather consistently maintained a policy of support for the right of employees to bargain collectively through instruments of their own choice. The *Standards for Social Work Personnel Practices of NASW* clearly states that participation in a strike "does not in itself constitute a violation of the Code of Ethics," and that the professional association "is opposed to laws or policies that prohibit strikes by employees." When a strike cannot be prevented, both management and the union are urged to staff essential services to avert threats to life and safety.

Alexander reviews the debate concerning the alleged incompatibility between unionization and professionalization. The latter is presumed to be directed to such matters as enhancement of standards and service to clients, while the former pursues matters of self-interest such as financial gain and improved conditions of work. Alexander explores the conditions under which the two are incompatible and under which they are complementary and reinforcing. In the face of declining membership in trade unions, particularly of the blue-collar variety, unions organizing professionals have shown dramatic gains. Alexander concludes that rejecting unionization because it is thought to be unprofessional is unsound in theory, in historical perspectives, and in the current reality.

Tambor examines administrative resistance to collective bargaining, which he sees as rooted in concepts of elitism, paternalism, and professionalism. He sets forth the reasons that motivate social workers to organize on the one hand and to resist organizational efforts on the other. Bargaining rights, the scope of bargaining, and issues of client service are examined through the experiences of social workers in New York City and Chicago. Tambor contends that social workers, like other workers, are wage earners, and sees them increasingly identifying their interests with collective bargaining and unions.

Issues concerning strikes by social workers and continued service to clients are probed by Lightman. Here again, professional vs. personal values and interests occupy attention. Lightman contrasts American and Canadian experience with strikes and the extent of unionization. In order to explore attitudes toward striking, he conducted personal interviews with members of the Metropolitan Toronto branch of the Ontario Association of Professional Social Workers. Although the subjects had limited personal experience with strikes, the vast majority had no objection in principle to striking. Quality of service was seen as a more important strike issue than traditional union concerns such as compensation and job security. Union demands, such as smaller case loads, are seen as enhancing client service.

D. ADMINISTRATIVE ETHICS IN SOCIAL AGENCIES

In making organizational decisions, administrators continually face the alternative of choosing what is thought to be the right thing to do or opting for what is organizationally expedient. When things go well and resources are relatively plentiful, such choices are easy to make. Doing what is right, as long as it is rooted in principles of competent professional practice, is relatively devoid of pain. When resources are constricted, the kinds of decisions one must make, such as curtailing programs and activities or choosing between equally worthy clients, are fraught with difficulty and anguish. In a benign political environment, activities that counter prevailing sentiment are more easily tolerated and encouraged. A regressive ethos calls for courage, skill, and determination when challenging the status quo. Yet such activity may have strong ethical sanction and beckon administrative leadership in times of stress and uncertainty.

Issues of these sorts involve, at the core, questions of ethics, that is, of right and good conduct. Such conduct needs to be shaped out of the identity of administrative purpose with client service integrity. In the professions, such principles of conduct tend to be incorporated in codes of professional ethics that become elaborated over time as experience and judgment mature.

In recent years, concern for ethical principles in the human services has spawned a growing literature and stimulated interest in professional conferences and academic curricula. Although clarifying the ground on which ethical considerations are nourished, the codes of conduct hardly provide final and conclusive guides for organizational behavior. In part, this is a consequence of the often-contradictory character of competing ethical postulates and of the ways in which assumptions derive from alternative ideologies and value premises.

The selections in this section discuss ethical behavior in social agencies. These concern both individual and organizational ethics, particularly as they reflect the current political and economic environment.

Levy presents a tentative framework toward codification of some of the basic requirements for ethical behavior in the management of social agencies. He includes managerial ethics in relation to organizational administration, to colleagues and clients, to sources of funding, and to the community. Implicit in the discussion is the relationship between canons of professional practice and ethical foundations. To be professional is to be ethical. In the hierarchy of values that support competent administrative practice, Levy suggests that ethical considerations are transcendent. Other dimensions of skill are clearly essential, but in this context are hardly sufficient.

The dramatic changes in the current social policy environment, with its extensive curtailment of federal and state resources for social program, form the backdrop for the next selection. Reisch and Taylor focus on an additional dimension of the pervasive phenomenon of cutback management—its ethics. They contrast ethical and technical responses to the demands of retrenchment, and suggest that these cannot avoid considerations of values, equity, and social justice. It is in the ethics of distribution that they locate the essential dilemmas of choice. They see the social allocation of goods, services, and benefits on the basis of efficiency and utilitarian criteria as wanting from the perspective of what is socially fair and just. Reisch and Taylor propose a set of guidelines for administering curtailed resources based largely on Rawls' concept of distributive justice, and include the political dimension of administrative action. One effect of acting on these guidelines is the enhancement of equality goals at a time when economic trends and politics are moving in an opposite direction.

A. Personnel Practices

16

NASW Standards for Social Work Personnel Practices

NATIONAL ASSOCIATION OF SOCIAL WORKERS, INC.

GENERAL PRINCIPLES

These standards are based on the principles that (1) effective social service depends on qualified staff and (2) staff members can give their best service when they work under conditions of employment that are conducive to the maintenance of high quality and quantity of performance. Since the provision of responsible services to individuals, groups, and communities is the paramount concern of the social work profession, these standards are issued with the understanding that they will always be applied within the framework of this fundamental concern of the profession.

For social workers to function at their best, every organization employing them should have policies pertaining to personnel administration developed by a cooperative process involving staff, board, and administration. These policies should be available to all members of the staff and governing boards. As standards of good practice, they apply equally to administrative personnel and, except when indicated, to professional and nonprofessional staff.

An agency's personnel policies should include a clear, practical plan for affirmative action to achieve a workforce that is free of racial or sexual discrimination. They should also allow for the nondiscriminatory administration of personnel matters.

Staff should participate in the development of personnel policies and in regular periodic review of them. The policies should include provision for hearing staff members' grievances and other provisions substantially similar to those that follow. These policies are endorsed by NASW and recommended by the association to practicing social workers, to employing agencies, and to the supporting public as being basic to good personnel administration and good social work practice.

These standards represent principles of sound personnel policies and practices. They are not intended to substitute for the formulation by specific agencies of their own personnel policies. However, they have been formulated to serve as a guide in the development of personnel policies by social agencies and other institutions employing social workers, such as health agencies, schools, and courts. When NASW has occasion to review personnel practices in specific organizations, these standards serve as a basis for recommendations to improve them.

As part of the NASW program for improving personnel policies, procedures have been established under which the association considers complaints filed by social workers against employers alleging violations of written personnel practices.[1] When complaints are filed against an employer who does not have written personnel policies, these standards are used in the process of adjudicating the complaint.

STANDARDS

1.0 Professional Ethics

The agency shall recognize and respect the NASW Code of Ethics for social workers. It shall uphold the responsibility of the social worker to abide by the Code of Ethics, as expressed in the preamble and in the specific principles for professional conduct the code contains. The agency's policies or regulations shall be consistent with the principles of sound professional conduct represented by the code. [EDITOR'S NOTE: See Appendix.]

2.0 Affirmative Action

Every employer shall prepare and make public a plan for affirmative action to achieve a workforce free of discrimination and prejudice. Public employers are governed in this by the Equal Employment Opportunity Act of 1972, as well as by other state and federal laws, and should follow the suggestions prepared to implement these requirements.[2]

Employers in the private and nonprofit sectors are also covered by Title VII of the Equal Employment Opportunity Act of 1972 in prohibiting discrimination. Affirmative action to eliminate present and future discrimination is not required by this act, but a plan should be prepared by every employer. Comprehensive guidelines and suggestions for the preparation of an affirmative action plan are available from the U.S. Equal Employment Opportunity Commission.[3]

The following elements represent the basic principles of an affirmative action program:

1. The agency should have a strong policy and commitment to implementing it.
2. Responsibility and authority for the program should be assigned to a top agency administrator.
3. The present workforce should be analyzed to identify sections or occupations in which minorities, women or men, are underutilized.
4. Specific, measurable, and attainable hiring and promotion goals should be set, with target dates for each area of underutilization.
5. In large agencies, each section manager should be responsible and accountable for helping to meet the goals.
6. Job descriptions, hiring criteria, and job classifications should be reviewed to assure that they reflect actual job needs.
7. The agency should actively search for minorities and women who qualify or can become qualified.
8. All personnel and employment procedures should be reviewed and revised to assure that they do not have a discriminatory effect and that they help attain goals.
9. Procedures or a system to monitor and measure progress regularly should be developed.

3.0 Nondiscrimination

In all personnel actions and relations, there shall be no discrimination based on personal characteristics that do not directly relate to the performance of an individual's duties. Such personal characteristics include race, physical handicap, sex, sexual orientation, color, age, residence, national origin, organizational membership, or political belief. Employers of social workers shall recognize the right of employees as professionals and private citizens to engage in social action and political activity. The rare situations in which discrimination or action based on these factors may be appropriate shall be specifically identified, justified in writing, and made known to all interested parties.

4.0 Selection of Personnel

Personnel shall be selected on the basis of professional competence, which is designed to assure appointment of persons best qualified to discharge the agency's function effectively. In recruiting personnel, the agency shall, at the appropriate time and place, make the following known to prospective employees:

1. Specific requirements of and salary range for the vacant position.
2. Qualifications sought in the candidates for the position.
3. The agency's commitment to affirmative action.
4. Personnel practices of the agency.
5. Any anticipated changes in agency structure and function having direct bearing on the position to be filled.

An agency recruiting to fill a vacant position shall inform members of its own staff who might be interested in and qualified for the position of its availability and allow such staff members to apply for the position. When a merit system is in effect, the agency shall hold promotional assembled or unassembled examinations for its own staff members in addition to holding open competitive examinations.

In the course of evaluating a candidate for a position, written references shall be obtained. Requests for references should state that the requesting agency will feel free to share references with the applicants. References provided with a request that they not be shared should be returned and not considered. Informal, verbal discussions of an applicant with a previous employer should not supplant open, honest reference-giving.

Appointment to a position shall be in writing, with duties, compensation, conditions of employment, and the place of the position in the general function and program of the agency set forth. After an appointment is made, any major change in the assignment or conditions of employment shall be confirmed in a letter to the employee. Letters of appointment, as well as letters regarding changes in assignment or conditions of employment, should be acknowledged by the employee in writing.

5.0 Probation

Probationary periods serve a dual purpose: to permit the employer to evaluate the employee's performance and to provide an opportunity for the employee to assess whether the agency provides a suitable setting for his or her professional interests.

When a probationary period is required, it shall be for a specified period of time. A minimum of three months and a maximum of six months is recommended for professional personnel. The end of such a period shall be marked by a mutual evaluation and by a clear decision by both employer and employee regarding the retention of the employee in the new position on the regular staff. Should the employee decide to terminate employment at the end of the probationary period, this decision should not be reflected adversely in the employee's references or record.

After satisfactory completion of the probationary period, all agency personnel policies and benefits shall apply retroactively to the date of employment with the agency.

6.0   Personnel Manual

Personnel practices and procedures shall be an integral part of the agency and shall be provided to employees on entering duty and readily available thereafter. The development and revision of the practices shall be the responsibility of the policymaking body, with participation by the staff (e.g., through staff and board personnel committees, a staff advisory committee, union representation).

The agency executive shall have the responsibility of implementing the policies and assuring that there is effective communication between the various staff and administrative levels. A specific procedure for preparing and amending the manual should be written.

The manual shall be reviewed at least biennially. Changes in the manual shall be set forth in writing and copies of such changes provided all employees. The manual shall include the following:

1. A description of the agency's functions, organizational structure, and administrative lines of authority and responsibility and how they are delegated or shared.
2. A clear statement of the agency's purposes and goals, including its commitment to affirmative action.
3. A clear definition of the ways in which new policies and/or practices or modifications thereof are established and implemented.

7.0   Grievances

Provision shall be made for a fair and impartial hearing if the employee believes he or she has been unjustly affected by a personnel action or policy of the agency. Such procedures shall be in writing and include the following:

1. Clearly defined procedures for due process, including a hearing, and the right to appeal. An opportunity for the employee to confer with supervisory and administrative superiors, as needed, shall be provided.
2. Provision for representation, when desired, by a staff member.
3. Provision for the protection of the employer's right to have a written statement describing the basis of the specific action giving rise to the grievance and the employer's right and responsibility to present in writing the specific basis for his or her dissatisfaction.

4. Opportunity for consideration of the alleged grievance by at least an intraagency committee or other group capable of providing judicious review. The appropriate committee or group should be specified in the agency's procedures.
5. Opportunity for the employee to present testimony before an impartial body considering the alleged grievance, directly or through witnesses, and to have a representative of his or her own choice.
6. A clear delineation of the person or persons having authority for making the final decision.

8.0   Labor-Management Relations

NASW reaffirms that social workers as employees shall participate in the formulation of personnel policies and procedures. NASW further reaffirms that members of the association may participate in this formulation through whatever instruments they choose democratically and reaffirms the responsibility of management to accept and work with the means chosen by the employee group.

Employees of nonprofit organizations and public agencies should be included under the protective enactment of state labor relations laws, including provisions that guarantee collective bargaining rights. NASW supports the collective bargaining process between organized labor and management as one means of providing a rational and coherent method of solving problems inherent in employee-employer relationships and thereby achieving conditions of employment conducive to optimum service to clients.

Professional values will guide the manner in which NASW members, whether as union members or part of management, participate in collective bargaining. Management and labor should be encouraged to adopt a procedure that approaches *continuous negotiations* as a means of avoiding the trauma of deadline-determined agreements. Labor and management are responsible for understanding and utilizing effectively all the tools at the disposal of those involved in bargaining in a free society—including mediation, arbitration, and the fact-finding panel or board—as a means of finding solutions to problems when direct negotiations have failed to provide an agreement between the employer and the union. The fact of participation in a strike by a member of NASW does not in itself constitute a violation of the Code of Ethics. NASW is opposed to laws or policies that prohibit strikes by employees.

NASW as professional association shall not engage in collective bargaining on behalf of its members or assume the technical responsibilities of mediation, independent fact-finding, or arbitration. This will not preclude use of individual social workers as mediators, fact-finders, or arbitrators. In the event of a labor dispute, NASW shall use its good offices to keep communications open and should know and encourage the use of competent resources for mediation, fact-finding, and arbitration. This does not preclude NASW's taking a position for or against either party in a specific conflict situation.

The agency management has ultimate responsibility for service to the people it has offered to serve. In the event of a work stoppage, however, both management and the union should work together to define and plan for staffing emergency services essential to the preservation of the lives and safety of people served by the agency. When there is a union contract, provision for emergency services should be included.

9.0   Classification Plans

To achieve the purpose and carry out the functions of an agency program effectively and efficiently, there shall be a classification of all positions based on their relative complexity and responsibility that will clarify the duties of the positions and serve as a basis for employment interviews, equitable salary administration, and other personnel purposes. NASW has prepared standards for both preprofessional and professional social work staff that should be used as a basic classification format within which the agency will need to establish its own classification structure.[4]

The classification plan shall include a statement or table showing the grouping of each position with other positions of a similar level of complexity and responsibility and a statement placing this grouping or classification of positions in proper relationship to other classifications of positions. It shall be in writing and be provided to staff. There shall be provision for continuing periodic review of positions and their classification.

A job description shall be prepared for each position and should include the following:

1. A title that accurately reflects the functions of the position.
2. A listing or description of the duties and responsibilities assigned and the quality and quantity of performance expected.
3. A statement of the minimum qualifications required to perform the duties of the position.
4. A clear statement of the responsibility for supervision of each level.

10.0   Salary Policy

In furtherance of its purpose to promote the quality and effectiveness of social work practice through service to the individual, the group, and the community, NASW seeks to develop and support policies, procedures, and programs that will help recruit and retain qualified and competent personnel to staff these services.

Of equal importance to creating an adequate supply of professionally qualified personnel is the retention of these people in the profession. Experienced and well-qualified personnel provide a basic core for the profession. Their accumulated wisdom and experience are needed to add to knowledge and skill and to raise standards of performance. These experienced workers are also essential for pre-service and in-service education and research. They provide essential leadership. Well-qualified persons must not be lost to more remunerative fields because adequate compensation for years of experience is not available in social work employment.

The association has adopted a salary policy that recommends a minimum salary level for the classification levels defined in the NASW *Standards for Social Service Manpower*. These minimums are periodically reviewed by the Board of Directors and are set to assure that the following are reflected: (1) changes in cost of living, (2) changes in standard of living, (3) increases in national productivity, (4) changes in salaries paid for positions requiring comparable education and experience, (5) assurance that the minimum represents a figure that is attainable and equitable, and (6) changes based on regional salary patterns. For the practitioner who meets the normal expectations of increased competence and responsibility, an annual increase in salary of 6 to 8 percent is recommended.

11.0 Pay Plan

There shall be a pay plan made up of a salary range for each class of position to assure that social workers receive equitable treatment in salaries and to assure efficient administration of an agency. The pay plan shall

1. Cover each group of positions in the classification plan.
2. Indicate the salary range for each class of positions and the amount and frequency of increments. It should also state whether increments are periodic or based on merit.
3. Include appropriate salary steps *within* and among job levels to reflect requirements of or achievements in education, training, and experience.
4. Provide for annual review and consultation with staff.
5. Provide for annual cost-of-living adjustments as fully as agency resources allow.

The salary range assigned to each job classification shall be high enough to attract and retain competent professional personnel. It shall take into account the extent and nature of the responsibilities, qualifications required, and rates of pay for comparable positions in other agencies or fields. Salary ranges for each classification shall provide enough latitude to allow a social worker to enhance performance and to continue in a position without being deprived of salary advancement or forced to take on a different assignment. When the beginning salary recommendations change, there shall be corresponding increases in the salary ranges for experienced workers at different levels of responsibility.

There shall be a systematic progression and a logical relationship between the salary ranges assigned to different classifications. When a social worker's duties and responsibilities are changed through promotion or increased significantly through a revised job description, the job should be reclassified and the salary increased accordingly. When the agency's salary ranges overlap, the principle of increased pay for increased responsibility shall apply. This principle would prevail even if the social worker received a salary on the previous assignment equal to or higher than the minimum of the salary range for the new classification.

There shall be provision in the pay plan for annual increments within each salary range. The annual increments shall be a specified percentage of the social worker's salary for all positions in the salary classification plan. The pay plan shall exclude payments "in kind" as part of total salary payments.

Additional merit increments should be given for unusual or superior performance that exceeds specific agency standards. If performance is unsatisfactory, regular increments can be withheld for a specified period not to exceed one year. Either improved performance or termination of employment in a specific position should result.

Temporary reclassification and pay adjustment shall be provided for regular employees who, in the absence of some other staff member, are assigned duties heavier than those they usually carry when such an assignment persists for a period exceeding the longest compensated leave possible in the agency.

12.0   Reimbursement of Expenses

Expenses incidental to the job shall be provided by the agency in addition to salary. Policies governing payment of such expenses shall be established to cover actual costs. For example, staff members shall be reimbursed for the following:

1. Costs incurred in connection with attendance at luncheons, conferences, and the like when attended at the request or direction of the agency.
2. Actual out-of-pocket expenses.
3. Mileage rates sufficient to cover actual costs of operating and maintaining a car.

4. Expenses incurred in purchasing liability insurance when such extra expenses arise from use of a personal car for business purposes.
5. Local transportation on agency business.
6. Expenses incurred in travel on agency business.

Reimbursement should be on the basis of written accounts detailing the nature of the expenses and amounts.

13.0 Secondary Employment

Secondary employment is employment on a paid basis engaged in by an individual in addition to a primary employment obligation. It can provide personal satisfaction and enhance professional competence.

NASW reaffirms that a social worker's remuneration from primary employment should provide the means to maintain a standard of living appropriate for professional personnel in the community. Secondary employment to supplement income for this purpose should, therefore, not be necessary.

When private practice is the secondary employment, the NASW standard for the private practice of social work—membership in the Academy of Certified Social Workers—is to be observed.[5]

The following provisions shall govern secondary employment:

13.1 AFTER REGULAR WORKING HOURS

1. An employee has the right to engage in secondary employment as long as it does not interfere in any way with his responsibilities to his primary employer. Agencies should have governing policies, including provisions that safeguard agency operations when secondary employment may entail conflict of interest or when there is evidence that it would negatively affect job performance.
2. Remuneration from secondary employment shall accrue solely to the employee.
3. When the primary employer's facilties and/or resources are used, the employee should obtain prior written approval. If reimbursement for such use is required by the agency, there should be a written understanding of the nature of such reimbursement.
4. The primary employer and the employee should establish a clear and written agreement which assures that the employee will not provide services in secondary employment to clients who otherwise would be served by the primary employer except when mutually agreed on.

13.2 DURING REGULAR WORKING HOURS

Activities such as teaching, conducting seminars, and speaking engagements for which the employee is reimbursed are illustrations of this kind of secondary employment.

1. An employee has the obligation to seek advance approval of his employing agency for this kind of assignment. Although such activity may have secondary benefits to the employing agency, the agency retains final authority for approval.
2. Remuneration from this type of activity shall accrue to the employee.
3. Agencies should have policies governing this type of employment. If such policies include a provision for reimbursement to the primary employer for the time the employee is actually absent, it may be in the form of deductions from earnings or by requiring the employee to utilize earned compensatory, vacation, or other leave time other than sick leave.

14.0   Use of Volunteers

The primary purposes for the use of volunteers shall be to enrich, extend, or otherwise to supplement the services of agency staff for the benefit of clients. When volunteers are used, the agency shall have a written policy that includes the following points:

1. A clear definition of the functions and activities appropriate for volunteer and paid staff.
2. Written descriptions of activity for each type of volunteer used and clear procedures that relate the volunteer to regular, paid staff.
3. Provision for reimbursement to volunteers for expenses, as appropriate.
4. Procedures for orienting and training as well as for monitoring the activities and contributions of volunteers to the service or program.
5. A statement of assurance that volunteers will not be utilized in any way that would decrease the use of paid personnel. It should be a fundamental personnel policy of any agency or institution making use of unpaid volunteers that such personnel will not be permitted to supplant regular, paid staff.

15.0   Staff Development

An orientation period shall be provided for any employee newly appointed to a position, whether coming from within or outside the agency, for the purpose of informing the employee of the specific job duties and their relation to agency function. The agency shall establish both policies and opportunities for ongoing staff development. Continued professional growth shall be expected by the agency of all professional employees. Formal means for professional growth become increasingly vital as requirements for maintenance of licenses become universal.

Opportunities for continued staff development shall be afforded through provision of the following:

15.1 INTERNAL AGENCY RESOURCES

1. Supervision and consultation from professionally qualified persons.
2. Availability of agency-acquired professional literature.
3. Regular, planned staff meetings for discussion of the agency's program and social work problems and methods in those agencies large enough to support them.
4. A structured staff development program with qualified training staff.

15.2 USE OF EXTERNAL RESOURCES

1. Links with educational institutions to provide opportunities for continuing education in social work, at both postbaccalaureate and postmaster's levels.
2. Use of adult community educational resources in a planned career development program for personnel with less than a baccalaureate degree who are providing social services.
3. Dissemination of information regarding conferences, institutes, workshops, and so forth related to the functions and goals of the agency.

15.3 EDUCATIONAL LEAVE

1. Provision should be made for leave during working hours to attend conferences, institutes, workshops, or classes to advance the employee's skills related to the functions and goals of the employing agency. Such attendance in accordance with agency policy shall result in no loss of pay or vacation time.
2. Provision should be made for extended leaves for educational purposes so that employees may continue to upgrade professional credentials and further develop professional skills. Provisions for educational leave should be such as to make it financially feasible for employees to take such leaves.

Terms of such leaves should be clearly set forth. The worker on leave should be considered an employee, with all rights and benefits protected.

15.4 FINANCIAL AID

It is the responsibility of the agency to make available to personnel information about opportunities for state, federal, or private grants-in-aid, scholarships, fellowships, or loans.

16.0 Financial Aid for Professional Education

Social work agencies and other employers of social workers should support programs of financial aid by contributing to university or community programs, developing their own programs, or supporting appropriate legislation at federal, state, or local levels designed to increase the professional social work labor force.

The establishment of restrictive conditions in the granting of financial aid or the imposition of employment commitments frequently limits the effectiveness of such programs. Experience and research in administration of financial aid programs have shown that social work students do not have sufficient knowledge of the range of social work methods or fields of practice or of their own skills and professional interests to choose among prospective job offerings at the beginning of their professional education. Therefore, the imposition of employment commitments should be discouraged.

When agencies establish programs of financial aid to students for professional education at the baccalaureate, master's or doctoral level, the following practices shall be observed:

1. The agency will help applicants evaluate all available opportunities and help them understand fully the terms of the agreement.
2. The grant will cover the full period required for completion of the degree without interruption. Agency support should be discontinued only if the student withdraws or is advised by the school to withdraw from professional education or if the terms of the agreement are no longer applicable.
3. The student who is an agency employee on educational leave will retain seniority rights and status with respect to employee benefits included in the agency personnel program.

A written agreement shall be made between the agency and the student, taking into account the following:

1. The amount of the grant and the period of time it covers.
2. Any commitment requiring the recipient of the grant to accept employment in the agency following completion of professional education should not exceed a period equivalent to that covered by the financial aid grant. When the student is on a work-study program and

continues in active service with the agency during part of his professional education, the time spent in agency service should be credited.
3. A clear statement of conditions under which the agency may terminate the agreement, including a statement of procedures to be followed if the student does not complete professional education or, for valid unforeseen reasons, is unable to fulfill the requirements of the agreement. If financial restitution is part of the agreement, terms for repayment should be specified, usually without interest.

17.0 Participation in Activities of Professional Organizations

Social work, like other professions, has undertaken professional activities largely through the voluntary participation of its qualified members. Individual members have viewed and should view such participation as part of their professional commitment. Agencies should encourage such professional activities and make time available to social workers for them.

Since the range of professional activities is broad and varied, the agency should grant the worker time off to participate in such activities when prior discussions have concluded that the professional activity coincides with the agency's specific goals and the time off will not jeopardize the daily functioning of the agency. In those instances in which the social worker has been assigned activities; chosen to serve on such bodies as national boards, commissions, task forces, or committees; or asked to present a paper or lead a professional institute, the agency should offer no impediment to the social worker's need for time off from agency responsibility. Time off for professional activities under these circumstances should not result in the loss of vacation, salary, or compensatory time.

18.0 Evaluations

As a basis for objective evaluation of performance, the agency shall set forth written standards of performance for all positions in its classification plan. Such standards shall describe the quality and quantity of performance expected for each job duty.

Each employee shall develop specific performance objectives, for the supervisor's approval and shall participate with the supervisor in the periodic review and revision of these performance objectives. Evaluations of performance shall be based on the agency's written standards for the position and the specific performance objectives. Evaluations shall be made by the person or persons who directly supervise the employee.

Evaluations shall be made annually, or on another agreed-on schedule, (1) when required for the professional development of the employee or the administrative needs of the agency, (2) when there has been a significant change in the performance of the employee, or (3) when the employee or the supervisor leaves the agency. When a probationary period is required, there shall be an evaluation at the end of that period.

The evaluation shall relate specifically to the performance of the job assigned to the employee and, when indicated, to such personal behavior as is not in accord with NASW's Code of Ethics.

The time of the evaluation shall be known in advance. Evaluation shall engage the joint participation of the employee and supervisor. However, the authority of the evaluator must be recognized on both sides and final authority belongs to the supervisor.

The evaluation shall be placed in writing and shall cover the points discussed in the evaluation conference. The employee shall be given the opportunity to read the evaluation, to sign it (signifying that he or she has read it), and to file a statement covering any points of disagreement. A copy of the evaluation shall be furnished to the employee. The employee shall have the right to obtain a professional review of an evaluation by higher administrative authority in the agency and to add information on his or her performance to the evaluation record.

19.0   References

A copy of the letter of reference shall be provided to the subject of reference on request. The letter of reference shall be prepared by the agency and reviewed by the employee prior to leaving the agency.

References provided by the agency

1. Shall be factually correct and include all pertinent data.
2. Shall state the relationship of the writer to the subject of the reference.
3. Shall be limited in content to material that has been made known to the subject of the reference during the course of his or her employment.

20.0   Personnel Records

A personnel record must be maintained by the agency for each employee. It shall contain the application, contracts or agreements, description of work assignments, performance ratings, and pertinent correspondence. It shall be open and available to the employee and contain no material or information that cannot be shared with the employee.

Material provided to or offered to the agency on a "confidential only" basis shall not be accepted or solicited by the agency or any members of the staff, except when required in law or federal regulation.

The written evaluation and the employee's statement, if any, shall become an integral part of the employee's personnel record. The personnel record shall be kept strictly confidential and be available to authorized persons only. No information on an employee or from a personnel record shall be furnished to persons outside the agency except when specifically authorized by the employee.

21.0 Temporary Employment

Employment for a limited period for specific purposes shall not necessarily be subject to the same conditions of employment that apply to permanent staff. The length of time for which one is employed and the scope, duties, compensation, and conditions of employment pertaining to the temporary position shall be clearly defined.

22.0 Part-Time Employment

Regular permanent employment on a part-time basis shall be subject to the same conditions of employment that apply to full-time permanent staff. Employees changing from full-time to part-time status for any reason should be specifically advised by the agency administration of the resultant changes in their pay, working conditions, or benefits.

23.0 Tenure

An employee who has successfully completed the probationary period in a position for which such is required and who continues to meet the agency's standards of performance shall have the right to continue with the agency except when dismissed for cause or in situations involving the reduction of staff. The policy of indefinite tenure shall be safeguarded by provisions for regular evaluations, specific conditions for termination of employment, and appeals procedures. In situations involving the reduction of staff, the order of layoff among employees of the same or equitable class shall be governed by seniority and the goals of affirmative action.

24.0 Promotion

In filling a vacant position the agency shall first advise its current employees of the forthcoming opening and give first consideration to the promotion of qualified employees within the agency. The promotion of employees shall operate under the same standard governing selection of personnel and the agency's affirmative action plan. That is, there shall be equitable consideration of all professionally qualified applicants without discrimination on such bases as physical disability, race, color, religion, age, residence, sex, sexual orientation, national origin, or membership in a union or an organization whose primary purpose is the protection of civil rights or the improvement of living conditions and/or human relations. Procedures for promotion shall provide for evaluation of persons on the basis of professional competence, which is designed to assure appointment of persons best qualified to discharge the agency's function effectively.

Promotion shall be based on evaluation of past performance, capacity for the vacant position, and the goals of affirmative action. When these factors are relatively equal for two or more employees, seniority shall be the deciding factor.

25.0   Hours of Work

A reasonable number of hours shall be stipulated as the regular workweek. It is recommended that the workweek not exceed 37½ hours.

Overtime on a regular sustained basis shall not be expected or required. When a significant amount of overtime cannot be avoided, provision for compensation should be made. Overtime compensation, paid in time, shall be at the rate of at least 1½ hours per hour worked.

When necessary tasks (case recording, preparation of required reports, and so forth) cannot be reasonably accomplished prior to a professional employee's termination with an agency, the employee and agency share a responsibility to make arrangements to assure completion of the work. Extension of the period of employment, use of compensated overtime, and use of the employee's own time may all be considered. In any event, a clearly understood arrangement shall be agreed on before termination.

Agencies shall make every effort to maintain hours of service that are responsive to community needs and provide opportunities for increasing the individual employee's efficiency. Variations from regularly assigned hours shall be mutually agreeable, insofar as possible, and shall be recorded in memorandums.

For agencies, institutions, or resident camps requiring evening or weekend hours, the plan of hours shall be clearly defined with the following limitations recommended:

1. No more than two work periods per workday.
2. No more than four evening work periods per calendar week.
3. A consecutive forty-eight hour period off in each calendar week.
4. At least one weekend of sixty consecutive hours off per month.

26.0   Annual Leave

A definite period of leave with pay shall be earned for services performed by all regular employees. An employee shall earn leave beginning in the first month of employment. It is recommended that such leave be at least fifteen days for the first year of employment, twenty-one days for the second, third, and fourth years, and twenty-seven days after the fourth year of employment. Such leave shall be accrued in days or hours per pay period.

To encourage the timely use of annual leave, agencies should establish a maximum level of accruable leave and take steps to assure that employees are able to take annual vacations and able to use leave that is accrued. The amount of leave accruable over two years is the recommended maximum amount. An employee leaving the agency shall be entitled to the annual leave due.

27.0   Sick Leave

The agency shall provide leave with pay when the employee is not able to work because of illness or when the employee's presence is temporarily required to care for members of the immediate family.

It is recommended that the rate be no less than twenty-four workdays per year, with the right to accumulate such leave. Recognition should be given to employees who do not need to use sick leave, including the possible arrangements of converting sick leave to other paid leave or for converting a percentage of unused leave to pay at the end of each year.

When an employee has used up accrued sick leave but continues to be absent because of illness, the employee shall be given the opportunity to substitute annual leave. If no annual leave has been accrued or if the employee chooses not to use it for the purpose of sick leave, leave without pay shall be granted for a specified period of time. During absence on leave without pay, the employee shall not accrue sick leave or personal leave but shall retain seniority rights.

28.0   Parental Leave

28.1   MATERNITY LEAVE

Provision should be made for sick leave and leave without pay as maternity leave. Inability to work because of pregnancy shall be considered a medical disability and the employee shall have the right to use sick leave for it. Employees requiring maternity leave shall request it at least sixty days before the date on which the period of leave is to begin. It is recommended that maternity leave be granted for periods up to a maximum of one year. The agency shall reinstate the employee returning from maternity leave to a position comparable to the one she vacated, and she shall be paid at prevailing rates when a suitable vacancy occurs in the staff.

28.2 PATERNITY LEAVE

Fathers whose assistance is needed in the care of children or the mother shall have the right to use leave or to be granted leave without pay if paid leave is not available.

29.0 Military Leave

Military leave shall be granted to employees who are inducted into the armed services. Employees on military leave shall be afforded the protection of their seniority rights and their status in the agency's retirement plan and shall be reassigned promptly on return to civilian life. Provision shall be made so that employees called to individual military reserve training shall suffer no loss of regular income and no loss of vacation time owed them. When an employee chooses alternative services as a conscientious objector or is imprisoned for refusal to serve, he shall receive the same consideration as the employee who accepts military service.

30.0 Jury Duty

Leave for jury duty shall be provided so that employees called to serve on juries suffer no loss of regular income and no loss of vacation time due them.

31.0 Sabbatical Leave

It is recommended that sabbatical leave for personal and professional development be granted to employees after six years of service excluding leave without pay. It is recommended that sabbatical leave consists of at least three months with pay in addition to the annual vacation. Sabbatical leave should be contingent on the employee's return to the agency for a period of at least one year following the leave.

32.0 Holidays

The personnel policy of the agency shall provide for the recognition of all legal and customary community holidays as paid leave time. Such holidays shall be specified in the manual. Employees authorized to work on holidays shall be granted premium pay at a specified rate.

33.0   Working Conditions

Working facilities shall be of such a nature as to afford employees a reasonable degree of comfort, to insure the maintenance of health, and to
make possible the discharge of duties efficiently. Working space and facilities shall afford both privacy for professional activities and dignity for
both employees and clientele.

34.0   Retirement

Retirement shall be defined as the termination of employment under a
specified retirement plan in effect in an agency when the employee has
reached retirement age and no longer wishes to work or is no longer
able to work.

Although the current practice is for planned retirement at the age
of 65, the abilities and needs of individual employees, as well as the functions and staffing requirements of the agency, should be recognized in
any retirement policy. Increasingly it is being recognized that employees
have the right to be employed after they reach age 65 if they are able to
perform satisfactorily. Consideration should also be given to shifting
such employees from full-time to part-time work, but such a shift should
be mutually agreed on. There shall be no discrimination against employees because of age.

The following standards shall be incorporated into the agency's retirement policies and practices:

1. The agency policy shall state the planned retirement age and contain
   provisions for retirement prior to the planned retirement age and for
   continuation of employment beyond such age when the individual's
   performance makes this possible.
2. As employees approach retirement age, there should be consultation
   services available to assist them in making the necessary transitional
   adjustment to retirement.
3. The executive or designated person shall be charged with the responsibility of determining with the individual the plan for retirement or
   continued employment. Such planning shall be initiated six months
   to a year prior to the planned retirement date. The final decision to
   continue employment beyond the planned retirement age is the responsibility of the employer.
4. There shall be a written confirmation of the agreed-on plan.
5. Provision that retirement initiated by the employer shall be handled
   as a grievance and subject to the same process and appeals.
6. Provision for election of retirement prior to or later than the planned
   retirement age, with appropriate adjustment of benefits.

7. Provision for retirement at full benefits prior to the planned retirement age when retirement is necessary because of total and permanent disability.
8. Provision for death benefits at least equal to the current annual salary if death occurs before retirement and while the employee is still on staff. This benefit shall be independent of the refund referred to in the section on pension benefits.

35.0 Pension Plan

The agency shall provide for a pension plan to be administered by a competent retirement system, insurance company, or bank. Employers will need to see that their pension plans meets the standards of the Employee Retirement Income Security Act of 1974. All plans should be fully funded. If the plan is a contributory one, the agency's contribution shall be equal to or greater than that of the staff. It is recommended that the pension plan include the following:

1. Provision that for all regular employees, entrance into the plan be mandatory after a specified period of employment of not more than one year, with optional provision for payment retroactive to the date of employment.
2. Provision for entrance into the pension plan without a waiting period if the employee has had retirement coverage elsewhere.
3. Provision for past-service benefits for employees who have rendered long-time service prior to adoption of the retirement plan.
4. Provision that benefits after twenty-five years of cumulative service be 66 percent or more of the highest three years of salary when the employee has given long-time service in one agency.
5. Provision for full and immediate credit to the employee of equities arising from the agency's and, in case of contributory plans, employee's contributions.
6. Provision for return of the employee's contribution plus interest if he or she leaves the agency and elects a cash refund or provision for return of this contribution to the beneficiary in the event of the employee's death before benefits have begun.
7. Provision for the *portability of pension benefits* or, at least, the retention of benefit rights beyond coverage under the plan.
8. The pension plan shall clearly identify its relationship to and be separate from social security benefits.
9. When legally permissible, employers should inform the employees of and make arrangements for tax-sheltered annuity plans when the employees choose this type of plan.
10. Provision for change of beneficiary.

11. Provision for various forms of optional settlement, including the joint and survivor option, guaranteed payments, and variable annuities.
12. Provision for continuance in the plan on an individual basis in the event that change in employment does not permit the individual to participate in a group retirement plan or in case of an approved leave of absence.

It is recommended that employees shall be apprised annually or biennially of benefits accrued to their account as of a given date. It is further recommended that there be a periodic review (at least every two years) of the entire retirement program.

36.0 Insurance Benefits

The agency shall finance, in whole or in part, insurance plans to help employees meet certain financial obligations. The employer shall provide sickness and accident disability insurance. When benefits are available to spouses and families of employees, the benefits shall be granted equally without regard to the sex of the employee or whether the employee is the principal wage earner of the family.

Insurance plans shall include the following:

36.1 HEALTH INSURANCE
Benefits for medical and hospital expenses, including social work services.

36.2 DISABILITY INSURANCE
1. Compensation (including workmen's compensation) equivalent to full salary and medical costs for a period of incapacity up to at least six months when such incapacity is a consequence of a disability incurred in the line of duty.
2. Continued compensation or disability payments for incapacity resulting from a disability incurred in the line of duty, the duration of which exceeds the six-month period referred to above.

36.3 LIABILITY INSURANCE
1. The agency shall provide professional liability insurance.
2. The agency shall provide liability and life insurance for work-related travel.

36.4 UNEMPLOYMENT INSURANCE
Agencies shall provide coverage for unemployment insurance for all employees.

37.0 Termination of Employment

37.1 LAYOFF
1. Layoff shall be defined as removal from a position owing to the abolition of the position because of reorganization or retrenchment.
2. The agency shall establish a formula governing the order in which employees shall be laid off. The formula shall be inversely applied if, at a later date, such employees can be rehired because of reorganization or expansion. Layoff and recall procedures shall conform to the standards included in the section on tenure.
3. The employee who is laid off shall receive severance pay in an amount related to the length of service.

37.2 DEMOTION
1. Demotion shall be construed as removal from a particular position with an offer of a position of lesser responsibility because of the employee's inability to perform in the position of greater responsibility or the abolition of the position of greater responsibility. (See Layoff.)
2. When demotion is offered to more than one employee as an alternative to being laid off, a formula similar to that prescribed to govern layoff shall govern the order in which employees are demoted. The formula shall be applied inversely in the event that those so demoted can at a later date be promoted as a result of agency expansion.

37.3 DISMISSAL
Dismissal shall be construed as the discharge of an employee from an agency because of unsatisfactory job performance, violation of contract, or certain acts contrary to the NASW Code of Ethics.

37.4 RESIGNATION
Resignation shall be construed as termination of employment at the volition of the employee. The employer shall not coerce an employee into resigning by threatening dismissal.

38.0 Termination Notices

38.1 TERMINATION BY EMPLOYER ACTION
1. The employer who terminates the employment of an employee shall give a reasonable amount of notice. It is recommended that the permanent employee be given at least thirty days' notice and the probationary employee at least two weeks' notice, except that when laid off,

the probationary employee shall be entitled to at least thirty days' notice.

2. Pay in lieu of notice may be granted at the discretion of the employer.
3. The employer shall give written notice of the action and the reasons for the action, and the employee shall acknowledge such notice in writing.

38.2 TERMINATION BY EMPLOYEE ACTION

1. The agency shall specify the amount of advance written notice required in instances of resignation and employees shall abide by agency requirements in this matter.
2. The employee shall provide written notice of the intent to resign as of a specific date and the employer shall acknowledge the receipt of this notice in writing.

NOTES

1. "Policies and Procedures," Part 1 of *Manual for the Adjudication of Grievances* (Washington, D.C.: National Association of Social Workers, 1973).
2. *A Guide for Affirmative Action* (rev. ed.; Washington, D.C.: Bureau of Intergovernmental Personnel Programs, U.S. Civil Service Commission, November 1972).
3. *Affirmative Action and Equal Employment: A Guidebook for Employers* (Washington, D.C.: U.S. Equal Employment Opportunity Commission, 1974).
4. *Standards for Social Service Manpower*, Policy Statement 4 (Washington, D.C.: National Association of Social Workers, 1974).
5. *Handbook on the Private Practice of Social Work* (rev. ed.; Washington, D.C.: National Association of Social Workers, 1974).

B. Affirmative Action

17

Affirmative Action and Job Security: Policy Dilemmas

SHIRLEY M. BUTTRICK

A conflict among legitimate rights carries a corresponding obligation to search for remedies that are as equitable as possible. It is in this spirit that the thorny relationship between affirmative action, unionization, and seniority (tenure) is here examined. For while the struggle has been to achieve affirmative action in hiring and promotion that struggle has taken place within an economy of expanding opportunity. Given a situation of contraction or a nogrowth, the issues involved in layoff, as well as in hiring and promotion, surface. The resulting polarization and escalation of racial tension make incumbent the search for solutions.

Do the demands to equalize employment by increasing the percentage of minority and female employees on corporate and university payrolls mean that they are entitled to some special consideration when cutbacks are made? How can layoffs proceed without compromising either the equal employment opportunity obligation (EEO) or the obligation to organized labor? How can promotions be handled in the presence of an increasingly tenured faculty?

To put the discussion in proper perspective, the significant legislation should be noted. Three federal laws and one executive order are important: namely Title VII of the 1964 Civil Rights Act; the Equal Pay Act of 1963 as amended; Title IX of the educational amendments of 1972; and Executive Order 11246 as amended by 11375.

Title VII of the Civil Rights Act covers all employers with fifteen or more employees. It makes it unlawful to discriminate against an individual in hiring and firing, or with respect to compensation, terms, conditions, and privileges of employment because of race, color, religion, sex, or national origin. The most important guidelines pertain to hiring and promotion criteria. Criteria must be spelled out in objective terms. Also, criteria which may seem to be neutral but which adversely affect women or minorities are unlawful unless the employer can demonstrate that the skills measured by the criteria—bona fide occupational qualifications—are actually necessary in the performance of the job. The 1972 amendments expanded the jurisdiction of the Equal Employment Opportunity Commission to include all educational employers, major educational public elementary and primary school systems as well as public and private institutions of higher education. The Equal Pay Act of 1963 prohibits discrimination in regard to wages or fringe benefits based on sex, and in 1972 this act was amended to cover executive, administrative, and professional employees.

Executive Order 11246 has included coverage of sex discrimination since October, 1968, when it was amended by Executive Order 11375.[1] The requirements of the executive order are based on the contractual relationship between the federal government and employers holding contracts with the federal government. As a condition of doing business with the federal government, the employer is required to meet a higher standard than that imposed on employers in general by Title VII. Under the executive order, all employers with federal contracts in excess of $10,000 must agree to take affirmative action to:

1. Eliminate all discriminatory practices against women and minorities.
2. Eliminate, through the establishment of goals and timetables, any underutilization of women or minorities in their work force whether or not the underutilization is a result of prior discriminatory practices.[2]

Employers with contracts in excess of $50,000 must, in addition, develop and maintain an Affirmative Action Plan (AAP). Employers are evaluated on their good faith efforts to meet these goals. In addition, employers awarded contracts in excess of one million dollars must have their AAP's audited and approved prior to issuance of the contract.

Title IX has been in effect since July 1, 1972, and covers sex discrimination in student admissions, treatment of students, and employment of faculty for all educational institutions receiving federal monies from grants, contracts, loans, and so forth. Through this legislation almost every educational institution—elementary, secondary, and postsecondary—is explicitly prohibited from engaging in sex-discriminatory practices. Because the final Title IX regulations were not issued until August, 1975, it is still too soon to determine how the Office of Civil Rights will move.

The main import of the Civil Rights Act is that it permits the Department of Health, Education, and Welfare (HEW) to investigate discrimination and compel its elimination on the basis of the financial relationship between the federal government and the institution; it does not have to wait until a complaint has been filed.[3]

There are some who are still unclear about the concept of equal employment opportunity and affirmative action. EEO refers to the right of all persons to work and to advance on the basis of merit, ability, and potential. Affirmative action represents a way of achieving that goal. This is why there is recognition of the need to analyze the work force, to identify practices that serve to deny women and minorities equal pay, equal privileges, and equal opportunity for employment and promotion. It follows also that conditions of underutilization of women and minorities must be identified and steps taken to correct such underutilization as well as other inequities. What has been misunderstood is that it is "illegal" to have an institution or a department "reserve" a specific position for a female or a minority candidate and thereby exclude other potential candidates from consideration.

While there is much established civil rights law in the area of hiring and promotion, legal guidelines with regard to dismissal and layoffs are only now beginning to take shape. For example, the National Association for the Advancement of Colored People (NAACP) is currently involved in litigation against the policy of determining layoffs, furloughs, and dismissals by seniority.[4]

Case law is also developing around the variety of issues involved in sex discrimination in employment. The courts appear to be moving in the same forceful manner they showed in their decisions on racial discrimination. However, since the bulk of the sex discrimination cases has been filed only during the past few years, most of the key decisions so far have been made at the lower or appellate court levels. The situation is further complicated by the fact that case law has progressed along two different legal paths: under Title VII of the Civil Rights Act and under the 14th amendment to the Constitution. Thus, case law is more highly developed in relation to the specific issues of hiring, promotion, and testing qualifications than, for example, to layoffs.[5]

Take, for example, the case of *Griggs* v. *Duke Power Company*. In that case, Chief Justice Warren E. Burger of the Supreme Court wrote, for a unanimous court:

> The objective of Congress in the enactment of Title VII was to achieve equality of employment opportunities and remove barriers that have operated in the past to favor an identifiable group of white employees over other employees. Under the act, practices, procedures or tests neutral on their face and even neutral in terms of intent cannot be al-

lowed if they operate to "freeze" the status quo of prior discriminatory employment practices.[6]

In *Albermarle Paper Company* v. *Moody* the Supreme Court made back pay a right of victims of discrimination in all but exceptional circumstances.[7] It also tightened the standards an employer must meet in order to use an employment test that disqualifies minorities at a higher rate than it does nonminorities.

More recently, in *Watkins* v. *Local No. 2369*, Federal District Judge Fred J. Cassibry held that the Continental Can Company's plant in Harvey, Louisiana, should not be permitted to use a seniority approach that had the effect of laying off forty-eight out of fifty black employees, mostly because all but two of them had been hired since 1965.[8] Another view appears to reject Judge Cassibry's line of reasoning. The decision of the Court of Appeals in the Seventh Circuit stated that Title VII speaks only to the future and that an employment seniority system embodying the "last-hired, first-fired" principle does not of itself perpetuate past discrimination. "To hold otherwise would be tantamount to shackling white employees with a burden of past discrimination created not by them but by their employer."[9]

In industry there is seniority born of unionization; in universities, tenure born of academic freedom. The issue involves the relationship between tenure, seniority, and affirmative action and the critical effect of employment and layoffs upon these relationships. The conflicting and competing claims all have merit. One cannot erode the progress of the last five years, but the claims of seniority of service are indeed serious ones. It is somewhat encouraging to find organized labor searching for some compromise; that is, for a system of plant-wide seniority rather than seniority by job category or by department. In the meantime, the consistent logic of the courts continues to be that people should not be adversely affected as a result of race or sex.

ISSUES

Even if the issue of layoffs in an economic downturn had not arisen, a problem would still exist in any field or area that was neither actively expanding nor in flux. Thus, we have reached the point in universities, for example, where the tenure decisions of the 1960s may burden the entry of new people into the system. In such a case, the issue will be even more sharply drawn as to whether existing criteria for entry, promotion, and tenure may be at odds with affirmative action criteria. Chait and Ford lean heavily in this direction. They point out that the typical assistant professor has between three and seven years to demonstrate qualifications for tenure. These are years, beyond the doctorate, where women are disadvantaged by childbearing and other responsibilities. Further, they see the Griggs decision as lending support to their view that "credentials" as a criterion for tenure may also be at odds with affirmative action.[10] They lean on a lower federal court decision, namely, *Armstead* v. *Starkville Municipal School District*, as providing additional substance for their view. In that case, the court declared that a public school board had unlawfully discriminated against blacks by tying teachers' appointments and retention to the attainment of a master's degree and specified scores on graduate record examinations that had not been validated as accurate predictors of job performance.[11] The implications of such decisions are that the employers (colleges) have the burden of showing that any given requirement has a clear relationship to job performance.

By 1972, colleges and universities with tenure systems (85 percent of the total) had a median of 41 percent to 50 percent of their faculties on tenure.[12] Given present circumstances, vacancies need to arise from turnover rather than from expansion. The clear effect of tenure, however, is to limit turnover and thus to come into conflict with affirmative action. Unions also offer job security, which vies with tenure. Moreover, academic freedom can just as well be safeguarded through "conditions of employment" clauses. Unlike tenure systems, unions can protect everyone within the bargaining unit and so shift the burden of proof on to management to demonstrate incompetence.

Regardless of one's opinion of the feasibility and desirability of unionization for institutions of higher learning, the fact is that by the fall of 1973, 212 postsecondary institutions had collective bargaining agents. While affirmative action sets up a challenge to the criteria and procedures used to accord tenure, unions also pose a challenge by taking on the traditional goals of tenure, namely employment security and the protection of academic freedom. Does this mean that affirmative action and unionization are themselves compatible? Not at all. Teachers' unions have historically supported fixed pay scales. Such "lock-step" systems are based on length of service and specified credentials. They tend to bar an administrator from offering different salaries to equally qualified employees. Given the realities of the market place, this lock-step system conflicts with affirmative action recruitment. To the extent that retrenchment leads to layoffs, seniority as practiced by unions (unless new formulas are found) will adversely affect minorities and women.

In a January, 1973, directive, William Hodgson, then Secretary of Labor, ordered the Bethlehem Steel Plant at Sparrows Point, Maryland, "to correct a seniority system that has been found to perpetuate the effects of past discrimination in the assignment of blacks to jobs in departments with limited advancement opportunities." As authority to act, Hodgson cited Executive Order 11246, the same order that governs affirmative action for colleges and universities.[13] Chait and Ford maintain that affirmative action and unionization are likely to bring an end to current tenure systems. Where affirmative action conflicts with unionization, they believe federal and state agencies will settle for affirmative action. Could be!

In the meantime, both unions and academic institutions have begun to search for ways to maintain the best of their tenure and seniority systems while permitting some innovation and flexibility.

DIRECTIONS

Universities have begun the process of rethinking and changing their traditional tenure commitments. The most pressing reason is financial. Some universities now require an extended probationary period, others have set tenure quotas, some offer only renewable contracts (which are usually renewed). The aim is to provide both financial and curricular flexibility, and in this respect, tenure guidelines and affirmative action plans have some elements of compatibility, at least in the short run. For that matter, unionization and affirmative action plans may be somewhat compatible in the long run. For as women and minorities become a more significant constituency, union policies which discriminate against them will have to undergo change.

As tenure has come under increasing attack, even its staunchest supporters have begun to consider the choices to be made in arriving at some reasonable guidelines. What are the choices and what shall the stated policy be? In a situation where there is little or no growth in the total number of faculty members, what are the limits to the tenuring-in process? What are the critical variables that must be considered?

The American Association of University Professors, justifiably uneasy with the setting of tenure limits, has identified several variables which must be considered, such as the annual attrition rate of those who have tenure, the annual promotion rate, and the fraction of tenured faculty lost by attrition who are replaced by nontenured appointments.[14] Each one of these variables represents a possible policy position which can affect the tenure ratio. For example, it is possible to achieve a tenure ratio of 0.67 by doing all replacements at the nontenured level, with a tenured attrition rate of 0.05 and an annual promotion rate of 0.10. It is also possible to keep the desired tenure ratio of 0.67 by replacing half of the tenured losses by tenure appointments if the attrition rate were 0.05. In that case, the promotion rate would have to drop to 0.05.[15]

All of this is intended to emphasize that there are choices to be made, that tradeoffs are possible between attrition, promotion, and replacement, and that it is useful to make such choices explicit. One way to decrease the tenuring-in problem is to raise standards. Or the annual promotion rate can be lowered, and a faculty member spend more time in a non-tenured rank. Greater turnover can be encouraged within the tenure ranks. The tenure ratio is itself a choice variable. But when an acceptable ratio has been chosen, a set of policies compatible with it should be stated. Such decisions involve knowing the tradeoffs that are involved and should be made with the full participation of faculty members.

The illustrations utilized for tenure decisions are also applicable to seniority decisions. New York City Human Rights Commissioner Eleanor Holmes Norton has been asking employers to consider cost savings by means such as a reduced work week, shift changes, payless work days, and job cuts across categories and departments to spread the burden. Certainly business, caught between minority and feminist organizations, organized labor, and the civil rights enforcement machinery, wants some formula that will allow layoffs without jeopardizing either its EEO obligations or its obligations to organized labor. All are in agreement that the issue is prickly. Yet all are equally agreed that traditional methods are no longer workable and that modifications in the seniority system are in order. Had the recession gone much deeper, there would have been no way to avoid a solution, however faulty. The problem is not easily resolved to anyone's satisfaction, for the clash of interests is potentially explosive. Serious ideas must be brought forward and pat answers discarded. It is to be hoped that this discussion will make a small contribution in that direction.

NOTES

1. Roslyn Kane, *Sex Discrimination in Education*, Vol. I. This report was prepared under contract No. 300–75–0205, Education Division, National Center for Education Statistics, Department of Health, Education, and Welfare, 1976.
2. Regulations issued pursuant to Executive Order 11246, 41 C.F.R. 60–2.
3. Kane, *op. cit.*, p. x–7.
4. The NAACP argues for "racial ratios," that is, it asserts that an employer should have the same proportion of blacks after a layoff as it had before the layoff.
5. For an excellent summary of selected cases, see Kane, *op. cit.*, Section XI, pp. 1–19.
6. *Griggs* v. *Duke Power Co.*, U.S. Supreme Court, 1971, 401 U.S. 424 S. Ct. 849, 28 L. Ed., 158 (1971).
7. U.S. Supreme Court, 10 FEP 1181, June 25, 1975.
8. *New York Times*, January 29, 1975, p. 17.
9. *Ibid.*
10. Richard Chait and Andrew T. Ford, "Affirmative Action, Tenure, and Un-

ionization," in Dyck Vermillye, editor, *Lifelong Learners: Issues in Higher Education* (San Francisco: Jossey Bass, 1975), p. 125.

11. *Armstead* v. *Starkville Municipal School District*, 325F. Supp. 560 (1971).
12. Chait and Ford, *op. cit.*, p. 126.
13. *Ibid.*, p. 129.
14. "Surviving the Seventies, report on the Economic Status of the Profession, 1972–1973. Part III: Tenuring-in." 59th Annual Meeting of the American Association of University Professors, AAUP *Bulletin*, LIX (1973), 198–203; Richard R. West, "Tenure Quotas and Financial Flexibility in Colleges and Universities," *Educational Record*, Spring, 1974, pp. 96–100.
15. See AAUP *Bulletin, op. cit.*, p. 20, for the formula which illustrates the limit to the Tenuring-in process where there is no growth in total faculty.

18

Three Key Issues in Affirmative Action

CATHERINE LOVELL

As we attempt to implement affirmative action policies, three key issues always arise. *First*, the distinction between affirmative action and "nondiscrimination"; *second*, why preferential hiring and the setting of target quotas are necessary to the affirmative action process; and *third*, why traditional standards of "quality" must be reexamined.

Until these issues are resolved, successful affirmative action programs cannot be implemented and substantial progress toward eliminating job discrimination will not be made. Their resolution will require fundamental shifts in individual values as well as changes in some of our collective norms.

UNDERSTANDING THE DIFFERENCE BETWEEN AFFIRMATIVE ACTION AND NONDISCRIMINATION

The distinction between affirmative action and nondiscrimination is the difference between the *active* and the *passive* mode. It is illustrated by the difference between management by objectives and incrementalism. All of our public agencies have been "equal opportunity employers" operating under fair employment practices laws for nearly 30 years. What those laws require are policy statements against discrimination. The absence of overt discrimination has sufficed to meet this standard. Action is left to the individual applicant. Affirmative action, in contrast, requires more than passive nondiscrimination by the organization—it demands active programs of broadly applied preferential hiring systems. It requires definition of objectives for redressing employment imbalances and implementation of plans for reaching those objectives.

Setting operational goals, and developing criteria for measurement of progress toward these goals, is much talked about these days in management theory. Administrators, however, still more often than not observe such decision rules more in theory than in the doing, particularly in situations of strongly conflicting objectives and values. Yet, goal setting, action programs, and evaluation are the modus operandi of affirmative action. Affirmative action demands more from organizational leaders than lack of prejudice and belief in equal opportunity; operationalizing affirmative action requires leaders to take action stances in which priorities are reordered and time and energy is allocated to affirmative action *above other goals.*

There are many reasons why such a shift is extremely difficult even if the administrator is basically unprejudiced. Many see affirmative action as a diversion from "real" organizational goals. How do we answer the director of a city public works department who says, "My job is to repair roads and keep the storm drains operating. I need the best engineers I can get for that. My job isn't to solve social problems"?

Questions of this variety must be satisfactorily answered if affirmative action is to go forward. Public managers must be convinced to broaden their perspectives and to redefine their standards of performance if the values inherent in affirmative action are to be upgraded to an operational level. This will require new standards for evaluating what is important in public organizations and strategic revisions of reward systems to support new standards.

WHY IS PREFERENTIAL HIRING AND THE SETTING OF TARGETS AND QUOTAS ABSOLUTELY NECESSARY TO THE PROCESS?

Affirmative action guidelines require specified objectives, usually translated into numerical quotas, as minimum goals for the employment of minority individuals and women. Numerical objectives have emerged for the present as the only feasible mechanism for defining with any clarity the targets of action and the criteria for evaluation of progress toward achieving them within a given period of time. Thus, the courts have upheld the validity of goals and quotas in civil rights enforcement efforts and have stated that color-consciousness and sex-consciousness are both appropriate and necessary remedial postures.[1]

Nevertheless, the issue of preferential hiring has assumed the proportions of a major national controversy. The issue is partly one of varying definitions of the situation. Preference and compensation can be seen as words of positive connotation or as words of condescension and disparagement. Preference can be defined as choosing the more highly valued candidate at a given point in time and circumstance, and compensation can be defined as redress for past failures to reach the actual market of human resources available to our organizations. From a very different perspective, these words in combination may be defined as "reverse discrimination."

The characterization of preferential hiring and quotas as reverse discrimination provides a crutch for those who would avoid the changes in organizational behavior required by management by objectives. Obviously, to the extent that quotas as targets for progress become job "slots" and maximums rather than minimums, they perpetuate race and sex discriminations. Otherwise, the argument is diversionary and should be treated as such.

Until we are ready to recognize that years of experience with passive nondiscrimination in the public sector have not substantially changed its white, middle-class, male-dominated employment patterns and until we are ready to set objectives wherein results are what counts, it is unlikely that change will take place. Yet, when people with differing perspectives are asked to agree on concrete goals, and must attempt to reach collective agreement on priorities, conflict becomes inevitable.

However, we have learned to submerge conflict in organizations by avoiding explicit goal statements. We escape confrontations by letting statements of *intent* substitute for *action* plans in the most controversial areas. Conflict is also avoided by allowing sub-units to pursue their primary objectives with as little pressure as possible on them to agree on or produce on broader system goals. To the extent that affirmative action clashes with individual values or requires diversion of resources from each sub-unit's highly ranked goals it is met with avoidance or outright resistance. A serious affirmative action program, therefore, demands substantial departures from traditional policy-making practices and managerial styles.

WHY MUST OUR TRADITIONAL STANDARDS OF "QUALITY" BE REEXAMINED?

Most attacks on preferential hiring programs are grounded in the assumption that the quality of performance and work standards will be severely diminished as a result of the systematic employment of minorities and women. They are also grounded in the assumption that few "qualified" Blacks, Chicanos, other minority individuals, and women are available. Both assumptions stand on the third assumption that present criteria of merit and procedures for their application can be accepted uncritically and have yielded the excellence intended. We have not asked ourselves why the use of certain standards has resulted in the virtual exclusion of women and minorities from many professional positions and almost all high-level positions. To the extent that the use of our present standards has resulted in this exclusion (or inclusion in only token proportions), our organizations have been denied access to important sources of intellectual and physical vitality. Thus, the logic of affirmative action says that where a particular criterion of merit, even while not discriminatory on its face or in its intent, operates to the disproportionate elimination of women and minority group individuals, the burden on the organization to defend it as an appropriate criterion rises in direct proportion to its exclusionary effect.

The problems raised by the quality issue are probably the most difficult of those faced in affirmative action. Questioning our accepted standards of quality strikes at tradition and destroys some of the most important groups of our individual self-definitions. The less secure the institution, occupational group, or individual concerned, the more threatening such examination becomes. Degrees and other labels provide a much more comforting definition of quality than does a continuing evaluation of job performance. The more the occupational group is involved in processes of professionalizing itself or is striving for higher status, the greater the tension between those processes and inclusionary requirements. All of these changes increase exclusivity. Attempts at implementation of affirmative action in police departments, for example, are running head on into the federally financed drive to "professionalize" according to traditional measures—particularly degree attainment.[2]

The case of several state colleges in California which are undergoing a change of status from colleges to "universities" provides us with another example. In this instance one of the main criteria for change of status is the number of Ph.D. degree holders on the faculty. Teachers with master's degrees who had been receiving excellent evaluations from deans, peers, and students are suddenly being reevaluated according to a more "professional" standard, i.e., the Ph.D. Job performance is the same, but some are now being dismissed or not advanced because external criteria have changed. Any attempt to implement affirmative action programs in this atmosphere of degree consciousness is difficult. Suggestions that alternative standards of faculty quality be considered (for example a bachelor's or master's degree plus experience, cultural knowledge, ability to relate to students, ability to serve as a minority role model, and warmth, energy, and decency) are met with fears about lowering standards and allusions to the importance of "quality." We see here two conflicting sets of standards about what is important and what quality means.

Organizational leaders dedicated to pursuing inclusionary policies must be prepared to meet the "quality" issue head on. The development of alternative measures of accomplishment is essential to the success of affirmative action programs at this period in time. A complex of social factors has combined to exclude minorities and women from the higher levels of formal educational attainment, and great numbers have pursued avenues of development other than that of formal education. Yet, their experience paths prepare them to bring new perspectives, different values, and perhaps even equal or higher capabilities to many public jobs. If, as we say, our objective is the best person for the job, we are *committed* to affirmative action.

Finally, in the broadest sense, a public employee group representative of the differing values and various perspectives in our total society is essential to public accountability. Any procedures which exclude multiple experience paths and disparate values from organizations *will* in these terms *lower standards* of public accountability as well as organizational effectiveness.

NOTES

1. For a summary of court decisions regarding quotas, see Herbert Hill, "Preferential Hiring, Correcting the Demerit System," *Social Policy*, July-August 1973, pp. 96–102.
2. For further discussion of this problem as it relates to an actively professionalizing sheriff's department, see Catherine Lovell, "Accountability Patterns of the Los Angeles County Sheriff's Department," *Institute on Law and Urban Studies*, manuscript, November 1973.

C. Labor Relations and Collective Bargaining

19

Professionalization and Unionization: Compatible After All?

LESLIE B. ALEXANDER

According to some observers, many social workers share a general feeling that the increasing unionization of social workers at both the M.S.W. and B.S.W. levels is a serious challenge to social work's professionalism.[1] The perception of unionization as "unprofessional" is a commonly held though untested assertion. The related view that unionization and professionalization are inherently antagonistic and mutually exclusive is problematic; it fails to account for the slow yet steady rate since the 1930s of unionization of professional workers of all types, including social workers, psychologists, lawyers, engineers, occupational therapists, and college professors.

Although membership is currently declining in blue-collar unions, many white-collar unions, including those that organize professionals, are showing dramatic gains in membership. As of 1978 it was estimated that about 30 percent of all professional and technical employees (excluding managers and the self-employed) were represented in collective bargaining efforts.[2] Union activity is strongest among professionals in education, government service, and the entertainment and communication industries and less prevalent among doctors, lawyers, scientists, and engineers. Since the early 1970s, unionization has also made great strides in the health care field. Although there is evidence of accelerating participation in unions by social workers, there are no firm statistics on the number of professional social workers belonging to the three major unions organizing social workers nationally: the American

Federation of State, County, and Municipal Employees; Service Employees International Union; and the National Union of Hospital and Health Care Employees.[3]

One way around the seeming paradox between the negative view of unionization for professionals and its growth is to examine unions and professions theoretically, as ideal types. Such a contrast is useful for two reasons. First, this comparison seems to underlie the widespread sentiment in social work that unions are unprofessional. More important, such a comparison of ideal types results in the inevitable conclusion that unionism and professionalism as principles, unionization and professionalization as processes, and unions and professional associations as modes of organization are, in fact, contradictory and incompatible. It is only when the realities are examined, both of the less-established professions such as social work and of the unions organizing them, that the compatibility and mutual reinforcement emerge. The paradox disappears and a more substantive debate about the pros and cons of unionization for professionals is possible.

The occurrence of unionization and professionalization as complementary processes, then, appears least likely when both are examined as ideal types exemplifying the most mature and successful of each. For example, the ideal model of unionization could be the automobile or steel workers' unions. The model of the industrial union, which includes all workers in a given industry regardless of skill or occupational specialty, is chosen deliberately, since it appears to underlie most discussions that contrast professions and unions. In addition, the major unions organizing social workers and many other professional workers have been industrial in form. The contrast between craft unions—organizations of workers engaged in a single trade and using similar skills—and professions is much less pronounced. The ideal model of professionalization might be law or medicine, especially as exemplified by self-employed, independent practitioners.

At this level of analysis, unionization and professionalization seem to have little in common, other than both being processes that represent collective, protective efforts in behalf of their membership and aimed at upward social mobility.[4] Useful dimensions on which to compare as ideal types the two organizational forms—the union and the professional association—are patterns of membership, overall philosophy, and tactics.

MEMBERSHIP

Regarding membership, unions have typically been associated with wageworkers involved in manual labor for low pay. The professional association on the other hand, is generally associated with middle-class people involved in nonmanual, more esoteric, prestigious, and lucrative work. Class and status differences have been stressed continually in the literature, beginning with Carr-Saunders and Wilson's classic work on professions in 1933. In their view, those aspiring to professional status should avoid unions at all costs:

> Indeed, association with that movement (labor) is generally regarded, even among the more economically dependent of professions, as calculated to depress rather than elevate their social status and is therefore avoided even in cases where one might expect it to be sought after.[5]

This resistance to unionization on the grounds of prestige has endured, forming part of what C. Wright Mills defined in the 1950s as the "principled" rejection of unions by many white-collar employees.[6] The following is another example of this principled rejection:

> The "after all, we are all workers" approach has served to alienate many professional persons from the labor movement who might otherwise be sympathetic. Unionism's endeavor to organize professional personnel by appeals to worker solidarity, when professionals regard themselves as a group set above the common herd, has been a tactic as self-defeating as it is persistent.[7]

The cleavage created by differences in status and image seems almost insurmountable.

Another important dimension of membership patterns relates to the exclusionary practices of both unions and professional associations. Both exclude potential members, but on the basis of more-or-less opposite criteria. Unions typically reject those above a certain level in the organizational hierarchy—for example, those defined as management—whereas professional associations tend to exclude members on the basis of insufficient education or experience.

For professionals who are union members, these exclusionary practices typically mean that eligibility for membership in their professional association is for their lifetime, whereas eligibility for union membership is short term, lasting only until the individual is promoted into management. Unions' eligibility criteria also result in a fair amount of turnover, with a large percentage of the membership being younger, professionally less experienced individuals who remain eligible for union membership only for a few years until they are promoted into management. Although promotion into management is detrimental from the unions' perspective, it is synonymous with advancement from the professional point of view.

PHILOSOPHY

There is also considerable variation in the overall philosophy and goals of the two modes of organization. In the union's ethos, a very real and inherent conflict of interest exists between union members and management. No such inherent adversary relationship exists in the professional ethos. In addition, although both modes have protective functions, union activity is more narrowly confined to this domain, focused primarily on improving wages, hours, and conditions of work. Whereas higher status is an expected though often-denied consequence of unionization, success on the instrumental dimension—the realization of economic and job benefits—is most critical to a union's success. Although the "expressive" or ideological purpose of unions is apparent and important, the primary function is to accrue economic and job-related benefits rather than to provide something in which to believe. The expressive dimension is clearly secondary in the majority of cases. Much more so than professions, unions are basically institutions of the job market whose development and traditions are greatly influenced by economic developments. The established professions lack this extreme dependence on outside economic influences.

The professional spirit, on the other hand, extends beyond narrow economic and protectionist issues.[8] Concern for the enhancement of standards, proficiency within the profession, reputation in the community, service to clients, and, above all, autonomy, are all within its expansive interest. Whereas the union's claims to financial gain are primary, the professional association lays claim first and foremost to autonomy and independence on the job. The union generally can influence only the conditions of work, leaving the determination of who does the work and the nature of its content up to management; professional autonomy, however, includes defining and controlling the nature of the work, not just the surrounding conditions. Autonomy, then, is a requisite for the full flowering of the service ideal, another important hallmark of the professions.

At an ideal level, professionals stress the primacy of the public good, whereas unions stress the primacy of private benefit. However, by definition, professionals are not as immune to financial lure as their rhetoric of service might imply. In fact, financial success and high prestige are inevitable and necessary requisites of full-fledged professional status. Though generally masked in professional rhetoric, substantial financial gain is indispensable to assure professional status.

Nevertheless, although the professional association does seek collective advancement, the professional ethos both allows, and in fact emphasizes, individual mobility. Striving for upward mobility is the rule rather than the exception. Among the professions, individual advancement is based on merit; however, unions stress seniority. Although union members are not without hopes for individual gains in status, this is not a part of the official union value system. Above all, union philosophy stresses egalitarianism and the good of the collectivity. As Haug and Sussman have stated, "the slogan of 'all for one and one for all' suggests disapproval for individual climbers."[9] In fact, the epitome of the professional is the autonomous individual practitioner, whereas the epitome of the unionist is the staunch group member.

According to an idealized perspective, in the unlikely event that professionals would unionize, their individualistic, elitist emphasis would favor a craft rather than an industrial union. Given a typical social agency, one would expect to find the professional social workers in one bargaining unit and the clerical and maintenance workers in another. Nonprofessionals would definitely be ineligible for membership in the professional bargaining unit, and the professionals would fight to keep it that way.

TACTICS

A final point of comparison involves the difference in tactics and rhetoric of the two modes of organization. The classic tactics of unions, which emerge from their basic and open power struggles with management, involve a range of applications of power—from slowdowns to pickets to strikes. Union rhetoric, which often involves a public admission of bitterness and hostility, commonly includes such terms as "arsenal of weapons," "open warfare," "enemies," "class solidarity," "demands," "grievances," "militancy," and "rights." The adversary tone is readily apparent. So also is the prevailing collectivist spirit.

Professional associations, on the other hand, are not as blatantly involved in power struggles but rather emphasize more cerebral tactics, such as developing codes of ethics, raising standards of practice, promoting good community relations, and expanding the knowledge base. Although some professional associations, notably the American Nurses Association, the American Association of University Professors, and the National Education Association, have engaged in collective bargaining, the more usual route for professional associations to take in solving economic problems is through formation of vocational bureaus, publication of minimal salary scales, and development of personnel committees and programs. Theirs is the rhetoric of "service," "individual merit," "standards," and "consensus." The overall tone is dignified, cerebral, and conciliatory.

In the same connection, the purpose and tactics of the professional association result in much less intimate involvement in the daily lives of members than the union has. The professional association deals more at the level of broad public relations. Unions, on the other hand, through their structure of locals and shop stewards and their emphasis on collective bargaining and redress of grievances, are much more involved on a day-to-day, intimate level with their members. Their protection is more immediate, more specific, and probably more effective.

INCOMPATIBLE VIEW

If unions and professions are judged by ideal standards, then the conclusions reached by noted authorities such as Northrup and Carr-Saunders and Wilson seem inevitable: the two are inherently incompatible. Their basic membership patterns, philosophies, and tactics are so irreconcilable that they could not coexist without each continually violating the sacred prerogatives of the other. For convenience this will be termed the "incompatible" view of professional unionism.

According to this view, which assumes ideal standards of unionism and professionalism, any type of unionization among professionals, social workers included, is an anomaly. Given that today less than a third of all professional employees are covered by collective bargaining agreements, many of which are negotiated by professional societies that eschew the label of "union," the argument could be made that this view conforms most closely to reality.[10] It certainly corresponds to the often-quoted rejoinder of many professionals to the idea of unionizing: "It just isn't professional!" However, this line of argument evokes ideal constructs and treats all professional union members as though their unionism and professionalism were each fully mature, when this is not, in fact, the case.

Nevertheless, some explanation is still needed for the group of exceptions: those persons claiming professional status who have also been unionized for the last forty years. At least two other rough models of professional unionism shed light on this seeming paradox. Neither is pure nor comprehensive, and they share some common features. Both orientations view unionism and professionalism as compatible under certain conditions. The first pattern might be called the transitional model and the second the hybrid model. Both orientations involve a certain reluctance and defensiveness in relation to unionization.

TRANSITIONAL MODEL

According to the transitional model, unionization and professionalization are compatible only when both processes are at early stages of development. However, professional development is always of greater interest. Although the aspiring profession is recognized as relatively weak on established indexes of professionalism, this insecure status is regarded as temporary. Full professional status is the ultimate outcome. In fact, unionism is not expected to become a permanent fixture at all, but rather will be shed as professional status becomes more secure. Unionization is regarded as a necessary and effective evil for wresting higher wages and better working conditions from management in the present.

This crude model makes certain assumptions. The union is expected to serve a purely instrumental function—the acquisition of economic and job security, both of which are requisites for secure professional status. The union is regarded strictly as a means rather than an end. This orientation assumes that as both unionization and professionalization mature, union and professional prerogatives will inevitably clash. But this does not matter, since unionization is only a transitional stage in the pursuit of full professional status.

This model perhaps best represents the widespread although unwritten assumption of some reluctant professional union members. It also corresponds to the reality that for many professionals, union membership will indeed be only transitory. When professionals are promoted to supervisory positions, they are generally classified as management and are no longer eligible for union membership. This transitional model is deficient, however, in several important respects. Although it contains elements of truth, it cannot account for the following circumstances, most of which were evident by the late 1940s. First, it ignores the reality that several aspiring professions, including social workers, teachers, nurses, and librarians, have not rejected unionization, even though their professional status is more secure now than in the 1930s and 1940s when they first began to unionize. Unionization is not a transitional phenomenon for these groups.

Second, the model is too optimistic about the prospects of many occupations for obtaining professional recognition, particularly in regard to the high status, high income, and autonomy associated with the established professions.[11] In a thorough and provocative review of the empirical evidence regarding patterns of professionalism, Epstein and Conrad point out the limited descriptive and predictive validity of measures of social work professionalism as either an independent or intervening variable. They conclude:

[A more empirically based, deprofessionalized model] would view claims to social-work professionalization as in fact expressions of social-work professionalism—an *ideology* associated with *aspiration* to professional status rather than as an expression of the central norms of social work as a "professional community."[12]

Third, this orientation fails to take into account the environmental constraints, especially the highly bureaucratized context, in which most professionals work. And fourth, it fails to account for an inevitable interactional process: when unions and professionals interact over time, unions become more professional and professionals become more proletarian. As a result, new hybrid forms of organization develop, drawing from both unions and professions, yet different from either in their classic sense. In other words, a process of diffusion takes place.

HYBRID MODEL

The hybrid model of organization, sketched briefly by Wilensky, seems to account better for the development of most unions of professional workers.[13] This approach assumes that many occupations aspiring to professional status will not achieve it in the traditional sense of the word, that is, in terms of the prestige, power, and financial success of the established professions such as medicine or law. The hybrid approach also judges these new professions on different terms—not merely as weak imitations of the established models but as different forms that should be judged on their own merits. The model assumes that when unions and professionals interact over time, each begins to assume some of the characteristics of the other; new forms emerge that borrow from, but do not entirely conform to, either the traditional union or the traditional professional model. The result might be one new form that combines the functions of a union and a professional association, or it might be two parallel forms. In the latter instance, union and professional forms remain separate but borrow from and influence each other. In both instances, the need for union protection, particularly in the areas of salary and working conditions, is seen as a permanent requirement.[14]

Much consideration has been given to the differences between the emerging professions, which are represented by the hybrid model, and the established professions. Whether referred to as the "new," "less-established," "emerging," or "semi" profession, social work conforms to the general pattern that emerges from this discussion. Obviously, the newer professions command less prestige, have shorter training periods, and are less lucrative than the more established professions of law and medicine. However, Wilensky's parsimonious discussion, which captures the basic arguments made by others, identifies two other critical points of comparison:

1. newer professions are salaried and housed in bureaucracies, both of which can threaten autonomy and the service itself, and
2. because their knowledge base is either too broad and vague or too

narrow and restricted, the claims of these professions to exclusive jurisdiction and autonomy are also threatened.

For example, Wilensky cites social work's broad yet vague knowledge base as being one of the major obstacles to full professional status.

Although the issue of social work's weak knowledge base is critical, it is much less controversial than the issue of the professional in the bureaucracy, which Perrow has described as "certainly the hottest single topic in the field of organizational analysis during the early 1960s."[15]

The topic of the professional in the bureaucracy is obviously a complex one, but for understanding the hybrid model of professional unionism, several points are important. First, as Wilensky, Freidson, and Perrow, among others, have cogently pointed out, it is incorrect to think of bureaucratization and professionalization as inverse processes. While recognizing certain real constraints of bureaucratic life, Freidson points out that, at least in the case of health services, many of the dysfunctional consequences attributed to bureaucratic organizations might be more accurately attributed to the professional organization of medicine.[16] In other words, many of the rigid, mechanical, and authoritarian attitudes and much of the inadequate coordination that alienate and depersonalize clients are due more to the dominance of the medical profession in health care administration than to the bureaucratic characteristics of health care.

Perhaps too much has been made, then, of the disparity between the two modes. Perhaps a bureaucratic setting is not as limiting to professional practice as has been traditionally emphasized. To quote Wilensky:

> There is another way to view what is happening to professionalism: it is not that organizational revolution destroys professionalism, or that newer forms of knowledge (vague human-relations skills at one extreme, programmed instruction at the other) provide a poor base for professionalism, but simply that all these developments lead to something new. The culture of bureaucracy invades the professions; the culture of professionalism invades organizations.[17]

If bureaucracies are threats to professionals, so too are professionals threats to bureaucracies. They lack appreciation for rules and regulations, they focus on the unique rather than the routine aspects of the client's situation, and they demand authority in matters relating to the client and the organization. Besides, the obvious reality today is that most professionals, physicians and lawyers included, practice within bureaucratic settings. The individual practitioner is becoming an anomaly.

The issue of bureaucracy has also been emphasized in the literature on professionals in unions. Almost all the authors in this field view the bureaucratic setting as predisposing professional workers to unionize, particularly when the bureaucracy becomes extremely large and impersonal. One of the classic works in the field, Kleingartner's *Professionalism and Salaried Worker Organization*, seems to make the bureaucratic context the critical variable by defining such occupational groups as teachers, nurses, and social workers as *salaried* professionals in contrast to *self-employed*, autonomous professionals such as physicians and lawyers.[18] Granted, newer professionals do not have the status or income of the established professions. Instead, in Kleingartner's terms, they maintain the rhetoric but lack the essence of professional status. However, in light of the reevaluation of bureaucratic influence, this point seems to have been overemphasized.

Given the hybrid model of organization, what characteristics distinguish unions of professionals from unions of blue-collar workers? Just as fundamental differences have been observed between established and emerging professions, so too have distinctive differences in structure and style been observed between unions of professional and blue-collar workers. For example, bargaining units in professional unions often tend to be smaller and more scattered; they also have a tendency—with teachers a primary exception—to reject the use of strikes and other more extreme pressure tactics in favor of arbitration and mediation.[19] The potential use of the strike, in particular, creates a serious dilemma for many professional union members. However, as Kleingartner has queried:

> If the union does not establish a strong collective bargaining mechanism, what can it do that the traditional professional association cannot do? And can the union be strong in collective bargaining unless it is willing to use the strike weapon?[20]

Use of strikes has always been a major issue in the debate within social work over unionization. Some recent data on the use of strikes by a select group of social workers suggest that for most of them, the threat of a strike is more a matter of form than substance, since no-strike (and no-lockout) clauses are commonly included in labor contracts covering social workers. Also, evidence suggests that many social work union members strongly favor arbitration over strike action.[21]

More recently, reflecting the ethics of professionalism, many unions of professionals have also demanded that the scope of collective bargaining be expanded to include such things as size of classes and caseloads, course content, and office space—prerogatives previously regarded as belonging to management.[22] In some cases, union members have also demanded that they be able to meet to discuss professional issues on work time.

Notwithstanding such structural differences that distinguish unions of professionals from those of blue-collar workers, perhaps most attention has been devoted to differences in style and tone, which reflect the middle-class, professional bias.[23] For example, among unions of professionals, the class struggle or inherent conflict between the union and management has usually been underplayed, with workers often expressing dual loyalty to both management and the union; euphemisms have been used (such as calling a grievance committee an "office relations" committee); middle-class organizers have been used; and merit, rather than seniority, has been stressed for promotions. Finally, unionization is presented as a way to promote, rather than impede, professional standards.

This appeal to potential members to view unions as a means of securing professional status reflects a certain defensiveness against the idea of union membership on the part of these professionals. However, it represents a much less standoffish and extreme reaction than that displayed by certain engineering and nursing associations in the 1940s and that persists today. In those two instances, the professional associations adopted strong and open campaigns to deter their members from joining unions and began to engage in collective bargaining themselves. Union affiliation was to be avoided at all costs.[24]

Such dramatic, defensive maneuvers reflect a principled rejection of unions that is not so much in evidence today. In fact, there is still evidence that professionals join unions for much the same reasons as blue-collar workers. Just as Mills predicted in 1951, Kleingartner concludes almost thirty years later:

> White-collar workers may join unions as a purely defensive act. However, increases in white-collar unionization depend also on the relative merits of the case rather than on an emotional experience. . . . They tend to see the union as an organization that can get things done. They may not like the unions, but neither is there much evidence of the traditional principled opposition.[25]

Although unions of professionals do have some distinctive structural and stylistic features, just like blue-collar unions, they are basically evaluated and valued on instrumental dimensions. The potential for professional unions to serve functions of association and social change is present just as it is for blue-collar unions; however, their primary purpose and emphasis is also the same as that of blue-collar unions: obtaining higher wages, better hours, and better working conditions.

CONCLUSIONS

The analysis of unions and professions as ideal types reveals the conditions under which the two modes are incompatible: when both unionism and professionalism are both at mature levels of development. When the structure and style of existing professional unions are examined, it becomes clear that unions of professionals are comparable to neither traditional professional associations nor traditional unions. Rather, a process of diffusion takes place. A new hybrid form of organization develops, drawing from, yet different from, both unions and professional associations in the classic sense. Recognizing this diffusion process resolves the seeming paradox in the unionization of professionals.

The professional associations of social workers have officially endorsed since the mid-1940s the right of individuals to bargain collectively and to be represented by a union of their choice.[26] Nevertheless, a principled or ideological rejection of unionization still persists among many social workers—the belief that joining a union "just isn't professional." Despite the growth of union membership among professionals of all kinds, including social workers, few writers have challenged this erroneous position in the professional social work literature; nor has it received much attention at professional meetings. Given the growing dissatisfaction among some service workers about the content and context of their work life, the potential for unionization seems ever greater.

A number of reasons exist for professionals of all kinds to reject unionization, such as the potential for rigidity in the addition of more bureaucratic apparatus in the form of the union; doubts about its ability to obtain significantly better wages and working conditions, particularly in the public sector; and general problems of worker-union alienation, such as the failure of some union leaders to reflect the views of their members or charges of financial improprieties on the part of some union leaders. However, equally convincing reasons exist for professionals to unionize. For example, the union can provide more immediate protection for workers than professional associations. Unions can also effect improvements in basic working conditions for professionals, thereby improving service delivery to clients. In addition, by broadening the scope of collective bargaining explicitly to include certain issues regarding the profession and social change, unions can also enhance service delivery. Furthermore, although they have generated significant controversy and had mixed success, definite historical precedents exist in social work for such an expansive view of unionism. Social work unions in the 1930s and 1940s espoused not only traditional bread-and-butter union issues, but also issues of domestic social reform, war and peace, and professional development as well.[27]

The primary point is that all these pros and cons are legitimate issues in professional unionization, and they should be raised to the level of open debate within the profession. To reject unionization because it is allegedly "unprofessional" is supported neither by the theoretical base, the historical record, nor the current reality.

NOTES AND REFERENCES

1. *See,* for example, Howard Hush, "Collective Bargaining in Voluntary Agencies," *Social Casework,* 50 (April 1969), pp. 210–213; Charles S. Levy, "Social Workers and Unions," in Levy, ed., *Social Work Ethics* (New York: Human Sciences Press, 1974), pp. 195–208; and Lawrence C. Schulman, "Unionization and the Professional Employee: The Social Service Director's View," in Simon Slavin, ed., *Social Administration: The Management of the Social Services* (New York: Haworth Press, 1978), pp. 460–468. Three recent pro-union works also mention this attitude. *See* Gary L. Shaffer, "Labor Relations and the Unionization of Professional Social Workers: A Neglected Area in Social Work Education," *Journal of Education for Social Work,* 15 (Winter 1979), pp. 80–86; Milton Tambor, "The Social Worker as Worker: A Union Perspective," *Administration in Social Work,* 3 (Fall 1979), pp. 289–300; and Jeffry Galper, *Social Work Practice: A Radical Perspective* (Englewood Cliffs, N.J.: Prentice-Hall, 1980), pp. 159–161. However, the perception of incompatibility between unions and professions does not appear widespread among MSW union members. *See* Leslie B. Alexander, Philip Lichtenberg, and Dennis Brunn, "Social Workers in Unions: A Survey," *Social Work,* 25 (May 1980), pp. 216–223.
2. Bureau of Labor Statistics, U.S. Department of Labor, *Directory of National Unions and Employee Associations, 1979,* Bulletin No. 2079 (Washington, D.C.: U.S. Government Printing Office, forthcoming), Table 14. Because technical and professional workers are lumped together, the number of professionals represented by collective bargaining is obviously less than 30 percent. *See also* Eileen B. Hoffman, *Unionization of Professional Societies,* Report No. 690 (New York: Conference Board, 1976), pp. 41–42.
3. Jerry Wurf, "Labor Movement, Social Work Fighting Similar Battles," *NASW News,* 25 (February 1980), p. 7.
4. *See* Marie Haug and Marvin Sussman, "Professionalization and Unionism: A Jurisdictional Dispute?" in Eliot Freidson, ed., *The Professions and Their Prospects* (Beverly Hills, Calif.: Sage Publications, 1973), pp. 89–104.
5. A. M. Carr-Saunders and P. A. Wilson, *The Professions* (Oxford, England: Clarendon Press, 1933), p. 329.
6. C. Wright Mills, *White Collar* (New York: Oxford University Press, 1951). For a more recent statement, *see* Magali S. Lawson, *The Rise of Professionalism* (Berkeley: University of California Press, 1977), p. 236.
7. Herbert R. Northrup, "Collective Bargaining by Professional Societies," in Richard A. Lester and Joseph Shister, eds., *Insights into Labor Issues* (New York: Macmillan Co., 1948), p. 157.

8. The ideas about professions in this section come primarily from Eliot Freidson, *Professional Dominance: The Social Structure of Medical Care* (Chicago: Aldine Publishing Co., 1970); William A. Goode, "The Theoretical Limits of
   Professionalization," in Amitai Etzioni, ed., *The Semi-Professions and Their Organization* (New York: Free Press, 1969), pp. 266–313; and Everett C.
   Hughes, "Work and the Self," in Hughes, ed., *Sociological Eye* (Chicago:
   Aldine-Atherton Co., 1971), pp. 283–427.
9. Haug and Sussman, op. cit., p. 102.
10. Hoffman, op. cit., p. 1.
11. *See* William A. Goode, op. cit., p. 267; Harold L. Wilensky, "The Profession-
    alization of Everyone?" *American Journal of Sociology*, 70 (September 1964),
    pp. 137–158; and Nathan Glazer, "The Schools of the Minor Professions,"
    Minerva, 12 (July 1974), pp. 346–364.
12. Irwin Epstein and Kayla Conrad, "The Empirical Limits of Social Work
    Professionalization," in Rosemary Sarri and Yeheskel Hasenfeld, eds., *The
    Management of Human Services* (New York: Columbia University Press, 1978),
    p. 178.
13. Wilensky, op. cit.
14. *See* Archie Kleingartner, "Collective Bargaining between Salaried Profes-
    sionals and Public Sector Management," *Public Administration Review*, 33
    (March-April 1973), pp. 165–172.
15. Charles Perrow, *Complex Organizations* (Glenview, Ill.: Scott, Foresman &
    Co., 1972), p. 55. The social work literature has followed the same pattern as
    the more general works: an overemphasis on the dysfunctional aspects of
    bureaucracy in the early 1960s, with more balance since then. *See*, for exam-
    ple, Peter M. Blau and W. Richard Scott, *Formal Organizations* (San Fran-
    cisco: Chandler Publishing Co., 1962); and Nina Toren, "Semi-Professional-
    ism and Social Work: A Theoretical Perspective," in Amitai Etzioni, ed., *The
    Semi-Professions and Their Organization* (New York: Free Press, 1969). *See also*
    Epstein and Conrad, op. cit., pp. 176–177.
16. Eliot Freidson, "Dominant Professions, Bureaucracy, and Client Services,"
    in Yeheskel Hasenfeld and Richard A. English, eds., *Human Service Organi-
    zations* (Ann Arbor: University of Michigan Press, 1974), pp. 428–448.
17. Wilensky, op. cit., p. 150.
18. Archie Kleingartner, *Professionalism and Salaried Worker Organization* (Madi-
    son: University of Wisconsin, Industrial Relations Research Institute, 1967),
    p. 50. However, Kleingartner does not emphasize the salaried relationship
    as much in his later article, "Collective Bargaining between Salaried Profes-
    sionals and Public Sector Management."
19. *See* Everett M. Kassalow. "The Prospects for White-Collar Union Growth,"
    Industrial Relations, 5 (October 1965), p. 40; George Strauss, "Professional-
    ism and Occupational Association," *Industrial Relations*, 2 (May 1963), p. 15;
    and Bernard Goldstein, "The Perspective of Unionized Professionals," *So-
    cial Forces*, 37 (May 1959), p. 323.
20. Kleingartner, *Professionalism and Salaried Worker Organization*, p. 55.
21. Alexander, Lichtenberg, and Brunn, op. cit., p. 219. For a historical per-
    spective, *see* Leslie B. Alexander, "Organizing the Professional Social
    Worker: Union Development in Voluntary Social Work, 1930–50," unpub-

lished Ph.D. dissertation, Bryn Mawr College, 1977. For more general discussions, *see* Levy, op. cit.; Tambor, op. cit., Shaffer, op. cit.; and Al Nash, "Local 1707, CSAE: Facets of a Union in the Nonprofit Field," *Labor History*, 20 (Spring 1979), pp. 256–277.

22. *See* Kleingartner, "Collective Bargaining between Salaried Professionals and Public Sector Management"; and Dennis Chamot, "Professional Employees Turn to Unions," *Harvard Business Review*, 54 (May–June 1976), pp. 119–127.

23. *See*, for example, the quarterly issues of *Interface*, published by the Department for Professional Employees of the American Federation of Labor–Congress of Industrial Organizations. This theme is also recurrent in the newsletters and bulletins of all the major unions that organize professionals. For a fascinating account of the accommodations made by a union local to social work professionalism, *see* Nash, op. cit.

24. Northrup, op. cit., pp. 134–143; and Hoffman, op. cit., pp. 40ff, 52–55.

25. Archie Kleingartner, "The Organization of White-Collar Workers," *British Journal of Industrial Relations*, 6 (March 1968), pp. 82–83. *See also* Mills, op. cit., p. 309.

26. *See Personnel Practices in Social Work* (New York: American Association of Social Workers, September 1946), p. 4. This pro-union position was revised and reaffirmed in 1968, 1971, and 1975. *See NASW Standards for Social Work Personnel Practices* (New York: National Association of Social Workers, 1968, rev. 1971 and 1976.)

27. *See* Alexander, op. cit.; Leslie B. Alexander and Milton Speizman, "The Union Movement in Voluntary Social Work: 1930–1950," *Social Welfare Forum, 1979* (New York: Columbia University Press, 1980), pp. 179–187; John Earl Haynes, "The 'Rank and File' Movement in Private Social Work," *Labor History*, 16 (Winter 1975), pp. 78–98; and Jacob Fisher, *The Response of Social Work to the Depression* (Cambridge, Mass.: Schenkman Publishing Co., 1980).

20

The Social Worker as Worker: A Union Perspective

MILTON TAMBOR

A few years ago, this writer was asked to speak to a social work administration class on collective bargaining and address the following questions: What effect does the adversary relationship, inherent in collective bargaining, have on the organization? What happens to such concepts as group leadership, motivation, and atmosphere for self-actualization and autonomy? What happens when responsibility for resolving agency problems is shifted to a third party? What are the implications of seniority systems for professionals? What impact does the high cost of preparing for and participating in organizations, as well as administering ongoing contacts, have on organizational priorities? What are the implications for the professional when nonprofessional members of a union have different concerns relative to outcomes of the collective bargaining process? What happens to the client when social workers strike?

Implicit in these questions are assumptions that deny that social workers have interests as workers and judgments that incorporate anti-union biases. These same assumptions and judgments are significantly reflected in social work education, the social work profession, and the social work literature.

Administrative resistance to collective bargaining is rooted in concepts of professionalism, elitism, and partneralism. Yet, social workers are mobilizing to unionize.

During the past 20 years, there has been massive union growth in the public sector. Approximately 50 percent of public employees are represented by unions and associations as compared to 25 percent in the private sector (Stieber, 1973). Within public welfare departments (Stieber, 1973), where many social workers are employed, the figure is as high as 69 percent. In the highly industrialized Middle Atlantic region,

90 percent are represented by unions or associations. With more than
one million members, AFSCME is the largest public employee union
(Cole, 1977) representing social workers. Recent figures from the
AFSCME Research Department indicate that 35,000 professional social
workers and approximately 55,000 human services workers are represented by that union.

Social workers are also members of the Service Employees International Union, state associations, teacher and faculty organizations, Local
1199 of the National Hospital Union, and, in much smaller numbers, a
few predominately private sector unions. In the voluntary sector, there
is a rich history and tradition of social workers and unions, beginning
with the United Office and Professional Workers of America organized in 1937 (Cole, 1977). District Council 1707 AFSCME represents
approximately 13,000 members in voluntary agencies, and there are
smaller AFSCME Local Unions of voluntary agency workers in Detroit,
Philadelphia, Milwaukee, and Los Angeles. The voluntary sector is not
as highly organized as the public sector. There is a multiplicity of agencies, many employing small numbers of workers with some unsure of
their continued funding, and with the exception of hospitals, most
unions are therefore reluctant to expend considerable organizing energy and resources in this area.

Unions are generally organized industrially, with the National Labor Relations Act and comparable state statutes and orders mandating
the largest possible units of employees with a community of interest.
Frequently, it means that all workers in the organization, excepting
management, may be in the same bargaining unit (Cole, 1977). In Canada, the estimate is that a majority of social workers are covered by bargaining agreements (Levine, 1975), and in British Columbia the figure is
above 90 percent (Martin, 1975).

Despite this accelerating participation of social workers in unions,
social work education has not incorporated this experience within the
professional curriculum. For example, in education and nursing, where
the associations act as bargaining agents, collective bargaining classes are
increasingly becoming an integral part of the class content. Only a few
schools of social work have courses in collective bargaining, and only in
some administration classes is this topic introduced.

THE POLITICS OF PROFESSIONALISM

Wagner and Cohen (1978) contend that defining social workers as professionals has definite political implications. Citing a strike (Rehr, 1960)
and the conflict with the Social Work Code of Ethics, they argue that social workers are expected to support the moral and political stance of

their agencies and abandon their personal and political values—specifically their class interests as workers. They conclude that the service ethic promotes institutional loyalty and the coinciding of the social workers' interests with management. In regard to the social workers' autonomy in their practice with clients, the exercise of agency control on caseloads, accountability, and content of practice are noted. Other studies (Rein, 1970) indicate that workers will comply with agency rules rather than their own evaluation of the clients' needs. As to the most minimal forms of job security, the unorganized social worker is more vulnerable than the organized blue collar worker, with no grievance procedure involving arbitration and seniority (Wagner & Cohen, 1978).

Within the profession, the elitist attitude still persists that in an industrial profit-making enterprise, collective bargaining is necessary, but that in a nonprofit agency, that same process cannot be applied (Hush, 1969). If social workers and administrators share the same background and goals, and if most social workers assume administrative positions at some point in their careers (Skidmore, 1978), then the perception of the union as an outside party threatening existing group-centered leadership serves a particular management interest. Such a perspective would also emphasize the different interests of professional social workers and nonprofessionals, rather than their common tie as workers.

In a struggle for improving salary and employment benefits, one social worker describes the shock of discovering the powerlessness of professionals (Schlachter, 1971) and the specific effects of paternalism. Security for the individual is determined by the relationship with the administrator rather than in association with one's colleagues. After achieving union recognition, this social worker summarizes the lessons learned: social workers can work collectively; social workers can act aggressively to pursue their interests as workers; and social workers can only be effective advocates of clients if they are capable of advocating for themselves as workers.

In the public sector and in large bureaucracies, these dynamics of professionalism have less impact. Workers have to deal with an impersonal organization—changing and conflicting regulations, a myriad of forms, communication breakdowns, etc.—and collective action is necessary. Since such bureaucracies and their top administrators may be responsible to city, county, and state governments, even upper level social work supervisors can organize together for particular purposes.

RESISTANCE TO UNION ORGANIZING

From this writer's experience, management, beginning with the election conference, will usually argue for extending the election date to allow ample opportunity for campaigning. The campaign may be organized around letter writing, staff meetings, or individual supervisory contacts. The theme is that unionization will result in a loss of benefits and the institution of rigid and formal relationships between staff and administration. Prior commitments to salary increases and job classification changes are withdrawn; workers may be told that existing benefits would need to be renegotiated; the use of time clocks may be threatened. One director concluded that a 15-minute rest period in a contract would require a possible disciplinary action for the employee if a minute more or less were taken. In a child care agency, the director announced that unionization would necessitate using monies available for salaries to pay management attorney fees.

Most administrators will respond as hard-line industrial managers, even though possessing liberal credentials (Fitch, 1950). A few executives can accept the union and collective bargaining. One agency director reported being besieged by other administrative colleagues and agency board members who viewed the union organizing as nothing less than a Communist conspiracy. Initially, he perceived that his leadership and integrity were being challenged, and that as a father-figure he had failed as well. However, with his strong commitment to the staff and the program, he decided to accept the decision to organize. He interpreted the collective bargaining process to the board and received support from important allies. Salary increases were implemented, and a collective bargaining agreement incorporating a number of flexible provisions was concluded. Currently, the union and the agency have been involved in areas of mutual interest affecting the funding and setting of salary schedules. Such accommodations will be more apt to develop if agency boards have greater representation by organized labor and as union representation becomes more legitimized.

There is less overt resistance to union organizing in public welfare agencies. In the industrialized states, there has been historically some form of union recognition. Unions and associations are fairly large and able to utilize political pressure effectively. The public welfare agency's response will often be to pit associations and unions against each other and will often prefer the association to the union as the exclusive bargaining representative of the workers. Within such large organizations, resistance and acceptance will vary within departments, among supervisors, and between rural and urban areas.

UNION ORGANIZING ISSUES

The organizing climate has been affected by broad economic and social conditions. The job market for social workers has tightened up, limiting job mobility. Severe budget cutbacks and reductions in social service are constant threats. Salaries for social workers have been unable to keep pace with inflation. The contract gains for teachers (Haughton, 1969) and other professionals have enhanced the collective bargaining process. However, specific issues at the workplace serve to trigger off an organizing drive. An unfair discharge, unilateral reduction of hours, and arbitrary layoffs are concrete examples in the organizing of community mental health centers. In other cases, social workers may see the awarding of promotions and merit salary increases as blatantly inequitable. The distributions of salary increments, not low pay, may be the key issue. New workers are hired at higher rates than those currently employed. Being a male and the primary breadwinner, for one director, were sufficient criteria for determining basic salary differences. In many agencies, staff personnel practice committees recognize that final authority rests with the management, with the agency having no obligations to bargain on grievances and benefits. One agency board announced to the staff personnel committee that other priorities compelled the agency to suspend further discussion for six months.

As this point, potential union organizers emerge within the agency and begin to articulate the grievances collectively. A profile of an effective social worker organizer, not influenced by the politics of professionalism, might include:

1. the organizer develops credibility at the workplace through job performance, knowledge of the agency, and rapport with coworkers;
2. the experiences as an activist provide the worker with organizing skills and an understanding of power relationships;
3. the organizer supports democratic decision making, is committed to uniting workers across occupational lines, and is prepared to assume planning and leadership responsibilities.

Public sector social workers have some basic protection in areas of job security and promotions, incorporated into the civil service system. Caseloads, physical working conditions, training, downgrading of services, and salaries are often the immediate issues. Since these bargaining units may be fairly large, unions and associations may compete extensively for representation.

COLLECTIVE BARGAINING LAWS AND THE SCOPE OF BARGAINING

Many social workers are not covered under comprehensive bargaining laws, and the scope of bargaining is expressly limited, particularly as it relates to client issues. These obstacles create impasses and increase the likelihood that professional social workers will resort to strike.

In the public sector, bargaining laws are fragmentary and follow no particular pattern. Only 11 states have comprehensive bargaining laws affecting all state and local government workers (Wurf, 1973). In some states, only local government workers are covered; and in a few others, only state employees are included. Wages and fringe benefits are not subject to bargaining in other states. Such legislation cannot conflict with civil service or other statutes. As such, civil service regulations preempt important bargaining issues that are negotiated in the private sector. In addition, when agreement can be reached at the bargaining table, governmental units may still refuse to relinquish their authority.

In contrast to the private sector, there are prohibitions against strike activity by public workers (Tanimoto & Najita, 1974). Restraints on strike activity and penalties against employees and employee organizations are prescribed under many laws, although some recent legislation grants the right to strike if essential services are maintained and if the health, safety, and welfare of the public are not threatened, i.e., Alaska, Minnesota, Oregon, and Pennsylvania.

Within the voluntary sector, the situation is similarly confusing. Depending upon the amount of interstate commerce, social workers might be covered under the National Labor Relations Act. As amended in 1974, private health care institutions are now included: hospitals, health maintenance organizations, health clinics, nursing homes, extended care facilities, or other institutions caring for the sick and aged. The Act explicitly protects the right to strike. Most other agency social workers would be covered under state statutes modeled after the Wagner Act, or treated similarly as other public employees. Not surprisingly, 25 percent of strikes and 33 percent within AFSCME involved recognition (Stieber, 1973). The strikes of social workers in New York City and Chicago in the mid-1960s concretely illustrate the impact of bargaining constraints and the limited scope of bargaining.

Following a work stoppage by the Independent Union of Public Aid Employees in 1966 and a demand for a collective bargaining agreement with Cook County, the Cook County Commissioner's Fact Finding Board issued a report which included the following interesting observations (Elson, Leibik, & Savers, 1960). First, union organizing of public workers had been accompanied by strike activity reminiscent of the wave of strikes following World War II. Second, in comparison to teacher unions, labor scholars knew and wrote less about social workers. Third, it would be in the best interests of the clients and community if social workers were provided with adequate protection and acceptable working conditions. Fourth, the main causes for strikes related to recognition and the right to bargain, grievances over working conditions with no recourse to arbitration, and a failure in the use of mediation, fact finding, and advisory arbitration at impasses. The Committee also heard testimony documenting the effect of collective bargaining in decreasing turnover and in attracting competent staff through higher salaries. For the Committee, the concept of collective bargaining implied a healthy bargaining relationship where disputes could be resolved by peaceful means. The Committee's recommendations included organizational privileges and a representation election which was subsequently held and won by the union.

In 1967, the IUPAE entered into negotiations with the Cook County Department of Public Aid, and the demands included salary plan changes, payment for Blue Cross, grievance procedure advisory arbitrators, job protection for temporary workers, and progression for clerical workers (Weber, 1969). The Union also proposed that the Department issue handbooks covering regulations for recipients and a rule change to permit the disbursement of checks to recipients without approval of the Central Office. Weber (1969) observes that unions of social workers are more than vehicles for improving wages and working conditions, but serve to reform the welfare system as well. The County Department's position was that client-service demands were outside the scope of bargaining, that the balance of the union proposals were in conflict with Civil Service and the Illinois Department of Public Aid, and therefore, that the County had no authority to make decisions in those areas. In April 1967, the majority of social workers engaged in strike action.

A settlement was subsequently agreed upon excluding policy demands and ratified by the Union. Meanwhile, the Board of Commissioners refrained from acting upon the settlement since money and issues beyond their authority were supposedly involved. The basic settlement was later scuttled; salary increases were reduced, increases in Blue Cross coverage were not provided, and advisory arbitration was withdrawn. Weber (1969) contends that the strike had limited impact. No essential services were denied, and community organizations and craft unions exerted minimal political pressure upon the Cook County Board of Commissioners.

The Social Service Employees Union entered into negotiations with New York City in 1964. Demands related to additional staff, reduced caseloads, career and salary plans, training, and improved physical plant conditions, i.e., overcrowding, ventilation, and space for private interviews (Kendellen, 1969). The City's position was that many issues, including additional staff and physical plant, were not negotiable. In 1965, the longest strike of public employees in New York City's history began. The strike ended on February 1, although strike penalties, including jailings and fines, were the last issues to be resolved. The Dean Committee recommended that all issues submitted by the Union be discussed through a fact-finding panel and that salary and classifications were subject to modification. The panel's recommendations incorporated many of the basic demands of the Union: limited caseload size, joint caseload committee, training, physical plant improvements, and a committee to review the entire status of collective bargaining and career and salary plans. The membership support, the Union's effectiveness in halting the agency operation, the contribution of Dean Schottland, and the important role of the New York City Labor Trades Council are cited as the key elements in winning the strike.

In the next negotiations, the Union proposed many client service demands which it argued would improve the caseworker's job. They included an annual revision of budgets in accordance with the Consumer Price Index, automatic clothing allowance, the right of recipients to fair hearings prior to suspension of assistance, telephone allowance for clients, and availability of residential treatment. The response was that only the City could determine the standards of service and the manner in which operations could be conducted. There were also doubts as to whether caseloads, staff reserves, and training programs would be negotiable. The ensuing strike was unsuccessful, as there was limited support, minimal attainable demands, and divisions on client-service issues.

Voluntary agency employers also reject client-service issues as outside the scope of bargaining and subject only to management rights. Standards of practice, proposals related to in-service training, caseloads, and agency board and staff committees may prompt a similar response. In one Family Service agency, a plan for being accessible to clients during evening hours was formulated without any consultation with the union. The union insisted that this issue be negotiated. The consequence was the establishment of evening hours with flexi-time provisions for social workers. Too frequently, however, the union is judged to be acting on the basis of narrow interests (Schulman, 1978). The irony is that professional social workers are supposedly trained to possess competence in advocacy negotiating but are denied this expertise across the bargaining table. Teachers, in contrast, have made significant inroads in regard to teaching methods, assignments, class size, and curriculum content.

An alternative for social work unions is to act outside the bargaining arena. Training in client advocacy was directly provided by a union as part of its steward education program. The issue of staff-client ratios was directly brought to the state legislature and action was taken. A booklet summarizing eligibility requirements for clients was prepared by a union. The publicizing of crowded conditions and long waiting periods for clients led to the decentralization of offices. Unions have joined in coalitions in struggle for community control (Tambor, 1973). Nevertheless, it would seem logical to conclude that the providing of social services presupposes common purposes, and some progressive administrators may enter into bilateral decision making with the union.

In summary, impasses between management and the union can often be averted by allowing for meaningful bargaining with no restrictions in its scope. The right to strike is fundamental to the bargaining process, a fact recognized by the social work profession (NASW Standards for Social Work Practice, 1971). In strike situations, emergency services can be provided independently or by mutual agreement of the parties (Warner & Hennessy, 1967; Ryan, 1970). The success of the strike may depend upon the essentiality of both the service and the job functions of those social workers (Lightman, 1978). When these factors are absent, however, the agency may be just as vulnerable as the union since questions relating to continued funding and support can be raised. Concomitantly, the nature of the service and its delivery may be constructively debated within a public forum (Warner & Hennessy, 1967). The New York City and Chicago social workers' strikes clearly indicate the vital function of organized labor's political clout, in addition to client and community support.

Before a strike, intervention through mediation and fact-finding can be most helpful. In New York City, the constructive role of the Dean Committee was noted. With economic issues, where the scope of the bargaining may be clearly defined, such factors as the agency's ability to pay, cost of living, and comparable salary rates may be considered by the fact-finder. Where the bargaining issues are more complex and the positions of management and union have been polarized, then voluntary arbitration, a mechanism not sufficiently used, may be most appropriate. The union and the agency agree, in essence, to submit the dispute to a mutually agreed upon third party whose decision is binding upon both parties. By understanding the full dimensions of collective bargaining, it should be apparent that neither social workers nor unions can be solely responsible for strikes. If a fair determination or accurate judgment is to be made, then each given situation would need to be evaluated independently. Since a strike may mean a no-win situation for management, union, and clients, then a mutual obligation exists to exhaust every possible means to arrive at a settlement.

CONCLUSION

Industrial social work programs are also linking the profession with workers and unions, an important new constituency (Efthim, 1976). With student placements in locals and the employment of social workers in unions, mental health agencies, and labor organizations such as

AFSCME District Council 37, schools of social work and the social work profession have become less isolated from unions and blue collar workers. As social workers become involved in joint labor-management mental health programs, particular knowledge of labor-management relationships, including the grievance procedure of the collective bargaining agreement, will be necessary (Perlis, 1978).

As attitudes within the social work profession toward collective bargaining and unions continue to change, their common purposes may be more readily understood. The editorial comments in *Social Work Today* in 1936 are just as relevant now:

> Readers of *Social Work Today* are fully aware of the genuine concerns of the trade union movement in social work with standards. . . .
> Have the professional bodies and the trade union organizations common purposes? Is there a meeting ground for cooperative effort?
> Any cursory examination of the program or demands of the trade union reveals their goals to be as clear and direct as those of the professional society—high standards of service and high standards of employment practices. . .

REFERENCES

Cole, E. Unions in social work. *Encyclopedia of social work*. New York: National Association of Social Workers, 1977.

Dulles, F. *Labor in America*. Northbrook: ARM, 1966.

Efthim, A. Serve the U.S. work force: A new role and new constituencies for schools of social work. *Journal of Education for Social Work*, 1976, *12*, 29-36.

Elson, A., Leibik, L., & Savers. C. Cook County Commissioners fact finding board report on collective bargaining and county public aid employees. *Industrial and Labor Relations Review*, 1967, *20*, 457-477.

Fitch, J. *Professional workers as trade unionists*. Address to National Conference on Social Welfare, 1950.

Haughton, R. *Collective bargaining, strikes, and public employees*. Presentation to Commonwealth Club of California, 1969.

Hush, H. Collective bargaining in voluntary agencies. *Social Casework*, 1969, *50*, 210-213.

Kendellen, A., *The social service employees union: A study of rival unionism in the public sector*. Unpublished doctoral dissertation, Cornell University, 1969.

Levine, G. *Collective bargaining for social workers in voluntary agencies*. Toronto: Ontario Association of Professional Social Workers, 1975.

Lightman, E. An imbalance of power: Social workers in unions. *Administration in Social Work*, 1978, *2*, 74-82.

Martin, M. *Social workers and collective bargaining in British Columbia*. Toronto: Ontario Association of Professional Social Workers, 1975.

NASW standards for social work personnel practices. Washington, D.C.: National Association of Social Workers, 1971.

Perlis, L. Industrial social work: Problems and prospects. *NASW News*. Washington, D.C.: National Association of Social Workers, 1978.

Rehr, H. Problems for a profession in a strike situation. *Social Work*, 1969, *5*, 22-25.

Rein, M. Social work in search of a radical profession. *Social Work*, 1970, *15*, 13-29.

Ryan, T. When an agency is struck. *Catholic Charities Review*, 1970, *54*, 3-10.

Schlachter, R. *The worker: A new self image*. Paper presented at the Ninety-Eighth Annual Conference on Social Welfare, 1971.

Schulman, L. Unionization and the professional employee: The social service director's view. In S. Slavin (Ed.), *Social Administration: The Management of the Social Services*. New York: The Haworth Press and Council on Social Work Education, 1978.

Skidmore, R. Administration content for all social work graduate students. *Administration in Social Work*, 1978, *2*, 61-72.

Stieber, J. *Public employee unionism: Structure, growth, policy*. Washington, D.C.: The Brookings Institution, 1973.

Tambor, M. Unions in voluntary agencies. *Social Work*, 1973, *4*, 41-47.

Tanimoto, H., & Najita, I. *Guide to statutory provisions in public sector collective bargaining*. Honolulu: Industrial Relations Center, 1974.

Wagner, D., & Cohen, M. Social worker, class, and professionalism. *Catalyst*, 1978, *1*, 25-56.

Warner, K., & Hennessy, M. *Public management at the bargaining table*. Chicago: Public Personnel Association, 1967.

Weber, A. Paradise lost: Or whatever happened to the Chicago social workers. *Industrial and Labor Relations Review*, 1969, *22*, 323-338.

Wurf, J. *A federal bargaining act for state and local public employees*. Washington, D.C.: The Coalition of American Public Employees, 1973.

21

Social Workers, Strikes, and Service to Clients

ERNIE S. LIGHTMAN

As divorce is to marriage, so a strike is to the collective bargaining process. Neither outcome is inevitable, nor even particularly desirable, but the possibility always exists that two parties in a relationship will be unable to reconcile their differences in a mutually satisfactory manner. Often the real victims are relatively uninvolved third parties, be they children, clients, or the public.

The analogy breaks down quickly, of course, for although marriage need not be a relationship based on conflict, collective bargaining is fundamentally adversarial in nature. It is based on the view that there are essential and fundamental differences of interest between employer and employee in any work setting.

Despite initial misgivings, many social workers now seem to accept the idea of trade unionism and their own membership in unions. Several years ago, Tambor cited figures from the Metropolitan Detroit Chapter of the National Association of Social Workers, in which 50 percent of the respondents indicated that they belonged to a union and nearly 75 percent approved of the idea of social workers joining unions.[1] Current data on the extent of union membership by social workers in the United States are not available, even as estimates. It is believed to be small but increasing rapidly, particularly among those with less than a master's in social work (M.S.W.) degree.[2] Recently, Oppenheimer suggested that the increasingly bureaucratic settings in which social workers are employed along with other white-collar professionals would make these groups amenable to the prospect of unionization.[3] Finally, labor laws in many parts of North America are such that growing numbers of social workers will find themselves placed in unions, often without much direct say.[4]

Even as the issue of unionism becomes less of a problem to many social workers, the question of the strike remains a major dilemma. Indeed, as more social workers find themselves belonging to unions, they will be faced by the need to develop an appropriate response to the strike. In the United States, direct experience with strikes by social workers is limited.[5] The literature, some of which is several years old, appears to focus almost as much on the appropriate response to someone else's strike as to the issues involved in a strike by social workers themselves.[6]

In Canada, by contrast, strikes by social workers, although not yet a common occurrence, are much more frequent than in the United States. This results in large part from more liberal laws governing strikes in the public sector.[7] These same laws have led to a generally higher rate of unionization among social workers in Canada. A 1975 estimate placed "the majority" of social workers in Canada as belonging to unions. It should be noted, however, that some of the most acrimonious Canadian strikes have involved the voluntary or quasipublic sectors (for example, Big Brothers in Toronto; Children's Aid in Sault Ste. Marie, Ontario, and in Hastings County; and Catholic Children's Aid in Toronto). Some observers suggest that the Canadian experience in this area could portend future occurrences in the United States.[8] In addition, the economic cutbacks and block funding affecting social services, coupled with a national ideological commitment toward deregulation and decontrol, could place social workers in a position in which they are both legally free to strike and virtually forced to do so in defense of their jobs, their clients, or both.

PERCEPTIONS OF STRIKES

Levine has noted that the operation of any enterprise, including a social agency, is based on the exercise of power. Employers have the power to make decisions while individual employees have little power to challenge this authority. It is in the nature of power that those who hold it will retain and attempt to augment it, until such time as a countervailing power arises to challenge this hold. The union represents such a countervailing force. When two potential sources of power in the workplace come into conflict, it is inevitable that differences will occasionally be unbridgeable. There follows escalation of conflict that results in a strike by the employees or a lockout by the employer. In either case, there is an exercise of pure economic, and occasionally, political, power, in an attempt by one side to force the other to accept its terms for settlement.[9]

This model of the collective bargaining process is not a normative

prescription, but a description of the essential nature of collective bargaining in North America today. Such a conflictual and power-based
approach toward decision making sits uncomfortably with many social
workers who prefer to believe that good faith and reasoned interchange
can resolve any work-related problem. At the same time, conflict and
power do not fit easily with many traditional social work values. Blugerman describes the dilemma: "The tenets of conflict are as different as
night and day from those of classic social work practice values. Power is
clearly not the main reason why we are in this work."[10]

The issue of striking, however, goes beyond a mere discomfort with
abstract notions of power and conflict. The strike by a social worker involves the withdrawal of labor, that is services, and the costs of this action may be borne, in the first instance at least, by the client. The social
worker, in general, is not believed to possess economic power, and the
union may be seen as the agent of the social worker's self-interest.[11] The
strike then indicates that self-interest has been assigned a higher priority
than the needs of those being served. A 1979 strike by British social
workers, most of whom were local government employees, lasted nearly
six months. A review of this time portrayed the conflict of values as:

> a clash between two opposed world views—the expressive caring tradi-
> tion dating from the Victorian origins of social work and the apparently
> instrumentalist attitude of the contemporary industrial trade union-
> ist.[12]

When social workers do go on strike, both union and management claim
that their primary concern is for the needs of the clients, and each party
blames the other for having allowed matters to deteriorate to the point
where a strike became necessary. The presence of innocent and often
disadvantaged victims in a social work strike, along with the general inexperience in the collective bargaining process on the part of both staff
and voluntary boards, may result in anger and hostility reminiscent of
the early union struggles of the 1930s.[13] In the long and bitter strike by
children's aid workers in 1979 in Sault Ste. Marie, for example, the provincial ministry of social services asked the Ontario Association of Professional Social Workers for help in recruiting social workers to the city,
reportedly at very high salaries, either to ensure continuity in the delivery of essential services or to break the strike, depending on one's particular viewpoint. The association declined to become involved. A 1980
strike by children's aid workers in Eastern Ontario resulted in newspa-
per advertisements seeking "contract workers for the duration of strike
by CUPE [Canadian Union of Public Employees] local 2197 only."[14]

APPROACHES TO STRIKES

On a daily basis, individuals can juggle or perhaps ignore uncertainties about unions, but the strike represents the symbolic throwing down of the gauntlet, the requirement to take a public stand. Ambivalence is no longer a viable option. The responses by social workers have been varied. Some have denied the strike as an option, either by explicitly stating that service needs must come first or by attempting to avoid being placed in a strike situation. Alexander et al. found respondents in their survey "overall strongly favor the most moderate of union tactics—arbitration—and strongly disapprove of the more forceful and traditional tactics such as strikes. . . ."[15] In 1960, Rehr discussed a hospital strike that did not involve social workers, and stated "professional responsibility takes precedence over . . . personal aims and views."[16] A different approach was taken during a 1970 municipal strike in Vancouver, British Columbia, when social workers attempted to have their services labeled by the union as "essential" so that continuity of checks to families on welfare could be ensured. The request was refused by the union, so that social workers who continued to work through the strike were "blacklisted."[17] More recently, attempts were made to organize nonmedical professionals in Ontario hospitals into collective bargaining units that would "not accept the notion of resort to economic force for the settlement of . . . disputes in the public sector. . . ."[18]

A second basic approach toward the dilemma of striking has been to redefine the union, and the strike, so that the two are seen not as agents of self-interest but as means to some broader social good. Galper, for example, sees the real goal as being radical change in society, with the union, and presumably the strike, as instruments to effect this positive change.[19] In 1971, Bohr and others found evidence of "pervasive change from an individual to a social view of altruism," the notion that under certain conditions the strike may be justified in terms of some probable long-term gain.[20] Bohr and his co-workers were describing a hospital setting in which the strikers were support staff, largely unskilled, and primarily minorities and women. The conflict over crossing the picket line, as these authors saw it, was not one between an act of caring and a political act but between two different forms of help.

Finally, one can simply acknowledge the strike as an essential component of free collective bargaining and attempt to ensure the minimum harm to clients. This is essentially the view of the National Association of Social Workers and has also been stated by others.[21] As one participant in the 1979 British social work strike said, "the strike made it a job like every other job, to allow us to identify with the people who we were visiting."[22] In this view, social workers are seen as workers like others, with needs to which an employer must respond. The uniqueness of the profession is denied and just as others in helping professions—physicians, nurses, and teachers—respond to unions and strikes, so too will social workers.

In all this discussion, however, there is a very little empirical data concerning how social workers actually respond to the idea of the strike. It is in an attempt to help build this data base that this study now turns. To do this, the chapter presents some baseline data on social workers and strikes. Personal interviews were conducted with 121 members of the provincial association of social workers in Toronto. Members were asked about their experience with and their attitude toward strikes, the conditions, if any, under which they would be prepared to withdraw their services, and which bargaining issues might induce this behavior.

METHODS AND SAMPLE

A random selection of names was drawn from the current membership list of the Metropolitan Toronto branch of the Ontario Association of Professional Social Workers to yield a sample of approximately 125 names. A letter of introduction on University of Toronto letterhead was sent to each of the names selected, informing the recipient of the purpose of the study and requesting participation. About a week later, one of thirteen previously trained M.S.W. candidates at the University of Toronto tried to make telephone contact to arrange a convenient time for a personal interview.[23] If contact could not be made, the respondent declined to participate, or other specific eligibility criteria were not met, another name was drawn at random from the list and another letter was sent out. This process continued until 121 people were contacted and interviews were completed. The reasons for exclusion included the following: the person's name was not in the current Toronto telephone directory; the letter of introduction was returned by the post office; the person was a social work student or faculty member at the University of Toronto; the address indicated a residence outside the boundaries of the municipality; and the person had not worked as a social worker during the previous four years.

The questionnaire itself was largely precoded to ensure for reliability, since there were thirteen different interviewers. The first section of the questionnaire sought demographic and historical information concerning unions and strikes; the second section contained attitudinal items using Likert-type scales; and the final section asked a variety of other attitudinal questions. The instrument was pretested on ten respondents, then shortened. Each of the 121 respondents was asked to sign a consent form as required by the University's Office of Research

Administration. Actual administration of the instrument took just over thirty minutes. The results were analyzed using the Statistical Package for the Social Sciences at the University of Toronto Computer Centre.[24] It is important to note that while the sample for this study was randomly drawn from the membership of the professional association, membership in this body is voluntary and restricted to those meeting certain (primarily educational) criteria. As a result the findings of this study cannot automatically be applied to the larger population of all social workers. There is no legal definition or regulation of social workers in Ontario and so the extent and even the direction of this possible bias cannot be determined; it is, however, generally believed that the more conservative elements of the profession and direct practice workers (not necessarily the same groups) tend to be overrepresented within the membership of the association.

Just over two-thirds (69 percent) of the sample was female and almost all the respondents (89 percent) had an M.S.W. degree or equivalent. Respondents worked in a wide variety of settings with the most frequent areas being medical (20 percent) and child welfare (18 percent). Nearly half (49 percent) worked in large organizations with more than 100 employees in total, but 37 percent of the respondents worked with fewer than ten social workers. Approximately two-thirds of the sample was employed in organizations in which primary funding came from government sources. Forty-two percent indicated primary employment in management positions, whereas the remaining 58 percent indicated line staff. Some of these organizational or structural considerations may have biased the reported attitudes of the sample. For example, management, who are excluded by law from membership in the union, might have more negative attitudes toward strikes than would line staff. The sample was dichotomized in a variety of ways: management and line staff; those in small (less than 100) and large organizations; governmental and nongovernmental employees; those in settings where some or all social workers were unionized and those where none was unionized. In each case, all the attitudinal questions reported later in the text were rerun using a chi-square test to observe for differences in the separate groups. Few individual items yielded significant results, and in virtually all the cases, none of the differences was significant. This would support the observation that it is the respondents' common experience and socialization as social workers which is relevant and not their particular work status or setting.

Respondents in general had limited prior experience with unions: sixty-two people (51 percent) from the sample said social workers in their organization were not currently unionized, and only twenty people (16.5 percent) from the sample actually belonged to a union. Only ten (8 percent) of the respondents had belonged to a union or association that went on strike during the time that they were members, and of these ten, six individuals went on strike; four did not.

AGREEING TO STRIKE

Perhaps the most basic question in the survey was whether there are any conditions under which a strike would (or would not) be considered an acceptable or appropriate action. To probe this area the questionnaire contained, mixed among other issues, a series of Likert-type statements suggesting various possible approaches toward the idea of going on strike. Respondents were asked to indicate agreement or disagreement on a five-point scale, which has been collapsed for present purposes to a trichotomy.

Survey findings indicate a wide variety of attitudes toward striking, as shown in Table 21–1. At one end of the spectrum nearly one in ten (8 percent) believed it is professional to strike "under all circumstances," while at the other extreme, nearly one in five (18 percent) reported that

TABLE 21–1. Attitudes of Respondents toward Striking ($N = 120$, percentage)[a]

Question	Disagree	Uncertain	Agree
It is professional for social workers to strike under all circumstances	83.3	8.3	8.3
It is professional for social workers to strike if adequate safeguards for the client are provided	15.0	5.8	79.2
It is professional for social workers to strike under extenuating circumstances	15.8	17.5	66.7
I would not go on strike under any circumstances	69.2	12.5	18.3
It is irresponsible to the client for a social worker to go on strike	52.5	15.8	31.7
Social workers provide an essential service [that] should not be interrupted by a strike	52.5	18.3	29.2

[a]One respondent failed to answer these questions. Columns may not total to 100 because of rounding.

he or she would not strike "under any circumstances." Over three-quar-
ters of the respondents (79 percent) approved the idea of striking if
"adequate safeguards to the client are provided." The more ambiguous
"under extenuating circumstances" retained virtually the same disagreement rate of 15 percent, but caused some of those who had previously agreed to the idea of striking to fall now into the "uncertain"
category.

The two remaining items in the table, referring to responsibility to
clients and essentiality of service, evoked the most mixed responses.
About 30 percent of the sample disagreed with the strike option in each
of these cases, in part because of the lack of explicit safeguards for the
clients; at the same time, over half the sample (52 percent) did not feel
striking was either irresponsible to the clients or that the service provided was of a sufficiently essential nature as to preclude the strike in
principle. It appears that there was a "hard core" of roughly one in five
respondents for whom a strike was not an acceptable alternative. The remaining 80 percent did not oppose the idea of a strike in theory, provided certain qualifying conditions were met. Even within this group,
however, there was substantial difficulty among the members over the
notions of responsibility to clients.

Specific Issues

What are the specific issues over which social workers might be prepared
to strike? Given the findings, one may anticipate reasons to strike that
would encompass client- and service-related concerns along with the
more traditional union goal of material gain. Whether client-related issues are more or less important than an issue of self-interest such as
wages is perhaps the most interesting of all the strike-related questions.
To explore this area directly, respondents were given "a list of issues
[that] might influence your decision to go on strike." They were then
asked to indicate "whether dissatisfaction in each of these areas prob-
ably/might/or under no circumstances would cause you to go on strike."
The results are shown in Table 21–2.

Traditional union priorities as these are conventionally understood,
such as wages and fringe benefits, were not the major reasons for which
social workers expressed a readiness to go on strike. Even the basic "survival" issue of job security, the single area in which unions are often perceived to exercise the greatest power, received the second highest response rate among the reasons that would "under no circumstances"
cause the respondent to go on strike.

At the other extreme, service-related issues, particularly quality of
service, evoked the most favorable response to the prospect of going on

TABLE 21-2. Issues That Would Cause Respondents to Go on Strike

Issue	Number[a]	Percentage		
		Probably	Might	Under No Circumstances
A majority vote of the union members	118	44.1	38.1	17.8
Wages	119	16.8	55.5	27.7
Fringe benefits (holidays, overtime)	119	11.8	38.7	49.6
Job security	119	28.6	41.2	30.3
Quality of service	116	51.7	34.5	13.8
Decision-making authority in organization	116	25.9	47.4	26.7
Caseload	117	21.4	50.4	28.2

[a]Numbers vary because not all respondents answered all questions. Columns may not total to 100 because of rounding.

strike. Over half the respondents (52 percent) indicated they would "probably" strike over this matter, while only 14 percent, or approximately one in seven respondents, reported that "under no circumstances" would he or she consider striking over quality of service. (It may be noted that this 14 percent response rate was even less than the 18 percent of respondents who had previously indicated that they would not go on strike under any circumstances.)

The importance assigned to a simple majority vote of the union membership on a decision to strike was perhaps unanticipated in the study and presumably reflects the substantial role assigned to staff meetings and collective decision making in the formulation of agency policy. At the same time, the more narrowly defined issue of authority and decision-making power within the context of the agency was much less critical.

Though caseload may be among the most important variables in predicting quality of service, it apparently was seen by respondents as more highly associated with wages and fringe benefits as outcomes of a total agency budget, and its size was cited least often after wages and fringe benefits as among the "probable" causes of strike action. Moreover, after fringes and job security, caseload was identified most frequently as an issue that "under no circumstances" would lead to a strike.

Salary-Caseload Mix

The results in Table 21–2 suggest that the general concept of quality of service was the most important probable indicator of the intent to strike, while traditional union concerns of wages, fringe benefits, job security, and work load were much less likely to lead to this outcome. Nevertheless, as agency and government resources directed toward social services continue to undergo increasing scrutiny, social workers may face additional dilemmas of choice with traditional union concerns. If financial resources are limited, would social workers prefer a given salary budget to be shared among a larger or smaller staff? The first alternative would imply more workers on the line, with smaller individual caseloads (and presumably better quality of service to clients), but individual salaries would be less; the second alternative would yield a smaller staff with higher individual salaries but also higher caseloads. Would an unacceptable response in this area lead workers to agree to a strike?

A final set of questions in this study sought to probe this trade-off directly and to explore its probable impact on a decision to strike. Respondents were asked to assume that they were working in a child welfare agency that had just received a 5 percent budget increase for the pending fiscal year. They were presented with three scenarios: a small or no salary increase for workers with caseloads remaining the same; a slight increase in salary (4–5 percent) with caseloads increasing by 7–10 percent; and a larger salary increase (7–8 percent) with increases in caseload of 10–12 percent. Seventy-four percent of the sample would "willingly" or "reluctantly" accept the first option that the remaining 26 percent would "not accept"; the acceptance figures for the second and third options were 60 and 36 percent, respectively. Given these three options as the only ones available, over half the sample would have been most ready to accept the first package. Respondents were then asked if they would consider going on strike in response to any of the options: 42 percent said no, 9 percent said "definitely," and the remaining 50 percent indicated "possibly." Of those reporting that they would consider the strike option, over half (57 percent) specified that the third choice —the high salary/high caseload mix—would most likely cause them to consider going on strike. Given the trade-off of salary for caseload, the clear priority on the part of the respondents in this study appeared to be the protection of the latter, even at the expense of the former.

Self-Interest vs. Altruism

One of the central tensions of social policy is that between self-interested motivation for human behavior on the one hand and actions on behalf of some larger group or community on the other. In his oft-cited

Hobhouse Lecture, for example, Macbeath presented, as the essential dilemma of social policy, the conflict between the self-regarding, or egoistical acts, of human beings and other, or altruistic, behaviors; Boulding used a similar approach fundamentally to distinguish economic from social policy.[25]

The trade union as an organization must confront this tension between self-interest and altruism and attempt to locate itself along a continuum between the two poles. It is probably fair to say that in most cases the primary goals and motives of a union are those of self-interest, marked by occasional forays in the direction of altruism. Indeed, Collard has stated that it is a "truly altruistic residual"—that extent to which motivation is not marked by self-interested behavior—that forms a major area of interest in social policy.[26]

Within the United States this altruistic component to union motivation is relatively small, at least in comparison with many other countries. Since its earliest days, the trade union movement in the United States has been characterized by what Samuel Gompers described as "business unionism," a concern with such "bread-and-butter" issues as wages, fringe benefits, job protection, and job security. Broader social goals have not been met through the workplace but have emerged through the political process largely independent of the union movement. In other countries egoistic and altruistic motivations coexist within the labor movement. Mishra has hypothesized that in a country, the larger the proportion of the work force that was unionized, the more developed would be the social welfare system.[27] In Britain, for example, the Trades Union Congress has long been part of the Labour Party. Both personal and social goals traditionally are pursued simultaneously on the collective bargaining and political fronts. In Canada, collective bargaining is conducted largely on the U.S. model, with many of the same "international" unions operating in both countries. Yet, at the same time, there does exist in Canada a tension somewhat similar to the British experience.[28] The Canadian Labour Congress maintains a formal institutional linkage with the third major political party, the New Democratic Party, and both personal and altruistic goals and motives are regularly articulated from within the labor movement.

CONCLUSION

Although the full extent of "altruistic residual" for union behavior is a matter of some dispute and may in fact be fundamentally unmeasurable, it is clear that the trade union as an entity illustrates the conflicting motivations of the social and economic markets. The author began with an assumption that on a micro level the individual social worker is faced with similar dilemmas of choice. In particular, the strike was seen as highlighting the conflict between self-interest and other-directed goals. The basic findings suggest that this tension may well be resolved by social workers in a way that differs fundamentally from those assumed to operate in the collective bargaining process. The values and priorities of social workers as expressed by the respondents in this study did not appear to be those of the self-interested economic person who is generally assumed to make up the membership of most unions.

Although most social workers appear to have no philosophical, ideological, or even professional objection, in principle, to the strike, there does remain a very strong concern for the needs of a client. Questions of service delivery were more important causes of possible strike action than were matters involving dollars and cents in the compensation package. Though comparative data from a sample of "average" workers—blue or white collar—are not available, it would be surprising to find wages, fringe benefits, and even job security presented as such unimportant inducements to strike. Likewise, a readiness to accept little or no salary increase in exchange for a constant work load size is not a finding that would be readily anticipated throughout the economy. Moreover, quality of service, however defined, probably would not be ranked so significantly on a wide scale.

As a final cautionary note, it must be remembered that the data are attitudinal. Relatively few respondents in this study had actually encountered a strike; thus, their responses must be taken as expressions of probable intent to act rather than reflections of past experience. As actual strike deadlines near, service goals could be traded off for more tangible monetary gains.[29]

The conclusion remains, however, that social work values did appear to influence the priorities of these social work respondents. In expressing a readiness to go on strike, these workers as a group not only seemed to place less emphasis on self-centered priorities than would be anticipated traditionally but seemed to give precedence to client-directed goals.

Notes and References

1. See Milton Tambor, "Unions and Voluntary Agencies," *Social Work*, 18 (July 1973), pp. 41-47.
2. Leslie B. Alexander, Philip Lichtenberg, and Dennis Brunn, "Social Workers in Unions: A Survey," *Social Work*, 25 (May 1980), pp. 216-223.
3. Martin Oppenheimer, "The Unionization of the Professional," *Social Policy*, 5 (January-February 1975), pp. 34-40.
4. Ernie S. Lightman, "The Ontario Labour Relations Board and Social Service Workers," *Canadian Welfare*, 52 (January-February 1977), pp. 5-7.

5. Gary L. Shaffer, "Labor Relations and the Unionization of Professional Social Workers: A Neglected Area in Social Work Education," *Journal of Education for Social Work*, 15 (Winter 1979), pp. 80-86.

6. For one of the few studies of actual strike experience by social workers, see Arnold Weber, "Paradise Lost: Or Whatever Happened to the Chicago Social Workers?" *Industrial and Labor Relations Review*, 22 (1969), pp. 323-338.

7. Gil Levine, "Collective Bargaining for Social Workers in Voluntary Agencies," *Ontario Association of Professional Social Workers Magazine*, 3 (March 1975), pp. 5-6.

8. "Symposium: Public Sector Labor Relations: A Canadian-U.S. Comparison," *Industrial Relations*, 19 (Fall 1980), pp. 239-324.

9. Levine, op. cit.

10. Michael Blugerman, "As I See It . . ." *Ontario Association of Professional Social Workers Magazine*, 3 (March 1975), p. 8.

11. Ernie S. Lightman, "An Imbalance of Power: Social Workers in Unions," *Administration in Social Work*, 2 (Spring 1978), pp. 75-84.

12. Mike Brogden and Mike Wright, "Reflections on the Social Work Strikes," *New Society*, 4 (October 1979), pp. 14-16.

13. John Hayes, "The 'Rank and File' Movement in Voluntary Social Work," *Labor History*, 16 (Winter 1975).

14. *Globe and Mail* (Toronto), September 19, 1980, p. 8.

15. Alexander, Lichtenberg, and Brunn, op. cit., p. 222.

16. Helen Rehr, "Problems for a Profession in a Strike Situation," *Social Work*, 5 (April 1960), pp. 22-28. This view was later challenged in a letter to the journal: Sheldon Zulkowitz, "More About Picket Lines," *Social Work*, 5 (October 1960).

17. Marjorie Martin. "Social Workers and Collective Bargaining in British Columbia," *Ontario Association of Professional Social Workers Magazine*, 3 (March 1975), pp. 34-35.

18. Michael Gordon. "Association of Allied Health Professionals: Ontario," *Ontario Association of Professional Social Workers Magazine*, 3 (March 1975).

19. Jeffrey Galper, *Social Work Practice: A Radical Perspective* (Englewood Cliffs, N.J.: Prentice-Hall, 1980), chap. 8.

20. Ronald H. Bohr, Herbert I. Brenner, and Howard M. Kaplan, "Value Conflicts in a Hospital Walkout," *Social Work*, 16 (October 1971), p. 40.

21. *NASW Standards for Social Work Practices* (Washington, D.C.: National Association of Social Workers, 1968, revised 1971 and 1975); and Milton Tambor, "The Social Worker as Worker: A Union Perspective," *Administration in Social Work*, 3 (Fall 1979), pp. 289-300.

22. Brogden and Wright, op. cit., p. 15.

23. Kit Breland et al., "Social Workers and Unions" (Toronto, Ont., Canada: University of Toronto Faculty of Social Work, 1980).

24. Norman H. Nie et al., *Statistical Package for the Social Sciences* (New York: McGraw-Hill Book Co., 1975).

25. Alexander Macbeath, *Can Social Policies Be Rationally Tested?* The Hobhouse Memorial Trust Lecture (London, England: Oxford University Press, 1957). See also Kenneth E. Boulding, "The Boundaries of Social Policy," *Social Work*, 12 (January 1967), pp. 3-11.

26. David Collard, *Altruism and Economy: A Study in Non-Selfish Economics* (London, England: Martin Robertson, 1978), p. 5.

27. Ramesh Mishra, *Society and Social Policy* (London, England: Macmillan, 1977).

28. John Coates, "Egoism and Altruism in the Canadian Trade Union Movement," (Toronto, Ont., Canada: University of Toronto Faculty of Social Work, 1981).

29. One participant in two of the Canadian strikes has indicated to the author in private conversation that service issues are almost always given up "in the crunch," and that in fact the result has been to make the social workers angrier and more willing to strike. See also Weber, op. cit.

22

The Ethics
of Management

CHARLES S. LEVY

Whether the social worker in an agency is the administrator, subexecutive, supervisor, or direct service practitioner, he or she affects, and is affected by, the structure and operation of the organization. This certainly legitimates attention in social work curricula to a wide range of administrative considerations.

I refer here to the technical as well as the humanistic and psychodynamic aspects of management. Whatever the administrative structure within which a social worker operates, there is much of an administrative nature to be known and to be done, and at the very least, to be sensitive to. There is money to be collected, spent, and accounted for. There are procedures to be followed and to be resorted to in the performance or facilitation of a service function. There are persons and institutions to account for and to. Management, in a word, is every social worker's business, whether directly or indirectly, and usually both. And management has its qualitative as well as its quantitative and technical features. Social workers relate not only to budgets, plants, records, and machines but also to clients, colleagues, cotenants, superiors, subordinates, supervisors, supervisees, consultants, board members, community members, insurance companies, government agencies, and so on.

At the foundation of the administrative responsibility and relationships of every social worker, at every level of an administrative hierarchy and in every social agency, is the ethical framework within which it is incumbent upon every social worker to operate. The ethical responsibility of the chief administrator will be different from that of the direct service practitioner, but both will carry it in some degree. As social workers, both will be bound by the code of professional ethics to which they will have subscribed, or which will be attributed to them by custom and usage. But, whether identified as social workers or not, by prescriptive definition of their roles in the organization, ethical responsibility of a rather specific nature will be ascribed to them. And each will ascribe to the other a rather specific order of ethical responsibility.

Within the limits of this presentation I can but suggest some of the requirements for ethical conduct in, and in relation to, management in social agencies. However, even that much should make readily apparent the amenability of expectations to codification.

MANAGERIAL ETHICS IN RELATION TO ORGANIZATIONAL ADMINISTRATION

By ethics is meant the value premises which are presumed to guide practitioners in the performance of their occupational functions, and which may be used to evaluate their conduct in performing them. Ethics constitutes the moral obligations which surround, infuse, and suffuse practitioners' occupational behavior. The ethics of management is appraised on grounds which differ from those associated with measures and manifestations of occupational competence, although these may very well coincide. Expectations in relation to both are functions of the practitioner's role, relationships, and assigned or assumed responsibilities. The bases for ethical judgment—both those which are used to guide ethical conduct and those which are used to evaluate it—include the duties of the practitioner, the occupational and social norms associated with those duties, the risks to others, and the opportunities for the practitioner which those risks generate (including the opportunity to exploit or abuse the advantage which the practitioner's duties make possible).

Loyalty to the organization is a minimal expectation; that is, it is the least that may be expected of staff members. It is not the be-all and end-all of their relationship to the agency, however. The expectation is conditional upon the adherence by both staff member and agency to their mutually understood commitments. It is not "my agency, right or wrong." Rather, the obligation has the character of what is owed to the agency by way of loyalty and devotion, so that differences concerning policy, for example, that existed at the time of the staff member's entry into the organization, are not suddenly and surreptitiously renegotiated with and through clients, or through politicized alignments with board members and others.

At the same time, staff members must be free to act responsibly, and with the use of normative channels, to influence changes in policy and practice which interfere with the optimal performance of the agency's service function, or which induce or settle for the neglect of human need or social justice. In fact, this may be regarded as of the highest order of loyalty and devotion to an agency, for it addresses the staff member's share of responsibility for the fulfillment of the agency's social commitments (strictly speaking, an additional though related ethical responsibility).

Procedures which are designed to expedite services, or account for them, are supposed to be adhered to. That is, staff members at all levels of administrative responsibility have the ethical responsibility to adhere to them, and to do so in an adequate and timely fashion to the extent that they affect or are affected by them.

It is incumbent upon staff members, as a matter of management ethics, to make things work in the administrative structure of the agency until they can be made to work better, and to implement the announced function of the agency to the full extent of their responsibility, plus a little more (the "extra mile" as it is put in theological circles and as it has been applied to ethics). A de facto change in policy or function, which stretches or subverts it (even in the ostensibly good cause of a client's need; for example, by conniving with clients in their infraction of eligibility requirements either for income maintenance or for clinical service) is unethical. If any requirements or preconditions for service are regarded by staff members as unjust or dysfunctional for particular persons, then the channel for modification is not in denying their existence or ignoring them, but in precipitating moves to effect changes in the interest of equity, or in response to changing needs and priorities.

In all of these cases in which staff members, even in a critical fashion, initiate movements toward change in policy, procedures, programs, or practices—precisely in what may be regarded as the fulfillment of ethical responsibility—the ethical assumption, the ethical principle upon which administrators are expected to act, is that those staff members will not be penalized or tainted for their pains. In such cases, administrators must look to their own ethics so that an ethical climate is nurtured and ethical conduct is manifestly valued.

Perhaps most fundamentally in the ethics of management, and perhaps the characteristic which most distinguishes the management of social service organizations and the management of profit-making ventures, is the congruence which should be aspired to between the ethics associated with the service of the organization and the ethics of its internal administration. Each feeds on the other and symbolizes the uniqueness of such organizations. If social justice, for example, is the watchword of social work, then it should be a matter of ethical course for justice to characterize all of the internal operations and relationships of the organization, and a matter of ethical course for each staff member to act accordingly, whatever his or her position in the administrative hierarchy.

There are no doubt many other principles of ethical practice relevant to the administration of social service organizations, but these suffice as illustrations.

MANAGERIAL ETHICS
IN RELATION TO COLLEAGUES

Loyalty to colleagues, like loyalty to a social agency, does not mean blind loyalty. It does not encompass every nefarious, destructive, and unethical act of which either may be capable. To begin on a rather negative note, staff members must feel ethically responsible to prevent, forestall, discourage, and stop the malevolent acts of colleagues as well as the employing organization as a whole. Means, opportunities, and procedures vary. There may be room for tact, notice, and so on, but the basic principle of ethical conduct by which staff members should feel bound is that they do not ignore or condone such conduct. Moreover, they are ethically obliged to do something about it. This is not a novel principle of ethical practice, for it occurs in most codes of professional ethics in one form or another. As a component of the ethics of management, however, it emphasizes not merely the responsibility owed to one's profession and to clients, but also the responsibility owed to the organization as a matter of administrative ethics.

The tendency to neglect the ethics of management often emerges in labor-management relations and negotiations. In such circumstances, ethical sensitivity is particularly required of administrators and agency staff members:

> As professional colleagues of union representatives . . . [administrators] are impelled to be considerate of the welfare of personnel, but as representatives of management they are obliged to be considerate of the agency's resources. . . . For effective labor-management relations, representatives of labor are obliged to represent labor and representatives of management are obliged to represent management [that is, it is their ethical responsibility]. . . . Hopefully . . . both union and management representatives will be guided by their concern for agency clients and by agency philosophy so that each will accord to the other maximum consideration, and each will strive to resolve differences amicably and considerately (Levy, 1964b).

There is much more that is positive about managerial ethics in relation to colleagues, however. From the basis for, and the manner of, hiring staff, through the supervision and evaluation of staff, and to the process of and provision for the separation of staff members and their transition to new or alternative employment, the administrator is subject to now familiar conventions of occupational ethics. The pressure on agency executives these days is such that they may be tempted to give greater priority to their own or to the organization's maintenance and survival than to their ethical responsibility to subordinates. It is times that try men's or women's souls, that test their own true ethical mettle. Unfortunately, ethics in relation to colleagues—especially when they are subordinates and subject to administrative control and power, as well as insecure in their positions in the midst of a tight labor market—seems to attain increased tenuousness with the increase of fiscal, job, administrative, and other pressures. Perhaps the highest order of ethics in management is the resistance to such pressures in dealing with colleagues, and the general resistance to the siren call of tempting powers.

The combination of power and pressure can be treacherous for subordinates. An administrator may neglect even the normative niceties of courtesy and consideration, as well as equity, when subjected to fiscal or board pressures. This can extend to his wielding wildly and arbitrarily the power at his disposal, and thus to the victimization of a subordinate by either precipitously firing, or so harassing the subordinate that the person quits in despair.

Of particular import in light of the luxury it sometimes represents for organizations is that aspect of ethical responsibility in relation to colleagues which has to do with the facilitation and enrichment of the opportunities of colleagues to succeed in the performance of their assigned functions; to grow and develop professionally; to assume increasing responsibility; to exercise initiative and exploit their own creativity; to improve their personal and family circumstances; and perhaps to move outward, onward, and upward in their professional careers. I could emphasize the practical consequences these processes can have for the organization in its functioning, in its evaluation by clients and community, in staff morale, and so on.

A major premise of managerial ethics is that what is prescribed is prescribed because it is valued in its own right, albeit in the context of practice, function, and organizational responsibility. What I have enumerated only briefly represents expectations or aspirations based precisely on values, and in particular, colleague-directed values. Some, in fact, may even be considered dysfunctional from an organization's point of view. An administrator, for example, might invest a lot of time, skill, and effort, not to mention emotional taxation, to help a student or subordinate develop professional skill and competence, only to lose that person to another organization, perhaps a competing one.

The ethical responsibility implied here is of an enlarged order, for it stems from the perspective of what another individual may be perceived as needing in one's own right, or being able to use beyond the immediate requirements of the organization. It implies humaneness and humanitarianism which exceed the scope of managerial concern. Obviously, if an administrator's response in this context is not only not of this lofty order, but actually extends to impediments and hindrances to job performance by subordinates, to guarantee and then penalize failure, then the result is almost classically unethical managerial conduct.

Again, other ethical responsibilities may be identified and defined, but perhaps these will serve to indicate the range of principles of ethical conduct which may be codified to guide and evaluate the acts of managerial personnel in social agencies

MANAGERIAL ETHICS IN RELATION TO SOURCES OF FUNDING AND OTHER RESOURCES

Receiving, soliciting, spending, and accounting for funds and other resources for the maintenance and operation of social agencies, and for the performance of their service functions, are processes which are replete with implications for the ethics of management. The more obvious ones come readily to mind. For example, administrators and fundraisers are not supposed to steal or embezzle funds. This is more than a moral imperative charged with intrinsic merit. It is an ethical expectation based on occupational trust. It is not merely valued behavior, but behavior valued in the context of relationship and responsibility to others.

There are less obvious ethical responsibilities which affect the administrator's fiscal and other transactions. In *Education and Training for the Fundraising Function* (Levy, 1973), I suggested that "even" fundraising affords opportunities and generates responsibilities of a qualitative and developmental nature, to the extent that these may be viewed as transcending the very practical demands and priorities which inhere in fundraising ventures on the social welfare scene. In that sense, these are ethical opportunities and responsibilities, although they may also advance the objectives for the ventures. They address the raising and spending of funds and the potentials and effects for human beings in relation to these processes. The ethics of management in relation to sources of funding and other resources includes both of these orientations to ethical responsibility: one has to do with the use of, and response to, all of the resources (human as well as financial) which are placed at the organization's disposal and for which administrators are held to account; and the other has to do with the humanistic considerations associated with the use of, and response to, the organization's resources.

Whatever the funding sources of the organization, the ethics of management requires scrupulous attention to the ways of acquiring funds, the ways of spending funds, the ways of accounting for funds, and the ways of evaluating the manner in which, and the purposes for which, funds have been and will be spent. No less is required in relation to the human resources that go into the operation and functioning of a social agency—staff, volunteers, trustees, and so on.

A high order of ethics is required in all of these connections. It is often said in fundraising and administrative circles that administrators should spend the organization's funds as if those funds were their own. This is hardly a sufficient standard for the purposes of ethical conduct in one's administrative capacity. For one thing, personal standards and values are much too variable. But, more importantly, the point at issue is not the economy with which funds are administered and expenditures made. Rather, the essential point is that administrators are obligated to see to it that funds and other resources are used for the purposes for which they are intended, with maximum productivity in relation to expenditures, and that they advance the service purposes of the agency. This implies the need for considerable competency and awareness of what is available at the least cost; of what is maximally related to the function or operation for which expenditures are to be made; of optimal, practical, and relevant accounting procedures for both income and expenses; of theories of welfare economics and the economics of organizational and communal, as well as governmental and societal, life. And in all of these connections, capacity to make maximum use of such competency and awareness is required.

All of this has to be assumed before confidence may be reposed in an administrator's ethical inclinations. Ethics becomes somewhat academic if competence for administrative practice is not possessed in the first place. Ethics implies value-based choices with respect to professional conduct precisely in the context of practice capacity. The presumption here is that the administrator will be in a position to make ethical judgments and decisions, and engage in ethical managerial interventions, if one knows what to do for professional and administrative purposes in the first place, and knows how to do it. This time, the "how" signifies the ethical use of the instrumentalities at the administrator's disposal and the very ethics of the instrumentalities to be employed.

Professional ethics implies skill and competence in implementing ethical choices. This does not mean that an administrator cannot be ethical without being competent. If one is, however, it is by accident. The competent, ethical administrator is ethical by intention. The competent and ethical administrator can make rationally ethical choices of intervention and validate them on systematically considered grounds.

Another reason for the emphasis on the transcendence of ethics in management is that, of all persons in a social agency, the administrator is the one with the least autonomy. The administrator's accountability is pervasive. It is not limited to particular persons or clienteles. Since it is organizationally induced, and since organizations are complex internally and in their relationships to the numerous external systems, administrators are highly exposed to responsibility, and to attributions of responsibility. Whether or not they delegate responsibility, administrators of organizations are the ones who are ultimately accountable for what is done in and by the organization and its personnel, as well as how and why it is done, and the myriad consequences which follow what is done.

One caution must be enunciated, however. Being zealous and scrupulous about the use of organizational resources does not mean the freedom to scrimp and save. These days, the inclination of an organizational executive to conserve resources is likely to earn for one initially the kudos of trustees and community. Reinforcement of such an inclination is all too likely to occur and thus encourage more of the same. Obversely, executives have been known to be fired, sometimes after years of ostensibly loyal and capable administrative service, and others hired precisely on the basis of the value placed on such inclinations. Routinely and mechanically applied, the tendency to pinch pennies can lead to invalid administrative conduct, and at times, unethical conduct. Short of spending money that an agency does not possess, an administrator might save money at the expense of the very service which is the reason for the agency's existence and, more seriously, exploit and demean employees, volunteers, and even clients in the process. These, too, represent transgressions of managerial ethics.

Early in my social service career, I witnessed a scathing attack by a board chairman on the administrator of a large service organization. The attack was a reaction to the administrator's proud reporting of substantial savings on plant maintenance. I thought the chairman was a bit self-righteous about it all, since his primary intent was to abuse the administrator whom he did not like in the first place, and his primary concern was that future budgets might be cut in view of the reality that the organization's budget was experientially determined and funds for local services came from national sources. These motives notwithstanding, his point was ethically if not also administratively relevant. The administrator would have to be considered guilty of unethical conduct if, in order to save available money and gain board approval, he hired fewer people than he had the budget for and that the organization needed. The persons who were hired would thus be exploited or maintenance service reduced, or both, and both ultimately would affect services to clients.

A similar consideration applies to the case of appointing professional and other staff members on the basis of what they are willing to settle for, rather than what is budgeted and available for the positions to be filled—and especially when inequities and relative deprivations are perpetrated as a result.

This does not, of course, mean that the ethics of management permits or encourages squandering. The ethics of management, to the contrary, requires the intelligent, conscientious, considerate, and careful use of funds and other resources which are available, but in the implementation of the policies and purposes of the social agency from both an administrative and ethical point of view.

MANAGERIAL ETHICS IN RELATION TO COMMUNITY AND SOCIETY

Only brief attention can be paid here to the ethics of management in relation to community and society, although this may be the most encompassing realm of ethical responsibility. The administrator is ethically responsible for whatever the social agency is accountable for—including the values associated with the service for which it has been created.

A reasonable starting point for the definition of the administrator's ethical responsibility is the function for which the agency is sanctioned and chartered. Practical pressures and considerations to the contrary notwithstanding, the administrator is ethically obliged to hew closely, and to see to it that the agency hews closely, to the sanctioned and chartered function of the organization. That function is not to be circumstantially or inadvertently changed. Rather, systematic and thoughtful involvement of persons or groups with authority and decision-making responsibility must be provided for. The very determination of what the agency's function should be is not to be arbitrarily made, for administrators share ethical responsibility for the validity of that determination in relation to prior needs in the community, and equitable judgments in relation to who has those needs. Quite obviously, functions which are destructive or discriminatory or otherwise unfair, unjust, illegal, or harmful, are ethically *verboten,* and no administrator should collaborate in initiating or implementing them.

The relevance and utility of the services of social agencies also require validation on ethical grounds. The community and the society have a stake in them, and that which is a stake for the community or society presents ethical responsibility for the administrator. Even when agencies do not rely on general community or governmental resources for support of the services they offer, administrators, along with their lay leadership, are subject to an ethical accounting. The fact that an agency is financially independent does not mean that it is institutionally autonomous. Neither are administrators autonomous in relation to community and society, even though they are afforded maximum autonomy and sanction by the agency in the representation of its interests. Although a rather extreme test of ethical conduct, both the initiation of a service and its subsequent implementation are ethically subject to the community's or society's responses, judgments, and priorities. It is to the administrator and to lay colleagues that the community or society must look for an accounting in this respect.

CONCLUSION

I have neglected the ethics of management as it pertains to the relationship between administrator and board, board committees, and other groups who are assisted in the performance of their planning, policy-making, problem-solving, and decision-making functions in behalf of the social agency and its clientele and constituents. This is hardly to suggest that this feature of management is either irrelevant or unimportant. It is sufficiently consequential, in fact, to merit extensive consideration. Ethical responsibility in this respect affects particularly that component of administrative practice which most closely approximates the helping process in social work, the ethics of which is applicable to it. In short, whatever, by way of ethical conduct, is expected of social workers in their relationships to clients would be expected of administrators in their work and with administrative groups. All of the humanistic and humanitarian considerations applicable to social workers in their relationships to clients apply to the administrator's relationships with board members, committee members, volunteers, and so on, although in form and operation there are appreciable differences.

The differences are minimized when management is compared with community social work, at least insofar as the practitioner's helping relationship to others is concerned. I have attempted to explore this linkage from a practice point of view (1962, 1964a). In both cases, the focus of the practitioner's work is not on what the clientele needs for itself, but what it needs in and for the fulfillment of responsibility in relation to, and in behalf of, others—in one case, the groups and classes of persons which the clientele represents and, in the other, the clients and constituents of the social agency whose needs and interests are administratively represented.

An exploration of the ethics of management in this regard would amount to covering the entire range of professional ethics. It is omitted here, but it cannot be overlooked.

In sum, then, the ethics of management in social agencies is a function—of organizational function. It is almost ironic that the service which an organization may choose to provide, freely and voluntarily, and occasionally even with its own resources, ultimately at times victimizes that organization and certainly its administrators. But, that is precisely the nature of the ethics of management.

REFERENCES

Levy, C. S. *Education and training for the fundraising function.* New York: Bureau for Careers in Jewish Service/The Lois and Samuel Silberman Fund, 1973.

———. The executive and the agency board. *Journal of Jewish Communal Service,* Spring 1962, *38*, 234–248.

———. *The executive and the Jewish community center board.* New York: National Jewish Welfare Board, 1964.(a)

———. Labor-management relations in the Jewish community center. *Journal of Jewish Communal Service.* Fall 1964, *41*, 114–123.(b)

23

Ethical Guidelines for Cutback Management: A Preliminary Approach

MICHAEL REISCH
CHRIS L. TAYLOR

Current economic conditions and the shifting political climate have produced fundamental and dramatic changes in government's role in solving social and individual problems. Retrenchment on a massive scale has begun with both the public and voluntary social services with limited preparation, planning or exploration of administrative alternatives. As a consequence, the political situation for social work, in the words of past NASW President, Nancy Humphreys,

> is so serious that we will never—as long as the [Reagan] Administration and the forces of the New Right dominate government—be able to hold conferences . . . where we do not also include a political agenda. Our jobs and the services to our clients that we represent are on the line in a way that has happened in no other time since the Depression. [*NASW NEWS,* June 1981, p. 1]

In this environment, "cutback management," which Levine (1979) defines as "managing organizational change towards lower levels of resource consumption and organizational activity" (p. 180), has been a popular topic. Yet, the literature on cutback management has paid little

---

Dr. Reisch is Assistant Professor, School of Social Work and Community Planning, University of Maryland, 525 West Redwood Street, Baltimore, MD 21201. Mr. Taylor is Director, Catholic Social Services, York, PA 17405.

attention to the potential impact of service reductions on recipients of services and makes few references to the ethical dilemmas for program administrators involved in planned retrenchment. In part, this gap reflects the limitations of social work research in these areas. As Levine (1978b) points out:

> at the present state of our knowledge about cutback management, strategies are easier to describe than to prescribe. . . . We need to be satisfied to raise appropriate questions and hope that later their answers can help managers cope with austerity . . . to investigate the major steps in the cutback process . . . [and to make] the strategic choices that an organization must make about confronting, planning, targeting and distributing. [p. 182]

The last issue—distribution—is the most troublesome for administrators, particularly in terms of its ethical aspects. Ironically, it has received the least attention in the growing literature on the subject of cutback management which has largely focused on five broad technological areas: long range planning, strategic choices, tactics and dilemmas; deregulation and sunset legislation; cutback leadership; the politics of retrenchment; and the relationship between organizational structure and retrenchment. Although a few articles ask ethical questions or begin ethical discussions, none outline an ethical framework for managing cutbacks. The emphasis has been, therefore, on tactical responses to retrenchment, which have been viewed largely as technical solutions to problems.

Although answers to these technical problems are critical, the development of ethical guidelines must keep pace with the growth of technology for the management of dwindling resources. Thus, this essay will deal in a preliminary fashion with the ethical problems of resource distribution as they relate to management in an era of scarce resources. How are the effects of large budget reductions to be allocated? Which programs have priority on remaining funds? How is the potential impact of cutbacks on varying populations to be assessed? All these are questions that involve ethical choices. If the social work profession is to retain its historical commitment to social justice, these distributive issues must be addressed.

To date, most of the literature on retrenchment has addressed such dilemmas as if they were "value-free." In fact, approaches to such administrative problems require difficult choices between conflicting value systems. It is in the resolution of such conflicts that ethics can play a key role. Without ethical guidelines, the process of program retrenchment becomes, in the current environment, a power struggle in which the least powerful and least articulate groups are at a significant disadvantage.

VALUES AND ETHICS

The literature of social work administration has long recognized that values and the ethical imperatives derived from them play a critical role in managerial behavior. In this context, values represent our beliefs about what is to be preferred in our administrative practice and ethics are the rule of conduct we establish based upon these preferences (Lewis, 1974; Levy, 1975). Values influence choices at every decision-making point at which administrators confront and provide ethical guidelines for the resolution of real or perceived conflicts. Decisions as to what issues are deemed appropriate for social intervention and the application of scarce administrative resources or service "technologies" are inseparably tied to values. Our conscious decisions to distribute shrinking resources in order to achieve particular ends are, therefore, political acts which clearly reflect our value preferences.

At present, it is all too clear that no national consensus exists on which social values are to be preferred in the implementation of program reductions. Indeed, in practice, persistent value conflicts can often be resolved only by reference to long-standing ethical codes. Such codes, however, generally focus on issues of microallocation in which the individual practitioner is believed to possess a certain latitude of choice. Macroallocatory issues are treated as if they are beyond the scope of individual practitioners and are referred to, if at all, in broad generalities. The NASW *Code of Ethics* (1981), for example, provides no specific principles for the administration of retrenchment and is open to much interpretation on this issue (Reamer, 1980).

Although administrative flexibility is needed in the cutback process, the absence of an adequate ethical model on which to base decisions about program reductions may leave too much room for interpretation. This can produce inequitable *distributive* results which clearly run counter to the practice principles outlined in the *Code*, a problem which is complicated further because many administrators who are determining the future of social programs and policies are not social workers and are not influenced by social work values. Decisions on program cuts are often based on definitions of administrative efficiency and effectiveness with a business rather than social welfare orientation (Lewis, 1978). Consequently, those programs are cut which are politically weakest but not necessarily the least effective or efficient in social work terms (Charnovitz, 1977; Levine, 1978). Terrell (1981) underscores the importance of ethical guidelines as an alternative to this modern version of the "survival of the fittest":

> Planning for austerity—altering programs in a humane fashion to accommodate losses due to budget reductions and inflation—is still sorely

needed for the years ahead . . . [in order to] offer opportunities for adapting intelligently to the 1980's rather than simply waiting out the bad years hoping for better. [p. 281]

Reamer argues forcefully that ethical guidelines cannot be based on intuition and practice wisdom alone, as is the case in most professional codes of ethics (Reamer, 1980). Reliance on the NASW *Code,* for example, leads to contradictory or ambiguous conclusions in the current situation; for while, generally, the *Code* supports resisting resource allocation schemes that have negative consequences for clients, it also expresses a contradictory position regarding "Responsibilities to Employers and Employing Organizations." Thus, Section IV, Part L, reads "The social worker should work to improve the employing organization's policies and procedures, and the efficiency and effectiveness of its services (and also) should adhere to commitments made to the employing organization" (National Association of Social Workers, 1980, pp. 25–26).

Whereas, in Section II, Part G, Number 3, the *Code* states "the social worker should not engage in any action that violates or diminishes the civil rights of clients." What does an administrator do, therefore, who is placed in charge of dismantling an organization that provides legal services for the poor? If one follows the mandate of one's employer, one is automatically acting to diminish opportunity for civil and legal rights of a targeted group of people. If one resists, there is another clear violation of the *Code* as well as considerable personal jeopardy involved.

The *Code* states else·where that the social worker should:

assist the profession in making social services available to the general public. . . act to ensure that all persons have access to resources, services, and opportunities which they require . . . act to expand choice and opportunity for all persons, with special regard for disadvantaged or oppressed groups and persons . . . advocate changes in policy and legislation to improve social conditions and to promote social justice. [National Association of Social Workers, 1980]

It is clear that the problems for administrators created by the need for cutback management compel us to make decisions which in their implementation place our practice in real or potential violation of such principles.

To go beyond the limitations of the *Code,* Reamer (1980) recommends that social workers focus on three specific issues and justify their resolution in a more compelling way than through intuition. These issues are:

1. the creation and justification of basic values to guide practice;
2. the definition of the limits on the moral obligation of social workers to aid those in need; and
3. the creation of principles to guide the distribution of scarce resources.

Although Reamer doubts "whether a moral principle will ever be available that will provide clear, unambiguous guidelines for ethical decisions" (Reamer, 1980, p. 540), the development of ethical guidelines for cutback management requires administrators to confront and attempt to resolve the specific issues Reamer identifies.

TRADITIONAL ETHICAL APPROACHES

Reamer has suggested the development of normative ethical guidelines to resolve the problems generated by the distribution of scarce resources (Reamer, 1979). On close examination, however, it appears that the argument he adopts tacitly accepts utilitarianism—the most popular of teleological or consequentialist approaches to social problem formulation and resolution (Reamer, 1979). The modern utilitarian position, popularized by Bentham and Mill, provided a philosophical framework for political efforts to reform the abuses of the Industrial Revolution. In so doing, proponents of utilitarianism developed an implicit justification of the social order and placed limits on potential social changes which would modify it.

In general, classical utilitarianism holds that an act is right if it promotes the greatest net balance of satisfaction for society. A utilitarian calculus presupposes the rational ordering of social goods to achieve this end. In the 19th and 20th Centuries this assumption has been linked with another: that the prioritization of social goals occurs through a process equally accessible to all members of society. The offspring of this marriage of assumptions is the belief that social policy and administrative decisions are the result of a goal-setting process which fosters generalized benevolence. Current statistics on the distribution of our nation's economic and social resources and the impact of recent cutbacks demonstrate that the consequentialist arguments of utilitarianism are particularly unsuited for an era of social program retrenchment if social welfare administrators wish to avoid the placement of undue hardships on the least advantaged segments of society.

Administrators are being asked to determine program priorities on the basis of a cost-benefit analysis. This approach to cutback management assumes that a formula can be developed to measure accurately the relative efficiency with which agency resources are applied to meet client's needs and that the impact of the reduction or withdrawal of agency financial resources in a particular area can be calculated in comparative terms.

Yet, many of the consequences of cutback management are qualitative, not quantitative, in nature. How are administrators, for example, to apply a utilitarian calculus to degrees of suffering or deprivation? Can the reduction of energy assistance funds and cutbacks in children's nutrition programs be compared in any quantitative manner? Can the short-term effects of the loss of legal services programs be measured against the long term consequences of a decrease in funds for maternal and child health centers? Do equal cutbacks produce identical consequences in different programs or even in similar programs within different communities? A utilitarian cost benefit framework does not provide satisfactory answers to such questions. It does not give administrators the tools to assess the extent and scope of such consequences and, in particular, how these consequences will affect the lives of those powerless groups in society whose needs can easily be subordinated to the needs of the majority.

For utilitarians, the object of social policy is to maximize the benefits to society regardless of how these benefits are to be distributed, except as distribution itself furthers the maximization of benefits or goods. Since the two major concerns of ethical inquiry—the "good" and the "right"—are defined independently by utilitarianism, this theory justifies a determination of the "goodness" of administrative decisions without reference to what is right. The net benefit to society—the "rightness" of administrative decisions—is calculated simply in terms of the maximization of what is good. For example, if the efficient utilization of agency resources (determined through a cost-benefit analysis) is defined as a priority social good, administrative actions can be ranked in value by criteria which assess the extent to which this predefined social good is maximized by particular administrative courses of action. Such actions may place the social benefits of retrenched programs at a lower point on the scale of desirable goods and may, as a result, fail to recognize any standards of rights which our clients may possess as members of the community.

Programs which address the most intractable problems in our communities may be the least "efficient" in cost-benefit analysis terms and become the first to be cut in periods of retrenchment. By assuming that "service commodities" produced by social welfare organizations can be counted like more tangible commodities produced by industry, approaches to cutback management which emphasize efficiency often ignore or discount the multiple service transactions in which the most disadvantaged individuals and families are involved. In addition, an accounting of agency "costs" which discounts the worker's skills as a "resource" and, thereby, ignores the impact of budget reductions on his/her ability to apply that resource for the client's benefit, further misinterprets the nature of the service transaction which occurs in social service agencies (Lewis, 1982).

"Utilitarianism," in Rawls' (1971) analysis, "does not take seriously the distinction between persons" (p. 27), and cannot assess the impact of social program reductions by any measure of justice. Finally, since the definition of the "good" in the current allocation of social welfare resources is made by individuals who often possess very different perspectives and personal resources from those who will feel the impact of cutbacks, the possibility that administrative decisions formulated on the basis of a utilitarian calculus can produce increased social inequality is obvious.

A utilitarian calculus creates no imperative of social justice since a concentration of goods benefiting the privileged and powerful can occur, leaving the majority wanting. As current policy and resource shifts reveal, under the rubric of "general societal benefit" social goods can accrue largely to the affluent and bypass or exclude minority populations. Consider, for example, the plight of the working poor who are unable to afford private health insurance but are now ineligible for government sponsored medical assistance. The classical utilitarian view would assess the benefit or harm to this population in terms of a calculus of gains or losses for the community. Yet, certain social goods, such as cost containment, are more easily quantifiable and are frequently valued more highly by policy makers or political leaders than other, more qualitative goods—the social value of health, for instance. As a result, the computation of social costs and benefits is biased from the outset by what it includes or omits as significant factors to be evaluated.

Without an ethic of distribution in such areas of social welfare as health care, many people will be denied the prerequisites even to compete in the marketplace for their share of the available social benefits. Although a more equitable distribution of benefits or goods would be one of high utility, there is no assumption in the current cost/benefit definition of utilitarianism that such results will or should occur. In an era of growing social and economic inequality, an administrative approach which does not consciously act to offset or reverse these developments would appear to be in direct contradiction of the historical legacy, if not the explicit ethical principles of the social work profession. Appeals to efficiency and aggregate utility may have a legitimate place in administrative decisionmaking, but these appeals are dangerous to justice in a period of resource scarcity and should be minimized.

Unlike utilitarianism which has been used to justify unequal distribution of societal resources and benefits, egalitarian theory challenges the assumption that society can be rightly ordered if it is based on social and economic inequalities. Egalitarians attack the belief in utilitarianism that inequality is a prerequisite to societal efficiency and individual freedom (George & Wilding, 1976).

Older egalitarian theory, however, espoused equality of opportunity in the formulation of policy and administrative decisions as a remedy to social inequality. According to George and Wilding, actions based on this premise produce inegalitarian results which are not much less objectionable than the consequences of the utilitarian approaches they replace. The emphasis on equality of opportunity espoused by older egalitarian theory can be seen, however, as the predecessor of a newer egalitarian approach based on greater equality of results or the maximization of social justice. In *A Theory of Justice,* Rawls (1971) develops his elaborate ethical system for operationalizing what he terms "distributive justice" as the central social value to guide social policy initiatives. His theory provides an alternate framework for the development of ethical guidelines in an area of program retrenchment, based on principles of social justice and guidelines consistent with social work values.

DISTRIBUTIVE JUSTICE

Rawls formulates his ethical prescriptions for distributive justice through a deductionist argument, in which the good and the right are not defined independently from each other. This argument is based on a general conception of justice which holds that "All social values . . . are to be distributed equally unless an unequal distribution of any, or all, of these values is to everyone's advantage" (p. 62). He then derives what he calls his Maximin Theory of two fundamental principles (pp. 60–61, 303):

1. each person has an equal right to the most extensive system of personal liberty compatible with a system of total liberty for all; and
2. social and economic inequality are to be arranged so that they are both:
   a. to the greatest benefit of the least advantaged consistent with the savings principle; and
   b. attached to positions open to all under conditions of fair equality of opportunity.

Rawls narrows the application of these principles through two "priority rules": the "Priority of Liberty" and the "Priority of Justice over Efficiency and Welfare." The first rule states:

"(a) a less extensive liberty must strengthen the total system of liberty shared by all; and (b) a less than equal liberty must be acceptable to those with equal liberty."

The second rule restores the existence of inequality and the application of efficiency in that:

> "(a) an inequality of opportunity must enhance the opportunities of those with the lesser opportunity; [and] (b) an excessive rate of saving must on balance mitigate the burden of those bearing this hardship." [pp. 302–303]

With the application of these caveats, Rawls modifies his general conception to justify unequal distribution of goods only when it is to the benefit of the least advantaged (p. 303). Rawls thus develops a synthesis of older egalitarian theories with their emphasis on equality of opportunity and newer egalitarian theories which focus on equality of results. Rawls maintains that these principles are those which would be derived by rational and disinterested individuals in what he terms the "original position," who are asked to construct principles of a social contract selected to further their own interests from behind a "veil of ignorance"—that is in a hypothetical situation in which each person is ignorant of his/her place in the "natural or social lottery" (pp. 12–13).

From these principles of justice, Rawls develops the *principle of redress*, which he argues establishes the basis for a more just distribution of social goods:

> Undeserved inequalities call for redress; and since inequalities of birth and natural endowment are undeserved, these inequalities are to be somehow compensated for. Thus, the principle holds that in order to treat all persons equally, to provide genuine equality of opportunity, society must give more attention to those with fewer native assets and to those born into the less favorable social positions. The idea is to redress the bias of contingencies in the direction of equality. [p. 100]

Within this framework of distributive justice, social program administrators must adopt the role of "imperial arbitrator"—to place themselves, so to speak, in a Rawlsian "original position." On the surface, this position resembles the role for administrators recommended by many of the writers on cutback management. Schmertz (1976), for example, states clearly that the administrator-as-arbitrator must consider the interests of the community as a whole as well as the interests of individuals and groups competing for scarce resources. Schmertz and others, however, provide no ethical guidelines for the consideration of community interests nor for any *definition* of the community and its interests. In contrast, Rawls' Maximin Theory provides not only ethical guidelines but presents these guidelines in a manner consistent with the philosophical tenor of social policy development in the 1980s: Like current policymakers, Rawls' theory has limited objectives and a desire to conserve as much as possible of the status quo.

GUIDELINES FOR CUTBACK MANAGEMENT

A preliminary list of recommendations for cutback management, derived from a perspective which emphasizes distributive justice, would include the following guidelines to serve as ethical prescriptions:

1. Consistent with the principle of redress, those programs which primarily benefit those least well off should be maintained, while working to restore programs that provide coverage to a broader segment of the community.
2. In order to allow all members of the community to participate in the most extensive system of total liberty, agencies have an obligation to provide services based upon need rather than calculations of cost-benefit.
3. To ensure the distribution of social and economic inequalities to the benefit of the least advantaged in the community, administrators should adopt a unitary, as opposed to a two-tiered system of service delivery. Although a two-tiered system appears to be an attractive method of providing at least a minimum of services to the most needy, a unitary mode of service delivery would prevent the evolution of a two-class pattern of program development in which the least advantaged received inferior quality or less accessible services.
4. The development of ethical choice mechanisms within agencies based upon the concept of distributive justice, not a utilitarian calculus, to identify trade-offs between programs, rates of marginal returns, etc.
5. Administrators have the duty to refrain from cutting or reducing programs which affect primarily the politically powerless who are least able to resist. This principle is compatible with the desire to promote fair equality of opportunity and to structure the distribution of resources in a manner which, *at a minimum*, will not deprive people of access to services.
6. Administrators have the duty to be politically active since politics and the political process are primary means for gaining support for just programs and policies.

This list could be refined and extended. Its purpose is to make a case for a critical connection between the daily practice needs of administrators for ethical guidelines and an ethical theory to support their development. The development of this preliminary list is based upon the assumption that social work administrators must act on the historic values of the profession to work for greater social and economic equality. These values must be reflected in the management of current budget cuts and in efforts to resist these cuts where resistance is possible. To do otherwise would mean a betrayal of our profession's past and our society's future.

IMPLICATIONS FOR PRACTICE

Guidelines 1 and 2 require that social agency administrators engage in a rigorous process of community needs assessment which includes an examination of the impact of present and impending budget reductions not only on their agencies but on the populations their agencies purport to serve. This examination should be assessed in light of the organization's mission, its current program and an evaluation of its "marginal activities." Administrators should ask themselves: "Are we providing services consistent with our initial program design? Is the process of delivering services linked to its ultimate outcome? Are services not only made more accessible, but are they, in fact, delivered to the least advantaged members of the community?" In our society, in which goals are increasingly confused with functions and in which social choices are obfuscated, this linking of need with program intent, process and outcome under a guiding principle of distributive justice provides a valuable ethic for administrators confronted with shrinking resources, conflicting guidelines and hostile forces on all sides (McTighe, 1979; Lewis, 1975).

Guidelines 3 and 4 involve increasing the accessibility of our programs to those clients whose needs are greatest; enabling all consumers of service to obtain help from a variety of programs more efficiently, so that we may deliver that help more effectively; and creating service delivery environments which treat each individual as relevant. We must seek to empower clients, rather than view them as unequal components in a broader societal equation. To accomplish these ethical ends in an atmosphere of shrinking means, we must explore the possibility of networking existing services; we must improve inter-agency communications; and we must develop more comprehensive information and referral systems. An area in which additional emphasis needs to be placed is on the provision of emergency services, in order that the least well off and least visible clients we serve are not victimized by political expediency. An ethic of distributive justice also requires an openness on the part of administrators to new service approaches, particularly those which integrate the skills of all human service disciplines within the framework of social work values and goals.

Guidelines 5 and 6 underscore the *political* nature of social work administration. Although the installation of rational choice mechanisms in data collection and analysis, for example, has much to offer administrators, we should be cognizant that the goals of social service delivery have political as well as technological aspects that are often overlooked in the current emphasis on technical solutions to our problems. In fact, many of the negative attitudes toward administrators which are shared by clients and staff are based upon an interpretation of the administrator's role which sprang from efforts to emulate business practices in social services management. We should not be surprised, therefore, that efforts to apply the techniques and value preferences of private enterprise to administrative practice in social work have not only met with mixed results but with resentment, if not open hostility, from staff and clients. This tension is likely to be exacerbated in the months and years ahead.

What we propose instead is for program administrators to work to build coalitions within our agencies and within our communities. This would not only serve the purpose of strengthening resistance to budget cutbacks, it would also encourage employee and client participation in planning and decision-making and, thereby, help retain the openness of our organizations with clients, staff and the community at a time in which increasing isolation would only add to the difficulties inherent in cutback management. The conceptualization of social issues within an ethical framework should be a process in which the development and implementing of strategies for resource allocation are demystified in the practice arena by the cooperation of providers and consumers of service. We must never forget that just as our program priorities must be human priorities, our agencies must be human scale institutions.

Another implication of guidelines 5 and 6 is that social workers need to become more active in electoral politics in their community, particularly as local political struggles take on heightened importance in the coming era of the "New Federalism." Social workers should support candidates committed to social justice and encourage others to organize and become politically active. Our traditional skills at coalition building, working with groups and interpersonal relationships, and our knowledge of our communities provide an excellent foundation for such activity.

CONCLUSION

The purpose of this paper has been to develop the outlines of an approach to ethical practice for administrators who must make program cutbacks. The work of Rawls and newer egalitarian theory provide a general ethical basis for administrative practice consistent with the mission and values of social work. An ethic of distribution fills

> the need for a new ideology that can legitimate and give ethical backing for government policies that are designed to create a socially just society . . . . The fact that the prospects of a socially just society appear remote should not make it any less worth striving for . . . .[Since] the piecemeal social reform of the last thirty years has failed to do more than scratch the surface of social and economic inequality, concentration on ways and means is likely to perpetuate such a situation. *The only escape lies in a*

reconsideration of fundamental social objectives. [George & Wilding, pp. 129–138; emphasis added]

Since solutions to problems of cutback management elude both technical and current ethical approaches, in the end, social work administrators must face some difficult political and professional choices. If overcoming the barriers of inequality is to remain a goal of social work, and if many current cutbacks reflect a return to an ideology of individualism which fosters that inequality, there appears to be only one choice for administrators which is consonant with the profession's historic values—that is, action based upon a principle of distributive justice that may eventually produce a society in which greater equality is a reality instead of a distant dream. The social work profession, therefore, needs to clarify its commitments. We assert that social workers should act immediately on the values they profess, values which emphasize greater social and economic equality. Management of the current budget cuts should reflect these values both in their implementation and in attempts to resist efforts to return our society to an era of more rigid class stratification and sharper inequalities.

Ultimately, the political and ethical issues of retrenchment are inextricably intermeshed. In the final analysis, without sufficient professional leverage in our communities, no ethical framework can be implemented. The development of an ethic of distributive justice, however, is more likely in its practice implications to generate the kind of community support necessary for its sustenance. Such an ethical framework can enable administrators to develop and refine new practice principles to guide their decision-making in the difficult decade ahead.

REFERENCES

Behn, R.D. Closing a government facility. *Public Administration Review*, 1978, *38*, 338-344.

Brewer. G.D. Termination: Hard choices—harder questions. *Public Administration*, 1978, *38*, 332-338.

Charnovitz, S. Evaluating sunset: What will it mean? *The Bureaucrat*, 1977, *6*, 63-79.

George, V., & Wilding, P. *Ideology and social welfare*. London: Routledge & Kegan Paul, 1976.

Glassberg, A. Organizational response to municipal budget decreases. *Public Administration Review*, 1978, *38*, 325-332.

Hitt, M. A., et al. Sunset legislation and the measurement of effectiveness. *Public Personnel Management*, 1977, *6*, 188-193.

Levine, C.H. More on cutback management: Hard questions for hard times. *Public Administration Review*, 1979, *39*, 179-183.

Levine, C.H. The new crisis in the public sector. In C.H. Levine (Ed.), *Managing fiscal stress: The crisis in the public sector.* Chatham, NJ: Chatham House, 1978 (a).

Levine, C.H. Organizational decline and cutback management: A Symposium. *Public Administration Review,* 1978, (b) *38,* 179-183.

Levy, C. *Social work ethics.* New York: Human Sciences Press, 1976.

Lewis, C.W. Cutback principles and practices: A checklist for managers. *Public Administration Review,* 1980, *40,* 184-188.

Lewis, H. *Combatting fictions in public policy and professional practice.* Baltimore: University of Maryland, School of Social Work and Community Planning, 1978.

Lewis, H. Management in the nonprofit social service organization. *Child Welfare,* November 1975.

Lewis, H. *Values, ideology and ethics in social work education.* Unpublished paper, 1974.

McTighe, J. Management strategies to deal with shrinking resources. *Public Administration Review,* 1979, *39,* 86-90.

National Association of Social Workers. *Code of ethics.* Washington, DC: NASW, 1980.

National Association of Social Workers. *NASW News,* June, 1981.

Rawls, J. *A theory of justice.* Cambridge, MA: Harvard University Press, 1971.

Reamer, F. Ethical content in social work. *Social Casework,* 1980, *61,* 531-540.

Reamer, F. Fundamental ethical issues in social work: An essay review. *Social Service Review,* 1979, *53,* 229-243.

Reisch, M. *Inflation and human issues.* Unpublished paper, presented to the Howard County Association of Community Services, Ellicott City, MD, February 1980.

Schmertz, E.J. The public safety and personnel cuts in New York City fire department: The role of the impartial chairman. *Employee Relations Law Journal,* 1976, *2,* 155-162.

Shefter, M. New York City's fiscal crisis: The politics of inflation and retrenchment. *The Public Interest,* 1977, *48,* 98-127.

Stewart, R.P. Watershed days: How will social work respond to the conservative revolution? *Social Work,* 1981, *26,* 271-273.

Terrell, P. Adapting to austerity: Human services after proposition 13. *Social Work,* 1981, *26,* 275-281.

Veatch, R.M., & Branson, R. *Ethics and health policy.* Cambridge, MA: J.B. Lippincott, Ballinger, 1976.

Wolfe, A. In defense of the state. *Social Policy,* 1979, *10,* 16-18.

PART III

Information, Computers, and Management

Editor's Introduction

Stimulated by pressure from funding, planning and monitoring agencies for accountability, and the developing availability at reasonable cost of technology and hardware, social agencies have sought increasingly to establish management information systems and procedures in their daily operations. Apart from such external demands, administrators are more and more aware of useful functions of a well-conceived sytem of data collection and dissemination as it serves the purposes of enhancing the quality of service delivery.

The following are among the *general* functions of social services information systems:

- planning and policy development
- decision-making
- coordination of client services

It is clear that these aspects of agency work require an adequate data base so that development can be rooted in objective reality rather than subjective judgment. In the absence of significant and accurate data, organizations move in a vacuum, unrelated to client need and community requirements.

There are other *specific* purposes to which systematic information can be directed—for institutional management, for service delivery, and for research, as follows:

Institutional Management

- budgeting
- program develpment
- program monitoring
- public relations
- evaluation
- cost analysis
- social and legislative action

Service Delivery

- referral and follow-up
- continuity of service

- clinical practice
- service integration and coordination
- tracking clients (to keep clients from getting "lost")
- recording
- staff evaluation

Research

- knowledge building
- social problem analysis
- program evaluation
- practice testing

The accumulation of service statistics has always been part of the social agency's activities, and they are generally included in annual reports and as documentation for budget requests from funding agencies. What is required is a systematic and purposive rationale that makes it possible to achieve many of the objectives suggested above. An adequate information system encompasses a series of processes, including systematic classification, indexing and coding, and data collection, storage, processing, retrieval, and transmission. This can be done manually, or through automated or electronic data processing. The choice between these alternatives is a function of volume, complexity (number of variables required for classification and retrieval), and cost.

Experience suggests that the establishment of a competent information system is best achieved through a collaborative process between service professionals and information specialists. The former are in a position to indicate the "what," "who" and "why" of the system. Knowledge of the substance of the particular program, its goals and objectives, its relevant elements, the purposes to be pursued, and the significant relationships between variables, provides guides to the specialist in designing the appropriate technology, the "how" of the system. Data thus becomes information when it is put to significant use. Administrators need to know the potentials of an information system, and how to use the technician productively. They need to determine what information is needed, for what purposes, who needs to provide it, and where to use it. They are in the best position, in consultation with the staff, to define the three major types of data required—patient oriented, program oriented, and personnel oriented. Research requirements need to be defined by appropriate personnel designing both evaluative and experimental protocols.

Well-designed and technically competent plans for data use are necessary but hardly sufficient for the establishment of an agency information system. Professionals in the organization need to participate in the operation as well as the planning of the enterprise. Unless staff members accept and adhere to the requirements of the design, the system cannot work. "Staff involvement in the study, design, and implementation stages [is] a necessary condition for success" (Nelson & Morgan, 1973). Many attempts at rational data use have failed, not so much because they are poorly designed, but because of resistance by the staff who had to provide the necessary data. Sometimes this resulted from lack of clarity about the information categories and coding system utilized. More generally, work overload and lack of conviction about the importance of the additional work requirements were at fault.

It cannot be stressed too much that acceptance of a new system must be carefully engineered. This is an important area of organizational change. A most significant role for the administrator lies precisely in this process of engendering compliance to the organizational requirements of a new information plan. A phased implementation process is clearly indicated, during which there should be continuous testing of steps in the technical design. Both professional and clerical feasibility are necessary, as is the step-by-step training of staff.

A good, comprehensive information sytem is often costly. It may take considerable time and effort to develop and adapt a sytem to tailor-made agency requirements. Start-up costs may be substantial in both financial and staff terms. Continuous operation of the system may similarly be expensive. These costs need to be considered carefully before an agency embarks on a full program. Pressure for accountability and auditing requirements by funding agencies. legislatures, and by governmental bodies purchasing services may suggest no alternative but to install a competent system. Professional considerations about quality of service and effective evaluation are also significant.

The selections in this section deal with particular aspects of information management including design, computerization, and system implementation. Two case studies illustrate problems and potentials in establishing and utilizing a schema for information handling. Weirich writes from the perspective of the administrator and of the critical choices that have to be made if the information system is to be useful and efficient. He explores approaches to design, and suggests that each step in the process must be taken in the context of the total organization. Technical experts make an important contribution, to be sure, but those who know the agency's needs and program must be intimately concerned with planning as well as implementation. In the process of developing a sound information system a multitude of factors needs to be considered, such as organizational politics and power, resource availability, ideology, technology, decision making, innovative dynamics, and change.

Schoech describes a microcomputer-based information system that addresses basic data management needs. He presents a series of basic concepts associated with such a system, poses a series of choices that must be made in developing the system, and reviews the limitations and constraints that inevitably accompany the installation of a new approach to information handling. Schoech here describes an in-house, on-line, interactive system that he feels can be used by most agency personnel after minimal training.

Kucic, Sorensen, and Hanbery discuss the decisions that have to be made in the process of developing an automated information system. They stress the importance of careful planning and preparation before introducing a computer to a human service organization. Specific suggestions are outlined for developing and evaluating requests for proposals issued to systems and computer vendors. Alternatives to purchasing or leasing computers are summarized. For a more complete review of computer use in human service agencies, see Slavin (1982).

The next two selections review the experiences of two social agencies in developing information systems. Phillips, Dimsdale, and Taft record the many steps taken in the process of establishing such a system in a family service agency. They pay particular attention to the technical structure of the system and the ways in which technical considerations are included in its development. The reports that are produced are described and their uses detailed with due consideration given to ensuring confidentiality. Although the case study is of a single agency, that agency was part of a consortium of organizations that pooled their resources in an effort that each member might have found difficult to achieve on its own.

Young describes a computerized management information system developed for a voluntary child-serving agency, which was intended to make information quickly available and adapted to make possible the assessment of the quality of services provided. The key importance of training the service delivery staff in the use of the system is made clear. Young specifies the objectives of the system, identifies the specific elements of the data base growing out of these objectives, and reviews briefly the overall operation of the system. The article is useful as an indication of the potential use of computer technology in providing information to administrators, supervisors, and direct-service personnel in enhancing service to clients, and in evaluating both service and program achievements.

REFERENCES

Nelson, C., and Morgan, L. "The Information System of a Community Mental Health Center," *Administration in Mental Health* (Fall 1973):28.

Slavin, S., Ed., *Applying Computers in Social Service and Mental Health Agencies,* New York: Haworth Press 1982.

24

The Design
of Information
Systems

THOMAS W. WEIRICH

The age of the computer has finally reached the social services. Many agencies are struggling to implement viable data-processing systems, while many others are contemplating such innovations. Funders are asking for ever more extensive reporting, and the public is increasing its demands for accountability. The need for information is so extensive that it is clear that the automated information system will be a fact of life for future social service administrators. Whether this will represent a burdensome intrusion into the administrator's realm or a useful tool to aid in management will depend in part upon the administrator's ability to manage the information system. This in turn will depend upon the administrator's understanding of the position of the information system within the agency context.

The purposes of this discussion are to present some of the essential administrative and organizational dimensions of computerized information systems, and to point out the special problems and prospects for the social services. Primary attention will be given to the administrator's point of view, based upon the premise that he or she will make the critical choices. This chapter will not be a technical discussion of computerization and computers, nor will it be a cookbook on implementation. The administrator can employ experts to cope with the technological aspects, but he or she must first be prepared to cope with the experts.

The main theme pursued here is that information systems must be understood within the context of the entire agency or organization. They are not independent operations, but instead interact with the other parts of the organization and its surroundings. The theme is clearly stated by Lucas (1975, p. 6):

An information system exists within the context of the organization; the problems of information systems are not solely technical in nature. Though there are technical problems and challenges, we have always been more successful in solving these problems than in dealing with organizational issues. It is our contention that *the major reason most information systems have failed is that we have ignored organizational behavior problems in the design and operation of computer-based information systems.* If steps are not taken to understand and solve these organizational behavior problems, systems will continue to fail. [Emphasis in original]

The situation in the social services is perhaps more difficult than elsewhere, for an organizational perspective on services is not fully developed. A discussion is needed, then, of the organizational issues in social services and how these inform the problem of computerized information systems.

It should be said that most agencies already have information systems of some sort. Those hurriedly scribbled case notes stuffed into a bottom desk drawer for future reference, or the boxes of case narratives stacked along the wall, differ only in sophistication and order from a well-oiled automated system. Most agencies have the rudiments of a management information system which can be used as starting points for automation. The essence of a management information system is the regular collection, processing, storage, retrieval, and presentation of standardized information deemed important to the organization. Historically these processes have been done by hand, but are now being gradually assigned to computers. Man or machine, the acid test for any information system is the degree to which it is actually used.

This discussion will be arranged around six major issues: organizational politics and power, resources, ideology, technology, decision-making, and innovation and change.

ORGANIZATIONAL POLITICS AND POWER

Political action occurs both outside and inside the social service organization. Two trends in the political context help explain the increased importance of information systems. The first is the rationalization of the decision-making processes in the public policy sphere. Planning, controlled program change, and evaluation are becoming more important and thus increasing the demand for extensive agency-level data. Program, Planning, and Budgeting System (PPBS), Goal Oriented Social Services (GOSS), and Zero-Based Budgeting are manifestations of the rationalization process, each representing a different approach to improved decision-making.

A second trend is the increased demand for accountability, in terms of both fiscal control and program effectiveness. After years of unquestioned growth produced few measurable results, the services are now being asked to account for money spent and to prove some impact is being made. This too requires the collection of agency-level information.

These external changes have created the need for agency-level information, and most service policies now require some formalized reporting. Since these information needs are continuous and regular, one-time sporadic reports are no longer sufficient. Permanent mechanisms are needed to supply data on regular schedules and in fixed formats, as well as for special requests. The tasks are growing too large to be handled by hand or with part-time clerical workers. As a result, social service organizations are searching for and implementing computerized information systems. And those that already have such systems in place are trying desperately to understand them. For most service agencies, all of this constitutes a major organizational change.

Since the establishment of an information system is a major internal change, it threatens organizational power structures, domains, and areas of autonomy. It will thus probably generate substantial amounts of resistance and possibly conflict. To overcome the resistances, the initiators of the information system will need an established and stable power base. The persuasion of an expert or an ideological argument will be sufficient in a few cases, but the exercise of formal authority will be required in most. The lure of additional resources or power may act as incentives for those outside formal authority structures (Lucas, 1975 pp. 16–19; Quinn, 1973, pp. 19–23).

One change in the power structure will be that information system operators will become important and influential actors. Management will become dependent upon the operators for the production of reports which satisfy external requirements and, to the extent the information system contributes to administrative practice, will look to the operators for advice. Line staff will use the system for record-keeping, identification data, or possibly referral help. The information system operators thus become the center of an essential communications network. They also will acquire authority to dictate certain organizational behaviors, such as the questions asked of clients and the categories used to define problems. In one agency both supervisors and staff frequently asked the information specialist for advice on how to code client problems. Eventually the standardization of the information system was internalized, and the precoded numbers for specific problems replaced more qualitative descriptions in normal conversion; unusual problems became "Code 99s."

The implementation of an information system increases the power of some organizational members while it reduces the autonomy of others (Quinn, 1973, pp. 9–12). Program accountability, for example, is more clearly defined, and substantial amounts of information can be produced to monitor performance. Those receiving the data have a continuous and "objective" supply of information which can be used to influence decisions. Program units, therefore, become more visible and must become more concerned with satisfying established performance standards. In one project, for example, a housing unit reported a large number of requests withdrawn by clients. Upon investigation it was found that the unit head feared losing staff if her unit had a poor performance record. To avoid reporting unmet needs for unavailable housing (even in a poor housing market), the unit head informed clients that there was little hope of placement and asked if they would like to withdraw the requests. Reporting large numbers of withdrawals seemed less threatening to this administrator than establishing a record of extensive unmet housing needs.

At the client-worker level, the flexibility of interaction may be reduced, with less discretion allowed in what information is elicited from clients. A computerized data collection form can become a determinant of the course of an interview, and a precoded list of problems and services can become a framework in which needs and actions are defined. Classification can easily become an end in itself, at the expense of the unique characteristics of each client.

Professional social service workers will no doubt resist these kinds of intrusions into their practice domains, and will resent the conformity that is implied. Missing information and incomplete forms can become a chronic problem, and some workers will insist upon narrative descriptions instead of precoded categories. One demonstration project established a workers task force to increase involvement in system design and reduce resistance to the use of forms and codes. This seemed to improve performance of information systems tasks and increase workers' understanding of the overall purpose of the system. The dependence of final reports upon each form and each coded message was clarified. Although such involvement is no guarantee of successful implementation, it can improve both understanding and commitment. Not incidentally, it is also a way to co-opt an important power block within the agency.

Service administration is itself an exercise in negotiating the tension between autonomy and control. Constituent parts of an agency fight to protect and improve their positions, while administrators push toward centralized control. Professions defend their areas of professional judgment and discretion. An information system must be established and survive among these larger political issues, and is never independent of them.

RESOURCES

Most social service administrators will realize that an information system requires extensive new resources, but some may not realize just *how extensive* the needs will be. Even in limited versions an information system is expensive. In one demonstration project, for example, a proposal for a complete system estimated developmental costs equal to the entire project's yearly budget, and this did not even include operating expenses. The proposal was politely rejected as fanciful.

An information system is labor intensive to develop and capital intensive to run. Planning, design, and implementation require costly specialized expertise. Few agencies have employees with the necessary skills, and trial-and-error development is out of the question. Outside technicians are thus the only answer. Since information systems for social services are not yet common, there are few real "experts" around. Experience with other areas, even in the human services, may not be directly transferable, forcing the administrator to choose a consultant with unclear evidence of competence. Even when a qualified consultant can be found, the social service administrator's inexperience with such technical work puts the agency at a disadvantage in specifying the terms of the work contract. One can easily be overwhelmed by the jargon, charts, and possibilities. Social service administrators will need some sophistication in the use of consultants, as well as an awareness of the potential and limitations of computers.

The operating technology for the information system is also expensive, requiring costly machines or machine time, specially designed forms, and various other supplies. Salaries must also be paid for the technicians who run and maintain the system, and for periodic updates of the system design. Often overlooked is the tremendous need for training, both during implementation and afterward. It is possible to contract the operation of a system completely or partially to an outside firm, including training tasks. Although this relieves the agency of some of the more technical problems the resultant loss of control may reduce the reliability and responsiveness of the system.

Since the need for new human and capital resources is so great, it is almost impossible to avoid increased spending. Most service agencies do not have a "surplus" for investment in automation, which means that present resources will have to be diverted or new funding acquired. Internal reallocations are likely to be challenged, since that would mean taking funds from direct services and increasing the administrative cadre. New funding means a change in economic dependencies, either intensifying the use of established funding streams or developing new ones. Collaboration with other agencies is one possibility, if agreement on a shared system design can be achieved. In one state a consortium of local agencies has been formed to share experiences and costs of information system development. Codes or procedures that have been tested in one locale are adapted to a new setting, avoiding both the pain and the expense of starting from scratch.

Many of the difficulties in obtaining the needed resources were experienced by one major demonstration project in social service integration. Initial attempts at system development were made by middle-level management people, who experimented with forms, codes, and record-keeping. It quickly became apparent that the task was too large and complicated for the non-expert, and that outside help would be needed. The agency could not hire its own staff, however, and had to rely upon external sources of help. Since it was the local branch of a state-administered department, the agency sought help from its parent organization. A limited amount of technical assistance was obtained, but this was ultimately ineffective in implementing the system. A state-level office of data-processing already existed, and it was reluctant to set up a local independent operation. Furthermore, the assistance given was sporadic, diverted by other priorities, and not attuned to local circumstances and needs. Trying a different strategy, the agency issued a number of purchase of service contracts, funded through special project monies and agreements with local governments. A contract with a data-processing branch of a neighboring college failed because of lack of attention and a mismatch in needed expertise. An individual consultant produced a grandiose design for the project, too sophisticated and expensive for its use. The project finally hired an individual consultant through a series of personal service contracts which stipulated close working relationships with project administration. Although the project finally established control over system development, it could not obtain funding equal to the task of implementation, and the system suffered from many setbacks and delays. The lack of resources and an inability to control available resources were at the root of many of the project's information system troubles.

The balance between control and expense will be one of the most difficult issues confronted. Those rich enough might be able to hire a complete staff and lease all necessary equipment thus avoiding control problems. Others may be completely dependent upon outside resources for system operation. The most typical, and possibly most desirable, arrangement will be a mixture of in-house staff and outside contracts. A systems analyst with a small clerical staff, for example, could handle the operation, maintenance, and interpretation of the system, while processing and storage could be purchased from outside providers. In this way, an agency could derive the benefits of computerized information processing, without shouldering the burden of capital investment.

IDEOLOGY

Conflicting values can produce many problems with information systems in the social services. Information systems imply a certain ideology, a world-view containing attitudes and beliefs about the way things are or should be. It assumes a way of thinking and acting and an approach to problem solution that are basically compatible with the systemic approach. Its values and norms define desirable organizational characteristics and behavior. These values may conflict with those of the social service agency, especially that of professionalism, and lead to misunderstandings and resistance. Prominent values often at issue are clarity, uniformity, permanency, and openness.

Clarity

A fundamental prerequisite of an operational information system is clarity. Organizational goals need to be clearly identified and operationalized into measurable objectives. Organizational activities need to be clearly defined and concise indicators of the extent of services must be established. Extensive numbered system codes for needs, services, and providers illustrate the need for detailed clarity. The implementation of an information system forces increased clarity in organizational characteristics (Quinn, 1973, pp. 12–16).

Social service organizations are typified by ambiguity rather than clarity. Goals are not always clear, and often consist of general value statements. Objectives are difficult to specify and are seldom stated in measurable terms, some defy operationalization; and official goals may not even reflect the actual operating goals of the agency. Services are difficult to divide into measurable units because many categories overlap.

In addition, it is frequently unclear how the information system will ultimately be used, a situation that was evident in the demonstration project mentioned above. Internal reporting requirements and the procedures for report utilization were never specified. Months were devoted to the specification of problem and service codes, while the articulation of the information system's mission with the organization's goal structure was neglected. The project's information system consultant attributed this to a basic misconception of what the information system was expected to do. The project's administration really wanted an "information management" system, not a "management information" system. The administration was motivated primarily by its need to respond to accountability demands and its desire to reduce paperwork. The most pressing organizational problems were the overwhelming information *processing* tasks, not the reform of decision-making processes.

Uniformity

If clarity is the primary conceptual expectation of an information system, then uniformity is the primary behavioral norm. To function reliably an information system must use a standardized language (i.e., definitions, terms, codes) and a routinized set of procedures (cf. Quinn, 1973, pp. 7–9). Furthermore, these must be employed consistently by all users; for without a high degree of conformity, the data will be unreliable, the system will have little credibility, and the products of the system will probably not be used (Lucas, 1975, p. 4). For the administrator this means an increased emphasis on organizational control of employee behavior, through rule-making, quality control monitoring, and enforcement.

A typical service organization, however, has high degrees of pluralism and non-conformity. Such diversity increases with the size of the organization, as the proportion of professionals and the number of specialty units increase. Each professional group and program unit develops its own definitions, language, and procedures. Underlying these are basic differences in delivery paradigms and professional orientations. Attempts to change these features to a single format suitable to the information system can generate strong resistance (Zaltman et al., 1973).

The demonstration project that has been serving as an example had two special problems in this area. First, the project had five geographically dispersed and historically distinct service centers. The management and staff of each center had unique characteristics (one center was dominated by mental health related people, for example, while another had mostly child welfare staff), and each developed its own orientation to the information system. System terms and definitions were interpreted differently, resulting in inconsistencies in the overall system. The second problem came with an attempt to integrate different professional groups into a single delivery structure. The groups held onto their service concepts and forced them into the information system. The most apparent results were separate lists of service codes for mental health and non-mental health activities, and a long list of mental health oriented diagnostic codes, many of which overlapped the more general service needs codes.

Permanency

An information system requires a relatively high degree of organizational stability during its development and implementation. It also needs permanency to be economically run. The design stages are long and the programming is complex. It is extremely difficult to establish a system for an organization that is constantly changing its central features. Time must also be allowed for "debugging" and refinement. The investments made in development, hardware, and supplies need to be stretched over a lengthy period of time. Although most systems attempt to be open to changes, realistically flexibility must be limited.

A social service agency, on the other hand, can be a very unstable entity, especially in the uncertain environment of the public organization. Basic structures and processes change over time, and new services and practices emerge in response to professional developments and community needs. Policies change, creating new lines of authority, demanding new forms of data, and reshuffling funding streams. Research and demonstration projects fare even worse, having far too short a life span. The administrator is faced with a basic dilemma between responsiveness to information needs and responsible information management. Uncontrolled program changes can make the information system useless, while over-protection of the information system can endanger program effectiveness and enforce program rigidity.

Openness

A final value assumption of an information system is openness. The assumption is that data needed by the system is available and readily given. A "complete" system needs a complete data base, and arbitrary barriers which impede that completeness must be avoided. Openness, however, need not mean that information is accessible to anyone. Once stored, the data base is usually protected from unauthorized entry; but such protection is not assured. A contributor may fear that the information given in confidence will later surface in unanticipated and unwanted ways. (The controversy over data banks and individual privacy is not limited to the social services, as there is also growing concern over credit, health, and educational records.)

Privacy is a central value in most social service agencies. The client-worker relationship is strictly confidential and held to be immune from intrusion. The rights of the client are paramount, and any attempts to expose personal information are resisted. Thus, social service workers may interpret extensive data collection as an intrusion into their professional domain and a violation of the client-worker relationship. The bonds of trust between client and worker are threatened, as are the prerogatives of professional discretion. To defend against these possibilities the service worker may purposely omit or change information, with the result that information is incomplete and unreliable.

Organizational privacy can also be threatened, since the performance of subunits becomes more visible when an information system is implemented. Without an information system subunits can retain information that might reflect negatively on their performance. With an information system, however, such information *automatically* goes to people outside of the unit, to superiors and possible competitors. The information is available for evaluation of the unit and as the basis for action against it. To prevent such negative repercussions the unit may resist participation or even "fudge" its unit reports. The housing unit mentioned above would have been more comfortable if it could have kept its problems with the housing market secret, but since the information had to be given, the least threatening reporting code was used.

These value conflicts have not received much attention in discussions of social service information systems, partly because administrators have not been sensitive to their existence. With the realization that system implementation affects some of the basic value foundations of their agencies, perhaps administrators can more effectively prepare for and confront such problems.

TECHNOLOGY

Information processing technology can be truly dazzling, and the inexperienced service administrator can be overwhelmed by the parade of the latest gadgetry, independent of its utility. Indeed, the future will probably see the incorporation of automation into service administration in creative and productive ways. In the meantime, however, there are fundamental issues which need to be confronted. One of the most important is the basic incompatibility between the technologies of information systems and social services.

Information system technologies are highly determinant; they are exact, certain, and predictable (Thompson, 1967). Their products are clearly defined, and the paths to their achievement are concise and reliable. Before a computer program can be run, the formats for all outputs must be specified in detail, each process and step must be precisely defined and interconnected with others, and the strict specifications for data input must be set. The complex electronics of the computer are intolerant; ask any beginner who has sat at a terminal trying to run the simplest of programs. Because of the interdependence of system parts, a small change at one point, such as a slight change in a data collection form, will have ripple effects throughout the system. Problems arise when such an exacting technology is joined with one that is almost the exact opposite.

Social service technologies are patently indeterminant. Goals and objectives are ill-defined, supported by low consensus, and sometimes conflicting. They change with the winds in the policy sphere, so that many administrators are reluctant to be tied to the specification required by an information sytem. Furthermore, regular reports can be all too revealing of agency performance.

The critical problem, however, is the extreme uncertainty of the connections between service goals and organizational activities. There are few proven solutions, and most delivery strategies are complex, changeable combinations of many approaches. Since indeterminancy makes it difficult for the information system to accurately mirror service delivery, problems arise in both design and interpretation.

This technological mismatch is especially apparent in demonstration projects. Here, change and development are organizational goals, and many projects emerge without any clearly defined delivery model. In this situation it is virtually impossible to design an information system that accurately catches the present project while it remains flexible enough for adaptation to future unknown changes. Some information system specialists recommend delaying design and implementation until an agency has stabilized and its delivery model has crystalized. Administrators know that this could be a long wait, and the more practical solution will be some concessions on both sides.

DECISION MAKING

One of the most frequently heard justifications for an information system is the potential contribution to decision-making. This justification stems from a basic value assumption, and the central premise of information sytems—rationality. People, management and workers, are assumed to be rational beings, solving problems and making decisions based upon facts, logical connections between means and ends, and expertise. The only limits to these processes are the lack of sufficient information and poor information-processing techniques. The establishment of an information system is intended to supply all of the needed data and to simplify processing, thus enabling people to make more rational choices. Indeed, the real zealots believe that *the* solution to poor decision-making is automation.

Contrary to this, however, most organizations and the people who run them are not perfectly rational. Their rationality is "bounded" by both internal capacities and external constraints (Simon, 1965; Thompson, 1967). Service administrators know that this is especially true of human service organizations (Hasenfeld & English, 1974). Decisions are often made on political grounds, for ideological reasons, out of tradition or habit, because of economic feasibility, from personal intuition or bias, or sometimes from simple expediency. Some decisions are never consciously made; things just seem to happen. Skilled administrators use an

informal "intelligence" network as the source of much information, and
no information system will replace these more qualitative inputs (Holland, 1976).

Thus, the rationalization of decision-making in the social services is
still incomplete. Nor is it specified how information systems are to be integrated into regular decision-making processes, let alone if it can be
done at all. Both management and workers lack experience in the use of
information systems, and the sophisticated techniques and potentials
are new and strange. Some speculate that automation is just too new in
the field of social services, as service professionals have not come to understand how it can be made to help them. One consultant reported,
"I spent months just holding hands and telling staff that it is not 'Big
Brother,' it is not '1984.'"

Given the precarious nature of social service organizations' environments, the indeterminancy of their technologies, and the state of administrative practice, non-rational decision-making is both understandable
and probably necessary. These circumstances, however, also force service administrators to be more realistic in their expectations of automated information systems. It should be clear that computerization is *not*
a magical solution to the problems of decision-making, and computer
printouts will not replace sound administrative judgment.

INNOVATION AND CHANGE

The organizational characteristics discussed thus far interact with the information system. To a very large extent they will determine an agency's
ability to implement. Without sufficient power and resources an administrator will not be able to initiate and sustain extensive innovation. A
hospitable ideological context will reduce resistance to the change, while
skillful political action will be needed to negotiate specific strategies and
conflicts. Finally, adjustments in service technology and decision-making
styles will be needed to make an information system more relevant.

In addition, these factors must be combined at an opportune time
and under the right conditions. For example, periods of external pressure for increased accountability may be a good time to seek additional
resources for system support, while outside demands also justify change
internally. On the other hand, institutionalization of an information system already designed may be easier during calm periods, when standardization is possible and few changes required.

Successful innovation will also depend upon the willingness of
agency staff to cooperate. Since the reliability of the system rests upon
the data collection efforts of staff, their performance is essential. Staff·

resistance can frustrate the fanciest of designs. Training is of course one change strategy, effective for educating staff in the potentials and limitations of automation and in learning required procedures. Early and continuous involvement in the design and refinement of the system will increase commitment to the project and reduce some of the mysticism of computerization. Contributions and criticisms from staff will help assure that the system will meet their needs as well as the administration's, and might reduce some of the more burdensome and unnecessary procedures. Administrators will also have to use consultants effectively, taking care to specify expectations clearly and monitor development. The organization of information system "task forces" at crucial agency levels, such as line staff, clerical workers, and managers, to review and help in design is a promising change strategy. At the same time, the danger of the information system becoming an independent end in itself should be avoided.

Ultimately, successful implementation will depend upon judgments by all participants, especially administrators, that the information system is worth the trouble (cf. Salasin & Davis, 1976). There has to be a payoff, or a yield. If the system actually helps people do their work, solve their problems, and make their decisions, then it will be appreciated and used. One of the best ways to increase support for an information system, to increase its usage, and to improve its performance, is to make it satisfy individual and organizational needs (Lucas, 1975). These needs should be identified at the very outset, and should remain in focus throughout.

At the present time the anticipation of real benefits from a computerized information system in the social services is problematic. A number of issues remain unresolved. First, the benefits for accountability and research purposes are the most apparent. Improved data bases and reporting will certainly help in the general evaluation and understanding of the services. On the organizational level the situation is less clear. There is no tradition of regular use of information system products, and the integration of a system into the everyday work patterns has yet to be accomplished. The benefits on the worker level, in case management for example, will have to be demonstrated and refined. The claims made for simplification of tasks and improved monitoring and follow-up will have to be sustained, and it is doubtful that the system alone will cause better service follow-ups if none were done before it.

On the management level, the utility of the information system for decision-making, evaluation, and planning is still unproven. Administrators and managers will have to "learn" how to use the system, especially if it is to be more than just a report-generating device. Such learning can not take place without an interest in and commitment to improved information management. Thus the steady commitment and support of top administrators are essential. Starting with a survey of informational needs for management decisions, and a review of existing ways information is obtained and processed, the administration can carefully build a new system.

CONCLUSION

The theme pursued here has been that social service information systems have to be understood within their organizational contexts. Service administrators will have to consider organizational factors as well as technical ones in their decisions to initiate, implement, and routinize new systems. Information systems can be magnificent, but they are not magic. The service administrator need not be mystified by their hardware, for in the end it is the administrator's hard work that will determine the system's usefulness. Although the computerized information system can certainly contribute to decision-making, it is no substitute for administrative judgment.

References

Hasenfeld, Yeheskel, and Richard A. English, eds. *Human Service Organizations.* Ann Arbor: University of Michigan Press, 1974.

Holland, Thomas P. "Information and Decision Making in Human Services." *Administration in Mental Health* 4, no. 1 (Fall 1976): 26–35.

Lucas, Henry C., Jr. *Why Information Systems Fail,* New York: Columbia University Press, 1975.

Quinn, Robert E. "Computerization and the Integration of Services: An Empirical Study." In *Services Integration: Selected Research Studies.* Cincinnati: Information Systems Center, 1973.

Salasin, Susan E., and Howard R. Davis. "Achieving Desired Policy or Practice Changes: Findings Alone Won't Do It." In *HEW Region III Evaluation Conference: New Perspectives, Summary of Proceedings,* Philadelphia, D.H.E.W., Oct. 19–22, 1976.

Simon, Herbert. *Administrative Behavior,* New York: Free Press, 1965.

Thompson, James D. *Organizations in Action.* New York: McGraw-Hill, 1967.

Zaltman, Margie, Gerald, Robert Duncan, & Jonny Holbek. *Innovations and Organizations.* New York: Wiley, 1973.

25

A Microcomputer-Based Human Service Information System

DICK SCHOECH

INTRODUCTION

Present computer technology far exceeds its use in human service agencies, and present technology is continuing to advance at a rapid pace. Technology is leading within the next five to ten years to a small, reliable computer with the capabilities of the larger systems of today. However, we need not wait for the future. The present market offers microcomputer systems capable of being used by a small human service agency or private practitioner at a cost less than that of one clerical position.[1] Human service agencies are ideally suited to benefit from the microcomputer's data processing capabilities since most agencies collect, store, and retrieve large quantities of data and information in the course of delivering services.

This chapter discusses how those delivering human service on the local level can use present microcomputer technology to address one of their basic needs, data management. It examines microcomputer technology and the concept of an information system, and discusses the choices and limitations associated with setting up a microcomputer-based human service information system. The microcomputer-based information system described can automate agency functions such as bookkeeping, client profiles, staff time and effort, needs assessment, information and referral, client tracking and scheduling, and program evaluation. Thus, while the system described is a powerful data processing tool, it avoids many of the problems inherent in our past experiences

The author wishes to thank Temple Baker for his technical assistance in the preparation of this article.

with information systems that were based on large, bulky, inflexible, costly, centralized computer technology.

Although the chapter describes a microcomputer-based information system designed for a small human service agency, the concepts are applicable to any agency or private practice with data management needs and can be used by larger agencies interested in developing distributed or decentralized systems.

A MICROCOMPUTER DATA PROCESSING SYSTEM

A microcomputer system (see Figure 25–1) consists of the following:

1. A standard typewriter keyboard and optional calculator keyboard to input information.
2. A TV-like screen to display the inputs and outputs of the system.
3. A microcomputer that functions like the receiver of an audio sytem. It includes processing, memory, and interface components. Microcomputer-based systems vary primarily in the size of the internal memory and the speed of the information processing.
4. An external memory in which information not being used by the microprocessor is stored. Sequential data can be stored on standard cassette tapes; however, the advantage of having random access to information makes a floppy disk storage system almost a necessity. A floppy disk is similar to a very flexible or floppy 45-rpm phonograph record. A 5 1/4 inch floppy disk can hold approximately 200 pages of double-spaced text.
5. A printer, if "hard copy" outputs from the system are needed.
6. Software, or the directions that make the microcomputer operate. Applications software consists of programs, or sets of instructions, that the user needs to solve a problem or perform a task, e.g., generating a report or performing a statistical analysis. Systems software controls the operations of the computer by performing tasks such as keeping track of where data files reside and translating applications programs into codes that the central processor can understand.

An information system is the link between data processing and the user of the information. Although there is widespread disagreement between professionals on exactly what constitutes an information system, for the human services, Burch and Strater's (1971) definition is very appropriate.

. . . a systematic, formal assemblage of components that performs data processing operations to (a) meet legal and transactional data process-

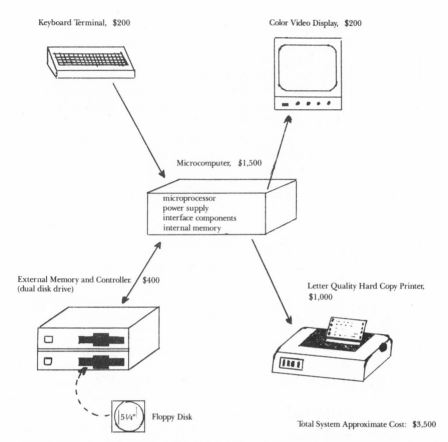

Keyboard Terminal, $200

Color Video Display, $200

Microcomputer, $1,500

microprocessor
power supply
interface components
internal memory

External Memory and Controller. $400
(dual disk drive)

Letter Quality Hard Copy Printer,
$1,000

5¼" Floppy Disk

Total System Approximate Cost: $3,500

FIGURE 25–1. A microcomputer data processing system and approximate costs

ing requirements, (b) provide information to management for support of planning, controlling and decision making activities, and (c) provide a variety of reports, as required, to external constituents. [p. 71]

An information system consists of a data base or a set of logically related files organized to improve access and minimize redundancy, a data base management system or software that manages the data, and hardware oriented towards providing information to the user (Davis, 1974). Information systems turn data (or facts) into information (or data that has been processed to achieve a purpose or enhance understanding). They perform such functions as originating-recording, classifying, sorting, calculating, summarizing, storing, retrieving, reproducing, and communicating (Sanders, 1970). Figure 25–2 illustrates how information subsystems can be combined to produce a total agency information system.

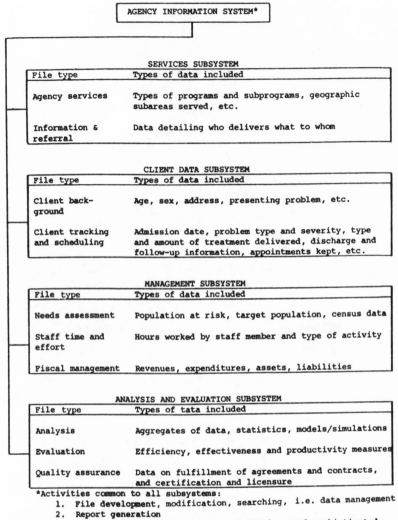

FIGURE 25–2. A generic human service information system

An information system may or may not be computerized. One agency may have a highly developed manual system, while another may have a computer-based, haphazard, and uncoordinated information gathering and retrieval effort. This distinction, although conceptually clear, is in practice harder to make, for "It has almost become an article of faith that the heart of an MIS (management information system) must be a computer" (Mason & Mitroff, 1973). Still, the distinction is necessary lest problems and procedures associated with developing an information system are attributed to the process of computerizing that information system, and vice versa.

Information systems have advanced significantly since the first business computer applications in the mid-1950s. Early systems were primarily housed in specialized electronic data processing (EDP) departments or subsumed under other functions such as accounting. They were used primarily for generating data and routine reports at the operational level, monitoring the movement of people or products through the system, developing models of systems, and automating routine decision making. Today, information systems have become much more flexible physically and informationally. In this expanded use, they are sometimes referred to as decision support systems (DSS) (Lucas, 1978; Keen & Morton, 1978; Carlson, 1977). With a DSS, managers can interact with data banks in highly flexible ways, e.g., generating graphs, retrieving information instantaneously, and using that information to query for trends or evaluate alternatives. This interaction can occur in a language and logic the decision maker is familiar with. Thus, a DSS is designed to enhance the decision maker's judgment on a continuous basis in all phases and levels of decision making.

Mason and Mitroff (1973) point to the necessity of viewing an information system in its overall context. Seen in this larger context:

> An information system consists of at least one PERSON of a certain PSYCHOLOGICAL TYPE who faces a PROBLEM within some ORGANIZATIONAL CONTEXT for which he needs EVIDENCE to arrive at a solution (i.e., to select some course of action) and that the evidence is made available to him through some MODE OF PRESENTATION. [p. 475]

Earlier information systems tended to focus on one psychological type, one class of problem, one or two methods of generating evidence, and one method of presentation. DSSs are developing the flexibility needed to address the variety of states of each of these variables. (For a more complete discussion of the concepts of information management in the human services, see Schoech, 1982.)

An information system, then, is simply a conceptual arrangement of data or a data management tool. Computerization allows for the rapid storage, manipulation, and retrieval of large volumes of data, making the information system a much more powerful decision-making tool.

CHOICES IN THE DEVELOPMENT OF A COMPUTERIZED INFORMATION SYSTEM

This section presents a series of choices that a human service agency must make in any effort to develop and implement a computerized information system.

How Comprehensive, Complete, or Total The System Should Be

A complete or total information system performs all the significant data processing operations of an agency. An information system having all the subsystems of Figure 25–2 would constitute a relatively complete system.

It is best to view a total system as a group of related but independent modules. The concept of a modular system is important for it allows gradual implementation, easier adjustment to the system by the agency, and minimal risk. A social service agency can rent a keyboard and video display, buy computer time, and try out one module of the system with a limited commitment of time, money, and energy. If this trial experience proves successful, the agency can then develop another module of its choice.

When developing a system from relatively independent modules, initial conceptual work on the total system should be completed in order to develop modules that will eventually tie together to form a network of modules or a total system. The most difficult conceptual work involves defining subsystems, boundaries, and interfaces, and viewing the information system as an integral component of agency decision making. Too often, as Mittenthal (1976) points out, this initial conceptual work is avoided, with unfortunate consequences.

> There is a sixth lesson to be drawn from the current infatuation with information systems. . . . Too often, information systems are bought without a clear specification of their purpose, or proper understanding of their relationship to other system components. . . . The danger is that, designed in a vacuum, an information system may not even be an effective tool, or at least its costs may outweigh its benefit. [p. 146]

What Module to Implement First

In deciding which module of an information system to implement first, an agency has several alternatives. First, it can computerize its most pressing data needs or those needs which are at present most difficult to handle by hand, e.g., large volumes of client data. Second, it can choose to computerize data and information that addresses the most pressing agency decisions that need to be made, e.g., program evaluation. Finally, it can computerize data and information of one of the most stable systems in the agency and one where the appropriate data is clearcut, e.g., payroll.

The basic considerations in these alternatives are how experienced in computers the agency is, how developed the present manual information is, and how much risk the agency can afford to take.

What Agency Data to Include in the Information System

This is one of the most difficult choices, and failure in this area "probably accounts for the downfall of more design efforts than any other factor except managerial participation" (Ross, 1976, p. 26).

Some authors suggest that an agency start automating information that relates to the major agency decisions that must be made. Others suggest automating based on the reports that an agency must produce. Carter and Newman (1976), in their discussion of data systems for a mental health center, suggest that an information system should be able to answer a series of questions on service, management, accounting, and evaluation (see Figure 25–3).

Given the turbulent nature of human service agencies, all three approaches should be examined with the following considerations. First, an agency information system need not do away with all paper files. If keeping a file by hand is easy and is causing no problems, then automating it may not be necessary. Certain files lend themselves to automation, others do not. Those that lend themselves to automation are those which contain large volumes of repetitive data that are frequently searched, manipulated, or rearranged.

Second, data takes on increased importance simply by being in the system. As Luthans and Koester (1976) point out, tenuous data may be viewed as iron-clad facts by those mystified by computers or those working in agencies unfamiliar with the data's limitations, e.g., planning bodies.

Third, the easiest data to computerize may not be the most useful for decision making. As Gorry and Morton (1971) have demonstrated, the easiest data to computerize is internal, routine data at the operational level, while the most pressing data needs involve strategic decisions of considerable risk and uncertainty that require data from the environment.

Finally, people tend to collect more information than they need. Although psychological studies point to the additional security this unused

Questions related to services

1. Does your agency have a way of identifying the target population?
2. Does your agency have a way of expressing the degree of client impairment in terms of general levels of disability or dysfunction?
3. Does your agency identify an array of services according to: (a) the target population(s) served, and (b) levels of functioning?
4. Has your agency identified complementary services which could have an impact on the clients you are serving?
5. Has your agency analyzed the coordination of its array of services for each target population with complementary services offered elsewhere in your community?

Questions related to the management of services

1. Can you substantiate a client's assignment to a level of functioning by some objective criteria?
2. Does your program have a systematic procedure for setting a timed sequence of intermediate objectives and long-term goals for each client and for relating these sequential objectives and goals to the client's level of functioning?
3. Does your agency have a systematic way to assign a planned sequence of services or therapeutic activities to accomplish intermediate objectives and long term goals?
4. Does your agency maintain a updated record of service contacts that show: (a) client's level of functioning, (b) type of service rendered, (c) amount of service (time), and (d) who delivered the service?
5. Does your agency have a regular review process that could be used to ascertain: (a) that services planned have been delivered, and (b) that client progress is occurring as expected?

Questions related to cost accounting

1. Does your agency have some criteria by which to distinguish between direct service costs and indirect costs?
2. Do members of your agency regularly report their indirect service activities relating to each target population?
3. Does your agency summarize the amount of each type of direct and indirect service delivered by various categories of personnel?
4. Does your agency keep records of expenditures that permits you to estimate direct costs per hour of service delivered?
5. Does your agency have a method for allocating or prorating indirect service expenditures to each hour of direct service?
6. Does your agency have a procedure for calculating expenditures for each client served?

Questions related to program evaluation

1. Does your agency have a policy for determining what information is appropriate for making decisions at various operational and administrative levels?
2. Does your agency use cost and outcome information to discover and solve problems in the service delivery system?
3. Does your agency regularly use procedures to test alternative solutions to service problems and to translate the results into program decisions?
4. Does your program assess the reliability and validity of the information used to manage and evaluate your program.

Note. From *A client-oriented system of mental health service delivery and program management: A workbook and guide* by D. E. Carter and F. L. Newman, U.S. Department of Health, Education and Welfare, National Institute of Mental Health, Series C, No. 12, Publication No. (ADM) 76-307, 1976.

FIGURE 25–3. Questions an agency data system should address

data has for decision makers, keeping unnecessary data is expensive and time consuming (Davis, 1974).

How to Segment Agency Files

This is the choice at which a microcomputer-based system and a larger system vary most widely. A larger system usually allows simultaneous access to many data files, whereas a microcomputer system typically has limited simultaneous access. In addition, a larger system can dedicate large sections of its internal memory to file manipulation, whereas a microcomputer system has a relatively small internal memory and therefore is limited to less sophisticated manipulations. Thus, creative external file arrangement is necessary if the microcomputer-based system is to have the data access, manipulation, and retrieval capacity necessary to meet the agency's needs.

By carefully examining agency forms and reports, one can begin to see which data frequently are used together and whether it is more feasible to store many files together chronologically on one floppy disk or segment files onto individual disks. Duplicating information on several files may sometimes be necessary and more cost effective than complex search procedures, but duplicate information may result in inconsistencies in data across files. A hard disk storage device, capable of containing the contents of 15-45 floppy disks, may be an inexpensive ($1,000-$2,000) addition to a system with data requiring more than one floppy disk.

How Conversational the System Should Be

A highly conversational system is designed to allow the inexperienced user to input, process, and retrieve information from the system. A conversational system prompts, queries, and instructs in language and logic familiar to the user. Different modules may require different levels of conversation, depending on who the potential users will be. A highly conversational system requires more sophisticated programming, and is therefore more costly, complex, and difficult to modify.

Who the Potential User Should Be

The answer to this question obviously depends on which module the agency is implementing and what equipment the agency can afford. Some modules are designed around the data and information needs of management, others around the needs of those who deliver the services. Highly conversational systems with multiple terminals can potentially be used by many staff. Probably the best advice is roughly to conceptualize the total system with different groups as potential users, and then finalize these plans based on initial experience and available funds.

What Computer Language to Use in Developing a System

An agency has the choice of using an assembly language or one of the more common high-level languages, i.e., COBOL, FORTRAN, or BASIC. Assembly languages, although efficient and flexible, are impractical because they require sophisticated programming skills. Each of the common high-level languages has different advantages. COBOL has traditionally been the preferred language for accounting and file manipulation, FORTRAN the language for computation, while BASIC was designed for time sharing (Lucas, 1978). Since all three languages are now highly developed and can theoretically perform most of the basic functions required of a human service information system, any language would be acceptable. Many data base management system software packages contain easy to use language eliminating the need for a high level programming language for all but the most difficult programming tasks.

How Compatible the System Should Be with Other Systems

Since a human service agency is part of a community service delivery system, compatibility with other systems has obvious advantages. Compatibility can occur in terms of hardware, e.g., similar computers; software, e.g., similar languages; and similar data formats.

The advantages of compatible software systems include using existing geo-coding programs to change client addresses into census tract or other geographic areas (Kluess & Moyer, 1978). Obviously, reporting to funding sources and other agencies would be simplified if agencies operated on systems that had compatible data formats. Disadvantages can occur since a system may become less responsive to internal needs as it adapts to the needs of a larger system. In addition, as Fried (1977) points out, crossing internal and external agency boundaries multiplies problems and increases the chances of failure.

Given the fact that most human service agencies are heavily influenced by their environment, serious effort must be made to assure maximum upward compatibility, especially where minimal internal sacrifices can be made. For as Schoech and Arangio (1979) point out, incompatibility of systems will only result in "further entrenchment of the fragmental service system that already exists" (p. 101).

Who Should Design the System

With few knowledgeable personnel available, this becomes a difficult choice. Compounding the problem is the fact that computer/information systems personnel and human service personnel usually speak two mutually incomprehensible languages (Quinn, 1976). Thus, considerable homework is necessary to avoid problems.

Consultants cannot be counted on to be totally objective, since promoting information systems is usually good for their business. If the consultant wants to make decisions for the agency rather than present choices between alternatives, the system developed may meet the needs of the consultant more than the needs of the agency. Ein-Dor and Segev (1978) indicate that much information can come to light by putting consultants interested in the project in an adversary situation. Paton and D'huyvetter (1979) present a wealth of information on setting up a consultant or vendor contract.

The factor that poses the greatest risk of all to a small agency, according to Neu (1976), is its long dependence on one individual as the very core of its development effort. Planning is required to insure that continuity can be maintained over the several years required to develop an adequately functioning system even with changes in consultants or key in-house personnel.

LIMITATIONS OF A MICROCOMPUTER-BASED INFORMATION SYSTEM

Information systems, like other technologies, seem to be a necessary evil. However, despite the frustrations and problems associated with their development and implementation, few see the possibility of functioning without them. The best strategy is to learn the capabilities and limitations of computerized information systems, so that they are not oversold and so that impossible results are not expected. The discussion of the following limitations is helpful for putting information systems in proper perspective.

An Information System Is not a Substitute for Sound Decision Making

This limitation is one of the most common listed by authors. In the computer-information system-decision making relationship, by far the weakest link presenting is that between information and its use in decision making. The skilled decision maker who knows little computer technology will be much more successful in using a computerized agency information system than an unskilled decision maker who is an expert in computer technology.

Although the End Results of Implementing an Information System Are Desirable, the Process Is Difficult, Frustrating, and Problematic

Information systems have a profound effect on any organization, but especially human service agencies, since they are usually unsystematic in their operation. The logic and precision required by information systems mean a radical change that causes stress and accentuates existing problems.

A Good Information System Will not Automatically Be Used (Noah, 1978)

In the final analysis, an agency information system is the user's system. To get quality information out, the user must have the knowledge to put quality information in. In addition, the user will not participate unless he or she has the confidence that the information will not be used detrimentally. Involvement and training are crucial to the system's use and, as Kraemer (1977) notes, it may even be necessary to avoid prepackaged systems simply to allow the user to learn through participation in the development effort.

An Information System Contains Only a Portion of the Data Needed for Agency Decision Making

Just as problematic as not using the data and information generated by a computerized information system is the over-reliance on that system. At this point in their development, agency information systems are able to capture only a portion of the information needed in agency decision making. For example, information from the informal organization and the organization's environment is typically left out of a system. Thus, an information system does not replace the need to use other decision making aids as political analysis or intuitive judgment.

Implementing a Complete Information System Involves a Long-term Commitment by Top Decision Makers to Substantial Organizational Change

The involvement and commitment of top decision makers throughout the several years needed to design, implement, debug, and reap the benefits of the system are seen by many as the key to a successful system (Bowers & Bowers, 1977; Cobb, 1976–77). The top decision maker must be willing to do the extra work required, e.g., secure a stable funding source, give moral support, attend important meetings, make crucial decisions in a timely fashion, delegate responsibility, keep communication channels open, and coordinate the conflicting interests.

An Information System Will Highlight
Agency Problems and Successes

The computerized information system functions as a spotlight on agency decision makers by quantifying and documenting what the situation is and how the decision maker reacts. Good management tends to look better and bad management looks worse. As Chapman (1976) points out, "An MIS is a powerful tool in the sense that it brings problems out into the open. Not all organizations are prepared to deal with stark reality" (p. 9).

Wilson (1966) suggests that the agency best suited to implement change is one that is superior or one that is failing. A failing agency must change or face extinction, while a successful agency can best withstand the pressures and risks associated with such a major change.

Cost Reductions Cannot Be Associated
with a Computerized Information System

Benefits of an information system have been extremely difficult to measure, although both business and government consider them worth the investment and problems involved. Rather than expect cost reductions, it is better to expect more accountable and improved service delivery and the ability to hold down future costs. The chance of future cost reduction can be increased by dove-tailing several computer applications, for example, running an information system and a word-processing system from the same microcomputer.

Hardware and Software Must Be Purchased
while the Market Is Undergoing Rapid Development

Since change in the hardware and software market will continue the present rapid advancement for at least another ten years, the tendency is always to wait until the next development hits the market. Compounding the problem is the limited standardization that exists across manufacturers of microcomputer systems.

Given this state of flux, choosing a microcomputer system can be compared to buying a car. It may be wise to buy a standard proven model from a reputable dealer rather than a new high performance system that may turn out to be one of a kind. Perhaps the biggest risk is purchasing from a company that is being driven out of business by fierce competition. A reputable dealer is the best bet against this occurrence, unless an agency has the time and expertise to examine a microcomputer manufacturer's stability (Cheney, 1979).

Any System Change Causes New Problems

Any time a change is made to improve a system, that change itself generates new problems. Although computerized information systems are tools that will help solve many of the information problems facing an agency, they generate their own set of problems as Gall (1975) points out.

> Systems are seductive. They promise to do a hard job faster, better and more easily than you could do it yourself. But if you set up a system, you are likely to find your time and effort now being consumed in the care and feeding of the system itself. New problems are created by its very presence. Once set up, it won't go away, it grows and encroaches. [p. 100]

What a computerized information system does is shift the problem areas. The assumption is that this shift is toward less severe problems and is in the best interest of the client.

It might be noticed that some of the most familiar problems associated with an information system have not been mentioned. This is because a microcomputer-based system avoids many of the problems traditionally associated with a larger system. For example, in regard to confidentiality and security, a microcomputer system can be more confidential and secure than a paper file system. The floppy disk can be locked up as easily as a paper file, and the system has the additional advantage of requiring a user code to obtain access to information. System failures are also less of a problem since broken components can easily be unhooked and exchanged.

CONCLUSIONS

Small human service agencies can at present benefit from the computer industry's efforts to corner the home computer market. We have moved from large, bulky, impersonal systems to those which are small, interactive, and oriented to the inexperienced user. Systems are becoming available which allow agencies to connect or network several microcomputers in order to share the same database, storage device, and printer. Although the smaller systems do not as yet have the capabilities of larger systems, they are powerful data processing tools capable of performing a variety of data management functions for smaller human service agencies and private practitioners. Applying low-cost computer technology to the delivery of human services will undoubtedly be one of the major tasks facing human service providers over the next decade.

NOTE

1. System costs vary depending on quality and options. Approximate costs for an average system are included in Figure 25–1. System and cost comparisons are available in many popular microcomputer magazines.

   In addition to the costs of the components in Figure 25–1 are the costs of developing the software and of keeping the system current with the organization. Developing software will probably cost more than the components and depends on factors as the number of files of Figure 25–2 which are automated, the ability to use or adapt existing software, the data manipulation capacity desired, etc. The yearly costs of keeping the system current with the organization (not to include expansion of the system) will usually cost approximately 20% of the initial sytem components of Figure 25–1.

REFERENCES

Bowers, G. E. & Bowers, M. R. *Cultivating client information systems,* Human Services Monograph Series No. 5. Washington, D.C.: U.S. Department of Health, Education, and Welfare, Project Share, June 1977.

Burch, J., & Strater, F., Jr. *Information systems: Theory and practice.* Santa Barbara: Hamilton Publishing Co., 1974.

Carlson, E. D. Decision support systems: Personal computing services for managers. *Management Review,* 1977, *66,* 5–11.

Carter, D. E., & Newman, F. L. *A client oriented system of mental health service delivery and program management: A workbook and guide.* Rockville, Md.: Department of Health, Education, and Welfare, National Institute of Mental Health, Series C, No. 12, Pub. No. (ADM) 76–307, 1976.

Chapman, R. L. *The design of management information systems for mental health organizations: A primer.* Rockville, Md.: Department of Health, Education, and Welfare, National Institute of Mental Health, Series C, No. 13, DHEW Publication No. (ADM) 76–333, 1976.

Cheney, P. H. Selecting, acquiring, and coping with your first computer. *Journal of Small Business Management,* 1979, *17*(1), 43–50.

Cobb, C. W. Problems and principles in the development of management information systems. *International Journal of Mental Health,* 1976–77, *5,* 103–120.

Davis, G. B. *Management information systems: Conceptual foundations, structure, and development.* New York: McGraw-Hill Book Company, 1974.

Ein-Dor, R., & Segev, E. *Managing management information systems.* Lexington, Mass.: Lexington Books, 1978.

Fried, L. MIS success story: Smoothing out people system. *Data Management,* 1977, *15,* 30–36.

Gall, J. *Systemantics: How systems work and especially how they fail.* New York: Pocket Books, 1975.

Gorry, G. A., & Morton, M. S. A framework for management information systems. *Sloan Management Review,* 1971, *13,* 55–70.

Keen, P. G., & Morton, M. S. *Decision support systems: An organizational perspective.* Reading, Mass.: Addison-Wesley Publishing Company, 1978.

Kluess, P. W., & Moyer, M. COMPIS, GDF/DIME and human resources: A local application. *Proceedings of the Urban and Regional Information Systems Association Conference,* 1978, 268–278.

Kraemer, K. L. Local government, information systems, and technology transfer: Evaluating some common assertions about computer applications transfer. *Public Administrative Review, 1977, 37,* 368–382.

Lucas, H. C., Jr. *Information systems concepts for management.* New York: McGraw-Hill Book Company, 1978.

Luthans, F. & Koester, R. The impact of computer generated information on the choice activity of decision makers. *Academy of Management Journal,* 1976, *19,* 328–332.

Mason, R. O., & Mitroff, I. I. A program for research on management information systems. *Management Science,* 1973, *19,* 475–485.

Mittenthal, S. D. A systems approach to human service integration. *Evaluation,* 1976, *3,* 142–148.

Neu, C. W. Small EDP shop risks. *Journal of systems management,* 1976, *27,* 36–39.

Noah, J. C. Information systems in human services: Misconceptions, deceptions and ethics. *Administration in Mental Health,* 1978, *5,* 99–111.

Paton, J., & D'huyvetter, P.K. *Management information systems for mental health agencies: A planning and acquisition guide.* Rockville, Md.: Department of Health, Education, and Welfare, National Institute of Mental Health, Series C, No. 15, DHEW Publication No. (ADM) 79–797, 1979.

Quinn, R. E. The impact of a computerized information system on the integration and coordination of human services. *Public Administration Review,* 1976, *36,* 166–174.

Ross, J. E. *Modern management and information systems.* Reston, Va: Reston Publishing Co., 1976.

Sanders, D. H. *Computers and management.* New York: McGraw-Hill Book Company, 1970.

Schoech, D. *Computer use in human services: A guide to information management.* New York: Human Sciences Press, 1982.

Schoech, D., & Arangio, T. Computers in the human services. *Social Work,* 1979, *24*(2), 96–102.

Wilson, J. Q. Innovation in organizations: Notes toward a theory. In J. D. Thompson (Ed.) *Approaches to organizational design.* Pittsburgh: University of Pittsburgh Press, 1966, 193–219.

26

Computer Selection for Human Service Organizations

A. RONALD KUCIC
JAMES E. SORENSEN
GLYN W. HANBERY

INFORMATION SYSTEMS (IS)

An information system (IS) is the collection of documents, procedures and steps used to identify, capture, record, process and report data generated by varied organizational transactions. To gather, store, process and report data, an IS may rely upon manual, automated or some combination of these methods. Many managers of small to medium-sized Human Service Organizations (HSO) mistakenly believe an IS is synonymous with a computer. A computer is a tool for processing and storing data and may or may not be appropriate depending on the circumstances. Managers are often tempted to make decisions about implementation (e.g., which computer do we buy?) *before* decisions about design are fully understood (e.g., what is the IS to do?). Aggressive sales approaches for computers and pre-packaged information systems can obscure important design decisions and may lead to an inappropriate pattern of decisions about the IS.

Several difficult questions face the designer of an IS:

- What are the user's information needs?
- What reports are to be generated?
- When are the reports to be produced?
- What functions will the system perform? (e.g., payroll, billing, statistical functions including productivity reports)
- What data will be captured?

These determinations can only be made by the ultimate users of the IS. Leaving these tasks to outsiders is to invite disaster because an outsider cannot decide what a manager needs from the IS. Outsiders can provide technical expertise, perspective and guidance; yet if the IS is to be used advantageously, the management and staff of the HSO must be intimately involved in the IS development.

OBJECTIVE

This paper focuses on decisions about the automation of an IS and how to purchase computers and computer programs. The systems development process has been discussed by Sorensen and Elpers (1978).

WHEN NOT TO AUTOMATE

Good reasons exist for automating, but many managers purchase a computer for a wrong reason. Examples include:

- "It's in the budget and if the money isn't spent, it will be lost." If spending the money is the only reason for automating, the best course is: *don't*; automation of an IS requires detailed planning and should never be done just because the money is there.
- "A number of HSOs of my size and function are automated." Computers aren't free; they are expensive and if improperly planned for can easily cause more harm than good.
- "The existing manual system is swamped and nobody can figure out what is going on. Reports are late and, worse, they are inaccurate and can't be easily corrected." If no one understands the existing manual sytem, a computer is not going to help. Automate an inadequate and poorly designed manual system and the result will be an inadequate and poorly designed computer system. Reports may arrive on a more timely basis, but they still will be inaccurate. Everyone will begin to maintain an "underground" manual system so as to have "correct" information and management's problems will be magnified instead of reduced.

DECISION TO AUTOMATE

Feasibility Study

The decision to automate is embedded in an evolutionary development of the IS and starts with a feasibility study or survey. This survey, for example, obtains an overview of the existing system, identifies the system strengths, weaknesses and user needs, prepares preliminary cost estimates and evaluates staff willingness to accept an automated system. Decisions to automate hinge on staff readiness to accept and use a sophisticated and automated IS (Paton & D'huyvetter, 1980). Lack of staff readiness is likely to have highly negative impacts on morale, turnover and organizational effectiveness. Some entities ignoring staff concerns have lost up to 75 percent of their clerical and support staff. A successful feasibility study is a positive prelude to an automated IS.

System Functions

The specification of system functions must be completed before the automation question can be addressed. For example, will the system be expected to do the payroll, billings, accounts payable, the general ledger, state reports, etc.? In many instances, a manual system can be more cost-effective and cannot be rejected outright. A computer system has four basic advantages over a manual one. A properly programmed computer system can:

- accommodate a much larger volume of transactions;
- process the transactions in a significantly shorter period of time;
- process identical transactions in precisely the same manner each time; and
- facilitate the storage of and rapid access to extremely large data bases.

Certain circumstances suggest automation (Shaw, 1981):

- the volume of transactions overpowers the existing manual system, even after redesign;
- reports are not available on a timely basis (i.e., in time to be used in decision-making);
- the organization is functioning but is not being managed in any responsible way;
- resource inflows have declined or cannot be traced adequately;
- costs are not in control or not meaningfully reported;
- information is incorrect or hard to correct.

The Final Decision

Any of the above could be caused by factors outside the control of a good information system so their presence is not a definitive signal to purchase a computer; however, the existence of one or more is a signal to look beyond mere adjustments and refinements of the manual system. At this stage a detailed cost-benefit analysis of optional solutions should be made. If the benefits of a computer system exceed the costs, if a manual system does not appear feasible, if the money is available and if management and staff have the patience to thoroughly plan the process, then an HSO should proceed to design and implement a computer-based IS.

Financial Aspects

Computer costs come in two batches. The first involves the cost of purchasing or leasing the physical equipment (hardware). The second involves acquiring programs (software) so that the machine can perform (e.g., generate a report on client admissions by age, sex and diagnosis), providing for ongoing maintenance of both equipment and programs, providing for staff, supplies, etc. As a general guide, the costs of the latter can be expected to be two to three times the cost of the former. For example, if a computer is purchased for $50,000, the support costs are likely to be an additional $100,000 to $150,000. Automation does not come cheaply no matter what the advertisements say.

COMPUTER SELECTION AND RFPs

The key to the acquisition of hardware and software is management involvement, careful planning and preparation. A feasibility study and preliminary systems design should have been completed and both should indicate the need for automation. Now the task is preparation of request for proposals (RFP) for submission to various vendors. Some vendors sell only hardware, some only software and some sell both, so a purchase could involve two vendors.

Software vs. Hardware?

HSOs often lack the internal technical expertise to perform a detailed analysis of computer needs. Software designed to meet the specialized needs of HSOs is in limited supply and developing the software from scratch can be expensive. There are a number of minicomputer manufacturers with proven track records who can supply the same basic hardware. Because of similarities in hardware, one strategy for HSOs in acquiring their first automated IS is to identify vendors who have *software* designed to meet specific needs or which is readily adaptable. This approach acquires the software first and then purchases the appropriate hardware to run the programs. While this strategy does not eliminate the need for an RFP, it does change its focus since some of the technical computer aspects will be less important.

Request for Proposals (RFPs)

An RFP is a written document describing your information needs to vendors. Vendors should be given a detailed idea of functions, reports and data capture considerations. The RFP must be more than a general two-page letter requesting bids on a system to provide general ledger accounting and client statistics. On the other hand, it should not be so specific as to hardware and software requirements so only one vendor can bid.

A well-prepared RFP will contain two types of systems requirements: *mandatory* and *desirable*. Mandatory requirements are absolute musts and are minimal acceptable capabilities. A mandatory requirement, for example, might be that total system cost cannot exceed $100,000 or the system must be operable within nine months of the contract signing date. Desirable requirements enhance the entire systems process but their absence would not be catastrophic. Examples might be the capability to support a particular programming language or ability of the hardware to fit into a specific space configuration.

Careful definition of mandatory requirements is important. If all requirements become "musts," vendor response to the RFP is seriously impaired since few will be able to meet all specifics. With careful thought few features need to be mandatory, and the more general the specifications, the greater the chance of obtaining a superior system (Joslin, 1977). Unfortunately, responses to general RFPs are more difficult to evaluate.

CONTENTS OF RFPs

RFP's should contain (Joslin, 1977):

- groundrules
- system specifications
- vendor support expectations
- technical questionnaire
- guidelines for vendor demonstrations (if permitted)
- contracting conditions
- general comments

Groundrules

This section outlines the purpose of the proposal, lists key dates, specifies how inquiries are to be handled, states the number of copies of the proposal to be submitted, specifies whether or not oral presentations will be permitted, states whether the system is to be purchased or leased, and outlines the proposal evaluation process. This enables vendors to highlight their features and avoids misunderstandings (Joslin, 1977). All important dates should be set forth, including:

- date vendor must indicate an interest in bidding
- date for withdrawal of RFP
- scheduled time for a bidders' conference (meeting for all interested parties to clarify issues—should be held within a month of getting RFP)
- proposal due date
- oral presentation dates
- award date
- contract date
- installation date

The RFP should require the final contract be signed by a corporate officer to avoid a vendor reneging on the grounds the person signing lacked sufficient authority to bind the company. The proposal itself should become part of the contract.

The payment schedule should be included in the RFP and a portion of the purchase price should be held in escrow until the system is fully operable and management is satisfied the contract has been fulfilled.

Systems Specifications

This section presents user needs by specifying functions to be performed, the reports (along with formats) to be generated, timing of reports, forms to be used, data capture requirements, and file layouts. An overview of the existing system should be provided for perspective, and it must be in sufficient detail to insure the vendor comprehends the needs. Mandatory and desirable features should be listed in this section.

Expectation of Vendor Support

The RFP should spell out the HSO's expectations for vendor support. Some vendors provide technical assistance through implementation as well as ongoing maintenance, while others do little more than deliver the equipment. Their claims should be documented along with referrals to satisfied customers who have recently purchased similar equipment. Take time to follow up the referrals to determine whether or not the vendor performed as promised.

Technical Questionnaire

A technical questionnaire can provide information useful for comparing hardware and software proposals across vendors. Lack of technical expertise may limit the value of this information to a given HSO, but outside consultants can help. The following items should be included in the questionnaire (Joslin, 1977):

- speed of all devices and components
- capacity of all devices and components
- language capabilities
- reliability of all devices and components
- expansion capabilities
- compatibility
- environmental factors
- software capabilities
- documentation provided

Request vendors to document their responses either with their own literature or by reference to technical literature provided by sources such as *Auerbach* or *Datapro* (viz., firms providing research reports and detailed specifications on a wide variety of computer systems).

Speed refers to the input and output devices as well as processing time. Since most systems are limited by the speeds of the input and output equipment, processing speed generally is not of concern to the mid-sized HSO.

Capacity considerations can be important particularly where the Central Processing Unit (CPU) and secondary storage are concerned. Since no processing can occur unless the program and the data are in core memory, core size can be a limiting factor. The operating system (OS) also must be in core. Therefore, most systems have secondary storage. The OS controls the movement of data from secondary storage to core, subsequent processing and the movement of data and results back to secondary storage. The vendor should be able to determine core requirements if HSO needs are fully understood.

Programming languages supported by each system are important. Applications packages (previously written software designed to do specific tasks and which might be adaptable to an HSO's needs) represent a means of minimizing programming costs. However, packages cannot be purchased if they are written in languages not supported by the hardware selected. Furthermore, some languages are easier to learn than others, so if management is considering training one or more staff members to be programmers, access to one of the simpler languages could be important. BASIC (Beginners' All-Purpose Symbolic Instructional Code) can be readily self-taught, whereas COBOL (Common Business-Oriented Language) is a more sophisticated language and is more difficult to learn.

Reliability includes two issues:

(1) error detection and correction capabilities, and
(2) expected downtime of the equipment.

Availability of maintenance services is of prime importance unless the machine has an extremely low incidence of downtime. The "best" system is useless if it is inoperable much of the time. Most of today's systems have excellent error detection and correction capabilities.

Since many organizations can be expected to grow, a system designed to meet today's needs may not meet tomorrow's needs. Therefore, the *expansion capabilities* of each vendor's equipment are important. Illustrative questions are:

• Can core be added?
• Can remote terminals be added?
• Can secondary storage be expanded?

Compatibility is important if an HSO already has some computer equipment or if the organization is considering purchasing some hardware components from other than the primary vendor. Can the vendor's equipment be used or adapted for use with other vendor's equipment?

Environmental factors deal with space, electrical, and air conditioning requirements, etc. Remodeling and/or rewiring can add significantly to the cost of a proposal and should be evaluated.

Since many HSOs lack in-house programming capabilities, knowledge concerning the vendor's *software support* is of use in evaluating the proposal. Does a vendor have packages to meet your needs or provide programming services? Documentation through technical literature and/or references to current customers should be requested.

After proposals have been received and reviewed, *vendor demonstrations* offer an opportunity for the vendors to present equipment under operating conditions and permit the HSO to review a potential acquisition. Issues such as timing, who is to pay for any travel, and set-up costs should be addressed.

EVALUATING RESPONSES TO RFPs

The most common vendor selection techniques are:

- Sole source
- Overall impression
- Cost only
- Weighted scoring
- Cost-value

Sole Source (SS)

The SS method refers to selection of one vendor (based on recommendations, advertising, prior experience, etc.) and deferring all decisions with regard to the end product to the vendor. No RFP is written, no competitive bidding occurs, and a feasibility study and a preliminary systems design may or may not have been completed. This technique often is used by those with little or no technical expertise under the mistaken notion the vendor "will take care of everything." Unfortunately, no vendor can be totally familiar with an HSO and managerial deferral of the overall systems design to the vendor is a great risk. The vendor will design a system perceived to meet HSO needs, but if experience is any indicator, the chances are very high those perceptions will not be the same as those of management and staff. The result is likely to be a suboptimal system (*Business Week*, Feb. 2, 1981).

Overall Impression (OI)

The OI method usually involves one person reading all proposals and subjectively weighing a variety of factors. Selection is based on overall impression. Final selection is highly dependent on personal factors. The proposal read in the quiet of the office may well be viewed more favorably than the one read at home while refereeing a sibling dispute. Given these potential problems, the technique cannot be viewed as highly reliable.

Minimum Cost (MC)

Problematic features of MC are the absence of effort to measure value attained and non-systematic consideration of extra features included in more expensive proposals.

Weighted or Point-Scoring (PS)

PS attempts to overcome the foregoing shortcomings. The most important aspects of the systems acquisition process are assessed and weights or points assigned to those items on a priority basis. Each vendor's proposal is evaluated in terms of each item and assigned rankings on a scale of zero to one. The rankings are multiplied by the weightings on an item by item basis and the resulting numbers are totalled for each proposal. The proposal with the highest number of points is awarded the contract.

Example of Point-Scoring Method.

Self-Help HSO decided to design and implement a computer-based IS. Three vendors submitted acceptable proposals which will be evaluated using the point-scoring technique. The IS Committee prepared a list of criteria comparing the proposals and ranked each vendor on a scale of 0 to 1 on each criterion. The criteria, assigned ranks and point scores, are presented in Table 26–1.

Primary problems of the method stem from the difficulty in establishing the weights and ranking the proposals. If weights are established prior to the release of the RFP (and not adjusted in response to the proposals received), the technique can be a useful one. The approach is superior to any previously mentioned and can be used by managers with limited technical expertise. In Table 26–1, Vendor A has the highest weighted score (viz, 344).

Cost-Value Technique (CVT)

A more sophisticated technique is the cost-value technique developed by Edward O. Joslin (1977). CVT attempts to explicitly recognize the value of desirable or extra features included by vendors as opposed to the mandatory requirements all proposals must satisfy. Any proposal not meeting one or more of the mandatory requirements is immediately disqualified. The cost of surviving proposals is adjusted by the value of extras. Extras may have positive value, no value or negative value (e.g., increased costs of operation).

CVT differs from the point-scoring method because each extra feature is examined and valued independently. Added features are treated in the aggregate under the po⁚ ⸱t-scoring system. The exercise of valuing the desirable requirements *forces* the purchaser to explicitly consider the worth of each extra and should result in more comparable comparisons.

CVT uses cost-value accounting where the total cost of each proposal is reduced by the added values and increased by additional cost of each added feature. These adjustments produce a derived cost for each

TABLE 26–1. Criteria, Weights, Rankings of RFPs and the Weighted Scoring of RFPs

Criterion	Weight	Ranking			Point Scores		
		A	B	C	A	B	C
Hardware Performance	50	.9	.8	.5	45	40	25
System Reliability	40	.6	.6	.7	24	24	28
Purchase Price	50	.8	.7	.9	40	35	45
Software Availability	50	.9	.8	.9	45	40	45
Vendor Support	70	.8	.4	.9	56	28	63
Documentation	50	.6	.9	.8	30	45	40
Expansion Capability	30	.7	.7	.6	21	21	18
Time of Availability	30	.9	.8	.9	27	24	27
Vendor Familiarity with HSO Operations	80	.7	.4	.3	56	32	24
Total	450				344	289	315

proposed system and the proposal with the lowest derived cost is selected. Cost-values can be established by reviewing price lists and technical literature and should be done at the time the RFP is written. The value of a particular applications program, for example, can be estimated by determining purchase cost from a software house or by estimating its cost if written by a contract programmer. Value may be the same as or less than cost. A given program might cost $5,000 to obtain, but if there is little or no use for the particular application, its value might be zero.

Two proposals differing in initial cost (viz, $66,500 vs. $73,000) become comparable after valuing extras ($63,600 vs. $63,300). Table 26–2 summarizes the technique (Joslin, 1977, adapted).

ALTERNATIVES TO PURCHASING/LEASING

An HSO needing automation but without sufficient funds or systems expertise has two other options:

1. service bureaus, and
2. time sharing.

Service bureaus provide computer related services for a fee. These firms usually do not perform systems analysis nor do they make more than mi-

TABLE 26–2. Cost-Value Selection Technique

	Vendor A	Vendor B
Cost		
Basic cost of system	$ 65,000	$ 70,000
Transportation costs	1,500	–
Site Preparation[a]	–	3,000
Total Cost (A)	$ 66,500	$ 73,000
Value		
Software Features	$ 3,500	$ 2,200
Early Delivery[b]	–1,000	5,000
Space Availability[c]	– 600	–
Vendor Support	1,000	2,500
Total Value of Desirable Features (B)	$ 2,900	$ 9,700
Cost of Basic Requirements (A)–(B)	**$ 63,600**	**$ 63,300**

[a]Site preparation refers to rewiring or other required changes.
[b]A positive value reflects early or timely delivery where a negative value indicates later delivery.
[c]Space availability refers to cost of providing adequate floor space.

nor changes to their application programs (e.g., payroll). Most specialize in accounting applications such as general ledger, payroll and billing. Service bureaus do represent a relatively inexpensive means of obtaining a limited computer capability while staff gain some familiarity with computers.

Time sharing enables many users to rent computer time and may be less expensive than outright purchase of hardware. The HSO still has to identify its systems needs and often has to obtain its own software. Time sharing avoids large cash outlays for equipment and eliminates many of the subsequent support costs, except for the software.

CONCLUSION

The decision to automate an information system is complicated. Without careful planning and preparation, introduction of a computer into an HSO could be costly and inefficient. A logical outgrowth of the planning process is an RFP and a careful evaluation of the vendor responses. Outsiders can provide technical expertise and perspective, but the systems development effort using automation must be compatible with and useful to the HSO.

REFERENCES

Business Week. A burst of critical feedback, February 2, 1981, pp. 68 & 71.

Joslin, E. O. *Computer selection.* Augmented edition. Fairfax Station, VA: The Technology Press, Inc., 1977.

Paton, J. A., & D'huyvetter, P. K. *Automated management information systems for mental health agencies: A planning and acquisition guide.* NIMH statistical report in the methodology series of the Division of Biometry and Epidemiology, 1980.

Shaw, D. R. *Your small computer: Evaluating, selecting, financing and operating the hardware and software that fits.* New York: Van Nostrand Reinhold Co., 1981.

Sorensen, J. E., & Elpers, J. R. Developing information systems for human services programs. In C. C. Attkisson, et al., (Eds.), *Evaluation of human service programs.* New York: Academic Press, Inc., 1978.

27

An Information System for the Social Casework Agency: A Model and Case Study

BRUCE A. PHILLIPS
BERNARD DIMSDALE
ETHEL TAFT

In the fall of 1976, the Planning Department of the Jewish Federation-Council of Greater Los Angeles charged its research specialist with developing some means of collecting service delivery data that would be accurate, flexible, and produce reports within time limits imposed by the decision-making process. As a result of preliminary exploration with the casework agencies funded by JFC, it was clear that these agencies were acutely aware of the shortcomings of their current manual systems; both in terms of providing planning data and in terms of providing internal management data.

All four major casework agencies (Jewish Family Service of Los Angeles, Jewish Family Service of Santa Monica, Jewish Big Brothers, and Jewish Vocational Service) agreed to develop a unified system which would encompass the needs of all of them. The Research Specialist began by working independently with each of the four agencies to begin to map out a common ground. After several months, it appeared that a unified information structure would be feasible and workable for the four casework agencies. A demonstration grant was secured to develop the system at this point. A systems designer was brought in to work together with the research specialist in coordinating the further development of a unified system.

In this paper, we will describe the development of the Jewish Family Service of Los Angeles component because the work characterizes the process as a whole.

IDENTIFYING INFORMATION REQUIREMENTS

The first step in designing an information system is to determine the information needed. This was accomplished by setting up an interdisciplinary task-group, made up of three components: the research specialist, the systems designer, and agency personnel. Their functions were as follows:

Research Specialist

1. Represented the information of the Planning and Budgeting Department.
2. Provided expertise on problems of data collection.
3. Coordinated JFS component with other agencies within the system.

Agency Director, Associate and Assistant Directors

1. Interpreted information required of agency by United Way.
2. Interpreted information most useful for setting and implementing agency policy.
3. Determining information usable for agency planning.

Agency District Directors

1. Interpreted information useful for worker, supervisor and district administration.
2. Provided expertise on data collection problems and procedures within District Office.

Systems Designer

1. Translated information requirements into data processing considerations.
2. Provided feedback to task group on feasibility and cost of suggestions made.

3. Design of system when requirements finalized.
4. Supervised programming and testing of final system.

The process of defining the system, then, involved exploration, feedback, synthesis, and negotiation. As the two technical personnel learned more about the agency (agencies), the agency personnel were sensitized to technical considerations. As a result, the technical personnel suggested new system applications based on a greater understanding of the agency, and the agency personnel focused more clearly on the relative significance of various requests as they became more familiar with system capabilities.

In addition, input was included from line workers, clerical staff as well as members of lay committees in the Planning and Budgeting Departments and the agency (agencies).

In order to promote creativity and an optimally useful system, task force participants were encouraged to "think big." When the lists of information required were laid on the table, it was clear that there was far more than could be included. In order to separate essential information from "would be nice to have," three criteria were developed.

1. *Usability:* How would the proposed information be used, and what sorts of decisions might be made on the basis of this information. There was strong feeling, for example, that certain kinds of clinical data should be included in the system. For example, information, about significant others in the client's immediate constellation of friends and relatives. On closer inspection, however, it became clear that this information would not be used for any application other than the worker's own edification. Instead, a new form was added to the case folder, summarizing this information for the worker's use.
2. *Appropriateness to Computerization:* Could this information be handled as well without being part of a computerized system? The telephone receptionist, for example, records requests for information by putting "hash marks" on a piece of paper. Since it was determined that no further detail was required (such as the kinds of information requested, the referral made by the receptionist, or the time taken in making the referral), it was deemed more appropriate to keep this process separate from the computer systems.
3. *Computer System Implications:* The most important of which is cost. Is the cost of collection and storage warranted by the usability of the information? Does inclusion of this data present any data collection or computer systems problems? The task group decided that five generic types of information met these criteria, and were essential for inclusion in the system:
   a. *Caseflow:* Data such as the number of open cases, number of new

cases, number of closed cases, number of active cases, and other monthly activity information.

b. *Case Profile:* For example, composition of the family being served, focus of service, family income, etc.

c. *Relation of Case to Larger Social Welfare System:* Here we were interested in tie-ins between the agency and the larger social service network. Included here is information relevant to source of referral, destination of referral out, other welfare services received (AFDC, SSI, etc.).

d. *Cumulative data about service modalities* used over the life of the case.

e. *The cost of direct service,* as measured by casework time spent on the case.

The discussion process described above can continue indefinitely. For this reason, the technical personnel established two criteria for determining finalization.

First, there was no longer any empirical way of resolving uncertainties. The only questions left were speculations about what might happen, or what might turn out to be the best information to have collected. This would become apparent only after a system was in operation for some time.

Second, there was already sufficient consensus achieved within the task group about the general structure of the system, so that individual differences appear to be minimal.

The source of referral codes are a good case in point. Much discussion had taken place over appropriate codes for source of referral. Some members felt there were too many, others felt the list to be incomplete. Still others disagreed with the whole classification schema. Because this issue did not affect the overall structure of the system, it was decided to use the codes as they had been developed so far and then see which ones actually were used, and what new ones might be needed.

The focus of services codes also illustrates the role of the systems designer. If up to 9 codes are used, the computer stores one digit, if between 10 and 99 codes are used, two digits are required. The systems designer pointed out that an exact set of codes was not important for systems purposes and new codes could be added later.

Once the system is finalized, the basic logic of the system cannot be changed without substantial expense. In the example of changing codes cited above, the basic logic of the system was unaffected. Adding essentially different information can alter the basic logic: for example, after programming had begun, some task group members decided to add a new piece of information requiring only one additional digit on the intake form. The systems designer pointed out that making this change would involve significant reprogramming, resulting in a substantial increase in programming cost (not to mention printing new forms). The impulse to redesign the system after it was underway created confusion, uncertainty, and almost negated the lengthy process that had gone before. Only the systems designer has the technical expertise to judge between a trivial change and a major one. Rather than debating the merits of this proposed change, the task group should have first consulted the systems designer about its practicability. As a result of this misadventure, it was decided to create a monitoring committee to review the system and propose changes for eventual production of a modified system based on actual experience with the present system.

In this first section we have used our own experience to develop a model for deciding on informational requirements. In the next section, we describe the administrative structure of the system along with the kinds of decisions that were made in determining it.

THE ADMINISTRATIVE STRUCTURE OF THE SYSTEM

The flow of information is based on the case cycle itself. Thus, when a case is opened, an intake document is filled out. The actual casework activity is recorded on contact slips. The case is closed by submitting a closing document, and can be reopened again with a new intake. In addition, there is an intake change form which can modify the contents of the intake sheet in the master file. (See the next section for more about the master file.) When a case is transferred to a new worker, for example, an intake change form would be used. In the following discussion, both the function and content of each type of document will be discussed along with the most pertinent decisions.

Intake Form

The intake form opens a case for the computer and also serves as a face sheet on the case. By combining the face sheet with the input document, we were able to avoid adding yet another piece of paper for the clerical staff to handle as part of the intake process. The workers had long desired some organized way of recording additional information about the client which was pertinent only to clinical aspects of the case. As a result of designing the computer intake form, a second form providing this background information was added to the intake process for inclusion in the case folder only. Thus, a long felt clinical need was addressed as a result of developing the computerized system.

In considering the actual content of the intake form, the task group found it necessary to make a disinction between a "case" and a "client." In the past, the agency itself had never been consistent in how it classified family members. In some instances, the entire family constituted the case, while in other instances each individual family member was considered to be a case (and given an individual case identifying number). Giving careful consideration both to how the data would be used and the implications for the system design, it was decided that the family should be the case, because the family is the specified unit of service for the agency. The systems designer translated this distinction into computer terms and made it possible to record information about the individual family members within the case. Thus, the system can count cases, clients, as well as other family members not seen as clients.

The task group then had to decide what information to collect about the case and what information to collect about family members.

Two constraints set limits on the amount of information to be included. First, it was desirable to minimize worker time involved in filling out the intake form. Each additional item on the intake increases worker resistance, collection costs (in worker time), and processing costs (in computer time). Second, it was felt that an increase in information would result in a decrease in accuracy. The task force agreed to include the following information components on the intake sheet (in order of their appearance on the form):

—Agency
—Form type (Intake)
—District within agency
—Case ID
—ID check (first three letters of principal client surname)
—Worker ID (worker to whom case is assigned)
—Date of transaction (i.e., date of request for service)
—Date of last close (if this is a reopened case)
—Source of referral
—Family income
—Zip code of residence
—Applicable insurance carried
—Tie-ins with public welfare system (such as SSI, AFDC, Medicare, etc.)
—Primary focus of service
—Secondary focus of service
—Number of children in the household ages 13-18
—Number of children in the household under 13
—Number of children in the household who are seen as clients
—Sex, marital status, client status, and date of birth for each adult in household

In order to reduce the amount of effort involved in filling out the forms, the first three items (Agency, Form Type and District) are pre-printed. Each worker is provided with an ID stamp and a date stamp. This is true for all the forms used in the system. A Rolodex is provided to each worker for looking up client ID's.

Two of these items required much discussion before a decision could be made. These are reviewed here in some detail because they illustrate the kinds of conceptual problems that are raised in the process of developing an information system. The focus of service for a case had traditionally been noted on the face sheet using standard FSAA codes. The possibilities inherent in a computerized system triggered a re-evaluation both of the standard codes and of the very process of defining focus of service. Because the focus of service can change over the life of an episode, the task group wished to have this case dynamic reflected in the system. Rather than record the focus of service at intake, the JFS participants in the task group wanted to record the focus of service for each contact. Then, the question was raised: "Why just one focus of service per contact, when, after all, two or three issues might be raised in the course of a session?" As the research specialist and systems designer pointed out, the worker time involved to record all this plus the additional storage costs made this approach unfeasible. Finally, even if these considerations were not obstacles, the likelihood that no single focus of service would ever develop from all this detail further argued against this approach.

Instead the technical members suggested that greater confidence be placed in the clinical judgment of the worker in determining focus of service which could be included in the system by adding a retrospective assessment of the focus of service made at the time of closing. It was also decided to stick with the basic FSAA codes and to augment them with special codes reflecting services unique to the agency (for the most part, these are concrete services provided by the agency such as conservatorship, locating board and care homes and the like).

Intake Change Form

The intake change form is used to change information originally submitted on the intake form. It is identical in appearance with the intake form with three exceptions. Document type indicates intake change (necessary for data processing), date of change replaces date of request for service, and new ID check replaces date of last closing.

Contact Slip

The largest single obstacle to implementation of the system was finding a way to collect data about case activity. Two of the central purposes of the system discussed above were to record the modalities used and the amount of time spent in direct service. The only way to accomplish this is to collect information about activity at the time it takes place. The most efficient method was immediately determined to be a contact slip filled out for each contact. The workers, however, resisted this idea, and a number of alternative methods were then explored, and tested, and rejected. Every other method ended up taking more time and being less economical than the contact slip (especially with pre-pointed fields and data stamps). The objection was less to the contact slip itself, than to the change it represented from the way the manual system operated (using a monthly summary sheet). Suddenly, the manual system which was generally agreed to be awkward, inaccurate, and inefficient seemed attractive. Ultimately, the executive staff of the agency had to decide that this would be the way to go. Interestingly, the contact slips have not been a problem; rather the major problem with the system is that the workers fill out contact slips for cases which they have neglected to open in the first place.

The contact slip, like the intake document, includes agency, form type, district, case ID, ID check, worker ID, and date of transaction (date of contact).

There are seven codes for type of contact listed on the contact slip: individual, joint (i.e., couple), family, home visit, group, significant telephone, and "other." The inclusion of "significant telephone" and "other" added two types of contact not included in the manual system. "Significant telephone" is used for direct service that takes place over the phone (as opposed to making appointments). "Other" is used for collateral activity on behalf of the case. While not direct in the strictest clinical sense of the term, this category allows for inclusion of all other activity related to the case, which results in direct service being provided to the client(s). The type of contact is coded as a single letter and entered this way on the slip. The time spent on the contact is recorded in hours and minutes. The contact slip also includes agency, form type (contact), district, client ID, ID check, worker ID, and date of transaction (contact).

Closing Form

The closing form summarizes information about the conclusion of the case. As with the other two forms, the closing document begins with agency, form type (closing), district case ID, ID check, worker ID, and date of transaction (date of closing). The closing document also records:

—who closed the case (worker, client, or both)
—reason for closing
—referral out (if closed by referral)
—basis and type of financial aid given (if any)

—fee information
—workers closing assessment of principal focus of service

The development of codes for reasons for closing, like the focus of service codes, triggered the agency to re-evaluate the implications of the traditional closing codes used. The first step in this process was a differentiation between clinical and concrete services. Concrete services are essentially closed by one code: "service completed," to indicate that the needed help was rendered. The clinical codes posed more of a problem. The old code "problem resolved" was recognized to be inappropriate for a short term agency (in addition to the clinical problem of this determination). "Situation improved" was substituted instead. In addition, to describe more realistically the reason for closing, the following codes were added: "client not satisfied with service," "service no longer desired/situation changed," "person(s) assessed as not treatable," "no resource in community/client refuses service."

These codes were worded so as to provide as much detail as possible without seeming to evaluate the worker. Evaluation is a separate process from management information. Moreover, if the closing document seemed to be evaluating the worker, all cases would end up being closed with "problem resolved."

In addition to clinical reasons for closing a case, it was realized that there also exist reasons for closing that are external to the case, and which have important implications for agency planning. These are "client cannot come to office due to transportation problem," "client cannot come to office during scheduled hours of agency or district," "client could not wait for service."

Finally, it was decided to differentiate between two kinds of referrals out: Type 1 (most appropriate service available elsewhere), and Type 2 (service requested is appropriate to agency, but not currently available). Type 2 was included as an early alert that the agency should consider services or programs not currently available, but which would be appropriate for the agency to deliver.

The second major decision had to do with information on financial disbursement. The executive staff of the agency wanted to know about the kinds of cases which received financial aid, the basis for its disbursement, and the specific type of aid given. These were accordingly included on the closing document. The amount of financial aid given was not made part of the system because the agency already had bookkeeping procedures which were tied in with the JFC accounting department.

The intake form is filled out by both the receptionist and the individual worker assigned the case. The worker fills out contact slip and closing form. Intake change is handled by worker where clinical information is concerned and by the clerical staff where administrative information is involved (such as transfer of a case to a new worker or district).

All documents are submitted for keypunching and computer input at the close of the month. During the following month errors are returned to workers and their corrections re-entered to the computer. Monthly reports are produced by the end of the month and forwarded to the appropriate recipients.

SYSTEM DESIGN

Non-technical persons involved in designing an information system typically tend to leave all technical consideration "to the expert." A rudimentary understanding of the computer side of an information system is well within the grasp of non-technical personnel.

Some knowledge of this area is particularly useful to the non-technical person in facilitating a better understanding of the capabilities, limitations, and procedures of computing. An overview of the technical structure of the SDIS is presented here in order to clarify those basic data processing considerations which form the framework of an information system. The discussion also stresses the relationship between agency policy and technical design.

Despite the complexity of detail involved in the data processing specification of an information system, there are really only four basic concepts involved: sort fields, master file, updating, and reporting.

Master File

The master file, like a paper file, consists of case records. The case record consists of case identifying information (ID and ID check) and a record of one or more "episodes." An epsode is an opening of a case. When the case closes this is a completed episode, otherwise it continues as an open episode. When the case reopens, a new episode begins. Thus, we are not limited to the most recent episode, but have the ability to analyze patterns of multiple openings and closings.

An episode contains all data from the intake form and the closing form (added when the case closes), as well as information developed from the contact slips. The contact slip contributes to the master file, the date of first contact, date of last contact, and cumulative counts of time spent and number of contacts for each type of contact listed on the contact slip.

Updating the Master File

Updating is the process by which the various forms add to or modify the information contained in the master file. For example, an intake form which indicates that the case is new would cause the creation of a new record, unless the system already has a case with the same case identifier, in which case an "error message" would be returned. On the other hand, if the case is said to be a reopened case, and there is no record of this identifier in the master file, another "error message" is returned. Similarly, a closing document cannot update an episode which is not yet open (or reopened).

The contact slips are used to update the cumulative count and time per modality as well as the dates of first and last contact of the current episode.

Reports

The master file is updated once a month when all documents filled out during the month are keypunched and input to the system. A program called "validate" locates errors (such as those mentioned above) and produces an error report. Once the errors are corrected (using a computer program called 'edit') the master file is then updated and the monthly reports are produced.

System Rules and Agency Policy

The errors programmed in the validation program were determined by the rules of the system. These rules were in turn based on the policies of the agency itself. A few such rules are discussed here for illustrative purposes:

1. *An intake form must have at least one contact slip.* Casework activity must take place in order to open a case. Otherwise the intake becomes part of the standard "no case made" file already maintained by the agency previous to starting the computerized system. From a systems point of view this saves the master file from being cluttered with non-cases by rejecting as errors those intakes not accompanied by contact slips.
2. *Only one opening and one closing are allowed for a given case within the same month.* The original impetus for this rule came from the system designer in order to avoid an excessive data processing burden. It became clear in discussion with the agency personnel that this also made good casework sense. If a case opens, closes, and then reopens within the same month, it probably should not have been closed to begin with.
3. *Contacts are recorded only for an open case.* This is a less obvious rule than is at first apparent. Workers will sometimes have a contact with a client after the case is closed. This rule reduces the temptation to continue contacts without reopening the case—a practice distinctly contrary to established agency policy.

At the end of the month all errors are sent back to the workers with messages such as "contact with unopened case," "intake of already open case," etc. When the errors have been corrected, the documents are re-submitted to the system so that the master file can be correctly updated.

Sort Fields and Reporting

All four documents begin with the same six pieces of information. These are called sort fields, and are used to organize the input data in such a way as to minimize processing costs. In addition, these sort fields make it possible to produce reports at various levels of specificity. The worker ID is used to produce a monthly summary of activity for each worker. In combination with the date of last contact and current date, the worker ID is used to produce a list of overdue cases (that is, cases which have had no activity for sixty days or more). The district sort field is used to sort the input data to produce district level caseflow reports and a summary of case activity for each district. The agency sort field separates the JFS data from the other agencies on the system (Jewish Big Brothers, Jewish Family Service of Santa Monica, and Jewish Vocational Service).

Buy or Build

Once the specifications for the system were agreed on, the task-group had to choose between purchasing an existing system or designing an original one. In order to reduce costs, a number of existing models were examined and ultimately rejected because they were not suitable. This includes the Statistical Package for the Social Sciences (SPSS) in Elliott R. Rubin, "The Implementation of an Effective Computer System," *Social Casework*, July, 1976, Vol. 57, No. 7, pp. 438–447. SPSS was found unusable because it is a "static" system. It sets up a complete "record," of data fed into it, but cannot easily alter this record once set up. For example, an agency using SPSS would have to cumulate activity over the life of the case (by hand) and then include the total as a part of the clinical record at the close of the case. We found this unacceptable because:

1. It involved unnecessary activity on the part of the worker in keeping track of case activity.
2. It would make monthly reports of caseflow and case activity impossible.
3. It could not be used for other special applications.

It is an excellent tool for the statistical analysis of data such as that exemplified by social surveys (precisely the purpose for which it is used in the Planning and Budgeting Department of the JF-C).

In the commercial field there are many applications which involve the creation and maintenance of a master file, procedures for updating it, and routines for producing required reports. Because none of these commercial systems were at all compatible with our needs, we found it necessary to create our own system. In sum, then, we decided not to compromise the requirements of our system in order to take advantage of an already existing package. Rather, we opted to develop a system that would meet the needs of the users.

REPORTS

The system produces two generic types of reports: standard monthly reports, and non-standard reports in response to specific requests. The monthly reports are run routinely and give an overview of the agency's activity for the month, while special reports are used to investigate a particular question in depth. In this section we will present some examples of each and will emphasize how they are related to the structure of the system itself. Because the applications of the system were a prime consideration in its design, an understanding of how reports are produced is useful to an agency contemplating the development of its own information system.

Routine Monthly Reports

At the end of the month the SDIS produces several standard reports which are described below.

General service report. This report gives a summary of caseflow by agency and district. Included are number of openings, closings, new cases, reopened cases, cases carried over from previous month, cases carried forward to next month, active cases, inactive cases, and overdue cases. "Overdue" cases are those which have been inactive for at least sixty days. This report provides the appropriate administrator(s) with an overview of the level of activity for the month.

Breakdown of active cases. This report, which is produced for both the agency and the districts, shows the number of cases which had 1 contact, 2–5 contacts, 6–10 contacts (etc.) during the month.

Breakdown by type of contact. This report presents the number of contacts and the total time spent on each type of contact during the month.

Breakdown of closed cases. This report presents the total number of contacts over the life of the case for cases which closed during the month. Because Jewish Family Service provides short term service, a majority of the cases should have had a cumulative total of five contacts or less.

Worker reports. Each worker receives three reports each month. A worker level version of the General Service Report is first, and shows individual caseflow. A worker level version of the breakdown of active cases report is second. This shows the time spent and number of contacts per type of contact for each worker. A detailed listing of the "overdue" clients in the individual worker's caseload is third. These worker level reports serve to give workers important feedback about their own activity during the month.

A Note on Confidentiality

Nowhere in the reports above or in any other part of the SDIS does the client's name ever appear. This is to ensure complete confidentiality. Only the client ID is listed on reports such as the overdue client report. In this respect the computerized system ensures greater confidentiality than the agency office where case files provide relatively open access.

Special Reports

The monthly case activity reports are produced dynamically—that is to say while updating the master file. Because input data is compared with the data in the master file, the monthly reports are produced as part of the master file update procedure. Special reports are static in the sense that they are based only on the contents of the master file. They are used to investigate various aspects of the client population, and in the next section we will present some examples of actual reports. Here we wish to describe how various pieces of information in the Master File can be used to create a special report.

The master file contains both the date of first contact and the date of last contact for the episode. Subtracting the former from the latter produces the duration of the case (measured in days). This would be done only for closed episodes, of course, as open episodes do not yet have the final date of contact. By bringing in date of birth we can compare case duration with age of client.

By subtracting the date of request for services from the date of first contact, we compute the waiting time from intake to initial casework activity. By cumulating time spent over the life of the episode, we can compute the cost of service.

We can compute the cost of service for age groups and for the various focus of service categories, or any other variable in the system. We could also compare the modalities most often used by the different age groups or focus of service categories. The inclusion of as simple an item as zip code makes it possible to carry out this sort of analysis on a geographic basis as well.

Clearly, all the possibilities are too numerous to describe here. In the initial design phase, careful consideration was given to the kinds of information to be used in special reports. The possibilities for in-depth analysis latent in the master file make the SDIS a valuable tool for evaluation and planning.

Sample Applications for Special Reports

Although the system is only nine months old at the time of this writing, it has already been used by both the Planning and Budgeting Department of Federation and the agency. Three such applications are discussed here: one requested by the Planning and Budgeting department, one requested by the agency, and one requested jointly.

The Planning and Budgeting department was interested in the volume and cost of service to the elderly (defined as 65 and older). Using date of birth to compute age, a report was prepared which provided the proportion of direct service time expended. Interestingly, in some districts the proportion of time taken up by the elderly was significantly greater than their proportion in the caseload, while in other districts the opposite was the case.

The program committee of JFS was charged with reviewing the district structure of the agency. One report run for this study compared the average time spent per case, the average duration of case (in days), and the average number of contacts per case in each district. Another report compared the focus of service and source of referral patterns for each district.

As the JFC of LA moves more toward decentralized planning and budgeting, both the agency and the Planning and Budgeting department will rely more heavily on a profile of the client population by area of the city. The availability of separate demographic data on the Jewish community of Los Angeles makes it possible to use the SDIS to compare the caseload of the agency with Jewish population of the city as a whole on the area by area basis.

COST EFFECTIVENESS

The cost effectiveness of the SDIS can be evaluated four different ways. First, the absolute cost of the system comes to about $2.00/episode including worker time for filling out the forms. The average cost per episode in direct service comes to about $40/episode. The system cost is about five percent of direct service costs. A second approach is to compare the total cost of running the SDIS with the total agency budget. In this comparison the SDIS constitutes about one percent of the total budget, while informing the agency about how much of the remaining 99 percent is spent. A third approach is to compare the cost of the SDIS with the old manual system. To begin with, the old manual system could not handle the kinds of routine monthly reports produced by the SDIS, so comparison is better based on the special reports. Because of the time involved, the cost of producing just one special report could easily amount to a substantial proportion of the yearly cost of operating the system. Further, it is doubtful that such a report would be ready in time for it to be used, not to mention the increased accuracy of an automated system.

Finally, one should take into consideration the benefits of the system which cannot be given a cost figure. The ability of an agency to learn about itself is an intangible commodity, but the most significant benefit of the system.

SUMMARY

In this paper we have briefly reviewed the process of developing an agency Service Delivery Information System in order to suggest a procedural model for other casework agencies considering such an undertaking.

We have tried to present not only an outline of steps, but the kinds of criteria used for making decisions about such a system. Particular attention was given to the technical structure of the system and the way in which technical considerations are included in developing a system.

In addition, reporting applications were selected which exemplify the utility of the system for the decision-makers who were involved in the design of the system. Attention was given to the production of reports from the information in the master file to evaluate the advantages of a flexible reporting capability and to suggest to the non-technical reader some of the ways in which the system combines data elements to produce required reports.

The small, medium sized, or even large agency may not have the funds available to produce such a system. However, a consortium of roughly similar agencies (from the point of view of structure and data processing) could divide the costs of developing a shared system, thereby reducing initial investment to a realistic amount. This, in fact, is what we have accomplished by developing a shared system for the social casework agencies affiliated with the Jewish Federation Council of Greater Los Angeles.

28

Management Information Systems in Child Care: An Agency Experience

DAVID W. YOUNG

As child care agencies become increasingly accountable to their funding sources, their communities and others, they are being called upon more and more to provide to third parties and to their boards of directors adequate information on the effectiveness of their programs. Additionally, many agencies continue to encounter administrative dilemmas that result from a growing complexity of service delivery patterns and from a continuing concern for the unmet needs of a constantly changing client population.

In part these problems stem from the traditional manner in which data are collected and presented. Statistical information in the child care field and in many social service fields is usually presented in a highly summarized manner, and often with a considerable lag between the time of an event and the time it is reported statistically. However, administrators of social agencies require both detailed and timely information. To be useful, this information must be presented in a format that:

1. permits a quick review,
2. facilitates the pinpointing of problem areas,
3. assists in the determination of responsibility for action, and
4. contains a capacity for followup and evaluation.

For example, in many child care agencies administrators receive a monthly or quarterly report summarizing the number of admissions, transfers and discharges. Although this information may be helpful for maintaining control over such factors as maximum population levels, it is only marginally useful for assessing the quality of service being delivered. More useful information would consist of reports that list the children involved, the appropriateness of the admission, the reason for the transfer, and whether the discharge was timely and as planned. This information would be even more useful if it were presented in a form that could be quickly scanned so that potentially inappropriate admissions, transfers or discharges were indicated. These instances could then be followed up and corrected if necessary.

THE TIME FACTORS

Manual preparation of reports that call for collection of a broad range of data, plus selection and presentation of portions of these data for administrative review and analysis, could be extremely time-consuming. Further, the development of special administrative reports presenting information concerning new agency emphases or new problem areas could be difficult. For example, an agency wishing to place increased emphasis on adoption might require a special list of all children who were under the age of 3 from families with an abusive parent, and in need of legal action to free them for adoption. In most agencies, manual preparation of such a list would require considerable effort from both casework and clerical staffs.

In an attempt to resolve this dilemma of the increasing need for detailed management information and the problem of delay in obtaining it by traditional manual methods, the Edwin Gould Services for Children agency of New York City has developed a computerized management information system. The system, called the Child Record System, contains a broad base of data on each child in care with the agency, and facilitates a wide variety of both regular and special analyses and comparisons. The latter characteristic allows the agency's administrators to determine more accurately the child's overall needs and the appropriate program to meet those needs, to evaluate more thoroughly the progress toward state child objectives, and to review more objectively the agency's ongoing programs.

The Child Record System was developed over a period of about 2 years,[1] and has been in operation for about 2 years. During these 4 years a great deal was learned about the application of management information system technology to the child care field. This paper presents some of that knowledge for professionals and others interested in the application of management information systems technology to the child care field.

The paper begins by reviewing the historical development and objectives of the system, discussing the basic decisions made by the agency in defining the scope and capabilities of the system. It then describes the overall operation of the system. Next the content of the data base and the process of report design are examined. Finally, the paper considers the potentials of the system and new directions being taken by the agency as a result of using the system.

HISTORY OF DEVELOPMENT

Conceptually, the Child Record System grew out of a variety of administrative problems confronting the management of Edwin Gould Services for Children. Specifically:

- As the agency's population expanded, the quantity of data to be maintained and tabulated was growing to unmanageable proportions.
- As service emphasis shifted from custodial foster care to adoption, aftercare and prevention, the information necessary for effective management of the new programs and services increased and changed in nature.
- As the size and turnover rate of the agency's population increased due to the new emphases, it became increasingly difficult for supervisors and program directors to be personally acquainted with each client and his or her needs and problems.
- As the quantity of information in each child's case record grew, due both to increased city and state reporting requirements and to new information being collected on biological parents and other involved persons, the effort required to summarize case information increased as well; the preparation of statistical analyses covering children with special characteristics or needs became an almost impossible task, thereby complicating program planning for these children.

Because of these problems and an administrative emphasis on full accountability for day-to-day decisions affecting clients, the decision was made to develop a computerized management information system.[2]

OBJECTIVES OF SYSTEM

At the outset, the agency's principal goal was to develop an information system that would retain and display when necessary the full range of objective case information on each child or on groups of children with similar characteristics. The hope was that such a system would facilitate program planning and eventually substitute for all but the narrative portions of each child's case record.

As the system developed, the agency's program directors began to focus on more explicit objectives. Among these were:

- to develop a variety of case management reports pinpointing problem areas and indicating situations requiring administrative attention or casework action.
- to give casework and supervisory staff useful and up-to-date reference information on each case in their caseloads.
- to summarize, tabulate and compare any given items in the case records at any given time, in order to prepare or assist in the preparation of special reports or population summaries.
- to prepare monthly control or "tickler" reports informing caseworkers and clerical staff of specific action required of them by the city or state on behalf of a client.
- to facilitate the access and summary presentation of data concerning specific areas of interest for certain categories of the client population, in order to assist in evaluating agency performance.

Early in the development process, the agency made three key decisions that had a major impact on the scope and usefulness of the system. The first was to accumulate a large data base on each child, covering a wide variety of potentially useful areas. This posed possible problems in terms of keeping the information current and accurate; however, it was believed that the advantage of having complete data available outweighed potential problems. Additionally, the large data base allowed the agency to make full use of a computer-based information system's capability to store and maintain large quantities of data without sacrificing the ability to "retrieve" and analyze any portion of the data base with speed and accuracy.

The second decision was to avoid use of standard report formats. It was felt that such formats would require the agency to analyze specific predetermined data elements that could become outmoded as agency objectives and client needs changed. Instead, the agency decided to develop a system providing complete flexibility of report formats and report design.

The third decision was to give the system an "end-result" as well as a "service-input" focus.[3] That is, caseworkers would be asked to designate a planned goal for each child and estimate a date for achieving it. This decision reemphasized the agency's concern with evaluation and overall program accountability.[4] Further, service needs of both children and biological parents became an integral part of the system.

In the 1 1/2 years following these decisions, considerable effort went into:

1. the development of the specific elements of the data base,
2. the construction of computer-readable codes,
3. the preparation of data entry forms,
4. the writing of computer programs, and
5. the instruction of caseworkers in the use of the system.

TRAINING THE CASEWORKERS

Caseworker instruction was perhaps the most important of these tasks, since the agency had placed a high priority both on giving the system a casework orientation and on involving caseworkers in the use as well as submission of information. Casework staff participated in many decisions concerning the nature and scope of the information system, and explanations of the data entry forms and coding structures were given at agency-wide meetings. Several other steps were taken to assist caseworkers:

- A special uncoded report—the Verbal Child Record Printout —was prepared to facilitate case reference and updating by caseworkers.
- An instruction manual was written giving detailed information on the use of the system by caseworkers.
- The system is used to help caseworkers prepare city and state reports.
- Many of the regular summary reports prepared from the system are distributed to the caseworkers, so that they are aware of the kind of information being utilized by the administrative staff.

The training of caseworkers to complete comprehensive information forms and to update data regularly began early in the design stage and is still in progress.[5] The agency believes this process has been aided by the emphasis placed on caseworker participation, particularly on "information feedback." Caseworkers either receive or have access to information supplied to supervisors and program directors.

The system was put into use in early 1971, and has been fully operational since. Because of the flexibility in both data base components and report formats, the system has also been an evolving one. New information has been added to the data base and new types of reports are regularly designed and prepared to meet agency and staff needs.

OVERALL OPERATION OF THE SYSTEM

Original Data Collection

Data collection for the Child Record System begins when a child is admitted to the agency. At that point the caseworker responsible for evaluating the child completes three data entry forms: an *Intake* form, a *Natural Parents* form and a *Foster Parents* form.

Following a staffing of each case and the transfer of casework responsibility from the intake to the undercare division, an *Undercare* data entry form is completed by the caseworker assigned to the child.

Report Preparation

Once each month a series of computer listings is prepared, giving detailed clerical information. These listings help clerical personnel and caseworkers to comply with city, state, and other reporting requirements. For example, clerical personnel receive listings of all children admitted, transferred within the agency, and discharged during each month. Caseworkers also receive listings of children in their caseloads for whom certain city or state reports are required.

Once each quarter a variety of case-management or other computer reports is prepared. One is the Verbal Child Record Printout, prepared for each child in care and sent to the caseworker in a binder containing the printouts for his or her complete caseload. Other reports such as an Analysis of Discharges, an Analysis of Plans To Be Completed in the Following Quarter, and an Analysis of Plans Not Completed on Schedule are also prepared at this time.

During each quarter, the system is used on an as-needed basis to prepare listings and reports in response to special requests, which may come from the administrative, casework or clerical staffs, or from the city or state. In some instances, information from the Child Record System itself is adequate to respond fully to the request. In others, Child Record information is distributed to caseworkers and clerical staff to assist them in preparing the reports.

Updating

Objective case information, such as caseworker changes, foster home changes, and status change, is updated monthly by the clerical staff. Updating of more subjective case information, such as problem appraisal, plan for the child, and service needs, is done quarterly by the caseworker. The caseworker reports any changes in or additions to a child's record by writing directly onto the corresponding Verbal Printout. The printouts are returned by caseworkers shortly before the end of each quarter; changes and additions are keypunched, and updated printouts are returned to caseworkers the first week of the next quarter (see the accompanying Systems Flow Chart).

DATA BASE CONTENT AND REPORT DESIGN

As mentioned earlier, two of the key decisions made in the development of the Child Record System were to accumulate a large data base, and to maintain flexibility in report design. To allow latitude in the creation of the data base, each child's record was designed to consist of about 2000 coded data positions.[6] Currently 1200 of those positions are in use, covering information in each of the following areas: basic identifying characteristics; service needs; recreation; IQ; remediation programs; vocational interests and needs; physical and mental health; adolescent sexual behavior; natural parents; and foster parents.

Additionally, the data base consists of a permanent record and a changeable record. Data known when a child first entered the agency is entered into both records. Thereafter, the changeable record is updated monthly and quarterly, as discussed previously, while the permanent record is left unchanged. This procedure was developed to facilitate computer-based comparisons between a child's characteristics at the point of admittance and at various points in the future.

Flexibility in report design is achieved by means of a computer program called the Report Generator.[7] The Report Generator is activated by three sets of cards:

- *The scan and select control cards,* which specify the characteristics a child's record must possess in order to be selected for a report;
- *The sort control cards,* which specify the order into which the selected records are to be sorted and the "hierarchy" of the sorted cards; and
- *The verbal control cards,* which specify what information from each selected record is to be printed on the report, the location in which it is to be printed, and if it is to be printed in coded form or not. If an uncoded form is desired, the verbal control cards specify what kinds of verbal designations are to replace the codes. The verbal control cards also determine the report headings to be used.

The flexibility thus created allows administrative and professional staff to develop reports without extensive assistance from computer experts. When interest is expressed in a particular problem or a particular

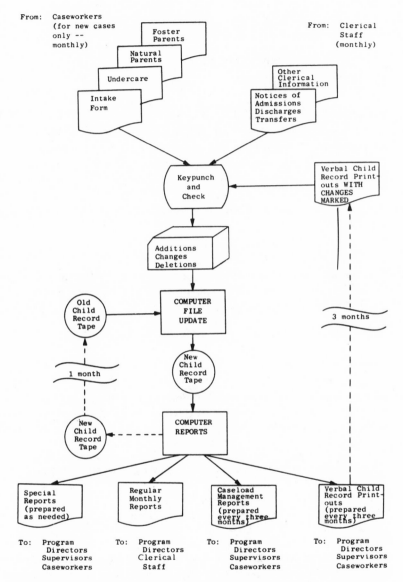

From: Caseworkers
(for new cases
only --
monthly)

Foster
Parents

Natural
Parents

Undercare

Intake
Form

From: Clerical
Staff
(monthly)

Other
Clerical
Information

Notices of
Admissions
Discharges
Transfers

Keypunch
and
Check

Verbal Child
Record Print-
outs WITH
CHANGES
MARKED

Additions
Changes
Deletions

Old
Child
Record
Tape

COMPUTER
FILE
UPDATE

3 months

New
Child
Record
Tape

1 month

New
Child
Record
Tape

COMPUTER
REPORTS

Special
Reports
(prepared
as needed)

Regular
Monthly
Reports

Caseload
Management
Reports
(prepared
every three
months)

Verbal Child
Record Print-
outs
(prepared
every three
months)

To: Program
Directors
Supervisors
Caseworkers

To: Program
Directors
Clerical
Staff

To: Program
Directors
Supervisors
Caseworkers

To: Program
Directors
Supervisors
Caseworkers

FIGURE 28-1. Child care record system—systems flow chart

381

category of child, a clerical person responsible for the operation of the system works with the child care professional to determine the specific information needed. A report format is designed, control cards are key-punched, and the report is prepared.

POTENTIAL OF THE SYSTEM; NEW DIRECTIONS

Owing to the built-in flexibility of the Child Record System, both in terms of report preparation and data base content, the system is constantly changing. Changes are usually in response to an expressed need from the casework or supervisory staff, but occasionally result from modifications in city or state reporting requirements. Additionally, the system has been modified on occasion to accommodate agency accounting functions. Finally, the agency intends to implement a full-scale planning, reporting, and evaluation system.

In sum, the Child Record System has been a useful tool to program directors, supervisors and caseworkers at Edwin Gould Services for Children. It has assisted them in meeting more effectively the needs of their clients, and in evaluating the overall results of their efforts thereby adding a valuable dimension to the agency's program and service accountability.

NOTES

1. Development funding for this and several other child care information system efforts in New York City was provided by the Edwin Gould Foundation for Children. Potential users of such systems may be interested in two monographs published by the Gould Foundation: *Child Welfare and the Computer: A Projection of Potential*, by Brandt R. Allen and Alexander B. Horniman, 1969; and *Child Welfare and the Computer: Four Years Later*, by Brandt R. Allen and David W. Young, 1973.
2. For a discussion of the system's beginnings, see "Case Costing in Child Care: A Critical Step Toward Increased Accountability in Social Services," by David W. Young, *Child Welfare*, LII, 5 (May 1973).
3. Emphasis on end results is generally lacking in the New York City child care system. This is in no small way a result of the city's system of reimbursement to voluntary child care agencies for services delivered. The reimbursement system financially penalizes an agency that discharges a child from care. See *Examination of New York City Child Care Reimbursement System*, by Brandt R. Allen et al., the 1971-1972 Prize Cases, Public Policy Program, John F. Kennedy School of Government, Harvard University, February 1972.
4. Work is under way in the agency to develop a more sophisticated evaluation system focusing on the relationship among goals, subgoals and service needs.

5. Caseworkers point out that time spent on forms cannot be spent with clients. An agency must recognize this "trade off."
6. Each record consists of 26 data cards with 80 columns per card, for a total of 2080 data positions. Card input is utilized so that system maintenance and operation does not require a computer professional. Once the cards have been read by the computer (the agency rents time—about 2 hours per month—on an IBM 360 Model 30), they are processed by a combination of magnetic tape and disk.
7. The early conceptual and design work for this computer system was performed by Thomas T. Goldsmith and James E. Hirst, management consultants to Edwin Gould Services.

Appendix

Code of Ethics of the National Association of Social Workers

AS ADOPTED BY THE 1979
NASW DELEGATE ASSEMBLY,
EFFECTIVE JULY 1, 1980.

PREAMBLE

This code is intended to serve as a guide to the everyday conduct of members of the social work profession and as a basis for the adjudication of issues in ethics when the conduct of social workers is alleged to deviate from the standards expressed or implied in this code. It represents standards of ethical behavior for social workers in professional relationships with those served, with colleagues, with employers, with other individuals and professions, and with the community and society as a whole. It also embodies standards of ethical behavior governing individual conduct to the extent that such conduct is associated with an individual's status and identity as a social worker.

This code is based on the fundamental values of the social work profession that include the worth, dignity, and uniqueness of all persons as well as their rights and opportunities. It is also based on the nature of social work, which fosters conditions that promote these values.

In subscribing to and abiding by this code, the social worker is expected to view ethical responsibility in as inclusive a context as each situation demands and within which ethical judgement is required. The social worker is expected to take into consideration all the principles in this code that have a bearing upon any situation in which ethical judgement is to be exercised and professional intervention or conduct is planned.

The course of action that the social worker chooses is expected to be consistent with the spirit as well as the letter of this code.

In itself, this code does not represent a set of rules that will prescribe all the behaviors of social workers in all the complexities of professional life. Rather, it offers general principles to guide conduct, and the judicious appraisal of conduct, in situations that have ethical implications. It provides the basis for making judgements about ethical actions before and after they occur. Frequently, the particular situation determines the ethical principles that apply and the manner of their application. In such cases, not only the particular ethical principles are taken into immediate consideration, but also the entire code and its spirit. Specific applications of ethical principles must be judged within the context in which they are being considered. Ethical behavior in a given situation must satisfy not only the judgement of the individual social worker, but also the judgement of an unbiased jury of professional peers.

This code should not be used as an instrument to deprive any social worker of the opportunity or freedom to practice with complete professional integrity; nor should any disciplinary action be taken on the basis of this code without maximum provision for safeguarding the rights of the social worker affected.

The ethical behavior of social workers results not from edict, but from a personal commitment of the individual. This code is offered to affirm the will and zeal of all social workers to be ethical and to act ethically in all that they do as social workers.

The following codified ethical principles should guide social workers in the various roles and relationships and at the various levels of responsibility in which they function professionally. These principles also serve as a basis for the adjudication by the National Association of Social Workers of issues in ethics.

In subscribing to this code, social workers are required to cooperate in its implementation and abide by any disciplinary rulings based on it. They should also take adequate measures to discourage, prevent, expose, and correct the unethical conduct of colleagues. Finally, social workers should be equally ready to defend and assist colleagues unjustly charged with unethical conduct.

SUMMARY OF MAJOR PRINCIPLES

I. The Social Worker's Conduct and Comportment as a Social Worker

A. Propriety. The Social worker should maintain high standards of personal conduct in the capacity or identity as social worker.

B. Competence and Professional Development. The social worker should strive to become and remain proficient in professional practice and the performance of professional functions.

C. Service. The social worker should regard as primary the service obligation of the social work profession.

D. Integrity. The social worker should act in accordance with the highest standards of professional integrity.

E. Scholarship and Research. The social worker engaged in study and research should be guided by the conventions of scholarly inquiry.

II. The Social Worker's Ethical Responsibility to Clients

F. Primacy of Clients' Interests. The social worker's primary responsibility is to clients.

G. Rights and Prerogatives of Clients. The social worker should make every effort to foster maximum self-determination on the part of clients.

H. Confidentiality and Privacy. The social worker should respect the privacy of clients and hold in confidence all information obtained in the course of professional service.

I. Fees. When setting fees, the social worker should ensure that they are fair, reasonable, considerate, and commensurate with the service performed and with due regard for the clients' ability to pay.

III. The Social Worker's Ethical Responsibility to Colleagues

J. Respect, Fairness, and Courtesy. The social worker should treat colleagues with respect, courtesy, fairness, and good faith.

K. Dealing with Colleagues' Clients. The social worker has the responsibility to relate to the clients of colleagues with full professional consideration.

IV. The Social Worker's Ethical Responsibility to Employers and Employing Organizations

L. Commitments to Employing Organizations. The social worker should adhere to commitments made to the employing organization.

V. The Social Worker's Ethical Responsibility to the Social Work Profession

M. Maintaining the Integrity of the Profession. The social worker should uphold and advance the values, ethics, knowledge, and mission of the profession.

N. Community Service. The social worker should assist the profession in making social services available to the general public.

O. Development of Knowledge. The social worker should take responsibility for identifying, developing, and fully utilizing knowledge for professional practice.

VI. The Social Worker's Ethical Responsibility to Society

P. Promoting the General Welfare. The social worker should promote the general welfare of society.

THE NASW CODE OF ETHICS

I. The Social Worker's Conduct and Comportment as a Social Worker

A. Propriety—The Social worker should maintain high standards of personal conduct in the capacity or identity as social worker.
  1. The private conduct of the social worker is a personal matter to the same degree as is any other person's, except when such conduct compromises the fulfillment of professional responsibilities.
  2. The social worker should not participate in, condone, or be associated with dishonesty, fraud, deceit, or misrepresentation.
  3. The social worker should distinguish clearly between statements and actions made as a private individual and as a representative of the social work profession or an organization or group.

B. Competence and Professional Development—The social worker should strive to become and remain proficient in professional practice and the performance of professional functions.
  1. The social worker should accept responsibility or employment only on the basis of existing competence or the intention to acquire the necessary competence.
  2. The social worker should not misrepresent professional qualifications, education, experience, or affiliations.

C. Service—The social worker should regard as primary the service obligation of the social work profession.
  1. The social worker should retain ultimate responsibility for the

quality and extent of the service that individual assumes, assigns, or performs.

2. The social worker should act to prevent practices that are inhumane or discriminatory against any person or group of persons.

D. Integrity—The social worker should act in accordance with the highest standards of professional integrity and impartiality.

1. The social worker should be alert to and resist the influences and pressures that interfere with the exercise of professional discretion and impartial judgement required for the performance of professional functions.

2. The social worker should not exploit professional relationships for personal gain.

E. Scholarship and Research—The social worker engaged in study and research should be guided by the conventions of scholarly inquiry.

1. The social worker engaged in research should consider carefully its possible consequences for human beings.

2. The social worker engaged in research should ascertain that the consent of participants in the research is voluntary and informed, without any implied deprivation or penalty for refusal to participate, and with due regard for participants' privacy and dignity.

3. The social worker engaged in research should protect participants from unwarranted physical or mental discomfort, distress, harm, danger, or deprivation.

4. The social worker who engages in the evaluation of services or cases should discuss them only for the professional purposes and only with persons directly and professionally concerned with them.

5. Information obtained about participants in research should be treated as confidential.

6. The social worker should take credit only for work actually done in connection with scholarly and research endeavors and credit contributions made by others.

II. The Social Worker's Ethical Responsibility to Clients

F. Primacy of Clients' Interests—The social worker's primary responsibility is to clients.

1. The social worker should serve clients with devotion, loyalty, determination, and the maximum application of professional skill and competence.

2. The social worker should not exploit relationships with clients

for personal advantage, or solicit the clients of one's agency for private practice.

3. The social worker should not practice, condone, facilitate or collaborate with any form of discrimination on the basis of race, color, sex, sexual orientation, age, religion, national origin, marital status, political belief, mental or physical handicap, or any other preference or personal characteristic, condition or status.

4. The social worker should avoid relationships or commitments that conflict with the interests of clients.

5. The social worker should under no circumstances engage in sexual activities with clients.

6. The social worker should provide clients with accurate and complete information regarding the extent and nature of the services available to them.

7. The social worker should apprise clients of their risks, rights, opportunities, and obligations associated with social service to them.

8. The social worker should seek advice and counsel of colleagues and supervisors whenever such consultation is in the best interest of clients.

9. The social worker should terminate service to clients, and professional relationships with them, when such service and relationships are no longer required or no longer serve the clients' needs or interests.

10. The social worker should withdraw services precipitously only under unusual circumstances, giving careful consideration to all factors in the situation and taking care to minimize possible adverse effects.

11. The social worker who anticipates the termination or interruption of service to clients should notify clients promptly and seek the transfer, referral, or continuation of service in relation to the clients' needs and preferences.

G. **Rights and Prerogatives of Clients—The social worker should make every effort to foster maximum self-determination on the part of clients.**

1. When the social worker must act on behalf of a client who has been adjudged legally incompetent, the social worker should safeguard the interests and rights of that client.

2. When another individual has been legally authorized to act in behalf of a client, the social worker should deal with that person always with the client's best interest in mind.

3. The social worker should not engage in any action that violates or diminishes the civil or legal rights of clients.

H. Confidentiality and Privacy—The social worker should respect the privacy of clients and hold in confidence all information obtained in the course of professional service.

1. The social worker should share with others confidences revealed by clients, without their consent, only for compelling professional reasons.
2. The social worker should inform clients fully about the limits of confidentiality in a given situation, the purposes for which information is obtained, and how it may be used.
3. The social worker should afford clients reasonable access to any official social work records concerning them.
4. When providing clients with access to records, the social worker should take due care to protect the confidences of others contained in those records.
5. The social worker should obtain informed consent of clients before taping, recording, or permitting third party observation of their activities.

I. Fees—When setting fees, the social worker should ensure that they are fair, reasonable, considerate, and commensurate with the service performed and with due regard for the clients' ability to pay.

1. The social worker should not divide a fee or accept or give anything of value for receiving or making a referral.

III. The Social Worker's Ethical Responsibility to Colleagues

J. Respect, Fairness, and Courtesy—The social worker should treat colleagues with respect, courtesy, fairness, and good faith.

1. The social worker should cooperate with colleagues to promote professional interests and concerns.
2. The social worker should respect confidences shared by colleagues in the course of their professional relationships and transactions.
3. The social worker should create and maintain conditions of practice that facilitate ethical and competent professional performance by colleagues.
4. The social worker should treat with respect, and represent accurately and fairly, the qualifications, views, and findings of colleagues and use appropriate channels to express judgements on these matters.
5. The social worker who replaces or is replaced by a colleague in professional practice should act with consideration for the interest, character, and reputation of that colleague.

6. The social worker should not exploit a dispute between a colleague and employers to obtain a position or otherwise advance the social worker's interest.

7. The social worker should seek arbitration or mediation when conflicts with colleagues require resolution for compelling professional reasons.

8. The social worker should extend to colleagues of other professions the same respect and cooperation that is extended to social work colleagues.

9. The social worker who serves as an employer, supervisor, or mentor to colleagues should make orderly and explicit arrangements regarding the conditions of their continuing professional relationship.

10. The social worker who has the responsibility for employing and evaluating the performance of other staff members, should fulfill such responsibility in a fair, considerate, and equitable manner, on the basis of clearly enunciated criteria.

11. The social worker who has the responsibility for evaluating the performance of employees, supervisees, or students should share evaluations with them.

K. **Dealing with Colleagues' Clients—The social worker has the responsibility to relate to the clients of colleagues with full professional consideration.**

1. The social worker should not solicit the clients of colleagues.

2. The social worker should not assume professional responsibility for the clients of another agency or a colleague without appropriate communication with that agency or colleague.

3. The social worker who serves the clients of colleagues, during a temporary absence or emergency, should serve those clients with the same consideration as that afforded any client.

VI. The Social Worker's Ethical Responsibility to Employers and Employing Organizations

L. **Commitments to Employing Organization—The social worker should adhere to commitments made to the employing organization.**

1. The social worker should work to improve the employing agency's policies and procedures, and the efficiency and effectiveness of its services.

2. The social worker should not accept employment or arrange student field placements in an organization which is currently un-

der public sanction by NASW for violating personnel standards, or imposing limitations on or penalties for professional actions on behalf of clients.
3. The social worker should act to prevent and eliminate discrimination in the employing organization's work assignments and in its employment policies and practices.
4. The social worker should use with scrupulous regard, and only for the purpose for which they are intended, the resources of the employing organization.

V. The Social Workers Ethical Responsibility to the Social Work Profession

M. Maintaining the Integrity of the Profession—The social worker should uphold and advance the values, ethics, knowledge, and mission of the profession.
1. The social worker should protect and enhance the dignity and integrity of the profession and should be responsible and vigorous in discussion and criticism of the profession.
2. The social worker should take action through appropriate channels against unethical conduct by any other member of the profession.
3. The social worker should act to prevent the unauthorized and unqualified practice of social work.
4. The social worker should make no misrepresentation in advertising as to qualifications, competence, service, or results to be achieved.
N. Community Service—The social worker should assist the profession in making social services available to the general public.
1. The social worker should contribute time and professional expertise to activities that promote respect for the utility, the integrity, and the competence of the social work profession.
2. The social worker should support the formulation, development, enactment and implementation of social policies of concern to the profession.
O. Development of Knowledge—The social worker should take responsibility for identifying, developing, and fully utilizing knowledge for professional practice.
1. The social worker should base practice upon recognized knowledge relevant to social work.
2. The social worker should critically examine, and keep current with emerging knowledge relevant to social work.

3. The social worker should contribute to the knowledge base of social work and share research knowledge and practice wisdom with colleagues.

VI. The Social Worker's Ethical Responsibility to Society

P. Promoting the General Welfare—The social worker should promote the general welfare of society.

1. The social worker should act to prevent and eliminate discrimination against any person or group on the basis of race, color, sex, sexual orientation, age, religion, national origin, marital status, political belief, mental or physical handicap, or any other preference or personal characteristic, condition, or status.
2. The social worker should act to ensure that all persons have access to the resources, services, and opportunities which they require.
3. The social worker should act to expand choice and opportunity for all persons, with special regard for disadvantaged or oppressed groups and persons.
4. The social worker should promote conditions that encourage respect for the diversity of cultures which constitute American society.
5. The social worker should provide appropriate professional services in public emergencies.
6. The social worker should advocate changes in policy and legislation to improve social conditions and to promote social justice.
7. The social worker should encourage informed participation by the public in shaping social policies and institutions.

Index